Lecture Notes
in Business Information Processing 179

Lecture Notes
in Business Information Processing   179

Series Editors

Wil van der Aalst
Eindhoven Technical University, the Netherlands
John Mylopoulos
University of Trento, Italy
Michael Rosemann
Queensland University of Technology, Brisbane, Qld, Australia
Michael J. Shaw
University of Illinois, Urbana-Champaign, IL, USA
Clemens Szyperski
Microsoft Research, Redmond, WA, USA

Giovanni Cantone
Michele Marchesi (Eds.)

Agile Processes in Software Engineering and Extreme Programming

15th International Conference, XP 2014
Rome, Italy, May 26-30, 2014
Proceedings

 Springer

Volume Editors

Giovanni Cantone
University of Rome Tor Vergata
Department of Computer Science, Systems and Production
Rome, Italy
E-mail: cantone@uniroma2.it

Michele Marchesi
University of Cagliari
Department of Electrical and Electronic Engineering
Cagliari, Italy
E-mail: michele@diee.unica.it

ISSN 1865-1348   e-ISSN 1865-1356
ISBN 978-3-319-06861-9   e-ISBN 978-3-319-06862-6
DOI 10.1007/978-3-319-06862-6
Springer Cham Heidelberg New York Dordrecht London

Library of Congress Control Number: 2014937905

Typesetting: Camera-ready by author, data conversion by Scientific Publishing Services, Chennai, India

Printed on acid-free paper

Springer is part of Springer Science+Business Media (www.springer.com)

Preface

Agile software development is now in its teens. It began by performing in relatively small pioneering organizations; then it gained the interest of medium-size companies, academia, and applied research institutions and laboratories; nowadays it runs in organizations of any kind, including major software and systems development companies.

Because of such a wide diffusion of agile development in industry, the need for collaboration between academics and practitioners increases, with the aim of improving the body of knowledge available to help managers, system engineers, and software engineers to take their managerial/economical, and architectural/project/technical decisions.

During its 15 editions, the XP conference has been a major supporter of the agile vision of software development. Year after year, the XP conference has been supporting the improvements and observing the growth of agile software development and providing evidence of the advantages that agile development can provide. In fact, these XP editions brought together industrial practitioners and researchers in the fields of information systems and software development. They examined the latest theory, practical applications, and implications of agile and lean methods.

XP 2014, in continuity with the past editions, provided a multidisciplinary platform for research and practice on various aspects of agile methods, increased the interaction and collaboration between practitioners and researchers, and discussed and rethought the relationships, synergies, compatibilities, and incompatibilities between agile and lean practices.

This book presents the regular papers, short papers, and the experience reports that the Research Program Committee accepted for presentation at XP 2014. We should point out that the acceptance process was very selective; specifically, more than 50% of the submitted papers and experience reports were rejected.

This book presents chapters concerning or rethinking agile and lean development research topics, including: contracting, maturity modeling, value-based software development, large-scale software development, methods, metrics, testing, challenges and perspectives, software development in practice and teaching at university. The experience reports come from both industry and research institutes, and their topics range from studying global architecture design approaches to investigating challenges involved when advancing software development practices.

Hopefully, we reached the goal of doing our best in serving the agile community by synthesizing the state of the art and practice and tracing its perspectives.

April 2014

Giovanni Cantone
Michele Marchesi

Organization

Conference Chairs

General Chair

Charlie Poole

Research Program Chairs

Giovanni Cantone   University of Rome Tor Vergata, Italy
Michele Marchesi   University of Cagliari, Italy

Workshops and Tutorials Chairs

Jutta Eckstein
Hakan Erdogmus

Research/Practice Chairs

Pekka Abrahamsson
Morten Elvang
Jaana Nyfjord

Short Paper Chair

Giulio Concas

Panel Chair

Steve Fraser

Executives & Managers Track Chairs

Diana Larsen
Jaana Nyfjord

Open Space Chairs

Diana Larsen
Andrea Provaglio

Program Design and Tech Demos Chair

Emily Bache

Lightning Talks Chair

Michael Leber

Local Team

Fabio Armani
Giorgio Natili

Volunteer Coordinator

Johanna Hunt

PhD Symposium Chairs

Davide Falessi
Xiaofeng Wang

Posters Chairs

Roberto Tonelli
Stefano Leli

Social Activities Chair

Cinzia Rosellini

Social Media Chair

Daniel Graziotin

Web Master

Martina Matta

Program Committee

Steve Adolph	WSA Consulting, Canada
Muhammad Ali Babar	IT University of Copenhagen, Denmark
Robert Biddle	Carleton University, Canada
Luigi Buglione	Engineering.IT/ ETS, Italy
Giulio Concas	University of Cagliari, Italy
Steve Counsell	Brunel University, London, UK
Ivica Crnkovic	Mälardalen University, Sweden
Simon Cromarty	Red Gate Software, UK
Steven Fraser	Tech Transfer & Research Relations Advisor, USA

Sponsors

ScrumAlliance®
Transforming the World of Work

F-Secure.

nitor

Media Sponsor

.NETCAMPUS

Organizers

Università di Cagliari

Table of Contents

Methods and Metrics

Testing and Beyond

Lean Development

Short Papers

Experience Reports

UX Design in Agile: A DSDM Case Study

Laura Plonka[1], Helen Sharp[1], Peggy Gregory[2], and Katie Taylor[2]

[1] The Open University, Walton Hall, Milton Keynes MK7 6AA, UK
[2] University of Central Lancashire, Preston PR1 2HE, UK
{laura.plonka,helen.sharp}@open.ac.uk,
{ajgregory,kjtaylor}@uclan.ac.uk

Abstract. Integrating User Experience (UX) design with agile development continues to be the subject of academic studies and practitioner discussions. Most of the existing literature focuses on SCRUM and XP, but in this paper we investigate a technical company who use DSDM. Unlike other agile methods, DSDM provides a configurable framework and a set of roles that covers the whole software development process. While elements of the UX design integration experience were similar to those reported with other agile methods, working practices to mitigate the challenges were identified using DSDM's standard elements. Specifically, communication challenges were mitigated by extending two of DSDM's standard roles. In addition, a change of focus between a design-led phase and a development-led phase of the project changed the communication challenges. Agile teams need to be aware that this change of focus can happen and the implications that it has for their work.

Keywords: DSDM, UX, agile roles.

1   Introduction

Adequately addressing the user perspective is critical for software system success [1], and good user experience design is fundamental to achieving this. How best to integrate user experience (UX) design into an agile project has been a concern of practitioners and researchers for many years [2, 3, 4]. The main agile methods do not provide robust support for this integration, leading to several experience reports and much debate in the UX community. Several approaches to integration have been suggested including aligning processes, utilising UX techniques alongside agile sprints, and co-location of experts. However challenges remain.

UX design is about designing "how the product behaves and is used in the real world... how it works on the outside, where a person comes into contact with it and has to work with it......every product that is used by someone has a user experience: newspapers, ketchup bottles, reclining armchairs, cardigan sweaters" [5]. This involves producing Wireframes, visual designs, interface widgets, user characterisations, and performing user research and usability testing.

In this paper we present a case study that explores the challenges faced by a company when integrating UX design into a Dynamic Systems Development Method (DSDM) project. We use an iterative research approach because it enables us to work

G. Cantone and M. Marchesi (Eds.): XP 2014, LNBIP 179, pp. 1–15, 2014.

closely with an organisation on challenges that are relevant to everyday practice. Dingsoyr et al [6] have called for more research that has industrial impact to build a body of knowledge about agile methods that is relevant to practitioners. DSDM is of interest because it has been studied less intensively than other agile approaches [7], yet it provides a particular perspective on project phases and team roles that sets it apart from other agile methods. The case study focuses on a high-tech software development company that has a core expertise in software delivery and subscribes to the DSDM method. This case study presents mainly the technical team's perspective since it was they who perceived the difficulty.

The main research question of this study is "What challenges are faced by a company trying to integrate UX design and DSDM agile development?" Addressing this question also allows us to discuss two follow-up questions "How does the DSDM framework support this integration?" and "What implications do the answers to these questions raise for DSDM and other agile methods?"

The paper is structured as follows: section two introduces the DSDM framework; section three summarises previous work on integrating agile and UX design; section four introduces the study site, and describes the research approach; section five presents our findings; and section six revisits the research questions.

2   The DSDM Framework

The Dynamic Systems Development Method (DSDM) is an agile framework for both project management and product delivery that grew out of the Rapid Application Development (RAD) tradition (www.dsdm.org). It was the earliest published agile method, and one of the founders, Arie van Bennekum, was an original signatory of the Agile Manifesto [8]. In contrast to early versions of XP and Scrum, which focused on engineering practices, DSDM sought to wrap the best aspects of RAD in a lightweight framework to ensure the delivery of business value. The method has evolved into the DSDM Agile Project Framework [9]. More details about how the different agile methods compare can be found in [7].

The DSDM framework covers the full project lifecycle including guidance on philosophy, principles, project roles, processes, practices and products. It is typified by key practices such as iterative and incremental development, MoSCoW (Must, Could, Should, Won't have this time) prioritisation, Timeboxing, Modelling, Prototyping and Facilitated Workshops. It is configurable so it can accommodate a range of project types and sizes; and is compatible with a variety of governance and programme office structures [9].

In this paper we give examples from DSDM Atern [9] because this version was used within our case study organisation. Atern consists of seven phases: Pre-project, Feasibility, Foundations, Exploration, Engineering, Deployment, and Post-project. In Pre-Project a proposal is formalised and prioritised in line with strategic goals. During Feasibility the business and technical viability of the project are considered. A high-level investigation of potential solutions is produced, as well as estimates of costs and timeframes. During the Foundations phase business needs are ascertained and high level requirements are identified, prioritised and linked to those needs, and resources are secured. Planning allocates high level requirements to increments (releases). Each increment consists of a number of smaller development timeboxes, the size of which is decided by the team. The first three phases are sequential and set the scene before the actual development begins. For each increment, Exploration and Engineering iteratively investigate solutions through the development of prototypes that build, test and document the solution. In Deployment the solution is made operational. The number of passes through this phase will depend on the number of increments scheduled and will be driven by business need. The Post-Project phase takes place after the last Deployment phase. It is used to assess project performance against business value and determine benefit realisation.

DSDM defines a full set of roles for project teams: Business Sponsor, Business Visionary, Technical Coordinator, Project Manager, Team Leader, Business Analyst, Solution Developer, Solution Tester, Business Ambassador, Business Advisor, Workshop Facilitator and DSDM Coach. The framework outlines the responsibilities required however these roles are filled in different ways depending on the nature of the project, but a key aspect is the importance placed on business involvement.

3   Integrating Agile Development and UX Design

Approaches to integration have been reported by both practitioners and academic researchers. They can be broadly divided into two categories: bringing people together, and aligning developer and UX designer work practices.

3.1   Bringing People Together

Cross-functional, co-located teams are regarded as imperative for agile to work. For example, a key practice in the XP agile approach is the 'whole team' practice. However this view is problematic. Firstly, it is often not feasible or desirable to co-locate UX designers and agile developers. For example because the organisation's core business does not support the direct employment of UX designers, or where the organisational culture keeps the disciplines separate: "UX designers work best when they are separated from the issues of software construction because these issues hamper creativity" [10].

Secondly, relying on cross-functional teams assumes that bringing people together leads to the integration of concerns, but does it? Ferreira et al. [11] found that integrating UX design and developers is an ongoing achievement, requiring articulation work and conscious effort day-by-day, so although co-location helps, it is not the whole story. They identified four aspects to this: integration as mutual awareness; integration as negotiating progress, integration as engaging with each other and integration as expectations about acceptable behaviour.

3.2   Aligning Developer and UX Designer Work Practices

Agile developer and UX designer work practices may be aligned in a range of ways such as: using techniques from one discipline in the other, combining agile and UX design processes, and recommendations derived from practice.

Techniques from UX design such as personas [12, 13], discount usability [14] and scenarios [15] have been reportedly used within agile projects. Personas can act as reminders to developers about who they are developing for, and hanging posters of personas in the development team area can make design work more visible to developers [13]. Looking at it the other way around, Kollmann et al. [16] describes the idea of a "Question Board", which is similar to an agile progress board but focuses only on design issues. They explain that it facilitates and triggers discussion about open questions and issues related to design. It also helps to avoid recurring debates and captures different perspectives. Sy [17] also suggests capturing design issues as story cards on a UX board to increase their visibility.

UX design has traditionally followed a process that includes big design up front – something that agile tries to avoid. Aligning these processes can therefore be a challenge. In response to this, Sy and Miller [18] proposed that UX designers work one timebox ahead of developers (see Figure 1), which has become very popular. This enables the design work to be completed ahead of development work yet be tightly coupled to it, as the user stories evolve.

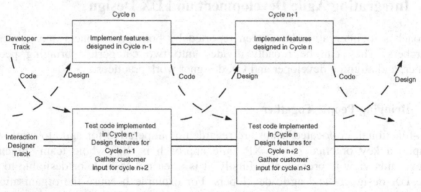

Fig. 1. 'Train tracks' development where UX designers work one timebox ahead of agile developers [15]

Several sets of recommendations have been developed by practitioners. For example, Jeff Patton has 12 recommendations for successful UX design integration [19] including "Research, model and design up front, but only just enough", and "Buy design time with complex technical stories". Nielsen and Norman [20] recommend development in train tracks, and emphasize the need to maintain a coherent vision.

4   Research Approach

This paper is based on a case study conducted by the Agile Research Network (ARN – see agileresearchnetwork.org), a network that conducts industry based research into agile methods. LShift, a hi-tech software development company, approached the ARN to investigate a challenge that they were facing: Integrating UX design into a DSDM project. The research was carried out between April 2013 and October 2013 using an iterative research approach that incorporates regular feedback points in which observations and findings were presented back to the development company [21]. This research approach was chosen based on two main considerations:

1. The research was conducted on a project that was running at LShift at that time. Studying a live project means that work practices and challenges that the team members face are constantly evolving during the course of the project and hence requires an iterative data gathering process to keep up to date with the changes.
2. LShift approached the ARN with a real-world challenge and the aim of this research was to generate research insights to address the research questions at the same time as providing research that helps practitioners [22]. In the context of this study, this means that we shared observations, findings, and relevant literature during the course of the case study.

4.1 Research Site

LShift is a hi-tech software development company that works across a broad range of industries, languages and platforms. They have tried many flavours of agile and subscribe to the DSDM method. At LShift all employees are co-located in an open-plan office. However due to the wide variety of projects they produce, the expert LShift software engineers regularly work with external experts and additional teams such as partner agencies or client-owned teams who are often not co-located for an entire project. This was the case for UX experts. LShift did not employ UX designers themselves. Instead their UX design work was done by a separate UX design agency that had some experience of agile but did not specifically subscribe to the DSDM method. The agency is a separate commercial entity, located in a separate building.

4.2 Data Gathering and Analysis

Our research approach consisted of four data gathering phases, two main feedback points and a jointly written report by the researchers and the company. Figure 2 shows a simplified timeline of our research approach. In practice, phases were iterated.

1. **First data gathering phase: Initial interview** At the beginning of the case study, three researchers interviewed the managing director and the programme manager to build an overall understanding of the project and to develop an initial picture of the as-is situation in the project and the perceived challenges. This interview served as a starting for the following observations.
2. **Second data gathering phase: Observations** During the case study, two researchers spent time at the LShift office observing the daily work practices of the development team and attending meetings. Table 1 presents an overview of the meetings attended. In addition, the two researchers had informal conversations with developers and project managers during lunch and coffee breaks. During all observations, extensive field notes were taken.

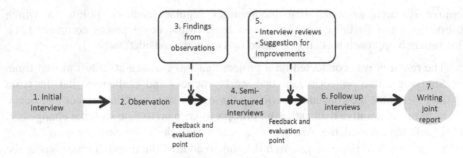

Fig. 2. Research Approach

3. **First feedback point:** At the first feedback point, initial observations and identified challenges were shared with LShift's management. The management supported us in identifying key stakeholders for interviews.

Table 1. Overview of observed meetings

# Observations	Type of meeting
5	Daily Stand-Up Meetings
1	Planning and estimation session
2	Retrospective (one with designers and one without)
1	Design Review Session

4. **Third data gathering phase: Semi-structured interviews** Semi-structured interviews were conducted with the identified key technical figures (developers, project managers, and a business analyst) and UX designers but subsequently the designers withdrew. The interviews were used to delve deeper into the identified challenges, to uncover additional challenges and to understand the perspectives of different key stakeholders. All interviews were audio-recorded and conducted by at least two researchers; each one lasted between 30min and 1 hour.

5. **Second feedback point: Presentation** Before the second feedback point, we (all four authors) analysed the interviews to understand the different perspectives on the challenges. We also reviewed existing literature to identify ways to mitigate these challenges. Subsequently, findings from the analysis and literature review were presented in a meeting that was attended by a large proportion of LShift's project team. In the meeting, project members confirmed the challenges we identified and discussed how to mitigate them using the literature review.

6. **Fourth data gathering phase: Follow up interviews** To keep track of the changes that took place after the second feedback point, follow-up interviews with the project manager and the managing director were conducted.

7. **Joint written report** As a final step of our research approach, a joint report with the company was written [23]. This final step allowed us to validate the interpretation of our observations.

The analysis of the data was conducted iteratively with a focus on articulating integration challenges. After each data gathering step, the data was analysed through group discussions, key themes were extracted and findings confirmed with the company. The findings of the each step informed further data gathering.

5   Findings

LShift recognized early on that developers and UX designers have different perspectives and goals, different processes, different commercial pressures, and different skills and knowledge. These differences manifested themselves during the "Feasibility and Foundations" phase and the "Engineering" phase. The next two sections present how UX design was integrated into DSDM during that phase, what challenges the project members were facing and how they addressed them.

5.1   Integrating UX Design during Feasibility and Foundations

For the project team the journey began at a very early stage. While the concept and business case for the new product was being developed, a number of user interface concepts were prepared which became a key part of the sales presentation. While it was understood by all that these were for illustrative purposes to bring the concept to life, they did create a set of expectations about the scope of the project and these expectations survived through the planning stages.

5.1.1   Working Practices during Feasibility and Foundations
From the beginning of the Feasibility planning stage, UX designers and developers together ran workshops to explore user journeys, produce a high level picture of what the product had to do and estimate the size of the design and development effort.

At the beginning of the Foundations phase, developers and designers were working mainly independently. LShift, the development company, who provided all the technical expertise and is the company with delivery responsibility, focused on fleshing out the high-level user stories, the technical analysis, infrastructure and architecture, the security design, and technical de-risking. Meanwhile, the designers created UX concepts and personas and collaborated closely with the client suggesting and deciding on designs without receiving technical input from the developers. The suggested designs were accepted by the client and consequently set their expectations.

5.1.2   Challenges during Feasibility and Foundations
LShift faced two main challenges during Feasibility and Foundations:

1.   Technical feasibility issues with design-led approach: To focus on the potential features of the product unencumbered by practicalities of having to deliver them, a design-led approach was chosen for the early stage of the project. Illustrating potential features using interface design mock-ups can be a very useful tool for providing a shared understanding of what's to be built. However, issues with this approach arose because UX designers and developers worked mainly independently, and designs were agreed with the client before developers confirmed their technical feasibility. This resulted in challenges because the client's expectations had been set, but some elements of the design had to be changed after developers discovered that they were not feasible.

2. Agile prioritization: The prioritisation of functionality in agile projects meant that the implementation of some features was delayed to a later increment than originally planned, and some features moved between timeboxes.

Whether the functionality changed because of technical feasibility issues or prioritisation activity, the result was the same: the client did not receive the functionality envisaged in the design illustrations, and this was a challenge.

5.1.3   Mitigations during Feasibility and Foundations
In order to mitigate this challenge, a developer was seconded to the UX team to work in a **Business Analyst role**, initially with a view to spend time with the design team and help assess the feasibility of design proposals earlier in the process. However, the initial planning of resources did not account for this extra, time-consuming task for the technical lead. This resulted in an extended Foundations phase because the technical tasks did not progress as quickly as expected.

5.2   Integrating UX Design during Engineering

During Engineering, the developers' work was broken down into increments comprising a number of three-week long time-boxes. The team held daily stand-up meetings and organised their user stories in a project management tool. The UX designers' work was also time boxed and they worked one sprint ahead of the development team (as shown in Fig 1). The designers organised their work during their timeboxes independently of the development team.

5.2.1   Working Practices during Engineering
During Engineering, developers and UX designers had to integrate their work with each other, organize the hand-over of designs and feedback on the designs.

The UX designers worked closely with the client through an iterative design process resulting in UX designs that were usually signed off by the client before being handed over to the development team. The developers received various documents. Usually designs were detailed, "pixel perfect"[1] and signed off by the client. However, occasionally developers received interactive wireframes. A design review to verify the implemented designs was conducted at the end of each increment.

Due to stakeholder constraints, the classic DSDM whole-team workshops were not run, but other communication-focused activities were in place.

Daily Communication: Designers attended the daily development stand-up meetings (either in person or on the phone). This provided a daily opportunity for communication and keeping up to date with each others' work.

The New Business Analyst (BA) Role: Identified during the Foundations phase this role continued to be a "communication bridge" between the developers and the client as well as between the developers and the design agency. Over time, this

---

[1] Pixel perfect design is the process of aligning and sizing all of the objects that make up a design to their exact pixel placements and sizes.

communication bridge worked more directly with the client to drive the business requirements and attended design meetings with the client to provide technical input.

Ad hoc and on-demand communication: Individual developers and designers could communicate whenever there was a need for it. Communication could also take place via email or through phone calls, and occasional face-to-face sessions were held between designers and developers to work through proposed approaches. This communication had no prescribed structure.

5.2.2   Challenges during Engineering

Although developers and designers had good opportunities to communicate regularly, both teams agreed that communication challenges and inter-related challenges regarding the level of detail in upfront design remained.

Communication between Developers and UX Designers

Communication is a broad topic, but here, four main questions capture the challenge.

1. What information needs to be communicated? UX designers and developers did not always realise that there was a need for communication. There was not enough mutual awareness of each others' activities, leading to mistaken expectations that caused frustration. For example, this led to the independent production of two incompatible solutions for the same feature: one from the developers and one from the designers. The designers did not know that the developers had developed a solution, and the developers did not know that the designers were designing the feature without knowing the technical constraints. This mix-up caused frustration when developers saw the design solution for the feature (signed off by the client) that did not consider their technical solution.
2. How and when best to communicate information? This question points to the need for agreed ways of working. As an example, developers sometimes needed to tweak designs after they had been handed over by the designers. How and when should this be communicated to designers: when the need for a change is first realised? once a proven alternative has been implemented and tested? or somewhere in between? Developers may not expect that an early notification will be helpful. From a designers' perspective a continuous feedback process on the designs may be attractive in order to maintain a coherent design and to inform future decisions about the design, but it may also cause a high level of interruptions as a design route may take a while to develop.
3. How to keep communication channels open? Although various channels of communication were set up, issues sometimes took longer than expected to be resolved, and this held up development work. This was particularly true when developers had queries about the designs. Some developers felt inhibited about phoning a designer to discuss the issue. Instead they used more indirect channels like email, or tried to resolve the issue within the development team for the sake of speed.

4. How best to keep the design implementation visible? Limited visibility of the design implementation posed challenges for designers. This happened because the design implementation was not regularly reviewed by the designers. In our case study, although designers had the opportunity to review the design implementation, formal design reviews were only planned at the end of each increment for budgetary reasons, and this proved to be too infrequent to catch all the changes. More formal or more frequently-organised reviews would have raised design implementation visibility.

Level of Detail in Upfront Design: Sometimes Less Is More
From the developers' perspective the initial designs were unnecessarily detailed. They gave five main reasons for this.
1. Prioritisation and de-scoping can lead to a waste of pixel perfect designs.
2. Some issues with the design will only be found once implementation starts.
3. Pixel perfect designs may increase resistance towards making design changes.
4. It is better to focus on functionality first and design as you go along because when developing new functionality, "any visual work … is a distraction."
5. Quality of designs can benefit from early input by developers with knowledge of design guidelines for the target platform.

5.2.3   Mitigations during Engineering
During the observation phase, LShift started to resolve the challenges by: introducing new roles and involving designers in development and vice versa. They also changed from a design-led to a development-led approach.

Introducing New Roles. Two standard DSDM roles were modified to help overcome challenges: the BA (Business Analyst) as communication bridge, and a Project Manager (PM) with experience of UX design and technical development.

The role was already introduced in Feasibility and Foundations. During the Engineering phase, this role developed into both a "communication bridge" between the developers and the client and between the developers and the designers to explicitly address the communication gap between them. This BA role was staffed by a senior developer, able to manage the discovery and communication of requirements, and to provide direct feedback on the technical feasibility of design ideas coming out of the meetings between designers and client. The BA also provided high-level requirements for the designers at the beginning of their sprints. Designers and developers perceived that the role improved communication.

A new person with experience of both technical projects and UX design was added to the team in order to take a classic DSDM Project Manager role. This was a departure from the company's usual model of employing a lead developer in the PM role, largely as a result of the size of the project and the amount of communication overhead around the design work. Doing so resulted in extra support for the extended BA role (described above), but also made sure that the designers' point of view was represented in the technical team.

Involving Developers in Design and Designers in Development. Visibility and transparency of the work by both parties was increased by:

- The designer attending daily stand-ups. Previously, although a designer attended stand-ups, different designers attended and they were often not the designer currently doing the work. Having consistency in attendance was perceived as positive, improved the communication and resulted in a quicker feedback loop.
- Providing access for designers and developers to all the stories being worked on at any one time.
- Releasing the implemented design to the designers once a week has led to iterative feedback coming from the designers to the developers.

From Design-Led to Development-Led Approach. Although the two mitigations discussed above improved the integration, a subsequent change of project requirements triggered a change of emphasis between development work and design work. Whereas previously a design-led approach was in play, a development-led approach was now needed. Technical spikes (prototypes) were developed and then shared with designers for their input. In more detail, this process involved:

1. Designers provided wireframes (not pixel-perfect designs) for the new functionality and these drove the conversation with the client and developers
2. Developers produced technical spikes (a 'walking skeleton') which cover basic functionality to complete a transaction or user journey to test a technical solution
3. Once the basic functionality was developed and agreed, the solution design was honed by the designers

This approach was perceived as useful since the design and the solution evolved together. Part of the reason for this switch of emphasis is natural as a result of the product concept maturing. There is a heavy emphasis on UX while the first requirements are becoming crystallised into new features, then as design patterns become clear, the development-led approach starts to become more prominent.

6   Discussion

This section returns to the research question posed above: "What challenges are faced by a company trying to integrate UX design and DSDM agile development?" In the next section 6.1, we discuss that the challenges found in a DSDM project are similar to the challenges in other agile teams. However, DSDM provides a different structure than other agile methods to address these challenges. We discuss this in section 6.2 and 6.3 focusing on the questions "How does the DSDM framework support this integration?" and "What implications do the answers to these questions raise for DSDM and other agile methods?"

In addition to the findings presented in this paper, a practitioners' perspective on the lessons learned from this study can be found in [23].

6.1   Key Challenges in UX Design and DSDM Integration

The challenges faced by our DSDM organization find resonances in existing literature, and so are not unique to this method, and some existing mitigation strategies have proved useful in this context.

Communication between Developers and UX Designers. The role of face-to-face communication between developers and designers is stressed by Isomursu et al. [24].

Several publications suggest involving developers and designers in each other's process. For example, Budwig et al. [25] describes an approach in which the developers conduct design work by creating paper mock-ups, presenting them to the customer and then feeding back to the usability engineers. Designers can also be more closely involved in the development process, e.g. in the sprint planning meeting [24] or the stand-up meeting [17]. In our case study company, a designer did regularly attend the stand-ups, but it was not always the designer actively working on the project. Communication improved when the right designer attended.

Design collaboration can also be encouraged through, e.g., a design studio [26, 27] in which developers, stakeholders and designers produce design sketches, present them and critique them in order to find the best solution. The aim is to develop technically-feasible designs, and to promote a shared understanding, shared ownership of the design solutions and team communication.

Level of Precision in Upfront Design: This challenge is also faced by others. The level of detail required depends on the communication process between designers and developers, but the main message is "just enough". There is little guidance on exactly how much is "just enough", and reliance often falls back onto frequent communication. However, in our case study, developers suggested five main reasons why "less is more" when it comes to design documentation ready for the start of developer involvement.

Larry Constantine's classification of outputs as "deliverables" versus "consumables" provides a useful perspective [19]. Deliverables need to be finished rather than modifiable. On the whole, designs are deliverables for designers and consumables for developers.

6.2   How DSDM Supports Integration

In the case study organization, the roles of the extended Business Analyst and the hybrid Project Manager were seen as key to overcoming the challenges. The DSDM framework focuses on roles and phases, and hence does provide some support in this area. However, as there is no explicit mention of UX design in DSDM and no UX designer role, teams have to work out their own approach to managing this issue.

DSDM's approach to roles is more detailed than that of other agile methods, and this enables project teams to explicitly identify and manage team members with different specialisms and different levels of responsibility. The roles involved during Foundations are primarily the higher level 'Project' level roles, such as the Business

Sponsor, Business Visionary and Project Manager. During Exploration and Engineering responsibility moves over to the lower level 'Solution Development' team, which contains roles such as the Business Analyst, the Business Ambassador, the Solution Developer and the Solution Tester.

In this case study two DSDM roles were adapted, one higher 'Project' level role, the Project Manager; and one lower 'Solution Development' role, the Business Analyst. In DSDM the Project Manager is responsible for business and technical delivery, high-level management, the outline delivery plan and resourcing specialist roles. The introduction of a Project Manager with a background in technical and UX management meant that the project level decision maker was sensitive to the team's UX challenges and was able to introduce new ways of working to improve the situation. The role of the Business Analyst in DSDM is to facilitate communication between the business and technical participants and to support Business Ambassadors and Advisors in thinking through requirements details. The extension of this role in the case study facilitated regular communication between the two teams.

These role adaptations were effective for LShift and could be attributed to the iterative research process with regular feedback points we initiated [21]. However, they were implemented fairly late on in the project and have yet to be fully evaluated. Others have also suggested introducing new roles to support team integration, e.g. Kollman et al have proposed a UX satellite [16]. An outcome from this work is a recommendation to the DSDM Consortium to include some explicit mention of UX design in the DSDM documentation along with some best practice guidelines that would help those using the method.

6.3   Implications for DSDM and Other Agile Methods

Three aspects of the findings here have implications for DSDM and other agile methods. Firstly, although UX design is not directly mentioned in the framework's description, DSDM does provide some support for the integration, but it could do more. Specifically, having standard roles that can be extended to address UX communication issues as discussed in the previous section is a useful starting point. However the roles are not configurable in DSDM at present, but maybe this would be appropriate.

Secondly, five reasons for reducing the amount of up-front design were identified by the developers at LShift. Explaining these to designers at the beginning of the project may lead to less resistance from them to minimize wasted resources. This may be useful for all agile methods, including DSDM.

Finally, the shift between design-led and development-led project phases is worth highlighting. In our case, the teams could not have started the project in a developer-led fashion because the product brand and image needed to be established first. However, once enough of the design had been developed and the common vision was established, the developers were able to tweak existing designs in response to evolving requirements. This difference has not been highlighted before in any agile context, and could be better supported in both DSDM and other methods.

7   Conclusions

This paper focuses on the use of DSDM, but regardless of which agile method is used, the integration of UX design and agile development is a challenge. This paper has highlighted challenges and practical mitigations from which both DSDM and other agile methods may learn.

DSDM's Feasibility and Foundations phases offered a good opportunity to identify and mitigate challenges in communication between different expertises. The sooner these challenges are mitigated, the fewer challenges will seep through to Engineering. Challenges that arose during these phases were addressed using extended versions of DSDM's standard pre-defined roles. DSDM might therefore be enhanced by including guidance and support for such extensions, the exact details of which are likely to depend on the specific context. Explicitly including roles to support communication such as the communication bridge and the hybrid project manager may enhance other agile methods too. Other agile methods may also learn from the challenges that arose during the Engineering phase, where most agile methods focus.

In this case study, UX designers preferred to produce 'pixel-perfect' designs early on. This concern is common to many agile methods, but the reasons are not so often articulated. Here we have highlighted five reasons for these concerns, and these are applicable in all agile methods.

The nature of any agile project may change from design-led to development-led. In this case study, the importance of the UX role within the team reduced as soon as the principles were set and the development team was operating well. This may change the power balance in the project and hence the dynamics that create the challenges in the first place. All agile teams need to be aware of these differences. This change from design-led to development-led has not previously been discussed in the literature and we suggest conducting further studies to investigate how the power balance between designers and developers evolves during the course of a project.

References

1. Abelein, U., Sharp, H., Paech, B.: Does Involving Users in Software Development Really Influence System Success? IEEE Software 30(6), 17–23 (2013)
2. Constantine, L.L.: Process agility and software usability: Toward lightweight usage-centered design. Information Age 8(8), 1–10 (2002)
3. Sharp, H., Robinson, H.M., Segal, J.: eXtreme Programming and User-Centred Design: friend or foe?. In: Proceedings of HCI 2004, 2nd vol. (September 2004)
4. Chamberlain, S., Sharp, H., Maiden, N.A.M.: Towards a Framework for Integrating Agile Development and User-Centred Design. In: Abrahamsson, P., Marchesi, M., Succi, G. (eds.) XP 2006. LNCS, vol. 4044, pp. 143–153. Springer, Heidelberg (2006)
5. Garrett, J.J.: The Elements of User Experience: User-Centered Design for the Web. New Riders Publishers, Indianapolis (2002)
6. Dingsoyr, T., Dyba, T., Abrahamsson, P.: A preliminary roadmap for empirical research on agile software development. In: Proceedings of AGILE 2008, pp. 83–94. IEEE (2008)
7. Abrahamsson, P., Warsta, J., Siponen, M.T., Ronkainen, J.: New directions on agile methods: A comparative analysis. In: Proceedings of ICSE 2003, Portland, Oregon, USA (May 2003)

8. Fowler, M., Highsmith, J.: The agile manifesto. Software Development 9(8), 28–35 (2001)
9. DSDM Consortium (2013), http://www.dsdm.org/dig-deeper
10. Ferreira, J., Sharp, H., Robinson, H.M.: User Experience Design and Agile Development: Managing cooperation through articulation work. Software Practice and Experience 41(9), 963–974 (2011)
11. Ferreira, J., Sharp, H., Robinson, H.M.: Agile Development and User Experience Design Integration as an Ongoing Achievement in Practice. In: Agile Conference (AGILE 2012), pp. 11–20 (2012)
12. Haikara, J.: Usability in agile software development: Extending the interaction design process with personas approach. In: Concas, G., Damiani, E., Scotto, M., Succi, G. (eds.) XP 2007. LNCS, vol. 4536, pp. 153–156. Springer, Heidelberg (2007)
13. Broschinsky, D., Baker, L.: Using Persona with XP at LANDesk Software, an Avocent Company. In: Proceedings AGILE 2008, pp. 543–548 (2008)
14. Kane, D.: Finding a place for discount usability engineering in agile development: throwing down the gauntlet. In: Proceedings of ADC, pp. 40–46 (2003)
15. Cho, L.: Adopting an agile culture. In: AGILE 2009, pp. 19–25. IEEE Computer Society, Los Alamitos (2009)
16. Kollmann, J., Sharp, H., Blandford, A.: The importance of identity and vision to user experience designers on agile projects. In: Proceedings of the 2009 AGILE Conference, Chicago, IL, USA, pp. 11–18. IEEE Computer Society (August 2009)
17. Sy, D.: Adapting usability investigations for agile user-centered design. Journal of Usability Studies 2(3) (2007)
18. Sy, D., Miller, L.: Optimizing Agile user-centered design. In: Proceedings of CHI 2008 Extended Abstracts on Human Factors in Computing, pp. 3897–3900. ACM, New York (2008)
19. Patton, J.: (2013), http://agileproductdesign.com/blog/emerging_best_agile_ux_practice.html (accessed September 6, 2013)
20. Nielsen and Norman group report (2013), http://www.nngroup.com/reports/agile-development-user-experience/
21. Gregory, P., Plonka, L., Sharp, H., Taylor, K.: Bridging the Gap Between Research and Practice: The Agile Research Network. In: Proceedings of European Conference on Research Methodology for Business and Management Studies (June 2014)
22. Avison, D.E., Lau, F., Myers, D., Nielsen, P.A.: Action research. Commun. ACM 42(1), 94–97 (1999)
23. The Agile Research Network in conjunction with LShift Ltd: Integrating UX design into a DSDM project: challenges, working practices and lessons learned (2013), http://agileresearchnetwork.org/ux-white-paper/
24. Isomursu, M., Sirotkin, A., Voltti, P., Halonen, M.: User Experience Design Goes Agile in Lean Transformation – A Case Study. In: AGILE 2012, pp. 1–10 (2012)
25. Budwig, M., Jeong, S., Kelkar, K.: When user experience met agile: A case study. In: Proceedings of CHI 2009 Extended Abstracts on Human Factors in Computing, pp. 3075–3084. ACM, New York (2009)
26. Gothelf, J.: Lean UX Applying Lean Principles to Improve User Experience. O'Reilly Media (February 2013)
27. Ungar, J., White, J.: Agile user centered design: Enter the design studio - a case study. In: CHI 2008 Extended Abstracts on Human Factors in Computing Systems, pp. 2167–2178. ACM, New York (2008)

Agile Principles in the Embedded System Development

Matti Kaisti[1], Tapio Mujunen[1,2], Tuomas Mäkilä[1],
Ville Rantala[1], and Teijo Lehtonen[1]

[1] Technology Research Center, University of Turku, 20014 Turun Yliopisto, Finland
http://embedded.utu.fi
[2] Oy LM Ericsson Ab, 02420 Jorvas, Finland

Abstract. Agile manifesto with its four values and 12 principles provides widely accepted definition of agile. Agile methods have been actively used in software engineering and other fields are starting to utilize agile development methods as well. Embedded system development combines software, hardware and mechanical engineering activities and thus has some characteristics and constrains which are not found in pure software engineering. These constraints have earlier been described to be leading to some reinterpretation of agile practices. However, understanding how these constraints affect the applicability of agile philosophy in embedded domain has not yet been systematically analyzed. Here we will discuss about agile methods and its applicability in embedded system development through the 12 principles of agile manifesto. We aim to capture the philosophy of agile rather than only individual practices, by presenting redefined principles for embedded system development.

Keywords: agile development, embedded system, embedded software.

1 Introduction

Agile methods are currently widely recognized and used in the field of software engineering. The Agile manifesto is commonly agreed to define agile software development [1]. There are many methods under the umbrella of agile that share the same philosophy as stated in the manifesto and thus it can be considered as the conjunctive factor between the different agile methods.

Each method has its own practices and they emphasize different issues. For example, Extreme Programming (XP) has many pragmatic practices where aspects such as extensive testing, code revision and pair programming are emphasized [2]. Alternatively, Scrum focuses more on managing projects where planning is difficult and relies on frequent feedback from development cycles with regular planning and review [3].

It is commonly agreed that iterative development is one of the core practices of agile development. Iterative development has been used already as far back as in the 1950's, but its widespread use has been limited until the agile movement in the 1990's originating from the software development world [4]. The iterative

G. Cantone and M. Marchesi (Eds.): XP 2014, LNBIP 179, pp. 16–31, 2014.

development approach was originally introduced as an alternative to a plan driven approach commonly labeled as the waterfall model [5].

In a recent systematic literature review (SLR) the state-of-the-art of agile methods in the embedded system and the embedded software development was studied by the authors [6]. The results of the review showed that most of the studies are experience reports and expert opinions, and no rigorous or controlled experiments have been done. However, these reports showed no fundamental issues why embedded development could not benefit from agile methods and practices. It is clear that there are some characteristics in embedded domain that challenge the applicability of agile development in embedded domain. In fact, many reports and experience opinions showed at least anecdotal evidence on the benefits of applying agile in embedded software development. It should be noted, that most of these studies concentrated on applying agile methods in embedded software development where software development is constrained by hardware. Our focus here is broader as we consider not just embedded software but embedded systems. These systems combine many fields of engineering that jointly create the system through collaboration where each field constrains others. To develop such a system in agile way we need agile system development and not only pure software development.

The characteristics that are relevant in understanding why agile methods might not be suitable as such in the embedded domain are discussed in Section 2. The Agile manifesto is based on four values which are backed up by twelve principles. We consider the four values to be too general as a basis for new agile method development for the embedded domain. Therefore, in Section 3 the suitability of the twelve agile principles in embedded system design is studied. The study is based on the emphasis of each principle analyzed in [7] and the characteristics of embedded system development. This paper combines information from literature and findings from an ongoing project (see acknowledgement) of the authors where agile methods are studied in the context of embedded systems development. In this project several case studies were conducted in companies developing embedded systems. We propose and discuss redefined agile principles for agile development of embedded systems in Section 3. The final section summarizes the findings.

2   Characteristics of Embedded Systems Development

Embedded system is application specific and it is typically defined to be a system consisting of mechanical and electronic parts in addition to application specific software. The applications of embedded systems vary from cell phones and navigation devices to cameras and medical devices to just name a few. The complexity of embedded systems has substantially increased which makes the development of such systems increasingly harder.

In this paper, the development of embedded systems is analyzed as a whole, including software, hardware and mechanical design. There are many issues that need to be considered when applying agile methods to embedded system development as the embedded domain differs in many aspects from pure software development. Some most common characteristics of embedded system development are discussed next.

2.1 Need for System Level Documentation

In agile methods the working software is promoted over comprehensive documentation. This is commonly interpreted as keeping the amount of documentation at a minimum and to start coding early without doing major up-front designs or architectures. In embedded systems this can not be avoided [8]. The view that system level documentation is required in embedded system development is also supported in [9], [10], [11]. There are many stakeholders and design teams involved in a project with different backgrounds and specialization. Different teams working in the same project also requires that the teams' work is synchronized which in turn requires some amount of up-front design documentation. Therefore there is a need to have better ways for communication and coordination between heterogeneous teams. The required documentation also leads to a problem of keeping the documentation up to date [8]. A document driven development is suggested as a way to share appropriate documentation and information between different stakeholders [11].

Additionally embedded systems are often developed for areas of application such as aerospace and medical devices where strict standards and regulations set requirements for their functionality and even for the development process itself. Heavy compliance approval processes may be required and therefore even small changes in plans or implementations have to be carefully considered. Compliance with standards also requires documentation to guarantee that the development process follows the guidelines and achieves the desired quality. However, several standards support incremental or evolutionary documentation which allows more agile development as the standards do not necessarily require big up-front design [12]. Even so, the nature of mission and life critical systems requires more documentation because they are commonly multi-year projects where there is a significant personnel turnover. For this reason tacit knowledge is not enough to transfer information between developers. Also, the products are long lived and of high quality that have to be maintainable. Usually there is a third party handling the maintenance. Therefore, there are needs to have precise high quality documentation present to transfer knowledge. [13]

2.2 Hardware-Software Interdependencies

Hardware and software parts are naturally tied together in embedded systems. Hardware and software require each other in the final verification and both parts have to be developed to some maturity before they can be tested together. Additionally, embedded system design requires substantial amount of experimenting with hardware and software e.g. due to the hardware timing constraints which can make the software behave in unpredictable ways. [8].

Electronics and mechanics design have long development cycles compared to software. Even though these cycles can be shortened with today's fast manufacturing processes, simulation tools, mechanical quick models, and with many off the shelf components, they are not expected to reach the cycle lengths of software development. Therefore, it may become an issue to fit these different domains together into a cyclic development flow.

2.3   Heterogenous Teams with Different Skillsets

Developers of each domain, such as software, electronics or mechanics, see the application mostly from their own point of view. A challenge is to combine these views to develop, test, and verify the application in the best possible way early. Mastering all these different domains at the same time is challenging or even impossible. Understanding the overall functionality is difficult and requires extensive experience or very close and efficient collaboration. However, overcoming this challenge through better understanding of the other domains is essential to create an environment which supports synergetic cross-domain innovation, and where communication is also effortless.

Agile methods commonly promote knowledge transfer within the team that leads to teams where tasks in a project can virtually be made by anyone. For example, agile methods promote a common code base and joint responsibility. Given the nature of embedded systems with many heterogeneous teams with different skills make it quite impossible to have such a knowledge transfer and commonly owned task base. Additionally, many different teams with specialized skills create difficulties in communication where misunderstandings can become quite common. This emphasizes close collaboration between different teams. The task is even more challenging should there be virtual teams or outsourced resourcing involved in the development process.

2.4   Inflexibility due to Real-Time Functionality

In embedded systems the software is commonly constrained due to resource constraints e.g. processor speed, memory and user interface. Real-time means that a function needs to happen in predictable ways, not that it is instantaneous. Hard real time requirements mean that if an action is not executed in a given time frame there could be a major failure in the system [14].

Maintaining synchronization of different parts of an embedded system is crucial for the whole system to work as designed. The time window for a certain task to complete can be very narrow and in many cases it can lead to a requirement of optimization. This introduces a challenge to design work, since even small changes in a feature or bug fixes in hardware or software may cause significant changes in the timings. This leads to a situation where efficient communication between the teams is emphasized and the ability to make changes becomes more difficult.

Real-time requirements are typical characteristics for any embedded system [8] and lead to necessary reinterpretation of agile methods and practices. For example refactoring needs to emphasize speed and low power consumption of the design rather than modular and readable code [15]. Timing-critical features typically have to be tuned carefully to operate as intended. In systems like these the correctness of the system functionality is guaranteed as long as every action is executed within a given timeframe [14].

3   Mapping Principles of Agile Software Development to Embedded System Development

Due to the characteristics of embedded system development discussed in the previous chapter, agile methods do not directly work in the embedded domain. There are many agile methods with various practices emphasizing different aspects. A widely recognized definition of agile capturing its philosophy is given by Agile manifesto [1]. The manifesto comprises four values and 12 principles. Since the four values are quite general and almost directly applicable to embedded system development, we focus on the 12 principles of the manifesto. In the following we will discuss how these principles apply in embedded domain and thus we aim to provide some guidance to developing an agile method for embedded domain. We also propose new principles which are more suitable for embedded system development, but still retain the essence of the original agile principles.

In Table 1 there are the 12 principles of the manifesto [1] and their corresponding emphasis given in [7]. We added a third column describing main challenges of each principle in the embedded system context. We have found that there are challenges in evaluating the product maturity, releasing the whole embedded system frequently and in accepting changes late in development process. In addition, due to the diversity of development teams there are challenges in communication and in aligning everyone's efforts in an efficient way. According to the emphasis of each principle discussed by [7] we grouped the principles in four categories which are progress of product development (principles 1, 3, and 7), control of change (principles 2 and 10), people (principles 4, 5, 6, 8 and 11), and improving the agility (principles 9 and 12).

3.1   Principles Concerning the Progress of Product Development

Agile methods underline the ability to measure reliably and continuously the status of a project through functional deliverables and suggest that slicing tasks in small pieces is a way to improve predictability and transparency. Creating small, self-contained tasks is not trivial in the embedded domain and new practices are needed to achieve this target.

Principle 1: Our highest priority is to satisfy the customer through early and continuous delivery of valuable software.
Principle 3: Deliver working software frequently, from a couple of weeks to a couple of months, with a preference to the shorter timescale.
Principle 7: Working software is the primary measure of progress.

Table 1. The emphasis and challenges of agile principles in embedded system development. The emphasis is from [7] and principles from the agile manifesto [1].

	Agile Principle	Emphasis	Challenge
1.	Our highest priority is to satisfy the customer through early and continuous delivery of valuable software.	Customer satisfaction, continuous delivery, value, early deliveries.	Definition of deliverable, long development cycles.
2.	Welcome changing requirements, even late in development. Agile processes harness change for the customer's competitive advantage.	Adaptability, competitiveness, customer benefit.	High cost of change late in development.
3.	Deliver working software frequently, from a couple of weeks to a couple of months, with a preference to the shorter timescale.	Frequent deliveries.	Definition of deliverable, the cost of delivering the whole system, long development cycles.
4.	Business people and developers must work together daily throughout the project.	Collaboration.	Multi-domain communication.
5.	Build projects around motivated individuals. Give them the environment and support they need, and trust them to get the job done.	Motivated individuals, good environment, support, trust.	Heterogeneous skills and teams.
6.	The most efficient and effective method of conveying information to and within a development team is face-to-face conversation.	Efficiency, communication.	Distributed development, multi-domain communication.
7.	Working software is the primary measure of progress.	Measure of progress via deliverables.	Frequent system releases.
8.	Agile processes promote sustainable development. The sponsors, developers, and users should be able to maintain a constant pace indefinitely.	Sustainability, people.	Heterogeneous skills.
9.	Continuous attention to technical excellence and good design enhances agility.	Focus on technical excellence, good design as enabler of agility	Refactoring, good design.
10.	Simplicity–the art of maximizing the amount of work not done–is essential.	Simplicity, optimize work.	Long cycles.
11.	The best architectures, requirements, and designs emerge from self-organizing teams.	Self-organization.	Heterogeneous skills, upfront system level design.
12.	At regular intervals, the team reflects on how to become more effective, then tunes and adjusts its behavior accordingly.	Built-in improvement of efficiency and behavior.	Heterogeneous teams.

The first agile principle assumes that the customer is satisfied by delivering valuable software. In the software development the goal is that software is throughout the development process "as ready as possible" and is incrementally built into the first fully-working version. It is self-evident that in embedded system development the first principle cannot be adopted as such, since the outcome of the development activities is more than just software.

To analyze the meaning and the validity of the principle in the embedded systems context, two questions have to be answered: 1) what is the equivalent concept to the "valuable software" in the context, and 2) can it be delivered early and continuously during the embedded system development cycle?

The first question is more complex than it firstly seems. The incremental development, that is taken for granted in software development, is not that straightforward in the embedded systems domain. If the measure of progress is considered to be a working system it could be that the first functional version of the system could become available very late in the design process. Thus the measure of progress would be available too late to allow the reliable estimation of product maturity and possible corrections in the design.

We suggest that in the agile embedded development frequent *demonstrations of progress* are taken into use. The demonstrations make the progress visible and, if possible, increase the understanding of the system under development, and therefore create value to the customer. The nature of demonstrations can vary. In early stages of the development a demonstration can be a pre-project, a proof of concept or even a document describing the system level design while in latter stages actual prototypes of the system are delivered. Even if documentation and plans can be accepted as demonstrations to some extent, the goal is to deliver working prototypes as early and as often as feasible.

What comes to the second question, the costs to manufacture hardware and mechanics prototypes nowadays are becoming lower compared to labor costs. Therefore, iterative development of hardware and mechanics is more feasible than it used to be, but nevertheless the iterations in these two domains are far longer that in software. Thus, the frequency of customer releases is heavily impacted by the speed of hardware and mechanical design. With the concept of redefining the deliverable it is possible to use e.g. dual targeting [16] to demonstrate the functionality of software and to improve the quality of hardware driver software even though the physical implementation of the system is not ready. Up-front prototyping and platform based design are hardware practices that can be used to get a working system and a demonstration. [17], [18]. In some cases it is fairly easy to deliver something working early. There is, however, difficulties in reaching the same pace or frequency of deliveries as in software engineering.

Laanti et al. summarize the emphasis of the first principle as customer satisfaction, continuous delivery, value and early deliveries [7]. Value builds up differently in embedded systems than in software, and it is possible that actual functional value will be realized only late during the development cycle. However, the customer can benefit from early and continuous delivery although the deliverable is not the working system. It is evident that by delivering some proofs of development advancements increases the customer's understanding into the development work and therefore, also the customer satisfaction during the development process. However, it has to be constantly kept in mind, that the ultimate goal and the fulfillment of customer satisfaction is the working system which creates additional value to the customer. Therefore, if there is a contradiction between the requirement of continuous delivery and the advancement towards the working system, the latter should be given priority.

As a summary, we need to either loose the requirement of early and continuous delivery in embedded systems development or define the "valuable software" differently than in software development context. The first principle could be changed in the embedded systems context as follows:

Proposal 1: Our highest priority is to satisfy the customer through early and continuous demonstrations which lead to the valuable system.

The third and seventh agile principle discuss the same topics as the first principle. Working software is in the core of all these three principles and therefore what is said above still applies. In the third principle frequent deliveries guarantee the visibility and the pace of the development work. Although in embedded systems development the reasonable development cycle might be longer than in software development mainly because of the functionality of the hardware is more difficult to slice into smaller pieces. Therefore, the cycle lengths should be stretched to their natural length. However, the suggested iteration range still applies even if it is likely that shorter lengths are not commonly met. The seventh principle repeats the message of the importance of working software as a measure of progress. As mentioned before, the concept of demonstrations that lead to a working system can be used as a sufficient substitute in the embedded systems development.

Laanti et al. summarize the essence of the third principle as frequent deliveries and the seventh principle as progress measure via deliverables. These core ideas behind the original principles can be restructured as follows:

Proposal 3: Deliver demonstrations leading to the working system frequently, from a couple of weeks to a couple of months, with a preference to the shorter timescale.

Proposal 7: Demonstrations and working systems are the primary measure of progress.

3.2 Principles Concerning the Control of Change

Agile manifesto stresses the openness to accept changes whenever during the development process to ensure customer's advantage [1]. However, in the embedded system development the cost of change late in the process can lead to substantial increase in cost and the sudden increase in the workload can significantly affect the release date. Therefore, new development techniques are needed to move the stance from reacting to changes to ensuring that the customer does not have a need for costly change late in development.

Principle 2: Welcome changing requirements, even late in development. Agile processes harness change for the customer's competitive advantage.

In the previous section, the concept of working software and its equivalent in embedded systems development was discussed. Another concept that works differently in embedded systems development than in pure software development are the changing requirements emphasized by the second principle. For example, in many cases the functionality of a software system can be removed by simply commenting out certain key lines from the source code. In embedded systems, changing or enhancing functionality of a performance optimized feature could result in a costly redesign due to software and hardware interdependencies. In real-time systems these kind of changes could even jeopardize the correctness of functionality.

Laanti et al. describe second principle to emphasize adaptability, competitiveness, and customer benefit [7]. Implementing this principle in embedded domain requires a domain specific approach to overcome the cost of change which is emphasized in embedded domain. One strategy to achieve adaptability is adding generality to the design. This is in contrast with for example Extreme Programming where simplicity over general designs is strongly advised. The assumption is that the cost of later modifications is smaller than the cost of making general designs since in software engineering most of the functionality is never used. In embedded domain this view is challenged since hardware sets limits how fast and flexibly the hardware iterations can be made. Strictly following the principle of simplicity would require much shorter hardware development cycles that are possible. This hardware iteration length boundary shifts the balance between simplicity and generality towards more general designs. More rigid and expensive the hardware iteration, the greater is the shift. Generality thus ensures that emerging customer requests could be handled as incremental design changes.

The lean software development approach provides a good tool for minimizing costs due to changing requirements in the embedded systems development. The fourth principle of the lean software development guides to *defer commitment*, which practically means that the work should not be started until the latest possible point. This way it is ensured that the latest and most correct information is at developer's disposal. [19]

Hardware inherently sets more limits and boundaries than software due to its inherent rigidity and longer development cycles. Additionally, the expenses of late changes in hardware more easily outweigh the benefits of the late change than in software. For this reason the project becomes less agile when it matures compared to software engineering projects. The software stays adaptable in the boundaries of the hardware constraints. This is the problem of embedded software development with hardware constraints. It has been previously discussed e.g. by [8, 16].

To fully gain agility in embedded system project we need to introduce ideas from hardware-software co-design [17]. It is important that hardware and software feedback loops are short and that the entire system, not just embedded software, is optimized. Both hardware and software set requirements to other domains. The common and inherent development phases of hardware are system design, design implementation, manufacturing and testing. These phases are clear points in the development that partially freeze the design. In each development phase it should be analyzed how the flexibility of the system is restricted after the phase has been completed. Through customer feedback from the demonstrations and implemented features it should be ensured that no unnecessary restrictions are made and that restricting decisions should be deferred as long as feasible. If not enough information is available to make a design choice, the requirement for simplicity should be relaxed. More general design choices should be implemented that allows late changes without a costly hardware re-implementation.

Based on this discussion, we can reformulate the second principle as follows:

Proposal 2: Defer making restricting design decisions to allow changing requirements, even late in development. This way the change can be harnessed for the customer's competitive advantage.

Principle 10: - Simplicity – the art of maximizing the amount of work not done – is essential.

Following Laanti's categorization, the tenth principle emphasizes simplicity and optimization of work. To avoid implementing anything that could be changed later on, the principle guides developers to commit only to work which is essentially necessary.

Simplicity in design is important just as well in embedded domain as it is in software engineering since it guides to avoid overly complicated solutions that are hard to document. There is, however, distinctions in embedded development that have to be understood. Previously, we have discussed long development cycles. Designing optimized, bare minimum functionality would easily lead to a situation where after the hardware is designed and sent to be manufactured, a new feature requirement arises.

To reduce the total amount of work to be done during the whole project it is good practice to reserve some extra functionality that has fairly high probability of being used even if this leads to fair amount of features never needed. This leads to a trade-off between additional cost and flexibility but, as we discussed in the context of the second principle, the target should always be to avoid disruptive modifications and to strive toward incremental changes. Practical means to implement generality in design work means utilizing non-optimal, general designs that can be more easily reused in different applications. This can be done with modular and general platform-design, which enables the implementation of functionality using software techniques rather than hardware implementations. As discussed previously, the capability of predicting the right amount of extra functionality is essential in implementing this approach efficiently.

As a summary, just as it is important to prioritize the work and to avoid overengineering, it is also essential to optimize the total amount of total work to be done during a project. Therefore, we suggest that the tenth principle should be reformulated as follows:

Proposal 10: Balance between simplicity – the art of maximizing the amount of work not done in a short term – and generality – the art of minimizing the total amount of work to be done in a long term – is essential.

3.3   Principles Concerning People

Agile methods promote people over processes. Emphasizing individuals puts the focus on people and their energy, innovation, and ability to solve problems and to work together towards a common goal. This is true also in embedded system development although there are some specific challenges created by teams with specialized individual skills, e.g. by dividing into hardware and software engineers.

Principle 11: The best architectures, requirements, and designs emerge from self-organizing teams.

In embedded system development top level design is required e.g. in order to have clear task allocation between software and hardware. Therefore, it is important that these teams have a joint system design or architecture. Additionally, there should be a leading role with the responsibility of the project having the supreme right to make important decisions should there be any conflicts between different teams and to maintain continuous interaction between teams [20]. As an example, in Scrum the Product Owner would make important product-related decisions that affect the teams, while the Scrum Master would facilitate the conflict mediation and continuous interaction between the teams. It is acknowledged that self-organization is still required, but the principle should also emphasize co-operating teams which allows the embedded system, not just its components, to have optimal implementation and not to have software and hardware overhead. We propose a slight change to this principle as follows:

Proposal 11: The best architectures, requirements, and designs emerge from co-operating and self-organizing teams.

Principle 8: Agile processes promote sustainable development. The sponsors, developers, and users should be able to maintain a constant pace indefinitely.

In an ideal development team everyone would be able to take on every kind of task. In embedded system development this, however, is not possible due to the differentiation and complexity of subsystem components that are needed for an application to be delivered. It is most likely, that there are areas of specialization that can be done efficiently only by few in the development team. This can possibly lead to management issues when specialized tasks are done in series. Delay in a critical part affects the rest of the developers causing the amount of work not done to pile up. For this reason sustainable pace can be more challenging in embedded context, but also, it can be the reason why it is even more important to pay attention to it.

Principle 4: Business people and developers must work together daily throughout the project.
Principle 5: Build projects around motivated individuals. Give them the environment and support they need, and trust them to get the job done.
Principle 6 The most efficient and effective method of conveying information to and within a development team is face-to-face conversation.

With heterogeneous teams a clear communication can be more difficult when there is no full understanding of a foreign domain. Therefore face-to-face communication is emphasized to make the communication more clear. However, in embedded systems domain it is quite usual that different design groups can be located on different sites. Therefore the face-to-face communication can be difficult, but modern communication tools allow communication in real time. Even though modern communication tools can alleviate the problem, most likely it can not be compensated altogether and thus following this principle requires special attention.

As a conclusion, the people related agile principles apply in the embedded systems domain, although some nuances have to be taken into consideration. Some principles are more difficult to follow and at the same time it can be more important to do so. The principle of self-organization is clearly the most challenging from all people related principles since the development teams contain individuals with clearly different skill sets and there is a requirement for top level design. That being said, *we propose to keep the fourth, fifth, sixth and eight agile principle intact in the embedded systems context.*

3.4 Principles Concerning Improvement of Agility

Agile methods encourage embracing customer initiated changes in product development and also promote that teams find better working methods and refactor their deliverables as long as it takes to fulfill customer's requests. In agile software development this is seen to improve agility as well as quality.

Principle 9: Continuous attention to technical excellence and good design enhances agility.

Striving towards good design through refactoring and modular code enhances agility in software development. Refactoring, especially in hardware design context, needs to be reinterpreted in embedded domain. Refactoring should emphasize speed and low power consumption while keeping the code as modular and readable if possible. [15].

In embedded systems the cost of change increases as the system grows more mature more strongly than in software engineering. This is true especially in real-time systems where the correctness of functionality of the system can be impacted even by small changes. Continual improvements during a product development should be limited only to those design phases that have not yet been completed.

Principle 12: At regular intervals, the team reflects on how to become more effective, then tunes and adjusts its behavior accordingly.

Investing in continuous development of skills improves multi-discipline team communication as team members become more familiar with other team's working methods. This helps to organize work in order to improve overall throughput. The outcome of reflection is twofold, firstly the improved communication helps to minimize unnecessary documentation and avoid misinterpretations. Secondly, understanding the work flow as a whole helps to optimize working methods of each team. The result is the best possible outcome from the product point of view instead of each team optimizing their own ambitions.

Even though some common agile practices such as refactoring do not fit as such in embedded context the principles behind improving agility are just as important in the embedded context than they are in software engineering. Therefore *we propose that that principles 9 and 12 remain intact in embedded system development.*

4   Summary

Suitability of agile principles in embedded system development has been discussed in this paper. There are some unique features in embedded system development that prevent the straightforward appliance of the original agile principles in the embedded domain. In this paper we presented the proposals for the agile principles in embedded system development which are presented in Table 2. The presented proposals were based on the emphasis of each principle and analyzed through the characteristics of embedded systems. These resulted in principle specific challenges that we summarized in Table 1 and discussed in Section 3.

Some of the original agile principles work in embedded domain as such and others require changes or reinterpretations. Additionally, the importance of some principles is emphasized differently in embedded context. We grouped the principles in four categories: progress of product development, control of change, people and improvement of agility.

The most notable differences are found in principles concerning the progress of product development. In embedded system development it is unfeasible to have frequent system releases due to long development cycles of hardware. Therefore, the definition of deliverable needs to be reinterpreted more loosely. By using hardware related practices it is possible to deliver frequently where the progress is measured via demonstrations.

Principles concerning the control of change also need different approach in the embedded domain especially with welcoming changing requirements even late in development. In hardware-intensive embedded system development late changes cannot be always accepted because of the high impact on cost and schedule since changes usually trickle down to many stakeholders and design teams.

The principles concerning people fit into embedded domain as they may fit into any domain. A discrepancy is found with self-organizing teams. In embedded domain there are commonly many distinct design teams collaborating on a

Table 2. Proposals for Agile Principles in Embedded System Development. Redefined parts of principles are emphasized.

	Proposal of Agile Principles
1	Our highest priority is to satisfy the customer through early and continuous *demonstrations which lead to the valuable system.*
2	*Defer making restricting design decisions to allow changing requirements*, even late in development. *This way the change can be harnessed* for the customer's competitive advantage.
3	Deliver *demonstrations leading to the working system* frequently, from a couple of weeks to a couple of months, with a preference to the shorter timescale.
4	Business people and developers must work together daily throughout the project.
5	Build projects around motivated individuals. Give them the environment and support they need, and trust them to get the job done.
6	The most efficient and effective method of conveying information to and within a development team is face-to-face conversation.
7	*Demonstrations and working system are* the primary measure of progress.
8	Agile processes promote sustainable development. The sponsors, developers, and users should be able to maintain a constant pace indefinitely.
9	Continuous attention to technical excellence and good design enhances agility.
10	*Balance between* simplicity – the art of maximizing the amount of work not done *in a short term – and generality – the art of minimizing the total amount of work to be done in a long term –* is essential.
11	The best architectures, requirements, and designs emerge from *co-operating* and self-organizing teams.
12	At regular intervals, the team reflects on how to become more effective, then tunes and adjusts its behavior accordingly.

project and the self-organization is mainly limited among the people working on the same, quite narrowly defined, domain.

Principles concerning improvement of agility are especially important in embedded domain since common practices, such as refactoring, are not trivial in embedded domain. Distinct development teams are unfamiliar with each other's work which has to be taken into account at each point of the adoption process.

The discussion and the proposed principles, presented in this paper, point out the main differences between software engineering and development of embedded systems. Based on the proposed principles it is also possible to examine the agility, as declared by the agile manifesto, of certain embedded system development practices. Each level and quarter of an organization should be aware of these presented principles to enable self-organization in the development teams.

As a conclusion, the twelve principles of the agile manifesto can be applied to embedded system development as long as their essence can be met with practices suitable for the context of embedded domain.

Acknowledgement. The research reported in this article has been conducted as a part of AgiES (Agile and Lean Product Development for Embedded ICT Systems) project. The project is carried out in collaboration with Finnish Institute of Occupational Health and industry partners BA Group, FiSMA, Lindorff Finland, LM Ericsson, Neoxen Systems, Nextfour Group and Nordic ID. The project is mainly funded by Tekes - the Finnish Funding Agency for Technology and Innovation.

References

1. Beck, K., Beedle, M., van Bennekum, A., Cockburn, A., Cunningham, W., Fowler, M., Grenning, J., Highsmith, J., Hunt, A., Jeffries, R., Kern, J., Marick, B., Martin, R., Mellor, S., Schwaber, K., Sutherland, J., Thomas, D.: Agile manifesto (2001), http://agilemanifesto.org/
2. Beck, K.: Extreme Programming Explained: Embrace Change. Addison-Wesley (1999)
3. Schwaber, K.: Scrum development process. In: 10th Annual ACM Conference on Object Oriented Programming Systems, Languages, and Applications (OOPSLA), pp. 117–134 (1995)
4. Larman, C.: Agile and Iterative Develpoment: A Manager's Guide. Addison-Wesley, Boston (2003)
5. Royce, W.W.: Managing the development of large software systems. In: Proc. IEEE WESTCON, Los Angeles (1970)
6. Kaisti, M., Rantala, V., Mujunen, T., Hyrynsalmi, S., Könnölä, K., Mäkilä, T., Lehtonen, T.: Agile methods for embedded systems development - a literature review and a mapping study. EURASIP Journal on Embedded Systems 15 (2013)
7. Laanti, M., Similä, J., Abrahamsson, P.: Definitions of agile software development and agility. In: McCaffery, F., O'Connor, R.V., Messnarz, R. (eds.) EuroSPI 2013. CCIS, vol. 364, pp. 247–258. Springer, Heidelberg (2013)
8. Ronkainen, J., Abrahamsson, P.: Software development under stringent hardware constraints: Do agile methods have a chance? In: Marchesi, M., Succi, G. (eds.) XP 2003. LNCS, vol. 2675, pp. 73–79. Springer, Heidelberg (2003)
9. Drobka, J., Noftz, D., Raghu, R.: Piloting xp on four mission-critical projects. IEEE Software 21(6), 70–75 (2004)
10. Gul, E., Taylan, S., Yuceturk, A.C., Yildirim, U.: Using xp in telecommunication software development. In: The Third International Conference on Software Engineering Advances, ICSEA 2008, pp. 258–263 (2008)
11. Luqi, Zhang, L., Berzins, V., Qiao, Y.: Documentation driven development for complex real-time systems. IEEE Transactions on Software Engineering 30(12), 936–952 (2004)
12. Theunissen, W.M., Kourie, D.G., Watson, B.W.: Standards and agile software development. In: Proceedings of the 2003 Annual Research Conference of the South African Institute of Computer Scientists and Information Technologists on Enablement Through Technology, SAICSIT 2003, pp. 178–188 (2003)
13. Sidky, A., Arthur, J.: Determining the applicability of agile practices to mission and life-critical systems. In: Proceedings of the 31st IEEE Software Engineering Workshop, SEW 2007, pp. 3–12. IEEE Computer Society, Washington, DC (2007)
14. Douglass, B.P.: Real-Time Agility: The Harmony/ESW Method for Real-Time and Embedded Systems Development, 1st edn. Addison-Wesley Professional (2009)

15. Smith, M., Miller, J., Daeninck, S.: A test-oriented embedded system production methodology. Journal of Signal Processing Systems 56(1), 69–89 (2009)
16. Grenning, J.W.: Test Driven Development for Embedded C. Pragmatic Bookshelf (2011)
17. Punkka, T.: Agile hardware and co-design. In: Embedded Systems Conference 2012, Boston, ESC–3008 (2012)
18. Cordeiro, L., Barreto, R., Oliveira, M.: Towards a semiformal development methodology for embedded systems. In: 3rd International Conference on Evaluation of Novel Approaches to Software Engineering, pp. 5–12 (May 2008)
19. Poppendieck, M., Poppendieck, T.: Implementing Lean Software Development: From Concept to Cash. Addison Wesley Professional (2007)
20. Womack, J.P., Jones, D.T., Roos, D.: The Machine That Changed the World. Simon & Schuster, London (2007)

Agile Software Development in Practice

Maureen Doyle[1], Laurie Williams[2], Mike Cohn[3], and Kenneth S. Rubin[4]

[1] Computer Science, Northern Kentucky University,
Highland Heights, Kentucky 41011, USA
doylem3@nku.edu
[2] Computer Science, North Carolina State University,
Raleigh, North Carolina 27695, USA
williams@csc.ncsu.edu
[3] Mountain Goat Software, Lafayette, Colorado 80026, USA
mike@mountaingoatsoftware.com
[4] Innolution, Niwot, Colorado 80544, USA
krubin@innolution.com

Abstract. Agile software development methods have been around since the mid 1990s. Over these years, teams have evolved the specific software development practices used. Aims: The goal of this paper is to provide a view of the agile practices used by new teams, and the relationship between the practices used, project outcomes, and the agile principles. Method: This paper provides a summary and analysis of 2,229 Comparative Agility™ (CA) assessment surveys completed between March 2011 and October 2012 by agile developers who knew about the survey. The CA tool assesses a team's agility and project outcomes using a 65-statement Likert survey. Results: The agile principle of respect for individuals occurs the most frequently, while simplicity occurs least. Progress/Planning is correlated strongly to nine principles. Conclusion: Subject to sampling issues, successful teams report more positive results for agile practices with the most important practice being teams knowing their velocity.

Keywords: agile software development, comparative agility assessment, agile practices.

1 Introduction

Agile software development is no longer considered a new idea, however showing the savings obtained from implementing an agile process is still largely through anecdote or case studies [1]. The agile manifesto defined principles, and since the inception of agile software development in the mid 1990s, teams have evolved the specific practices used [2].

The goal of this paper is to provide a view of the agile practices used by new teams, and the relationship between the practices used, success Outcomes, and the Agile Principles. We present a view into the state of the practice in agile software development based on extensive analysis of 2,229 completed Comparative Agility (CA) surveys.

G. Cantone and M. Marchesi (Eds.): XP 2014, LNBIP 179, pp. 32–45, 2014.
© Springer International Publishing Switzerland 2014

This paper contributes the following:

- Identification of the most and least popular agile practices.
- Identification of the agile principles that most influence other principles and successful project outcomes.
- Identification of individual survey statements that occur more frequently among successful teams than unsuccessful teams.

2   Comparative Agility

CA is a survey-based assessment tool, developed by three of the four authors, used by individuals and organizations to compare their own agility implementations to others. Any practitioner can visit the CA website[1] and, in exchange for investing his or her time to complete the survey, receive a free report that compares his or her survey results to the complete industry dataset. Alternatively, teams can request[2] to have a customized collector. These team members then individually take the survey using a team-specific survey URL.

At the highest level, the CA approach assesses agility across eight *dimensions*: Teamwork; Requirements; Planning; Technical Practices; Quality; Culture; Knowledge Creating; and Outcomes. The survey respondent is presented with 65 statements. Each statement is an agile practice for which the respondent indicates the truth of the statement relative to their team or organization. For example:

- Upfront planning is helpful without being excessive.
- Team members leave planning meetings knowing what needs to be done and have confidence they can meet their commitments.
- Teams communicate the need to change release date or scope as soon as they are discovered.
- Effort spent on planning is spread approximately evenly throughout the project.

Throughout this paper, we refer to the statements as "practices" interchangeably. The survey statements are considered practices because each statement indicates a practice the team would decide to include in their agile development process. CA respondents choose the appropriate response to the statement using a 6 point Likert scale: not applicable, false, more false than true, neither false nor true, more true than false and true. Individual survey responses were excluded from analysis when 'Not Applicable' was chosen. The remaining responses are assigned ranks of 1, 2, 3, 4, and 5 respectively for all analyses.

CA was designed to lead to actionable results. Sample comparison output is shown in Fig. 1 and the individual respondent or team receives information on the number of standard deviations of their response(s) versus the dataset mean. When an organization can see how it compares with other organizations, improvement efforts can be focused.

---

[1] http://www.comparativeagility.com/

[2] Those wishing to obtain a customized collector should contact the third author of this paper.

Initially, the CA consisted of 125 statements. The CA was shortened in 2010 through a systematic elimination of highly correlated and repetitive questions. Seven questions on project outcomes were added to the new CA to enable analysis of the practices teams use with their project results. This paper analyzed the newer survey instrument.

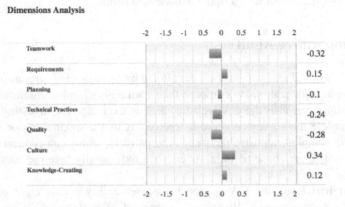

Fig. 1. Comparative Agility Dimension Analysis

3   Related Work

Williams et al. [3] published an overview of industry trends in agility based upon 1,235 respondents of the original 125-statement CA. This 2010 paper also explored in depth on the results of four industrial teams who responded to the CA via customized collectors, explaining why their results were relatively high or low based upon interviews with the teams. The paper discussed the resultant process improvement reactions and plans of these teams subsequent to reviewing their CA results. The work in this 2014 paper differs in the surveys analyzed and includes a statistical analysis of the agile principles and survey statements that were not part of the 2010 work.

Chow et al. [4] developed and analyzed a survey to examine success factors in agile software projects. They evaluated hypothesis based on success in quality, scope, timeliness and cost. The results showed that delivery schedule, agile software engineering techniques, team capability and project management process were the top four critical success factors in successful teams. This CA analysis differs in examining the agile principles, as well a examining a larger pool of practices.

VersionOne[3], an agile project management tool producer, has conducted an annual global survey of agile adoption and practices since 2006. VersionOne publicizes this survey at conferences and via email campaigns asking people to participate. Each year the survey has provided an aggregate report on the status of organizations currently implementing or practicing agile methods. Ambysoft[4] conducts similar

---

[3] http://www.versionone.com/
[4] http://ambysoft.com/surveys

surveys. This paper also reports on the status and demographics of survey-responders, but also provides statistical analyses of the survey results.

Two other assessment frameworks have been used to evaluate agile software development teams with published results. One is the Extreme Programming Evaluation Framework (XP-EF) [5]. The purpose of the XP-EF is to provide a structure for a case study such that the results of multiple, independent case studies can be combined and compared to create a family of related studies. For example, the results of case studies of industrial Extreme Programming (XP) teams at IBM and others were structured via the XP-EF [6].

The other assessment framework is the Shodan survey [5]. Similar in intent to CA, the purpose of the Shodan survey is to assess the extent to which a team adopts the practices of Extreme Programming. The published works detail specific case studies only. Additional published case studies (e.g. [7, 8]) examine agile development, which provide in-depth analysis of a single company.

ThoughtWorks *Agile Assessments*[5] and Dr. Agile *Assessment*[6] provide surveys similar to CA for the purpose of providing individuals and organizations information on their agile adoption and practices. These organizations have not published aggregate data, so we cannot compare to their results.

4   Data Collection and Demographics

The industry-wide data reported in this paper is based upon 2,229 completed CA surveys taken between March 26, 2011 and October 12, 2012. The survey database indicates that 3,339 surveys were attempted or taken during this timeframe, but 1,110 of these surveys were eliminated because not all of the 65 Likert statements had a response. In other words, a survey was deemed incomplete and omitted from the analysis if even one statement was skipped since the option 'Not Applicable' was available for all statements. Individual survey statements with the 'Not Applicable' response were not analyzed. Surveys were not eliminated when demographic questions were skipped. In this section, we report the overall demographics for all valid surveys and present the reported industry, team size, team experience, project types, and other general demographic information.

There were a large number of demographics collected and a subset of these are now discussed. A majority (78%, N=1,735) of the responses came from teams who asked for their data to be analyzed via a customized collector. Generally, teams that request a customized collector are being coached by one of the authors so that their data can be analyzed as a separate group. In other cases (22%, N=494), individuals found the CA survey site, such as after seeing articles written about the survey [5]. Based upon these circumstances, the respondents are considered to be part of agile teams or teams beginning an agile transition.

A broad range of industries participated in the CA assessment. Thirty-one (31) different industries were identified by respondents, including bio-technology, tourism, and game development. Table 1 lists the top five reported industries.

---

[5] http://agileassessments.com/
[6] http://www.dragile.com/

Table 1. Top five industries

Industry	Count	% of Responses
Web/Software Development	968	29.0%
Manufacturing	159	4.8%
Finance/Banking/Accounting	132	4.0%
Telecommunications/Networks	108	3.2%
Non-Profit/Trade Association	95	2.8%

Ninety-five percent (2,127) of the surveys had a response to the question *"Which best characterizes this project?"* Table 2 lists the most popular project types.

Table 2. Project Type

Project Type	% of Responses
Software, application or solution that will be used internally within my organization	37.9%
Web Development	33.8%
Embedded software/systems/devices	13.3%
Other	7.9%
A project being developed by one company for another company	7.1%

Ninety-seven percent of the survey respondents provided the number of people working on their project team including managers, developers, testers, and designers. Many teams had fewer than 10 (33.6%) people while 7% of the teams had more than 50 people. Table 3 summarizes the agile team sizes.

Table 3. Team size as percentage of all respondents

Team Size	% Total
1-10	33.6%
11-25	23.5%
26-50	10.0%
51-100	3.8%
More than 100	3.7%

Another demographic question was answered by 95% of respondents and queried: *"How long has this group been doing agile development prior to starting this project?"* Over 59% (1308/2229) of the respondents indicated the group had been doing agile for a year or less which is likely a manifestation of the survey being taken by new teams being coached by the authors. Table 4 summarizes the results of this question.

Table 4. Team's Experience

Team's Agile Experience	% Total
0-6 months	38.5%
7-12 months	21.8%
Longer than 1 year, less than 2	21.2%
Longer than 2 years, less than 3	10.6%
Longer than 3 years	7.9%
Left Blank	2.9%

In summary, the demographics presented here show that the analysis results discussed in this paper apply to a variety of agile projects and primarily to new teams.

5   State of the Practice

The state of the practice reports the project outcomes experienced by teams, the agile practices, as measured by the survey statements, in practice and presents and discusses the most popular and unpopular reported statements. Understanding the state of agile software development with respect to the twelve agile principles provides us with a quasi-metric of how current agile development compares to the vision stated in the twelve principles.

5.1   Project Outcomes

Seven CA statements assess the outcomes of an agile project are listed, along with a keyword in Table 5.

Table 5. CA Statements evaluating project outcomes

CA Statement	Keyword
The team has produced higher quality products since we started using an agile approach.	Higher quality
The team has been more productive since we started using an agile approach.	More productive
Our customers have been more satisfied with the functionality of our products since started using an agile approach.	Customer functionality
Our customers have been more satisfied with the usability of our products since we started using an agile approach.	Customer Usability
The team has had higher morale since we started using an agile approach.	Higher Morale
Our business has recognized greater economic value since we started using an agile approach.	Greater Economic Value
We have delivered functionality to users more quickly and/or more often since we started using an agile approach.	Delivered Functionality Quicker

The percentage of response type is plotted in Fig. 2 to provide a snapshot of the project outcomes when embracing agile development when compared to previous approaches.

The outcomes "more productive" and "delivered functionality to users more quickly" occurs the most frequently and have more positive than negative responses. The least occurring outcomes relate to customer satisfaction, both with functionality and usability. Of the 2,229 surveys analyzed, 1,593 (71%) reported at least one positive outcome, 636 (29%) of the surveys had only negative outcomes, and 516 (23%) reported all positive outcomes, as defined by responses of "true" or "more true than false."

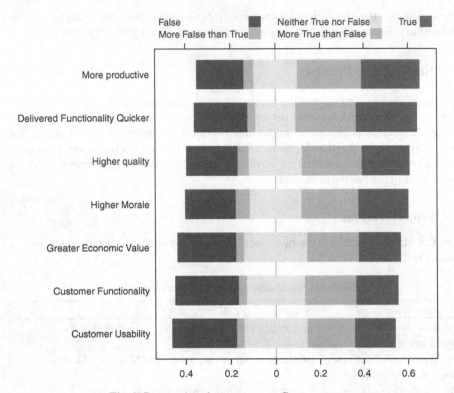

Fig. 2. Reported project outcomes, Count percentage

5.2   Agile Principles

The CA statements were mapped to one of the twelve agile principles defined in the Agile Manifesto [9]. Although statements may address more than one principle, each was assigned to the one principle that the statement most influenced. Table 6 presents the number of CA survey statements per principle and a keyword. The keyword is used in subsequent discussions.

The survey statements were grouped and the percentage of Likert-Scale responses are shown in Fig. 3. It is worth nothing that there are five principles, highlighted in Table 6, that have similar response percentages with a large number of positive responses. All but three principles (emergence, excellence, and simplicity) report at least 50% of teams are practicing the agile principle. The agile principles with the largest positive results are Individuals, Business, and Face-to-face. The CA statements for Individuals address team autonomy, support, and respect. The two statements with the most positive responses for Individuals are: *"Estimates are created collaboratively by the people who will do the work."* and *"Team members are kept together as long as possible."* Business statements evaluate how much the customer is involved in the development process. *"The product owner is available to discuss upcoming features and work-in-progress"* and *"One or more of scope, schedule, or resources is allowed to change during a project."* are the two statements with the most positive responses. Face-to-face survey questions target the availability of team members to meet in person. There are five statements evaluating this practice and the top two statements are *"Whole teams, including the ScrumMaster and Product Owner, have no more than 12 people on them."* and *"Team members communicate in a high-bandwidth manner without undue interference."*

Table 6. CA Survey statements per principle

Principle	Keyword	Num of statements
Our highest priority is to satisfy the customer through early and continuous delivery of valuable software.	Outcomes	7
Welcome changing requirements, even late in development. Agile processes harness change for the customer's competitive advantage.	Change	4
Deliver working software frequently, from a couple of weeks to a couple of months, with a preference to the shorter timescale.	Frequently	1
Business people and developers must work together daily throughout the project.	Business	5
Build projects around motivated individuals. Give them the environment and support they need, and trust them to get the job done.	Individuals	12
The most efficient and effective method of conveying information to and within a development team is face-to-face conversation.	Face-to-face	5
Working software is the primary measure of progress.	Progress	8
Agile processes promote sustainable development. The sponsors, developers, and users should be able to maintain a constant pace indefinitely.	Sustainable	7
Continuous attention to technical excellence and good design enhances agility.	Excellence	11
Simplicity—the art of maximizing the amount of work not done—is essential.	Simplicity	1
The best architectures, requirements, and designs emerge from self-organizing teams.	Emergence	2
At regular intervals, the team reflects on how to become more effective, then tunes and adjusts its behavior accordingly.	Retrospective	2

The principle of Simplicity stands out because it has more negative responses than any other agile principle. Simplicity is defined as the 'art of maximizing the amount of work not done' [9] which is evaluated with one statement: *Team members don't have to work on tasks that they deem to not add value.* These results may indicate that teams are not completely freed of bureaucratic or other non-value tasks when they use agile practices.

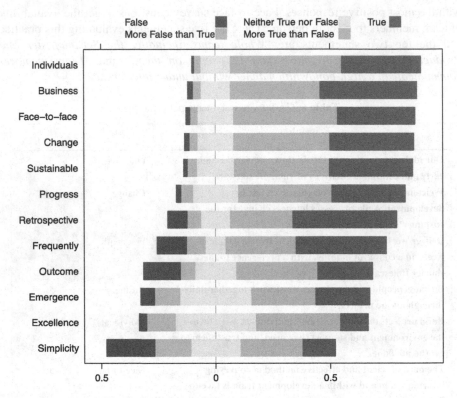

Fig. 3. Applying Agile Practices, Percentage Count

5.3   More and Less Popular Agile Practices

We analyzed the responses to the 58 non-Outcome statements. A survey response is considered positive if the practice was marked as "true" or "more true than false." The survey statements with the most positive responses are listed in Table 7.

Table 7. Most popular practices

CA Statement	% Positive	95% lower limit	Agile Principle
Estimates are created collaboratively by the people who will do the work.	85%	84%	Individuals
All work is done in iterations of no more than 30 days.	84%	83%	Progress
Whole teams, including the ScrumMaster and Product Owner, have no more than 12 people on them.	83%	81%	Face-To-Face
Team members communicate in a high-bandwidth manner without undue interference.	80%	79%	Face-to-Face
Team members are kept together as long as possible.	80%	78%	Individuals

Table 7 includes the 95% lower-limit of positive responses to the questions for generalization to the population of teams converting over to agile development. In other words, given assumptions of normality and random sampling, we are 95% sure that 84% of new agile teams are collaboratively developing estimates.

The practices embodied in the least positive statements are listed in Table 8. Similar to the previous analysis, we are 95% sure that no more than 25% of development teams have implemented pair programming. This is in agreement with previous studies. The next lowest, at no more than 27%, is that agile teams have no manual testing at the end of each iteration. This may be due to the large number of web applications requiring multiple browser version testing.

Table 8. Least popular practices

CA Statement	% Positive	95% upper limit	Agile Principle
Code is written using pair-programming.	23%	25%	Excellence
At the end of each iteration there is little or no manual testing required.	25%	27%	Excellence
Most code is written using unit test-driven development.	38%	40%	Excellence
Bonuses, annual reviews, and compensation promote team behavior.	40%	42%	Individuals
Team members don't have to work on tasks that they deem to not add value.	43%	45%	Simplicity

The agile principles associated with these statements reveal that while "Individuals" has the most positive responses of all the principles, there is room for improvement since at most 42% of the agile teams provide compensation to promote team behavior. Three of the five statements address the agile principle of excellence, and excellence is the second least popular agile principle for all of the survey questions. The practice of agile excellence, as measured by pair-programming, unit-testing, and automated testing are not practiced by most new agile teams.

6   Analysis of Principles and Outcomes

All statistical analysis and tests used are designed for ordinal data. A Spearman rank, r, correlation analysis was performed for all correlation computations. The Spearman rank correlation coefficient was selected because Likert-scale data is measured at the ordinal level. Data of this form violates a necessary assumption for the use of the parametric Pearson correlation coefficient, so a nonparametric correlation is used for analysis. A correlation, r, between two dimensions indicates that r^2 of the variability in one is attributed to variability in the other. Since multiple comparisons were performed, the Bonferroni correction was applied to control the false discovery rate. All correlations are deemed significant only when $p<=0.0002$ for the sample sizes analyzed in 6.1 and 6.2.

6.1   Outcome Correlations

The most strongly correlated statements among all 65 statements in the CA survey occur between the Outcome statements. A large number of surveys had no positive outcomes and, therefore, provide no information regarding the relationships between project outcomes. As a result, correlations between outcomes were computed only using surveys that had at least one successful outcome (1,714 surveys).

The correlation matrix for Outcomes is shown in Fig. 4. The correlation results are displayed as is a lower-triangular matrix with correlation values, r, represented by the size of the square. The larger the square, the more strongly correlated the pair of outcomes. The diagonal is an example of r=1. There were no negative correlations in this analysis. A correlation between two items is considered strong when its value is at least 0.5. All correlations are significant to p<0.0002.

The strongest correlation between two outcomes is for customer more satisfied with usability and customer more satisfied with functionality (r=0.78. Teams report delivering customer satisfaction with functionality and usability together or they are delivering neither. The smallest correlation is between higher morale and delivered functionality to users more quickly (r=0.46), meaning team members report higher morale delivering more frequently. The only other weak correlation is between delivering functionality to users more quickly and delivering higher quality. This is still a positive correlation, however it may reflect the tradeoff that often exists between quality and speed.

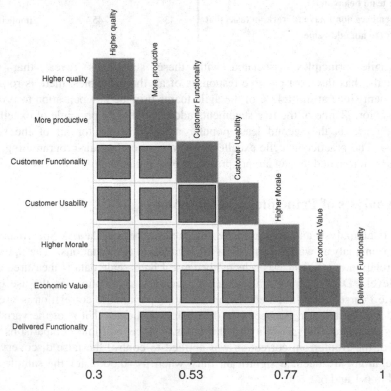

Fig. 4. Outcome Correlations

6.2   Principle Correlations

Correlations for the twelve agile principles were computed for the 2,229 surveys and are shown in Fig. 5. All correlations are significant with p<=0.0002.

All correlations are positive. The six agile principles of Progress, Sustainable, Individuals, Business, Change and Excellence are strongly correlated with each other. Face-To-Face is also a part of this group although its correlation to Excellence is weaker at r=0.45. This result means that teams embracing any one of these agile principles are embracing all of the others.

Progress is correlated strongly to the most dimensions and also to Outcomes (r=0.53). Progress may well be a bellwether of project success indicating projects who are tracking progress are seeing more positive outcomes, while projects not tracking progress are not seeing positive outcomes. In addition, teams that are monitoring progress are also committed to the other principles of agile development.

The principles of Frequently and Retrospective are not as strongly correlated, although interestingly they are highly correlated with each other. Retrospectives are occurring when there are more frequent releases perhaps indicating a fuller commitment to the team process changes necessary for agile development.

The two practices with the weakest correlations are Simplicity and Emergence indicating that changes in these practices do not explain changes in the other practices or outcomes. This result may be due not to the practice itself, but because these

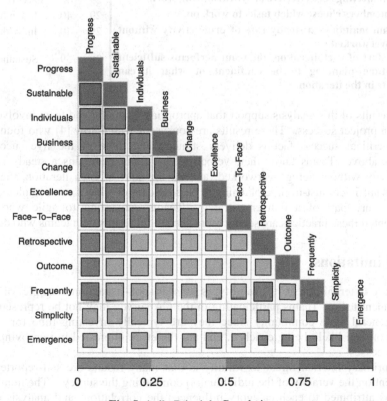

Fig. 5. Agile Principle Correlations

are both harder principles to measure. In addition, there are just three questions (1 for Simplicity and 2 for Emergence) in the survey measuring these practices.

6.3   Statement Analysis

Analysis was done to determine differences between successful and unsuccessful teams. A confidence interval was computed for the differences between answers for each statement between teams that had positive outcomes to teams that did not. All results are significant with $p < 0.001$.

Table 9 contains a list of the practices showing the largest differences between successful and unsuccessful teams. The table contains the 95% confidence interval (lower limit, upper limit) for the reported differences and its agile principle. This first row of this table states that successful teams responded with a 4 or a 5 to the statement 'Teams know their velocity' at least 33% more often than unsuccessful agile teams.

Table 9. Practices of successful teams

Practice	ll	ul	principle
Teams know their velocity.	33	45	Sustainable
Standup meetings are effective at synchronizing work.	29	40	Face-To-Face
Team members choose which tasks to work on.	29	40	Individuals
The team maintains a steady rate of productivity without being overworked.	29	40	Individuals
At the start of each iteration, the team performs sufficient just-in-time planning to be confident of what it can complete in the iteration.	28	39	Sustainable

The results of this analysis support that appropriate planning and team involvement results in project success. These results are consistent with Chow [4] who found that the top critical success fact is delivery strategy and three of the five successful practices above (Teams know their velocity, The Team maintains a steady rate of productivity without being overworked, and At the start of each iteration, the team performs sufficient just-in-time planning to be confident of what it can complete in the iteration.) are part of a delivery strategy. Teams converting to agile who have implemented these practices are seeing more successful results than teams who do not.

7   Limitations

The main external threat to validity is this is not a random sample of agile development teams. Teams participating in the CA survey may not be representative of the general agile community since they are typically investing time for survey completion, are likely being coached, and are therefore interested in improving their agile processes.

The primary internal threat to validity is that many results are self-reported and dependent on the veracity of the individual(s) completing the survey. The number of questions attributed to each category influences the correlations and analysis of the

CA dimensions and agile principles to outcomes. The addition or elimination of survey questions for each principle may alter the results. The CA assessment analysis treated all surveys independently. Teams from the same companies or surveys completed by multiple members of the same team can skew the results.

Another threat to validity is that surveys were taken by different employees on the same agile team and/or employed by the same company. Chi-square results shows that the company has some impact on results although no there were no obvious patterns.

There may be a "cap effect" with regard to the two-sample confidence intervals. For example since at least 83.7% of respondents answer one statement with a 4 or 5, it is that much more difficult to have a larger difference between the success/no success groups. Conversely with statement having fewer positive results, looking at all of them it is 59-63% it is easier to have a bigger difference there between the two groups.

The CA assessment does not differentiate between the methodology used to implement agile software development and this may also impact the results.

Acknowledgments. Thank you to the many reviewers and editors of earlier versions of this paper including Dr. Jane Huffman Hayes, Dr. Laurie Williams' research team, John Slankas, Barbara Doyle, Dr. Brooke Buckley, Dr. Janet Burge, and Sue Noble. The Burkhardt Consulting Center provided a thorough review of the data analysis. Brittany Campbell provided technical support in meeting LNCS style guidelines. Northern Kentucky University provided financial support to the first author for travel. The Scrum Alliance provided financial support for the second author.

References

1. Taft, D.K.: Agile Software Development Hits Stride After Years of Evangelism. In: eWeek (2013)
2. Williams, L.: What Agile Teams Think of Agile Principles. Communications of the ACM 55(4), 71–76 (2012)
3. Williams, L., Rubin, K., Cohn, M.: Driving Process Improvement via Comparative Agility Assessment. In: AGILE 2010, Orlando, FL, pp. 3–10 (2010)
4. Chow, T., Cao, D.-B.: A survey study of critical success factors in agile software projects. Journal of Systems and Software 81(6), 961–971 (2008)
5. Williams, L., Laymen, L., Krebs, W.: Extreme Programming evaluation Framework for Object-Oriented Languages – Version 1. In: N.C. Science (ed.) TR-2004-18, North Carolina State University (2004),
   http://www.csc.ncsu.edu/research/tech/reports.php
6. Krebs, W.: Turning the Knobs: A Coaching Pattern for XP through Agile Metrics. In: Wells, D., Williams, L. (eds.) XP 2002. LNCS, vol. 2418, pp. 60–69. Springer, Heidelberg (2002)
7. Pikkarainen, M., Passoja, U.: An approach for assessing suitability of agile solutions: A case study. In: Baumeister, H., Marchesi, M., Holcombe, M. (eds.) XP 2005. LNCS, vol. 3556, pp. 171–179. Springer, Heidelberg (2005)
8. Theunissen, W.H.M.: A case-study based assessment of Agile software development. University of Pretoria (2003)
9. Beck, K., et al.: Principles behind the Agile Manifesto (2001) [cited 2013]

Technical Dependency Challenges
in Large-Scale Agile Software Development

Nelson Sekitoleko[1], Felix Evbota[1], Eric Knauss[1], Anna Sandberg[2],
Michel Chaudron[1], and Helena Holmström Olsson[3]

[1] Department of Computer Science and Engineering
Chalmers, University of Gothenburg
nellysek@gmail.com, gusevbfe@student.gu.se, eric.knauss@cse.gu.se
[2] Ericsson AB
[3] Malmö University

Abstract. This qualitative study investigates challenges associated with
technical dependencies and their communication. Such challenges frequently occur when agile practices are scaled to large-scale software development. The use of thematic analysis on semi-structured interviews
revealed five challenges: planning, task prioritization, knowledge sharing, code quality, and integration. More importantly, these challenges
interact with one another and can lead to a domino effect or vicious
circle. If an organization struggles with one challenge, it is likely that
the other challenges become problematic as well. This situation can have
a significant impact on process and product quality. Our recommendations focus on improving planning and knowledge sharing (with practices
such as scrum-of-scrums, continuous integration, open space technology)
to break the vicious circle, and to reestablish effective communication
across teams, which will then enable large-scale companies to achieve
the benefits of large-scale agility.

Keywords: Technical dependencies, Large-scale agile, Cross-Functional
Teams (XFT), Qualitative research.

1 Introduction

Due to attractive characteristics such as flexibility, responsiveness and team
empowerment, agile development methods have been increasingly adopted by
large-scale development organizations. In emphasizing the use of iterations and
development of small features, agile methods have increased the ability for software development companies to accommodate changing customer requirements
and fast changing market needs [1]. In particular, agile methods have shown
their capacity in empowering development teams, improving their relationship
to customers, and allowing an increased focus on informal communication and
coordination rather than focusing on formal communication and documentation
of their practices [2]. As one of its basic principles, agile development provides
simple, rapid, and incremental solutions to big problems by breaking down complex features into smaller ones [3]. This allows for small, cross-functional teams to

G. Cantone and M. Marchesi (Eds.): XP 2014, LNBIP 179, pp. 46–61, 2014.
© Springer International Publishing Switzerland 2014

work on smaller tasks and well-defined areas of development and hence, improve both efficiency and speed.

However, while agile development methods and the breakdown of complex tasks were originally developed to improve small-scale development, and to support co-located teams, they are being increasingly adopted by large-scale development organizations with globally distributed teams [3]. In such settings, the agile breakdown of complex tasks poses a big challenge due to complex technical dependencies between teams [4]. These dependencies can be seen in various ways, such as, dependencies between activities in the development process, dependencies among different software artefacts, and dependencies across teams and team members [5]. Looking back at the agile basic principles, teams should communicate directly in a face-to-face conversation [6], a situation that is rarely the case in large-scale distributed software development. Instead, the complexity of technical dependencies increases with the size of the company, and in large-scale software development the challenge therefore becomes how to minimize technical dependencies that have a negative impact on team performance, as well as how to enable communication and management of technical dependencies between teams.

Based on this identified challenge of technical dependencies in large-scale software development, this study addresses the following research questions:

RQ1: What are the challenges associated with technical dependencies between teams in a large-scale agile software development?
RQ2: What affects the likelihood of a challenge to occur?

The **contribution** of the paper is twofold. First, and based on case study research, we identify the challenges that exist in relation to technical dependencies between teams in large-scale distributed development. Second, we provide a set of recommendations on how software development companies can manage these challenges in order to mitigate the impact of these on development team performance. While our findings are based on a single case study, we believe that our findings are relevant to other organisations in which communication and coordination between teams is a critical task.

The remainder of this paper is structured as follows: Section 2 describes agile teams and how agile team practices are increasingly applied in large-scale software development. The section also introduces the notion of technical dependencies and how these can be communicated in teams and in between teams. Section 3 describes the research site and the case study research methodology that we applied in this study. In Section 4, we present the findings from the interview study. Finally, in Section 5 and 6 we discuss our findings as well as provide a set of recommendations to help organisations address the challenges we identified in relation to technical dependencies.

2   Background: Large-Scale Agility, Technical Dependency, and Communication

2.1   Agile Teams

During the last decade agile methods have dramatically changed the way software development is performed, as well as the ways in which software teams are organised. Unlike traditional development methods characterized by plan-based execution of sequential phases, agile methods focus on managing unpredictability and change. In doing so, agile methods advocate small development teams in which all necessary competences are represented, i.e. cross-functional teams consisting of software developers, testers, architects etc. Typically, these teams take responsibility for the development of a software feature from the moment that a requirement comes from a customer, until that requirement is translated into software functionality that addresses that customers need. During development of a feature, the development team works in close collaboration with the customer in order to allow for rapid feedback loops, collaborative decision-making, as well as continuous integration and deployment of code changes [7]. In this way, agile teams seek to avoid cumbersome and time-consuming processes and instead focus on taking an end-to-end responsibility for feature development and that continuously validate if the functionality they develop correspond to customer needs. Typically, this is referred to as empowerment of teams [7]. Although agile methods differ in details and techniques, overall agile principles such as flexibility, empowered teams and customer collaboration lie at the heart of all of them.

2.2   Large-Scale Agile

For more than a decade, agile development methods have demonstrated their success in establishing flexible development processes with short feedback loops and consideration taken to evolving customer needs [2,8]. Due to successful accounts [9,10], these methods have become attractive to a broad variety of companies. Currently, large software-intensive organizations are in the process of deploying agile methods, and attempts to scale agile methods can be identified [11,12,13]. However, the applicability of these methods is not without challenges in large-scale development of software intended for a mass-market [14]. As recognized by Badampudi et al [15], organizations often discover misalignments between methods when attempting to use agile methods in a large-scale setting. According to the authors, the reason for this is that many large-scale companies practice agile in a way that is not consistent with the original agile ideas, and that the translation of the original ideas to a large-scale setting is difficult. Also, the shift towards agile is difficult for companies that are used to heavyweight sequential processes and companies that are confronted with interdependent teams and stakeholders located at different locations [15]. Often, development teams lack a shared understanding with other teams due to communication and coordination challenges, lack of documentation and complex decision-making processes among distributed stakeholders.

Another difficulty, and as reported on by Heikkila et al. [14], is the challenge related to cross-functional team creation. In their research, the authors identify difficulties with creating generalist teams that can implement features in all components of the software. As recognized in their study, organizations usually realizes that many components in a large-scale system are technically very difficult and interdependent, and require years of experience to be fully understood by developers. As a result, many large-scale organizations experience long lead times before the development teams can implement anything useful in a component. The authors conclude that identifying who has the required extensive experience and expertise to perform a task is still a challenge in a large organization adopting agile methods.

Finally, creating user stories that can be developed in a single sprint is reported on as challenging because of the complex nature of large-scale software systems [14]. Often, internal and external dependencies affect the way in which agile practices can be applied in large-scale development settings, and many organizations experience inconsistencies with the way in which agile practices are adopted. As recognized by [16], the understanding of the contingencies, i.e. how and when agile practices are applicable under variations in project size, business domain, and team configurations surrounding large-scale agile development is important.

2.3   Technical Dependency

The large number of interdependencies among activities and artefacts in the software development process is one of the major challenges in large-scale software development, which includes a large number of developers and development teams.[17]. Babinet and Ramanathan identify the following challenges of technical dependencies [18]:

- Unpredictability, were teams find it difficult to know beforehand what changes, issues, surprises, failures and successes they will come across during the development of a feature.
- Conflicting priorities, such as a team depending on a component that has lower priority in the backlog of another team.
- Difficulty in understanding overlapping and short release cycles, and teams constant changing of priority in each sprint.

To address these technical dependencies, Babinet and Ramanathan recommend release kick-offs, dependency identification exercises, Scrum-of-Scrums, virtual architecture teams, status reports and a number of other activities that help team communication and knowledge sharing [18]. In similar, Souza et al. propose tools with which technical dependencies can be analyzed and visualized so that these are better understood and therefore, easier to communicate among development teams [19].

2.4   Communication

Communication is often described as fundamental for organizational success [20]. Effective internal and external communication stimulates the performance of a development organization [21]. However, while communication is central to all organizations it also poses major challenges. As recognized by Johansson et al., a message can be properly communicated but the intended receiver may choose to interpret the message as invalid [22]. Also, to select a message at one point and deliver that message at another point is problematic [23]. As experienced in most organizations, inter-team communication is a challenge that grows with the size and complexity of the organization.

3   Research Method

3.1   Research Setting

The case study was conducted at Ericsson AB. Ericsson provides communications networks, telecom services, and support solutions used in global communication. It is ranked the fifth largest software supplier in the world with 950 million subscribers in over 180 countries. In this section, we map and describe the concepts of *cross-functional teams (XFT)* and *technical dependencies* from an Ericsson perspective.

Cross-functional Teams. A cross-functional team (XFT) is a team which has all core competences needed for the development and release of a feature. At Ericsson AB, XFTs generally follow the same working practices and include roles like system manager, system designer, function tester, system testers, and architect. In addition, each XFT has a scrum master, agile coach, and an operative product owner (OPO) on a part time basis and the team works in an open space which facilitates easy communication among teams. Each of these XFTs consists of 5–9 team members who have up to three roles in their team and some team members are associated with several teams in different roles. XFTs do not have team leaders but should be self-organized and work together with other XFTs on features which have a life cycle of approximately 500–1000 hours (a release consists of 20–80 features). Features are broken down into work packages which are developed in sprints of ~3 weeks. During the sprint, a XFT takes full responsibility for the development of a work package, breaks it down into user stories and tasks, and is in charge of handling planned and unplanned technical dependencies. Our study focusses on the 30 XFTs responsible for the development of one specific embedded software product that has been developed during a period of more than 10 years with a design base of more than 1 Million lines of code.

Technical Dependencies. At Ericsson, technical dependencies are relationships and interactions between artifacts and teams during product development. Examples include situations when a developer/team needs information regarding technical aspects of a system developed by another developer/team in order to progress the development work. Technical dependencies can occur during design-time, compile-time, and run-time and affect areas like source-code, architecture, hardware, and tools. At Ericsson, there are two types of technical dependencies: *Planned technical dependencies* are identified during the planning phase. Managers, program officers and product owners are responsible for identifying and scheduling planned technical dependencies, i.e identifying the tasks to be done in parallel or in sequence across teams, and communicating them to teams before development begins. *Unplanned technical dependencies* occur unexpectedly during the actual development of a product, for example due to improper implementation of the original plan.

3.2 Research Approach

This paper reports on a three-months case study at Ericsson AB plus a follow-up questionnaire[1] three month later. A qualitative research approach was chosen to investigate our research questions from a social, technical and organizational context. As qualitative research approaches aim to investigate and improve the understanding of phenomena in their real-life context [24], and especially when the purpose is to explore peoples' experiences and perceptions, we found it particularly well suited for our interests.

3.3 Data Collection

We interviewed 9 employees at Ericsson AB who were selected qualitatively based on insider knowledge about skills, experience, and organizational distribution from a population of 300 software engineers [25]. Our 9 interviewees have an average working experience of 10 years and about 3 years in agile practices, since Ericsson is gradually, team by team, transitioning to agile. In their work, they follow the most common agile practices like sprint-demo, retrospectives, daily stand-up meetings (~15min), and backlog grooming. Table 1 shows the roles the interviewees hold. A semi-structured interview approach was used to collect data because it has inherent properties that allow the interviewer to improvise and explore interview questions further [24]. Thus based on the progression of the interview, questions can be adapted and relevant follow-up questions posed [24]. The interview guide[2] helped us in ensuring that all questions were covered irrespective of the order in which they were followed. The interview questions mainly focused on planned and unplanned technical dependencies faced by XFT teams. Some of the interview questions are about the impact of incompatible components, how technical dependencies are located, communicated, resolved, and so forth [26]. We recorded the conversations while interviewing and transcribed these voice recordings verbatim to reduce the risk of corrupt data which can happen when transcribing during the interview [27].

---

[1] https://dl.dropboxusercontent.com/u/13255493/
   Tech-Depend-Questionnaire.pdf

[2] https://dl.dropboxusercontent.com/u/13255493/
   Tech-Depend-Interview-guide.pdf

Table 1. Interviewees and their roles / responsibilities

ID	Role	Responsibility
P1	Software designer	SW development
P2	Software designer and scrum master	SW development, facilitate team work
P3	Function tester	Functional testing
P4	Software designer	SW development
P5	Software designer and scrum master	SW development, facilitate team work
P6	Scrum master and architect	Team support, technical leadership
P7	Software designer and scrum master	SW development, facilitate team work
P8	Function tester	functional testing
P9	System manager, scrum master, and Function tester	Give directions, facilitate team work functional testing

After analysis of the interview data, we collected additional data to be able to confirm our findings based on a questionnaire that presented our findings as statements in a short questionnaire with a likert scale to measure the agreement of the initial interviewees with challenges, their dependencies, and proposed solutions.

3.4 Data Analysis

We analyzed the data collected from interviews base on the thematic analysis approach [27], an accepted method with wide-spread use in scientific and social science research consisting of six phases [27]. Please refer to [26] for details and examples of the data analysis.

1. Familiarizing with the data: We transcribed and read the data from the 9 interviews.
2. Generating initial codes: We coded the data from the perspective of the research questions.
3. Searching for themes: We grouped the initial codes we generated into different groups that we refer to as *initial themes*.
4. Reviewing Themes: We reviewed the initial themes, regrouped and refined them by cross checking the interview data with the generated codes in Phase 1 and 2. We then extracted and refined 5 themes in Phase 3.
5. Defining and naming themes: In this phase we reached a consensus about the five themes, which, in accordance to our research questions, we named the *main challenges* and present in the results section.
6. Producing the report: In this paper, we present and discuss the five main challenges and make recommendations.

3.5 Threats to Validity

As recognized by Maxwell [28], qualitative researchers rarely have the benefit of previously planned comparisons, sampling strategies, or statistical manipulations that control for possible threats to validity. While this can be acheived in quantitive research, qualitative researchers must try to rule out validity threats after the research has begun by using evidence collected during the research itself to make alternative hypotheses or interpretations implausible. One important aspect of validity is construct validity [24] that reflects to what extent the operational measures that are studied represent what the researcher has in mind, and what is reflected in the interview questions and themes. To address this critical aspect, we started each of our interviews with an introduction part in which the researchers shared their understanding of agile practices and technical dependencies with the interviewee. For example, we shared different definitions of the agile concept and we discussed the agile manifesto to get a shared understanding for the values that underpin agile development methods. Also, we shared our understanding of technical dependencies and why it is important to consider these in a large-scale development setting. In this way, the researchers and the interviewee had a shared understanding of the topic before the interview started, and we could proceed with asking questions without having to worry about the interviewee being unsure about the context we studied. With respect to external validity, i.e. to what extent it is possible to generalize the findings, our contribution is related to (1) the drawing of specific implications and (2) the contribution of rich insight [29]. Based on our interview findings, we present implications in a particular domain of action, i.e. in a particular software development company. Our study brings together empirical insight that allows for a deep understanding of this particular company, and the findings we present should be regarded as insights valuable for other companies interested in understanding the impact of technical dependencies in large-scale agile development.

4 Analysis and Interpretation

4.1 Technical Dependency Challenges in Large-Scale Agile

With respect to RQ1, (*What are the challenges associated with technical dependencies between teams in a large-scale agile software development?*), the analysis of the interview data revealed five main challenges: the planning challenge, the task prioritization challenge, the knowledge sharing challenge, the code quality challenge, and the integration challenge.

Planning Challenge. A perfect plan for software development would minimize the occurrence of technical dependencies. Uncertainty, which is inherent to software development, is one reason why creating and following such an optimal plan is practically impossible, but our interviewees also indicate potential for realistic improvement. This is reflected by the following quote from one of our interviewees:

> *"[Managers] do not plan and allocate tasks to teams in an appropriate way because they do not know much about the code and do not involve in the actual coding."*

Our interviewees mentioned that sometimes tasks that should have been assigned to a single team were instead split and assigned to several teams, thereby creating unnecessary dependencies. Insufficient planning leads to unplanned technical dependencies during the actual product development. Such unplanned technical dependencies across teams do not occur frequently, but when they occur, they seriously impact development and lead to changes in requirements and time-plan. Our interviewees also said that it is difficult to locate the root cause of unplanned technical dependencies.

Task Prioritization Challenge. According to our interviewees, the *task prioritization challenge* a result of the *planning challenge*. When unplanned technical dependencies arise, teams have to update their sprint plan to account for changes in requirements and time-plans. These changes arise for example from new requests for components from other teams that were not planned before and often lead to conflicts in the product backlog. Two problematic scenarios given by our interviewees characterize the prioritization challenge:

(1) When teams have to implement a component which was not in their backlog and (2) when they have to deliver a component in their backlog earlier than scheduled since another team realized that they were dependent on the component.

According to our interviewees, the above scenarios led to re-prioritizing tasks in their backlog.

> *"[...] constant changing of priorities makes our burn-down charts look bad."*

Our interviewees stated that changing priorities in their backlog usually destabilizes their work plan, because they need to assign resources to the unplanned requests, thereby leading to delays and late deliveries.

Knowledge Sharing Challenge. From the perspective of our interviewees, knowledge sharing among the XFTs is vital to enable good communication and coordination. If knowledge is not properly circulated, communicating technical dependencies will suffer, as indicated by some of the problems raised by the interviewees.

- Some interviewees do not have the opportunity to say what they want in company meetings (e.g. tasks presentation meetings), because of the multitude of people in the meeting. The interviewees claimed they do not get opportunity to express their burning issues or raise vital questions.
- Experienced personnel is involved in difficult tasks and often too busy to be approached.

Our interviewees also expressed some concerns about some of their colleagues attitude and ability to share knowledge, including the following problems:

- Protectiveness: Some team members are protective of their work and do not want to provide support to others.
- Bad teachers: Some team members know much about the code, but are simply not good at explaining it.

– Laziness: Some team members do not want to share knowledge because they fear that others will start seeking help from them more often.
– Over specialization: Some team members prefer to focus on their own task, thereby not having adequate knowledge of the entire product, which in turn leads to inefficient communication about dependencies.
– Lack of communicativeness: Some team members are too shy to either ask or provide information during meetings, thus causing important information to be ignored.

Another problem related to knowledge sharing occurs when team members do not understand, ignore, or forget what was discussed in a meeting:

"During development some people forget easily what was agreed upon in scrum meetings. Then, they are not be able to work accordingly."

From the perspective of our interviewees it is clear that such problems with knowledge sharing create a major challenge for communicating technical dependencies.

Code Quality Challenge. In software companies, good code quality will lead to quality products that can compete favourably in the market. However, in large scale software development, maintaining good quality code remains a challenge. Our interviewees stated that despite the existence of Subversion (SVN) control tools, too many people involved in the same code make changes in the code which can end up as conflicts in other teams. Their common view was:

"Such changes make it difficult to maintain a stable version of code, hence reducing code quality and creating more technical dependencies."

Function testers specifically shared an opinion that such changes make testing more complex because they have to rewrite test cases many times. The prevailing view among our interviewees was that providing good quality code is difficult because of technical dependencies.

Integration Challenge. In large-scale agile software development, merging of work packages is a problem because of the many self-organized teams working to deliver an integrated working product to the customers. Our interviewees demonstrated a scenario in which teams develop work packages independently for 2-3 months without knowing what is happening in the main branch. At delivery, teams get conflicts since many changes have been made in the main branch, hence creating dependencies which at times may only be resolved by engaging other teams. Despite tool support, this is a challenging task.

Other concerns expressed by interviewees were about incompatible dependent components they received from other teams that resulted in merge conflicts. According to our interviewees, incompatible components often cause teams to either re-plan or re-develop their work, thereby leading to late deliveries. It appears that the integration challenge is a result of not handling technical dependencies in a good way.

4.2 Likelihood of Technical Dependency Challenges

With respect to our RQ2 (*What affects the likelihood of a challenge to occur?*), we first tried to achieve a better understanding of the nature of the challenges we identified. By doing this, we then found that in fact the likelihood of a challenge to occur is affected by the presence of other challenges, for example if the planning challenge is not resolved, then it can lead to other challenges.

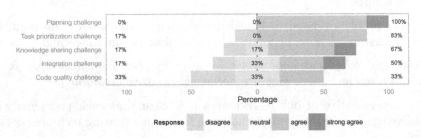

Fig. 1. Agreement of interviewees with challenges ("It is challenging to ...")

Understanding the Nature of Challenges. For understanding the nature of the challenges we discovered, we asked our interviewees which challenges they consider to be most dominant in their daily work. Fig. 1 shows that planning and task prioritization are recognized as most challenging.

During discussion and analysis of our findings, we also recognized that some of the challenges we found are more technical in nature (code quality and integration challenge), while others can be characterized as communication challenges (see axis Fig. 2). In fact, the *knowledge sharing* challenge refers to the mindset of engineers, which is mostly related to communication. *Task prioritization* and *planning* refer to work practices and relate both to communication and technical challenges. *Code quality* and *integration* are mostly technical in nature and require technical actions.

Relationships and Interdependencies. Based on the improved understanding of the challenges, a critical study of the main challenges by the authors revealed that during the development of a product, the challenges interact with one another to form a domino effect which leads to the technical dependency loop (Fig. 2).

These relationships between challenges cause a vicious circle. Consider for example the planning challenge: By suboptimal planning, unnecessary technical dependencies are introduced. These cause problems that surface as task prioritization challenge, which in turn increase the integration and code quality challenges. Bad code quality can put additional pressure on teams which are then reluctant to share knowledge. This in turn makes planning even more difficult. These circular relationships are bidirectional, e.g. in the example above, unresolved prioritization issues in the teams' backlogs seriously impair adequate planning.

4.3   Recommendations

In order to break through the vicious circle, one has to start with mitigating one challenge and then continue to exploit the positive influence on other challenges. Our interview data suggests that the knowledge sharing challenge is a good starting point. Improved knowledge sharing between technical and management staff on different levels can significantly improve the ability to create a good plan, and then in turn help addressing the other challenges.

We were especially interested in how our interviewees rate the dependencies and were specifically asking, whether a solution for the planning (respectively: knowledge sharing) challenge would positively impact other challenges as well. Fig. 3 indicates that a solution for the knowledge sharing challenge would have more impact on the other challenges. The figure also shows that the code quality

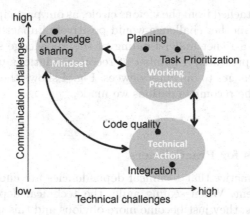

Fig. 2. Challenges associated with technical dependencies can be classified as communication and technical challenges. These challenges affect each other.

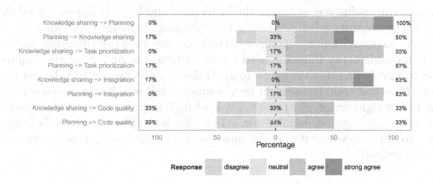

Fig. 3. Rating of challenge dependencies by interviewees

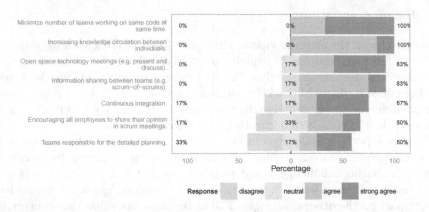

Fig. 4. Agreement of participants with recommendations

challenge is a bit detached from the vicious circle, as our participants do not agree that a solution for another challenge would positively impact the code quality.

In order to gain a richer understanding of the knowledge sharing and planning challenge, we presented a number of recommendations from literature for mitigating the challenges to our interviewees. Fig. 4 shows the agreement of our interviewees with the recommendations we made.

5 Discussion

5.1 Implications for Practitioners

It is not new for practice that technical dependencies are cumbersome in large software development. When scaling agile, the technical dependencies do not become more or less, they just become more obvious and this is actually a possibility for practice to deal with them. Here we have come to understand challenges associated to technical dependencies and the domino effect this can create. By embracing this knowledge of the domino effect, practice can break the vicious circle by improving one or two of the challenges and by that improving all challenges. For example, when improving the Planning challenge by making sure the planners have sufficient competence of the code, the Task prioritization challenge get less problematic. Planners need to understand the quality of the impacted code to make correct estimations (e.g. stinker code is known to take ten times more time than code included in lean components), which then helps prioritize task in the right order. For practice, it is of high importance to understand not only the challenges on detailed level, but also how they impact each other in order to improve where it gets the most impact. This study gives practice such understanding.

5.2 Implications for Research

Eklund and Bosch propose a model for defining interactions necessary for agile teams together with a set measures facilitating agile development in a context where the full product cannot be agile [30]. These interactions can be seen in four categories; requirements, project gates, integration & validation, and delivery. The more teams understand such interactions, the less technical dependencies (as discussed in this paper) they will encounter. In contrast, unplanned technical dependencies can surface in late and inefficient clarification of features and requirements, as discussed in related work on patterns of continuous requirements clarification [31].

Cataldo et al. show that lack of socio-technical congruence, i.e. the fact that social relationships such as communication of developers is not aligned with technical dependencies between them, leads to bad software quality [32]. Damian et al. discuss similar observations from a case study where organizational structure is not in line with the partitioning of requirements, thus leading to unsatisfied communication needs [33]. Both works hint on potential for organizational optimization, which however is especially difficult in volatile, complex, and large-scale agile environments.

Promising avenues for future research therefore include (i) investigating ways to measure interaction and knowledge sharing quality and providing actionable feedback to agile teams and (ii) gain a better understanding how organizational change can support minimizing technical dependencies.

6 Conclusion and Outlook

In this qualitative study, we identified five challenges associated with technical dependencies in large-scale agile software development: planning, task prioritization, knowledge sharing, code quality, and integration. More importantly, we found that these challenges interact and can lead to a domino effect or vicious circle: If an organization struggles with one challenge, it is likely that the other challenges become problematic as well. A follow-up questionnaire confirmed the relationships between challenges as well as that mitigating one of the challenges can have a positive impact on the other challenges and ultimately promises to break the vicious circle. Our results indicate that activities should focus on mitigating the knowledge sharing and planning challenges to reestablish effective communication across teams, which will then enable companies to achieve the benefits of large-scale agility. Although the findings in this paper are based on a single case study, we believe that our findings are relevant to other companies transitioning towards large-scale agile development practices.

References

1. Fogelström, N.D., Gorschek, T., Svahnberg, M., Olsson, P.: The impact of agile principles on market-driven software product development. Journal of Software Maintenance and Evolution: Research and Practice 22, 53–80 (2010)
2. Highsmith, J., Cockburn, A.: Agile software development: The business of innovation. IEEE Computer 34(9), 120–122 (2001)
3. Kettunen, P., Laanti, M.: Combining agile software projects and large-scale organizational agility. Softw. Process 13, 183–193 (2008)

4. Beck, K.: Embracing change with extreme programming. Computer 32(10), 70–77 (1999)
5. Curtis, B., Krasner, H., Iscoe, N.: A field study of the software design process for large systems. Commun. ACM 31, 1268–1287 (1988)
6. Beck, K., Beedle, M., van Bennekum, A., Cockburn, A., Cunningham, W., Fowler, M., Grenning, J., Highsmith, J., Hunt, A., Jeffries, R., Kern, J., Marick, B., Martin, R.C., Mellor, S., Schwaber, K., Sutherland, J., Thomas, D.: Manifesto for agile software development (2001), http://www.agilemanifesto.org (accessed on December 3, 2013)
7. Highsmith, J.: The great methodologies debate: Part 2. Cutter IT Journal 5 (2002)
8. Larman, C., Vodde, B.: Scaling Lean and Agile Development: Thinking and Organizational Tools for Large-Scale Scrum. Pearson Education Inc., Boston (2009)
9. Abrahamsson, P., Warsta, J., Siponen, M., Ronkainen, J.: New directions on agile methods: a comparative analysis. In: Proceedings of the 25th International Conference on Software Engineering, Portland, Oregon, pp. 244–254 (2003)
10. Olsson, H.H., Alahyari, H., Bosch, J.: Climbing the stairway to heaven: A multiple-case study exploring barriers in the transition from agile development towards continuous deployment of software. In: Proceedings of the 38th Euromicro Conference on Software Engineering and Advanced Applications, Cesme, Izmir, Turkey (2012)
11. Kerievsky, J.: Industrial xp: Making xp work in large organizations. Executive Report in Agile Project Management 6(2) (2005)
12. McMahon, P.E.: Extending agile methods: A distributed project and organizational improvement perspective. In: Proceedings of the 17th Annual Systems and Software Technology Conference, Salt Lake City, UT (2005)
13. Lagerberg, L., Skude, T., Emanuelsson, P., Sandahl, K., Stahl, D.: The impact of agile principles and practices on large-scale software development projects: A multiple-case study of two projects at ericsson. In: ACM/IEEE Int'l Symp. on Empirical Software Engineering and Measurement, Baltimore, Maryland, pp. 348–356 (2013)
14. Heikkila, V.T., Paasivaara, M., Lassenius, C.: Scrumbut, but does it matter? A mixed-method study of the planning process of a multi-team scrum organization. In: ACM/IEEE Int'l Symp. on Empirical Software Engineering and Measurement, Baltimore, Maryland, pp. 85–94 (2013)
15. Badampudi, D., Fricker, S.A., Moreno, A.M.: Perspectives on productivity and delays in large-scale agile projects. In: Baumeister, H., Weber, B. (eds.) XP 2013. LNBIP, vol. 149, pp. 180–194. Springer, Heidelberg (2013)
16. Dingsøyr, T., Moe, N.B.: Research challenges in large-scale agile software development. SIGSOFT Softw. Eng. Notes 38(5), 38–39 (2013)
17. de Souza, C.R.B., Redmiles, D.F., Mark, J., Penix, G., Sierhuis, M.: Management of interdependencies in collaborative software development. In: Proc. of Intl. Symp. on Empirical Software Engineering, pp. 294–302 (2003)
18. Babinet, E., Ramanathan, R.: Dependency management in a large agile environment. In: Proc. of Agile Conference, pp. 401–406 (2008)
19. de Souza, C.R.B., Quirk, S., Trainer, E., Redmiles, D.F.: Supporting collaborative software development through the visualization of socio-technical dependencies. In: Proceedings of the 2007 International ACM Conference on Supporting Group Work, Sanibel Island, Florida, USA, pp. 147–156 (2007)
20. Dainton, M., Zelley, E.D.: Applying communication theory for professional life: a practical introduction. SAGE Publications Inc. (2005)

21. Sosa, M.E., Eppinger, S.D., Pich, M., McKendrick, D.G., Stout, S.K.: Factors that influence technical communication in distributed product development: an empirical study in the telecommunications industry. IEEE Transactions on Engineering Management 49, 45–58 (2002)
22. Johansson, B.J.E., Persson, P.A.: Reduced uncertainty through human communication in complex environments. Cogn. Technol. Work 11, 205–214 (2009)
23. Shannon, C.E., Weaver, W.: The Mathematical Theory of Communication. University of Illinois Press (1971)
24. Runeson, P., Höst, M.: Guidelines for conducting and reporting case study research in software engineering. Empirical Softw. Engg. 14, 131–154 (2009)
25. Creswell, J.W.: Research Design: Qualitative, Quantitative, and Mixed Methods Approaches. SAGE Publications (2009)
26. Sekitoleko, N., Evbota, F.: Technical dependencies in practicing agile in large-scale software development organizations: A case study conducted at Ericsson AB. Bachelor thesis, University of Gothenburg, Sweden (2013), https://dl.dropboxusercontent.com/u/13255493/Tech-Depen-Report.pdf
27. Braun, V., Clarke, V.: Using thematic analysis in psychology. Qualitative Research in Psychology 3, 86–94 (2006)
28. Maxwell, J.: Qualitative research design: An interactive approach. Sage, Los Angeles (2013)
29. Walsham, G.: Interpretive case studies in is research: nature and method. European Journal of Information Systems 4, 74–81 (1995)
30. Eklund, U., Bosch, J.: Applying agile development in mass-produced embedded systems. In: Wohlin, C. (ed.) XP 2012. LNBIP, vol. 111, pp. 31–46. Springer, Heidelberg (2012)
31. Knauss, E., Damian, D., Poo-Caamao, G., Cleland-Huang, J.: Detecting and Classifying Patterns of Requirements Clarifications. In: Proceedings of 20th International Requirements Engineering Conference (RE 2012), Chicago, USA, pp. 251–260 (2012)
32. Cataldo, M., Herbsleb, J.D., Carley, K.M.: Socio-technical congruence: a framework for assessing the impact of technical and work dependencies on software development productivity. In: Proceedings of Second ACM-IEEE International Symposium on Empirical Software Engineering and Measurement (ESEM 2008), Kaiserslautern, Germany, pp. 2–11. ACM (2008)
33. Damian, D., Helms, R., Kwan, I., Marczak, S., Koelewijn, B.: The role of domain knowledge and hierarchical control structures in socio-technical coordination. In: Proc. of IEEE Int. Conf. on Software Engineering (ICSE), San Francisco (2013)

How Can Agile and Documentation-Driven Methods be Meshed in Practice?

Lise Tordrup Heeager

Aarhus University, Denmark
lith@asb.dk

Abstract. Agile methods are becoming increasingly popular in software development; even by organizations complying with quality standards. The literature reports on scattered examples of organizations that have succeeded in meshing agile and documentation-driven methods. However, due to a lack of empirical research, it is not well understood how to implement a meshed software development practice. To increase the understanding of how to do this, this paper presents two case studies of the development of safety-critical software. The first case study presents challenges of adopting quality assurance in an agile software practice. The second case study shows how agile practices are adopted in a documentation-driven practice compliant with the US Food and Drug Administration standard. Based on a framework that identifies nine practice areas in which the methods differ, the challenges of and possibilities in implementing a meshed software development practice is presented.

Keywords: Agile Software Development, Documentation-Driven Software Development, Safety-Critical Software Development, Scrum, FDA.

1 Introduction

Within software development, much focus has been and still is on the methods for developing software. Software developers have and still are struggling to find the best way to develop software. The two overall approaches of software development are; 1) the agile methods, such as Scrum [1] and Extreme Programming (XP) [2] and 2) the documentation-driven methods, such as the waterfall model and Structured Systems Analysis and Design Method [3]. Quality assurance standards such as CMMI [4] and FDA [5] also represent the documentation-driven methods. While the agile methods offer flexibility the documentation-driven methods offers predictability [6]. Some hybrid methods that seek to mesh both types of methods do exist; examples of such are The Relational Unified Process (RUP), or the spiral model. RUP is an iterative method with high focus on risk, but adaptable on the amount of documentation [7]. The spiral model is an evolutionary software process model which includes controlled and systematic aspects [8]. Despite these hybrid methods it is still not clear how to achieve a mesh in practice and due to the differences between the agile and the documentation-driven methods, meshing is very challenging [9]. Several practitioners are still seeking a way to mesh the agile and documentation-driven methods [10]. So far very little empirical data documents the alleged compatibility,

G. Cantone and M. Marchesi (Eds.): XP 2014, LNBIP 179, pp. 62–77, 2014.

and it is not well understood how these methods can be meshed in practice. Hence, the following research question has been formulated: How can the agile and the documentation-driven methods be meshed in practice?

This research question takes a practical viewpoint of how to mesh, in order to provide empirical evidence regarding if and how this can be done. It was studied via case studies of the development of safety-critical software. The strict requirements of the quality standards required when developing safety-critical software makes it difficult to adopt agile practices, since the differences between agile and documentation-driven methods are heightened. Researchers are therefore discussing whether or not agile methods are suitable for such projects, at the same time more and more organizations developing safety-critical software are interested in adopting agile practices in order to increase the flexibility of their software practice.

The paper is structured as follows; in section 2 the theoretical background is presented; through practice areas the differences and similarities of the agile and the documentation-driven methods are clarified. Section 3 defines the concept of meshing. In section 4 the research design and the case studies are described. Section 5 presents the analysis of the cases and in section 6 the results of the analysis is discussed. Finally the results are concluded on in section 7.

2 Agile and Documentation-Driven Methods

Many agile methods have appeared over the years. The Dynamic Systems Development Method (DSDM) [11], is identified as the first agile method [12]; followed by eXtreme Programming (XP) [2]. Among other agile methods is Scrum [1]. Today, Scrum and XP are the two most well-known and popular agile methods. Each of the agile methods has specific features, but also common characteristics: Through an iterative, test-driven software development process with frequent customer feedback, the agile methods seek high software quality. The short iterations, multi-disciplinary teams, knowledge sharing and continuous integration allow better control over the project and increase visibility [13]. To enhance knowledge sharing, they advocate an informative workspace, which includes information radiators [14]. Agile methods rely on the competencies of the software developers [15]. Refactoring (redesigning and rewriting software) is also advocated by the agile methods, as it serves to correct poorly written and redundant code [16].

Several terms are used for the traditional, documentation-driven software methods. I suggest the use of the term 'documentation-driven' which indicates that the methods use the documentation of its practices in various ways, for example for the sharing of knowledge and for proving the quality of the product. Furthermore, the amount and reliance on documentation seems to be one of the greatest differences between agile methods and the software practice suggested by the quality standards [17]. The objectives of documentation-driven methods are to create predictability, repeatability and optimization [6]. Documentation-driven development is often associated with the Waterfall model, also known as the systems development life cycle consisting of sequential development stages. The V-model is a variation of the Waterfall model; it has the same sequential structure but links the development phases to the software tests [18]. The methods Structured analysis [19] and Modern Structured Analysis [20] both provide structured techniques to the analysis phase.

2.1   Practice Areas of Agile and Documentation-Driven Methods

The agile and the documentation-driven methods have several differences, but also some similarities; this section highlights these. In a review of the literature; nine practice areas in which the methods differ have been identified (see table 1).

Table 1. The agile and documentation-driven practice areas

Practice area	Agile development	Documentation-driven development
Management strategy	Self-managing teams.	Control by management.
Customer relations	Customer involvement through the whole development.	Customer is involved during the early phase of the project.
People-issues	Focus on the social aspects.	Rely on documentation.
Documentation	Working software over documentation.	Highly reliant on documentation.
Requirements	Requirements defined in user stories.	Requirements are documented.
Development Strategy	Iterative development strategy.	Sequential development strategy.
Communications and knowledge sharing	Person-to-person communication (personalization).	Documented, explicit knowledge (codification).
Testing	Test of each increment, focus on test-driven development.	Late testing and rely on test plans.
Culture	Social and team-oriented.	Plan-oriented.

The agile and the documentation-driven software development methods are based on different project *management strategies* [12]. Adopting agile methods requires a change from command and control management to leadership and collaboration [21], [22], which requires a reorientation for the developers and for management [23].

Another difference between the agile and the documentation-driven methods is *customer relations*. Both the documentation-driven methods and the agile methods highly value the satisfaction of the customer. In documentation-driven methods the customer is mainly involved during the early phases of the project, while agile methods involve the customer throughout the whole development process [24]. The customer involvement in agile methods is therefore much greater [25].

The agile methods focus on the social aspects of software development [26] and *people-issues* are at the heart of the agile movement [27]. This heavy reliance on human factors poses challenges when adopting agile practices [28], it is a significant departure from the focus on plans of the documentation-driven methods [29].

While the agile methods tend not to *document* enough, the documentation-driven methods tend to be over documented [24]. However, the agile methods do not cast all documentation aside [30], and it is not necessary to write piles of documentation in order to comply with, for example, CMMI [31].

The agile and the documentation-driven methods handle the *requirements* differently, which also can cause problems when meshing [32]. Agile methods rely on user stories written by the customer in a plain business-like language. Such user stories cannot be used directly in safety critical projects. Instead each story must be translated into functional test cases [33].

To ensure adaptability, agile methods advocate an iterative *development strategy* [34]. Adopting an agile, iterative development strategy requires major alterations to work practices [22], [35]. In contrast to the documentation-driven methods, which have separate coding and testing phases, the agile methods include the testing and debugging of the written code in the iteration [36].

Knowledge sharing is an important part of both agile and documentation-driven methods [37]. While the agile methods rely on person-to person *communication and knowledge sharing*, documentation-driven methods focus on documented knowledge [38]. The frequent meetings (stand-up meetings, planning meetings and retrospectives) proposed by the agile methods serve as ways to informally communicate and share knowledge, enhanced by the self-managing developer teams. The documentation-driven methods favour division of labour, hence use role-based teams and the knowledge is shared in the documents [38].

The agile and the documentation-driven methods have different strategies for *testing*. Test-driven development has become popular within the agile community [22]. In XP, testing is a core practice and development is mostly test-driven [2]. It is also suggested that there is testing of all parts of an increment and that completion is determined by the increment passing all tests. In documentation-driven methods testing is done late in the process and is based on detailed test plans [39].

The *culture* in documentation-driven organizations is plan-orientated, whereas the agile cultures are more social and team orientated [40]. When adopting agile practices in a documentation-driven organisation, the organisational culture has to change from policy and procedure-based to freedom of development and management by team members [21]. Research has described adoption of agile methods as a culture change [26]. A change of organizational culture requires a change of people's mind-sets [23].

3   Meshing

Several concepts have been used to describe the compatibility of the agile and the documentation-driven methods; for example: mixed [41], hybrid [6] and combined [12]. In this paper the key concept used is meshed which by the dictionary is defined as: [to become entangled or entwined] [42]. This concept suggests that it is possible to implement an entangled practice where the elements of the agile and documentation-driven methods are not easily identified. Figure 1 depicts the definition of meshing. At each end of the line the pure form of respectively agile software development and documentation-driven software development is placed. In the middle of the line a span of compatibility is placed. Compatibility is achieved by implementing both agile and documentation-driven elements in a software practice; the practice becomes meshed. A mesh can be primarily agile or primarily documentation-driven (hence placed on respectively the right or left side of the line, within the span of compatibility). To identify the mesh of a practice, the nine practice areas presented above are used. Each of these may have different meshes. Even though some practice areas are not meshed an overall mesh of the software practice can still be achieved.

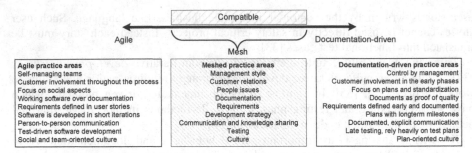

Fig. 1. The mesh of agile and documentation-driven practice areas

4   Research Design

The research design consists of two complimentary, interpretive case studies [43]. The first case study is of a small, agile software organization trying to mesh by adopting the quality standard GAMP (a standard for safety-critical, medical devices with software) [44]. The second case study involves a large pharmaceutical organization trying to mesh by implementing elements of the agile method Scrum into their FDA [5] compliant practice. For an overview of the case studies see figure 2.

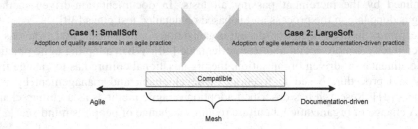

Fig. 2. The case studies

4.1   Case 1: SmallSoft

The first case focuses on the process and challenges of adopting quality assurance in a small, agile software organisation in Denmark. They were forced to adopt quality assurance by their primary customer as they by law were to be able to assure the quality of the safety-critical software. The project included the majority of the 15 software developers employed in the organization. At the beginning of the research study, the software organization expressed great frustration because of the requirements of the quality assurance standard as one of their primary goals was to maintain the agility. Hence, they had a need to mesh their practice.

The system development process was initiated in 1998 and in October 2004, the software organisation decided to initiate the adoption of the quality assurance as they realised that the customer would soon make a demand for quality assurance. The GAMP4 standard was suggested by the customer organisation later the same year. Two years later, in December 2007, the software organisation went through its first external audit. They failed this audit.

The software development practice was primarily agile in following way: The software was built in iterations of one month, in close cooperation with the customer. Each month an administration meeting between the software organisation and the customer representatives took place. At these meetings the requirements for the kernel version of the device were discussed, determined and prioritised. The requirements for the local adaptations were accepted at all times primarily by email or phone. All requirements were written by or in cooperation with the customer and formed as user stories, specified in electronic forms. The knowledge sharing within the developer team was done primarily through face-to-face communication, the software developers were sitting close together and worked in pairs; and very little documentation was done. Testing was done continuously.

4.2   Case 2: LargeSoft

The second case describes how a clinical product with embedded, safety-critical software is developed in a large pharmaceutical company. The focus was a software group consisting of approximately 30 managers, developers and testers. The development also involved clinical researchers responsible for the drugs, process engineers responsible for production facilities, mechanical engineers responsible for the product's mechanical functions in dispensing the drugs, and embedded hardware engineers responsible for the computer chips and the communication controlling the mechanics. Due to high level of safety-criticality of the device, the project had to comply with several quality standards (e.g. FDA). The project had run for years and was at the time of study entering the stage of refining the product.

This case study focused on how the software group was implementing a software development practice that meshed a documentation-driven FDA-compliant process and elements of the agile method Scrum. This software practice consisted of iterations of 2 weeks; an iteration was initiated with a planning meeting, including a retrospective of the previous iteration and planning of the future iteration. The developers were divided into two sub teams, which were coordinated by the Scrum Master. The testers were organised in their own sub team controlled by a test manager. The two sub teams of developers worked on the same product backlog. Two Scrum boards on the walls were used to display tasks and other relevant information. The developers primarily coordinated within the sub teams at the daily stand-up meetings. The developers were responsible for unit testing and reviewing the code during each iteration; the test team conducted the integration tests before the code was handed to the system engineering group in charge of the system tests.

4.3   Data Collection and Data Analysis

The data from each case study was collected and analysed sequentially. Each case study consisted of two phases and was conducted over a longer time period of approximately 1-2 years. A significant amount of data was collected: 36 qualitative interviews, observations and document studies (see table 2).

Table 2. Overview of the data collection in case studies

#	Case	Duration	Data collection
	SmallSoft: A small, agile software organisation	Phase 1: August 2007 – December 2007	4 qualitative interviews, observations and a document study
		Phase 2: January 2008 – June 2008	5 qualitative interviews, and a document study
2	LargeSoft: A large pharmaceutical organisation	Phase 1: November 2008 – June 2009	15 qualitative interviews, observations and a document study
		Phase 2: January 2010 – August 2010	12 qualitative interviews, observations and a document study

Data Collection and Analysis of SmallSoft

In the first case study, *phase one* had the purpose of gaining initial understanding of the challenges faced by the software organization in adopting the quality assurance. Four diagnostic interviews [45] were conducted, these included: the project manager and three developers from the software organization. Observations were made of the software organization over four months, building personal knowledge of the case. At the end of the first phase a quality seminar was given by a researcher. This seminar included all of the employees from the software organisation.

The initial data analysis showed that studying the adoption process from only the side of the software organisation did not reveal a full picture of the situation. In the *second phase* the focus was shifted and the adoption process was studied from an interorganizational perspective. Five qualitative interviews based on semi-structured interview guides on interorganizational relationship [46] were conducted. These interviews included: the project manager and a developer from the software organisation, as well as two users of the system and a customer representative.

All interviews were recorded and transcribed. The data collected was analyzed using Atlas.ti. This was done iteratively both in-between the phases and after the second phase. The focus of the analysis was on the software practice and its changes and progress. The practice areas served as an analysis framework. The findings were written up and presented in a report for validation.

Data Collection and Analysis of LargeSoft

In the second case study, *phase one* focused on the software practice. The phase consisted of 15 qualitative, diagnostic [45] interviews and a seminar presentation. The interviews were based on semi-structured interview-guides, that included the subjects: FDA requirements, agile software development and general strengths and weaknesses. The interviews included the project manager (two interviews), the software architect (two interviews), a software tester and developers from both sub teams. At the end the findings were written into a report and presented to the software group in a seminar.

The *second phase* focused on the improvements of the software practice that had been made by the software group since the first phase. The phase included 12 interviews with the project manager, the software developers, a tester, the new software architect, a coordinator between the software group and other groups of the project and a consultant specializing in Scrum, affiliated to the software group for 5 months. Furthermore, observations were conducted to verify the procedures and outcomes of the planning meetings and stand-up meetings.

All interviews were audio recorded, transcribed and analyzed using Atlas.ti. The focus of the analysis was on the software practice and identification of agile and documentation-driven elements. The practice areas served as an analysis framework. The full analysis was written up, presented in a report for validation.

5   Analysis of the Mesh in the Case Studies

Using the definition of meshing; the mesh of each practice area in the two case studies as well as the overall mesh of the two case studies will in this section be analyzed.

5.1   The Overall Mesh in the Case Studies

This section describes the overall mesh in the two case studies. The declared goal of the software developers and managers, in both case studies was to achieve a mesh. In practice not all developers and managers were evenly eager to mesh, which in the analysis is identified as a big barrier.

Meshing in SmallSoft
Despite their efforts to achieve a mesh the development practice in SmallSoft remained primarily agile. Hence, on the line on meshing, SmallSoft is placed on the left side outside of the span of compatibility (see figure 3). The external audit showed that the excessive documentation required by the quality standard was the main reason why the mesh did not succeed; the amount and quality of documentation produced on requirements and for knowledge sharing purposes was not enough. Frequent customer contact was maintained at monthly administration meetings and by email or phone. The communication and knowledge sharing between the developers was primarily based on personalization [47], they worked close together. The analysis of the customer relations showed a great trust between the parties. Due to this trust neither the developers nor the customers felt a need for a more documentation-driven customer relation and or a need for more documentation.

Meshing in LargeSoft
During the time of study the software group increased the agility of the software practices and achieved a mesh; the mesh was however primarily documentation-driven. Hence, LargeSoft is on the line of meshing placed on the right side inside the span of compatibility (see figure 3). The software group was successful at implementing an agile software development practice embedded in the documentation-driven project. The analysis showed that the software developers were not able to establish a contact to a customer and implement a well-functioning product owner role. Due to the excessive amount of documentation required by the FDA standard the practice area on documentation was very difficult to mesh. The case study also showed that handling the requirements in an iterative manner was difficult. This challenge arose due to a sequential treatment of the requirements specifications (forced by the

sequential development strategy of the overall project). The software group meshed the practice area on development strategy by embedding an iterative software practice in the sequential project. The communication and knowledge sharing strategy was in practice primarily personalized but also codified as much knowledge was documented. The testing was done in the late stages of the project and was based on thorough test plans, hence primarily documentation-driven.

5.2   The Mesh of the Practice Areas

The two case studies made it possible to provide contributions on six of the practice areas: 1) customer relations, 2) documentation, 3) requirements, 4) development strategy (only LargeSoft), 5) communication and knowledge sharing and 6) testing (only LargeSoft). Table 3 gives an overview of the mesh (or lack of) for these six.

Table 3. The agile and documentation-driven practice areas

Practice area	Mesh in SmallSoft	Mesh in LargeSoft
Customer relations	No mesh was achieved and the customer relations of SmallSoft remained primarily agile. Due to high trust between SmallSoft and their customer no need was found for standardizing this process.	No mesh was achieved and the customer relations of LargeSoft remained primarily documentation-driven. The product was developed for a market; no time was allocated for an internal product owner.
Documentation	No mesh was achieved and the customer relations of SmallSoft remained primarily agile. The requirements of the GAMP were not met, mainly due to the amount of documentation required.	A mesh was not achieved on documentation in LargeSoft, they remained primarily documentation-driven. The approval and change of a document was time-consuming; the main challenge of meshing.
Requirements	No mesh was achieved and the customer relations of SmallSoft remained primarily agile. The requirements written by customers could not be approved by GAMP.	The requirements practice in LargeSoft was meshed, the mesh remained primarily documentation-driven. Requirements were redefined in late in the project.
Development Strategy	-	The development strategy in LargeSoft was meshed, but remained mainly documentation-driven. Iterations were found advantageous, but were affected by long-term milestones.
Communications and knowledge sharing	No mesh was achieved, the customer relations of SmallSoft remained primarily agile. The communication was primarily face-to-face; no incentive for using documents for knowledge sharing.	A mesh of communications was achieved in LargeSoft, they remained primarily documentation-driven. Much communication was face-to-face, but documents were also used for knowledge sharing.
Testing	-	No mesh was achieved; the testing practice of LargeSoft remained primarily documentation-driven. Testing had little focus from management and was postponed.

6   Discussion

In this section, six propositions based on the analysis of the case studies are presented and discussed according to the literature. Figure 3 summarizes the findings.

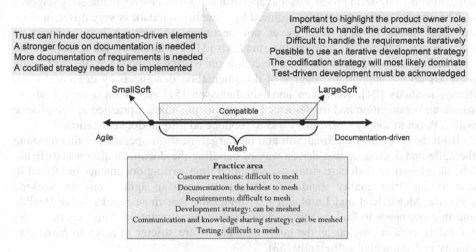

Important to highlight the product owner role
Difficult to handle the documents iteratively
Difficult to handle the requirements iteratively
Possible to use an iterative development strategy
The codification strategy will most likely dominate
Test-driven development must be acknowledged

Trust can hinder documentation-driven elements
A stronger focus on documentation is needed
More documentation of requirements is needed
A codified strategy needs to be implemented

SmallSoft   LargeSoft

Compatible

Agile   Documentation-driven

Mesh

Practice area
Customer realtions: difficult to mesh
Documentation: the hardest to mesh
Requirements: difficult to mesh
Development strategy: can be meshed
Communication and knowledge sharing strategy: can be meshed
Testing: difficult to mesh

Fig. 3. The findings of this paper

6.1   Customer Relations

Proposition 1: The practice area of customer relations is difficult to mesh. Trust between the software organization and its customer can hinder the adoption of documentation-driven elements. Implementing an agile product owner role in a documentation-driven project it is important to have the support of the management.

So far, the literature on agile software development and on meshing does not focus on how to implement a well-functioning customer relation. The literature does acknowledge that the outcome of a project is influenced by the customer relations [46], [48]. No research focuses on the influence of the customer relations on the adoption of documentation-driven elements in an agile software organisation. The case study of SmallSoft showed how close customer relations have great influence on meshing; it can both advance and hinder this. When trying to create a mesh it is therefore very important to be aware of how agile customer relations influence the implementation of documentation-driven practice areas.

The literature acknowledges that maintaining a close, agile customer relation requires a lot of time and involvement, which makes it hard to implement [49]. In LargeSoft the software group struggled to implement the product owner role of Scrum. The product was developed for a market and an immediate customer was therefore not associated. To solve this issue Murru et al [50] propose filling this role by an internal person or share it between an internal and an external person. In LargeSoft, filling the product owner role by an internal person proved difficult, as adequate time needs to be allocated the person assigned the product owner role. Showing that the management needs to acknowledge the importance of this role.

6.2   Documentation

Proposition 2: The practice area of documentation is the hardest to mesh. The amount of documentation required by quality standards is not supported by the agile focus. Handling the documents in a light and iterative manner may be difficult in a project controlled by long-term milestones and approval of the documents in the early stages.

The amount of documentation required by a quality standard is very different from the agile focus [24]. It is however not necessary to write a large amount of documentation to comply with quality standards [31]. Furthermore, the agile principle of working software need not be a rejection on writing documentation. Still, agile methods do not support the degree of documentation demanded by documentation-driven methods [24]. Kähkönen and Abrahamsson [51] report on a case study in which an organization had implemented a light documentation practice in compliance with XP, but to satisfy CMMI they had to produce additional documentation.

Both the case study on SmallSoft and on LargeSoft show specifically that meshing the agile and documentation-driven way of handling the documentation was difficult. The developers in both case studies spent much time writing documents and found it, due to the strict quality standards, difficult to keep an agile focus on working software. McMichael and Lombardi [52] underline that most standards are flexible and that one needs to find the appropriate level of documentation. This may be harder for safety-critical projects as the quality standards are stricter in order to make sure quality is documented sufficiently [53].

6.3   Requirements

Proposition 3: The practice area of requirements is difficult to mesh. The main challenge is the different emphasis on the amount of documentation needed and the difficulties of handling the requirements specifications iteratively.

One major challenge to meshing the agile and the documentation-driven methods is the way requirements are handled [32]. Both the case study of SmallSoft and on LargeSoft specifically showed how meshing the practice area of requirements was difficult due to several issues. User stories written in a plain business-like language cannot be used directly as requirements by an organization wishing to comply with a quality standard [53]. Instead, each user story needs to be translated into functional test cases [33]. SmallSoft experienced that requirements written by the customers could not be approved by the GAMP standard. Furthermore, this case study showed how due to a close, trusting customer relation the need for further documentation of the requirements was not perceived.

The agile and the documentation-driven practice areas on requirements are pursuing similar goals, but the major difference is the emphasis on the amount of documentation needed [24]. This is supported by the findings of this paper. The case study on SmallSoft showed that, handling the requirements in an agile manner did not comply with the requirements of documentation. The case study on LargeSoft also showed that the documentation of the requirements was hard to mesh. Even though the requirements were gathered at a big upfront analysis, the software group needed a iterative requirements process. They therefore attempted a mesh by changing the requirements and documents hereof in the late stages of the project. Doing so is expensive and a more iterative requirements gathering is therefore preferable [2]. Previous literature suggests that a mesh can be pursued by introducing a requirements engineering phase in the beginning, but still adjusting requirements iteratively [54]. Handling the requirements specifications in an iterative manner was, however, difficult for LargeSoft due to official approvals of the documents.

6.4   Development Strategy

Proposition 4: The practice area of development strategy can be meshed. This can be done by embedding an agile, iterative software development strategy in a documentation-driven project. Such a practice has several advantages but it does pose some challenges, as the long-term milestones will affect the iterations.

Previous literature proposed that the development strategies of the agile and the documentation-driven methods were incompatible [22]. The analysis of software practice in LargeSoft showed that it is possible to mesh the development strategies by embedding an iterative agile software practice in a documentation-driven project controlled by milestones. The milestones did, however, affect the content of the iterations and forced the documents to be approved in the early stages of the project. Boehm and Turner [32] advocate that the milestones are realigned and redefined to better fit an iterative approach. An empirical study of how to do this is however not presented. The literature acknowledges the advantages of iterative software development [55]. The advantage of developing the software in iterations in order to be able to define the requirements up front is highlighted [55].

6.5   Communications and Knowledge Sharing

Proposition 5: The practice area of communication and knowledge sharing can be meshed. Creating a mesh between the agile personalization strategy and the documentation-driven codification strategy is advocated. A mesh will likely be dominated by the codification strategy, due to the requirements of the quality standards.

The literature on meshing the agile and the documentation-driven practices do not deal with the issue of meshing the practice area on communication and knowledge sharing strategies. The literature on knowledge management reports on meshing communication strategies. In line with the case on LargeSoft, it is suggested to have a knowledge sharing strategy that consists of both personalization and codification; a distribution of 80%-20% is advocated [47]. These finding have been supported by for example Kautz and Thaysen [56]. Both SmallSoft and LargeSoft found it advantageous to have a primarily personalized communication strategy, but were, due to the quality standards, forced to have/introduce a dominating codification strategy.

6.6   Testing

Proposition 6: The practice area of testing is difficult to mesh. Implementing an agile, test-driven practice requires that both developers and the management realize the advantages of test-driven development.

Implementing agile practices such as test-driven development is a way to mesh the agile and the documentation-driven methods. It is argued that documentation-driven methods already focus on test and quality of the software, while the test-first and continuous integration proposed by the agile methods will be helpful in finding the problems earlier rather than later [32]. One case study reports on Scrum and CMMI level 5 being meshed; they underline how the test practices of Scrum (test-driven development and automated tests) supported the iterations and were an important part of the quality assurance [57]. Explicit quality plans were used to ensure testing was done in the right manner. The literature does not propose that implementing agile test-driven development may be difficult due to the different focus in documentation-driven projects in the implementation phase, as the case study of LargeSoft showed.

7   Conclusion

The purpose of this paper was to answer: how can the agile and the documentation-driven methods be meshed in practice? The research is based on two interpretive case studies focusing on safety-critical software development and at the same time attempting to achieve a mesh between the agile and the documentation-driven methods. The first case study showed how an agile software organization attempted to implement a meshed practice by introducing documentation-driven elements; however unsuccessful. The second case study showed how a software group in a documentation-driven project implemented a meshed (but primarily documentation-driven) practice by introducing agile elements from Scrum.

Based on the literature, nine practice areas of meshing were identified 1) management style, 2) customer relations, 3) people-issues, 4) documentation, 5) requirements, 6) development strategy, 7) communication and knowledge sharing, 8) testing and 9) culture. The case studies provided contributions on six of the nine practice areas; showing the following. A) Meshing the practice area of customer-relations is difficult. An agile customer relation can hinder the implementation of the documentation-driven customer strategy due to a high level of trust between the parties. Implementing agile customer relations can also be difficult in a documentation-driven project if such a relation is not prioritized by the management. B) The practice area of documentation is the hardest to mesh; the amount of documentation required by documentation-driven methods is not supported by the agile methods. C) The practice area of requirements is difficult to mesh. The challenge is related to the documentation of these. D) The practice area of development strategy can be meshed. A software organization can mesh the agile and the documentation-driven methods by using short iterations within long-term milestones. The iterations will however be affected by the milestones as the passing of these are dependent on certain activities, for example writing documentation. E) The practice area of communication and knowledge sharing strategies can be meshed, but will most likely be dominated by the documentation-driven codification strategy. F) The practice area of testing is difficult to mesh. Both developers and management need to realize the advantages of test-driven software development

References

1. Schwaber, K., Beedle, M.: Agile software development with scrum. Prentice Hall, Upper Saddle River (2001)
2. Beck, K., Andres, C.: Extreme programming explained: Embrace change, 2nd edn. Addison-Wesley Professional, USA (2004)
3. Hares, J.S.: SSADM for the advanced practitioner. John Wiley & Sons, UK (1994)
4. Chrissis, M.B., Konrad, M., Shrum, S.: CMMI guidelines for process integration and product improvement. Addison-Wesley Longman Publishing Co., Inc., Boston (2003)
5. U.S. Department of Health of Health and Human Services: FDA U.S. Food and Drug Administration 2011 (2010)
6. Boehm, B.: Get Ready for Agile Methods, with Care. Computer 35, 64–69 (2002)
7. Kruchten, P.: The rational unified process: An introduction. Addison-Wesley Professional, Boston (2004)
8. Pressman, R.S.: Software engineering - A practitioner's approach. McGraw-Hill Publishing Company, UK (2000)
9. Heeager, L.T.: Introducing Agile Practices in a Documentation-Driven Software Development Practice: A Case Study. Journal of Information Technology Case and Application Research 14, 3–24 (2012)
10. Boehm, B., Turner, R.: Observations on Balancing Discipline and Agility, pp. 32–39 (2003)
11. Stapleton, J.: DSDM: Dynamic Systems Development Method, p. 406 (1999)
12. Dybå, T., Dingsøyr, T.: Empirical Studies of Agile Software Development: A Systematic Review. Information and Software Technology 50, 833–859 (2008)
13. Mahanti, A.: Challenges in Enterprise Adoption of Agile Methods - A Survey. Journal of Computing and Information Technology 14, 197–206 (2004)
14. Cockburn, A.: Agile software development: The cooperative game. Addison-Wesley Professional, Boston (2006)
15. Aaen, I.: Software Process Improvement: Blueprints Versus Recipes. IEEE Software 20, 86–93 (2003)
16. Vogel, D.A.: Agile Methods: Most are Not Ready for Prime Time in Medical Device Software Design and Development. DesignFax Online, pp. 1–6 (2006)
17. Heeager, L.T.: The Agile and the Disciplined Software Approaches: Combinable or Just Compatible? In: Anonymous Information Systems Development, pp. 35–49. Springer (2013)
18. Hilburn, T.B., Townhidnejad, M.: Software Quality: A Curriculum Postscript? 32, 167–171 (2000)
19. DeMarco, T.: Structured analysis and system specification. Yourdon Press, New York (1979)
20. Yourdon, E.: Modern structured analysis, Prentice Hall PTR, USA (1989)
21. Misra, S.C., Kumar, V., Kumar, U.: Identifying some Critical Changes Required in Adopting Agile Practices in Traditional Software Development Projects. International Journal of Quality & Reliability Management 27, 451–474 (2010)

22. Nerur, S., Mahapatra, R.K., Mangalaraj, G.: Challenges of Migrating to Agile Methodologies. Commun. ACM 48, 73–78 (2005)
23. Moe, N.B., Dingsøyr, T., Dybå, T.: A Teamwork Model for Understanding an Agile Team: A Case Study of a Scrum Project. Information and Software Technology 52, 480–491 (2010)
24. Paetsch, F., Eberlein, A., Maurer, F.: Requirements Engineering and Agile Software Development, p. 308 (2003)
25. Huo, M., Verner, J., Zhu, L., et al.: Software Quality and Agile Methods, pp. 520–527 (2004)
26. McAvoy, J., Butler, T.: A Failure to Learn in a Software Development Team: The Unsuccessful Introduction of an Agile Method. In: Information Systems Development, pp. 1–13 (2009)
27. Galal-Edeen, G.H., Riad, A.M., Seyam, M.S.: Agility Versus Discipline: Is Reconciliation Possible? pp. 331–337 (2007)
28. Esfahani, C., Cabot, J., Yu, E.: Adopting Agile Methods: Can Goal-Oriented Social Modeling Help? pp. 223–234 (2010)
29. Vinekar, V., Slinkman, C.W., Nerur, S.: Can Agile and Traditional Systems Development Approaches Coexist? an Ambidextrous View. Inf. Syst. Manage. 23, 31–42 (2006)
30. Baker, S.W.: Formalizing Agility: An Agile Organization's Journey Toward CMMI Accreditation, pp. 185–192 (2005)
31. Bos, E., Vriens, C.: An Agile CMM, pp. 129–138 (2004)
32. Boehm, B., Turner, R.: Management Challenges to Implementing Agile Processes in Traditional Development Organizations. IEEE Software 22, 30–39 (2005)
33. Beznosov, K.: Extreme Security Engineering: On Employing XP Practices to Achieve 'Good enough Security' without Defining It (2003)
34. Larman, C.: Agile and iterative development: A manager's guide. Addison-Wesley Professional, Boston (2004)
35. Senapathi, M.: Adoption of Software Engineering Process Innovations: The Case of Agile Software Development Methodologies. In: Sillitti, A., Martin, A., Wang, X., Whitworth, E. (eds.) XP 2010. LNBIP, vol. 48, pp. 226–231. Springer, Heidelberg (2010)
36. Cohn, M., Ford, D.: Introducing an Agile Process to an Organization [Software Development]. Computer 36, 74–78 (2003)
37. Chau, T., Maurer, F., Melnik, G.: Knowledge Sharing: Agile Methods Vs. Tayloristic Methods, pp. 302–307 (2003)
38. Chau, T., Maurer, F.: Knowledge Sharing in Agile Software Teams. In: Lenski, W. (ed.) Logic versus Approximation. LNCS, vol. 3075, pp. 173–183. Springer, Heidelberg (2004)
39. Boehm, B.W., Turner, R.: Balancing agility and discipline: A guide for the perplexed. Addison-Wesley Professional, Boston (2003)
40. Dahlberg, H., Ruiz, F.S., Olsson, C.M.: The Role of Extreme Programming in a Plan-Driven Organization, pp. 291–312 (2006)
41. Boehm, B., Turner, R.: Using Risk to Balance Agile and Plan-Driven Methods. Computer 36, 57–66 (2003)
42. Oxford Advanced Learner's Dictionary: Oxford Advanced Learner's Dictionary 2011 (2011)
43. Walsham, G.: Interpretive Case Studies in IS Research: Nature and Method. European Journal of Information Systems 4, 74–81 (1995)
44. The International Society for Pharmaceutical Engineering: GAMP Publications 2011 (2010)

45. Iversen, J., Nielsen, P.A., Norbjerg, J.: Situated Assessment of Problems in Software Development. ACM SIGMIS Database 30, 66–81 (1999)
46. Goles, T., Chin, W.W.: Information Systems Outsourcing Relationship Factors: Detailed Conceptualization and Initial Evidence. ACM SIGMIS Database 36, 67 (2005)
47. Hansen, M.T., Nohria, N., Tierney, T.: What's Your Strategy for Managing Knowledge? Harv. Bus. Rev. 77, 106–116 (1999)
48. Das, T., Teng, B.S.: Trust, Control, and Risk in Strategic Alliances: An Integrated Framework. Studies 22, 251–283 (2001)
49. Paulk, M.C.: Agile Methodologies and Process Discipline. Crosstalk-The Journal of Defense Software Engineering 1, 15–18 (2002)
50. Murru, O., Deias, R., Mugheddue, G.: Assessing XP at a European Internet Company. IEEE Software 20, 37–43 (2003)
51. Kähkönen, T., Abrahamsson, P.: Achieving CMMI Level 2 with Enhanced Extreme Programming Approach. In: Bomarius, F., Iida, H. (eds.) PROFES 2004. LNCS, vol. 3009, pp. 378–392. Springer, Heidelberg (2004)
52. McMichael, B., Lombardi, M.: ISO 9001 and Agile Development, pp. 262–265 (2007)
53. Wright, G.: Achieving ISO 9001 Certification for an XP Company. In: Maurer, F., Wells, D. (eds.) XP/Agile Universe 2003. LNCS, vol. 2753, pp. 43–50. Springer, Heidelberg (2003)
54. Namioka, A., Bran, C.: eXtreme ISO?!? pp. 260–263 (2004)
55. Rising, L., Janoff, N.S.: The Scrum Software Development Process for Small Teams. IEEE Software 17, 26–32 (2002)
56. Kautz, K., Thaysen, K.: Knowledge, Learning and IT Support in a Small Software Company. Journal of Knowledge Management 5, 349–357 (2001)
57. Jakobsen, C.R., Johnson, K.A.: Mature Agile with a Twist of CMMI, pp. 212–217 (2008)

Contracting in Agile Software Projects: State of Art and How to Understand It

Shi Hao Zijdemans[1] and Christoph Johann Stettina[1,2]

[1] Leiden Institute of Advanced Computer Science, Leiden University,
Niels Bohrweg 1, 2333 CA Leiden, The Netherlands
[2] Centre for Innovation The Hague, Leiden University,
Schouwburgstraat 2, 2511 VA The Hague, The Netherlands

Abstract. The iterative nature of Agile methods paves the way for new and more dynamic contract arrangements in software development projects. However, while new types and adaptations of existing contract types have emerged in practice, a shared view on these arrangements is missing in literature. In this paper we review common contract types discussed in Agile and traditional project management. Based on existing literature and empirical data collected during a workshop and semi-structured interviews we present a preliminary framework to help understand and choose contracting practices in context.

Keywords: Agile project management, contracting, procurement practices.

1 Introduction

Agile project management is becoming increasingly popular in and outside the domain of software development [1]. While an Agile approach brings advantages to both the software supplier and the customer, it also introduces new challenges. Major challenges when implementing Agile methods in traditional software development organizations are caused by the necessity to adapt existing practices to fit the iterative nature of Agile projects in context [2]. Contracting is one of such domains of practice potentially affected by agile methods [3].

Contract negotiation is a crucial part of a software development project, because it has an influence on the entire project, its practices, the underlying patterns of action and governance structure. It can be challenging for a software supplier and customer to find a common ground of trust without prior collaborations. A good contract agreement is important for further relations [3]. Still, frequently we encounter (small) software companies that are unaware of existing contracting practices and the possibilities they offer.

Fixed-price contracts have been used frequently with Agile projects. Here, the high level of uncertainty in software projects, and the flexibility that is intended for the Agile approach conflict with the planning-driven nature of fixed-price contracts [3]. Therefore, the Agile contracting problem has gradually received more attention [4]. Alternative practices or contracting frameworks have been

G. Cantone and M. Marchesi (Eds.): XP 2014, LNBIP 179, pp. 78–93, 2014.

proposed in literature, but every project is different and therefore we believe that there is no one silver bullet for the Agile contracting problem.

Although an initial discourse can be found in literature, the discussion on contracting in Agile projects is scattered across practitioners literature and individual cases. Current contributions are limited to single case studies discussing individual frameworks in practice, and predominantly covering the perspective of software developers. This paper contributes an analysis of major contract types discussed in Agile and traditional project management literature. Empirically collecting the perceptions of different stakeholders such as legal advisors, Agile coaches and business owners we present a preliminary tool to understand and help choosing an appropriate configuration of contracting practices in context.

2   Related Work

In an attempt to counter contracting challenges in Agile projects, multiple contract types have been discussed in literature. In this section we review the contract types in Agile and traditional project management literature and their application in Agile contexts.

Fixed-Price Contracts Besides a prespecified price, a fixed-price contract contains a fixed deadline and an assumably complete specification of the software system in question. In practice a complete specification is rather difficult and costly to create (e.g. customer often cannot specify requirements accurately [4]) and hinders innovation (e.g. design changes in evolving system are only possible via expensive and often troublesome change requests). The supplier is financially responsible for any cost overruns. Therefore it is recommended that the supplier does not consider this contract type unless the system requirements are clear and unambiguous [5].

Target-Price Contracts In target-price contracts the risk of overruns are shared between the customer and the supplier [6]. The contract contains a target of effort (in man hours), a negotiated profit on the project and often a deadline. If the actual amount of hours exceeds the target, the customer pays 50% (or another agreed upon percentage) of the extra costs. And vice versa, if the actual amount is less than the target, the customer pays 50% of the difference between the actual amount and the target. This contract type can also be set up with a minimum and maximum amount of hours that can be charged.

Time & Material Contracts In Time & Materials contracts the supplier is paid based on its hourly rate [7]. At prespecified time intervals (e.g. monthly) a bill is sent to the customer, containing the amount of man hours and the total price according to the supplier's hourly rate. T&M contracts do not contain a complete specification of the system, and the project can be ended whenever the customer wants. The risk in T&M projects is carried by the customer; the supplier is paid fully for every hour, and therefore does not have an incentive to complete the project quickly [3]. The only meaningful incentive is high competition and the prospect of follow-up contracts [5].

Cost-plus contracts In cost-plus contracts, the customer pays for all the supplier's costs plus an additional fee that contains the profit [8]. There are different options to construct the fee. *Cost-plus-fixed-fee* contracts have a pre-specified fixed profit fee [5]. In *cost-plus-incentive-fee* contracts, suppliers receive a higher profit fee if they meet or exceed a specific target performance, which is agreed in advance by supplier and customer. This introduces an incentive for the supplier to keep the costs down [5]. Whereas the incentive fees are based on objective calculations comparing certain measures (e.g. costs, delivery time), *Cost-plus-award-fee* contracts utilize a more subjective fee. Award fees can be earned when the supplier meets significantly higher levels of performance, quality, timeliness or responsiveness in the project [5]. Cost-plus contracts require that the supplier's books be audited [5].

We will now present frameworks dedicated to contracting in agile software projects available in existing literature.

Agile Fixed-Price Contracts This book specifically devoted to Agile contracts [9] provides a contract model for 'Agile Fixed-Price Contracts'. The book gives a detailed guide on the setup, the tender phase, and the practical aspects of project management for Agile fixed-price contracts. This contract type contains a fixed price ceiling and the scope of the software system is left variable. It incorporates interesting features, such as 'exit points' and a 'Checkpoint phase'. Exit points are predefined points in time where the parties may terminate the project in a controlled manner. A Checkpoint phase is a period of x sprints or a performance scope of y storypoints, that act as a test phase of the cooperation between customer and supplier.

Agile Contract Primer - Multi-phase variable-model The *Agile Contract Primer*[10] provides suggestions for better understanding of IT lawyers' perspective, and multiple suggestions for IT lawyers are given to get a better understanding of the implications of the Agile methodology and systems thinking. The article also discusses *Multi-phase variable-model frameworks* which take into account that the uncertainty and risk profiles of software projects change over time. In a multi-phase framework, any phase can use any contracting model. For example: choose fixed-price for the first phase, where the Product Backlog is created and hence the most uncertain phase of the project is traversed, and then switch to T&M.

adVANTAGE The 'adVANTAGE' pricing model combines elements of fixed-price and T&M contracting models [3]. In this contracting model, the software supplier is paid for their effort after each sprint. The contract provides an idea of the overall scope in terms of user stories, time and budget. The required effort for each user story is estimated in the beginning of the project. These estimates are used in all sprints as an orientation point for the bill, as the actual effort for each user story is compared to the estimated effort. The final price for each sprint is compensated according to any differences in the actual and estimated effort (like target-cost contracts). The customer can prioritize, eliminate or add user stories at the beginning of each sprint, and in doing so, has to take into account the supplier's price estimates and its own budget ceiling.

Collaborative Agile Contracts Thorup and Jensen (2009) [11] proposed and tested this model in two commercial projects. The biggest distinctive feature of this contracting model is that the payment is delayed until a certain criterion is fulfilled [11]. In most contract types this criterion is a calendar date, however in Collaborative Agile Contracts, the criterion is to reach a predefined milestone where the customer is getting value from a specific delivered increment of the system. Generally both parties would like to reach these milestones as quickly as possible. The supplier's efficiency will be rewarded with a quicker payout. The customer will think more carefully when deciding what features he/she wants to have implemented, because all the increments will be paid for separately. Further, Concha et al (2007) [12] propose an approach called "Agile Commitments" which provides complementary practices for Agile projects. One of the objectives of Agile Commitments is to define and specify the commitments between the customer and supplier, which can provide a baseline for contract negotiation.

Current literature discusses a variety of contract types, however, the evaluation in projects following Agile methods is sparse. While contracting is discussed on the level of entire frameworks, our literature analysis points out that contracting types resemble a mix of distinct practices. Such concrete practices are fixed-price agreements or payments-per-sprint, often accompanied by further incentive and governance mechanisms. Based upon the literature reviewed above we find it appropriate to pose the following research question:

1. *What contract types and the contained concrete practices are suitable for different Agile project contexts?*

3 Method

Following our research goal we want to create an understanding of contracting practices in real world projects. To pursue this goal, we chose to conduct an inductive case study research approach as commonly proposed by literature [13,14]. Qualitative case studies allow to look at complex problems in context while developing rich and informative conclusions.

3.1 Data Collection: Workshop and Semi-structured Interviews

In order to establish an appropriate understanding of the topic matter we first conducted a scientific workshop for Agile professionals. The 45-minute workshop took place in context of a conference on Agile methods and was held with 8 participants. This pre-study allowed us to collect many perceptions on Agile contracting in a short amount of time, and gave us a general idea of current practices in use. Based upon the workshop results and existing literature we created an interview guide and conducted semi-structured interviews. The face-to-face interviews took place between April and June 2013 with five participants in different organizations. We interviewed participants from a variety of roles to ensure an inclusion of different perspectives on the topic. The interviews had an approximate duration of 60 minutes and took place at the participants' workplace. Before each interview, we asked the participant for permission to record the interview. We mentioned that all data from the interview will be anonymized. All interviews were voice recorded and transcribed. We further asked participants to provide process descriptions if available.

The structure of the semi-structure interviews was as follows: We started with general questions about the participant, the organization, their knowledge on (Agile) software development and contracting. We then continued with questions related to their experiences with contracts in Agile projects and challenges they are facing. Example questions were: *How does the process of acquiring projects look like in your organization (from initial project request to start of development)? What are important aspects to consider when contracting Agile software projects? What are the challenges you are facing with current contracts in Agile projects? What do you think could be improved in your current way of contracting software projects?*

The interview questions were continuously revised in course of the study. Given the variety of backgrounds of participants, we altered the questions according to a given situation (e.g. special knowledge in a particular area or limited in another). For example, with one of the participants who is a jurist in R&D, we skipped some of the more technical software development questions.

3.2   Data Analysis

To analyze the data from the interviews, we applied a qualitative data coding technique similar to that of Grounded Theory (GT) by Glaser and Strauss [15]. We used the coding technique, in contrary to GT, however, we used semi-structured interview guides based on existing literature and findings from the previously conducted workshop. The method is especially suitable for areas of research that have not been studied in great detail before. Such would allow us to collect rich information while enabling direct exchange with the practitioners.

All interviews have been fully transcribed. After the transcription, we performed 'open coding' [15] using the tool *Open Code* [1]. There, the transcripts were analyzed line by line and inspected for recurring key themes. Each key theme was then assigned a 'code' (i.e. a descriptive label), which forms a level of abstraction in analyzing the transcripts. By constantly comparing the codes against each other (i.e. Grounded Theory's *constant comparison method*), we categorized the codes to extract underlying concepts. An example:

Quote: *"In calculating our price, we ensure that there is a certain financial buffer for us, we use it for contingency planning. We define that buffer upfront based on our expectations and if along the way the customer [makes change requests] then we can be easier about it.*

Key Theme: *"Contingency planning for fixed-price projects"*
Code: Fixed-price modifications
Category: Fixed-price

---

[1] http://www.phmed.umu.se/english/
divisions/epidemiology/research/open-code/

4   Results

In this section we present the results collected. An overview of the participants is given in Table 1. In order to preserve the participants' confidentiality, we assign a an ID to each participant (P1-P5). All interviewees have several years of experience with contracting and contract negotiations in software projects. The majority of participants apply Scrum in their projects. P1 is a jurist in a legal department and does not apply any project management framework directly. P2 is familiar with agile methodologies, however, rather than implementing a particular method the company applies a few agile practices such as iterative development and frequent customer reviews. The size of the organizations varied heavily among the participants; from 10 to 145.000 employees. Supportive quotes will be provided, which have been translated from Dutch.

Table 1. Interview participants and descriptive variables

Participant	Type of Organization	Size of Organization	Function	Agile method	Experience
P1	R&D	Large	Jurist	-	Legal advisor in contract negotiations
P2	Web Development	Small	Co-owner	-	Contract negotiation with customers
P3	Auditing, Tax Advisory, Consulting	Large	Partner	Scrum	Contract negotiation with customers
P4	Consulting & Training	Large	ScrumMaster, Coach	Scrum	Training and consulting on business agility and performance improvement
P5	Software Development	Large	Agile consultant	Scrum	Research in Agile

In Figure 1 we present an overview of all the categories that we have distinguished from the different codes. To provide a quantitative view, all the categories were assembled and ranked by the the amount of codes they contained (Fig. 1). We divided the categories into two groups: *concrete practices* and *affecting factors*. As we can see in the figure, the majority of codes is related to concrete practices discussed by our participants. In total we found 330 codes distributed over 31 categories.

During the coding we identified the major challenges in Agile projects mentioned by our participants as:

1. *Lack of Customer Involvement: if the customer is not involved in the project enough, it will be more difficult for the supplier to develop the right system.*
2. *Difficulties in Scope Change: if the entire scope of the project has been completely specified in the contract, scope changes become very difficult.*

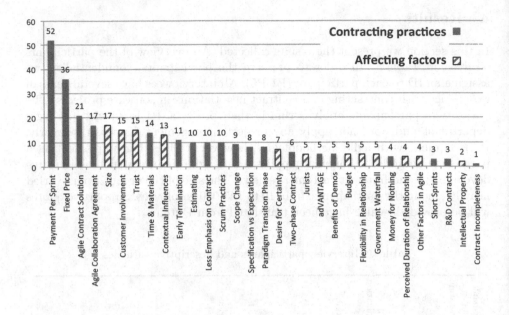

Fig. 1. Overview of the categories and the amount of codes they contain

3. *Lack of Trust: Before the project has started, customers tend to lack trust in that, by using the Agile approach, the supplier can deliver the right system without having to specify the system completely upfront.*
4. *Too much Trust: When the project is started, customers tend to have too much trust in that the supplier will deliver a good system, which in turn leads to less effort being put in the project by the customer.*

4.1   Concrete Practices in Use

Is this section we will report on the practices discussed by our participants. By such we mean observable patterns of human action such as 'payment per sprint'.

Fixed Price. 'Fixed Price' was mentioned many times. Besides the challenges regarding fixed-price contracts that have been described in related research literature (e.g. the customer's desire for certainty and upfront specification), another important distinction was often emphasized: the distinction between *specifications* and *expectations*.

> "*it's way more important to meet the expectations than the specifications. Of course you do need specifications, but those should be more like goals: 'what is the intended goal of the system?'. That is, however, difficult to state [formally], but it's better to verify the system against the goals instead of the specifications.*" - P4.

Payment per Sprint. Among the participants that actively use Agile methods, the opinions on payment per sprint varied widely. While P4 has *"never seen contracts done in that way"*, P3 currently uses this method of payment with success, and is confident that this is a very effective way of handling the payments in Scrum projects. In contrary to the adVANTAGE pricing model [3], this organization uses a fixed price per sprint.

> *"Billing is easy; I want to do that per Sprint. I want to do the billing as soon as possible... however it doesn't always work, because before you know it you're behind 2-3 weeks. But in general...there will be a bill per Sprint, and we try to do this as close to the end of the Sprint as possible. It is a fixed amount per Sprint by the way, so whether or not we make the exact agreed hours or not, that doesn't matter. This also has to do with the current economic conditions. Every company is trying to invoice quickly these days, because payments are taking so long."* - P3.

Benefits. P3 believes that one of the benefits for the supplier is the fast payment, and thereby some reduction of risk. The benefit of payment per sprint for the customer is the flexibility that can be offered in multiple aspects of the relationship. In the contract an agreement is stated for a certain amount of sprints. Every time the agreed amount of sprints has been completed, the customer can buy more sprints. At the start of the project customers can agree to buy a small amount of sprints to get introduced to the Agile approach. In these sprints the customer can witness the Product Backlog being created and managed, and he could receive the first part of the system.

> *"I always say 'You only get on board for one sprint, and when you're dissatisfied with a sprint, we can always just say goodbye'. Those are always enlightening insights for the customer."* - P3.

P3 elaborates that it is of course the idea to build the desired system together, but it is best to offer options like these to the customer just in case the collaboration works out differently. Another benefit that was mentioned by P3, is that the payment directly follows the acceptance of the sprint, which makes the payment more 'natural' for the customer.

> *"It's very logical right? You have a sprint, you get a report with the sprint, you get a demo with the sprint, well then it's pretty logical to add a bill to the sprint as well."* - P3.

Disadvantages. P4 stated that a disadvantage could lie in the fact that such a contract could create a short term vision. When there is a contract for a couple of sprints, the supplier will likely focus on these sprints and try to please the customer by presenting as much functionality as possible. This would tempt developers to put the quality of the system at risk by creating a technical debt, leading to poor software architecture.

P3 mentioned that this payment structure requires discipline in the financial aspect. He stated that his environment — one of the largest professional services organizations in the world, that mostly does financial advisory — plays a role in the successful realization of this payment method.

" However this requires discipline in the financial aspect, something that IT people are not very good at. I am being helped with that by my environment; in this house they always know everything financially." - P3.

Agile Collaboration Agreement. When all the features have been formally specified upfront, then there is very little room for any scope change. P5 stated that it is essential to solve this problem, and that ideally in Agile contracts *"scope change should be freed"*. To free scope change P5 suggested forming a joint-venture, or setting up 'Collaboration Agreements' for Agile software projects.

"One way is to form a joint-venture. Then the software supplier gets a share of the profit...I believe this is a possible way to do it. Another option is aimed towards Collaboration Agreements..that would contain things like the responsibilities and expectations of the parties" - P5.

The importance of proper collaboration and trust in Agile projects was also mentioned by P3 and P4. They believe that the customer should monitor the progress of the project more. According to them the responsibilities and expectations of the customer should be clarified and stated in Agile contracts for more effective collaboration, and a higher chance of project success.

"I think the best would be a pure Agile way, in which you, as a customer, can watch over the progress...very frequently...And of course, when you see that the team performs well, then you give them a bit more freedom, but if you get the impression of 'this doesn't suffice', well then as a customer I would be on that a bit tighter...And it's very possible to state that in a contract I think." - P4.

P3 emphasized that *"on the one hand customers should have more trust, and on the other hand they should have less trust"*. They should have more trust in the fact that they can get a good end result without a complete upfront specification. *"They should have less trust that, once they have started the relationship, the supplier will make it all alright. They have to critically watch the supplier"*.

Early Termination. Something that was often mentioned, was the 'Money for Nothing' part of Sutherland's 'Money for Nothing, Change for Free' [16], which is an agreement that in the case when the customer decides to terminate the project early (because he is satisfied enough with the delivered increments of the system), he will pay 20% of the remaining budget to the supplier. This can partly be seen as a bonus for delivering enough business value sooner than expected. The other part is a risk premium, since the supplier's resources have to be reallocated unexpectedly (P5). P4 and P5 both have not seen this being put to use very often, although they both believe that this element is required in the ideal Agile contract.

P3 reiterated the possibility to terminate a project early due to ongoing challenges. However, he was not familiar with the idea of customers terminating a successful project early. Even though a customer might be satisfied with the deliverables, budget and personnel have already been allocated. This makes it rather unlikely to stop a project before the planned end date.

> *"I have never seen that in a contract. It's very funny, because it's actually very logical to do it like that. That's very good. Although it can be seen that many customers have a lot of trouble with de-scoping, it's very hard to decide that you don't want something, even though it barely has additional business value. Customers are not used to that."* - P3.

Two-phase Contract. To handle the 'time and money' aspect of Agile contracting, P5 recommended a 'Two-phase Contract', which is inspired by the *Cone of Uncertainty* (McConnell, 1997). Especially in the beginning of a project, there is a lot of uncertainty (about the scope, price, duration etc.). This gradually declines along the duration of the project. Two-phase contracts take this into account and divides the project into two phases. The first phase is a relatively short phase aimed at getting through the initial uncertainty and creating a base of trust between the customer and supplier. P5 recommended to use fixed-price for this phase since it is relatively short, and the required effort can be estimated relatively easily. In this phase the productivity of the team is witnessed by the customer, there is a more accurate view on the requirements, the main impediments have been identified and an increment of the system has been delivered. When those elements are already in place, the parties could basically make any contract type work well for the second phase (e.g. fixed-price, T&M etc.).

4.2 Affecting Factors

Size. The size of the organization (supplier side or customer side) and the size of the project all play a role in determining whether this method of payment is feasible. P3 explained that smaller projects have an upfront total price estimate, and a planning of the sprints.

> *"But smaller projects, there you first have a total price estimate and a planning of the sprints. So formally they also buy sprints, but there is a bit more specification of the system....so a bit more towards a waterfall-like description of the end result. But when I look at other Agile contracts, this is pretty Agile."* - P3.

P2 (Web development) did not see any added value in doing the payments per cycle for his organization, because he does not have very complex cases.

Government Waterfall. Something that was mentioned by multiple participants was the regulations that are associated with software projects for the government. Governmental software projects should always have a complete upfront specification, price estimation and deadline.

"The contract model, that's where you really see the friction between waterfall and [Scrum]...And especially in the government, all the standards are aimed towards waterfall-like constructions, where everything is specified very clearly. " - P3.

Further, as dictated by EU regulations, no bilateral communication between principal and service provider is allowed before the contract has been awarded

Customer Involvement. An aspect that often poses a big challenge in Agile projects is the lack of customer involvement [17]. P3 explained his current experience with regard to customer involvement, and underlines its importance.

"We also invite the customer, and if he joins in more than once a week, then that can be seen as often. Something that also happens often is that the product owner goes and works at the customer's site. In that case he is present [with us] less than you'd ideally want to, but then that's also understandable." - P3.

Understanding Jurists. When asked what current challenges are in contracting from jurists' perspective, P1 stated that when jurists are making a contract for (two) parties, they often don't really know what the underlying intentions from these parties are. This somewhat limits them in their ability of setting up correct and accurate contracts.

"What I often encounter is that many times jurists don't know, what the intentions are of the parties." - P1.

This was confirmed by P5, who explained that he had conducted a workshop at a Dutch organization of jurists. This workshop aimed to get the jurists thinking about possible solutions. So far they believe that a solution based on Collaboration Agreements is the most feasible, and P5 said to believe that it is largely a matter of time before the effect of 'Agile Collaboration Agreements' is discovered.

5   Discussion

Following the description of main contracting types and the perceptions of our interviewees towards those, we will now proceed to discuss these types and their suitability in different context in Table 2.

According to McLeod and MacDonell [18] there are four main factor categories contributing to software development project outcomes, these are: Project Content, Institutional Context, People and Development Processes [18]. The factors influence the suitability of a contract type for a particular project (e.g. projects with ambiguous requirements can be well combined with exit arrangements, governments generally require fixed-price contracts). During contract negotiation some of these factors are easier to adjust than others (e.g. development process and project content are generally more flexible and easier to adjust than institutional context). Here we acknowledge the strong influence of contracting practices on the development process, as a contract can enforce a specific software development process. Following this line of thought, we consider Project Content, Institutional Context and People as independent factors that determine a project context. The contract practices then have to be selected accordingly based on these first three factors.

Further, based on our discussions with participants and contract elements in literature (e.g. incentives, uncertainty mitigation [5,9]) we made a distinction between four categories of contracting practices as depicted in Table 2: 1) Contract Basis, 2) an Incentive element 3) an Uncertainty Mitigation element and 4) an Governance element. The contract basis contains agreements on fairly basic contracting matters: the pricing model, delivery date and the scope of the system. However, since these basic agreements have proved to be insufficient in many project contexts, different variations and additions have been adopted in practice to overcome these challenges. The incentive element contains practices that focus on the unfair risk distribution that has often been associated with software development [3][7][9][10][11]. Leveraging additional incentive with a specific party can be used to balance the risk distribution for a project. The uncertainty mitigation element focuses on mitigating the uncertainty concerning the price, scope or deadline estimates that have to be made in the project. The introduction of a governance element to an Agile contract is focused on establishing a collaboration between the parties that is required for Agile software projects. This primarily aims to increase the amount of customer involvement in the project.

Contract basis In our interviews we found that fixed-price contracts are mainly used in projects for the government, or small projects. Despite of the negative connotations that fixed-price contracts have received in literature [3][9][10][11], fixed-price contracts have proved to work well in small projects, due to the fact that the requirements can generally be specified more accurately if the scope is small. Further, fixed-price agreements have been mentioned as efficient for small projects, as suppliers can avoid efforts associated with payments per sprint such as additional administration and billing.

We found that payment per sprint can be a good solution to increase the quality of the end result when the requirements are ambiguous, since this allows the scope to be specified incrementally. However, this can be regarded as unnecessary to implement in small projects, in which fixed-price contracts can also be used, since payment per sprint does not provide the customer with certainty about the price, and the time of delivery.

T&M contracts are not popular in Agile projects [3][7], because they put all the risk on the customer's side. However, we found that when there is mutual trust (i.e. supplier tries to work efficiently, and customer trusts this), T&M contracts can provide a very easy and straightforward payment structure.

Incentive Target-price contracts provide incentive for the supplier to deliver the system quickly, while not assuming all of the project risk (as is the case with

Table 2. Preliminary framework for understanding contracting practices as affected in project contexts. Practice contributes benefits predominantly for: Project Owner (◐), Supplier (◑), both (●), none (○).

	Contracting Practices					(affect Development Process)			
	Contract Basis			Incentive		Uncertainty Mitigation			Governance
	Fixed-Price / Scope	Time & Material	Pay per Sprint	Target-Price	Incentive Fee / Bonus Penalty	Exit Arrangement	Risk Buffer	Two Phase	Collaboration Agreement
Project Content									
Focus on Budget	◐	◑	◑	●	●	●	●	◑	○
Focus on Quality	○	●	●	●	●	○	●	●	○
Focus on Time	◐	◑	○	●	●	●	●	●	○
Ambiguous requirements	○	●	●	●	○	●	●	●	●
Large Size Project	○	◑	●	●	●	●	●	●	●
Small Size Project	●	◑	○	●	○	○	●	○	●
Institutional Context									
Government	●	○	○	○	○	●	●	●	●
People									
Uncertain Customer Involvement	○	○	○	○	●	○	○	○	●
Low Trust	◐	○	●	●	●	●	●	●	●

fixed-price contracts), since any cost overruns are shared evenly. Pricing models can be expanded with an incentive fee (i.e. provision for the adjustment of the total profit), that provides the supplier with an incentive to deliver the system more quickly or to reduce the costs. It is not recommended to use incentive fees when the requirement for the system are ambiguous [5].

Uncertainty Mitigation In our interviews we found that a risk buffer is a practice that is often used by the supplier to mitigate the uncertainty that revolves around the estimates that have to be made in fixed-price contracts. This buffer contains a part of the budget and a part of the project time span, and can be used by the supplier to handle any 'unforeseen' change requests in the last phases of the project. The customer does not need to be aware of this.

In our interviews and in literature [10] we found that the flexibility of the Two-Phase contract makes it a suitable contract type in different contexts of Agile projects. After the first phase (i.e. the most uncertain period of the project), the budget and time estimates for the rest of the project can be made more accurately. The breakdown into two phases can be particularly helpful in large projects with ambiguous requirements. Two different pricing models can be applied in this contract type, and these can be selected according to project circumstances (e.g. preferences of the customer).

Governance A collaboration agreement can be included in a contract when the amount of customer involvement is uncertain or expected to be low (e.g. if the customer is new to the Agile principles). In the Agile approach, the customer has an important role during the project, which is often not understood. A collaboration agreement helps create a common understanding by explicitly focusing on the responsibilities and expectations of the collaboration, and having the customer formally agree on this.

Based on the main challenges identified in our data (lack of customer involvement, difficulties in scope change, lack of- and too much trust), collaboration agreements can help by: Including collaboration expectations in contracts and creating an understanding of Agile values across the parties. Further, as collaboration agreements define how the teams work together expectations towards documentation and testing can be added. Especially as there is quite some uncertainty in Agile methods regarding documentation requirements [19,17], clarifying these expectations here can be helpful.

Although the contracting practices each have their benefits, many of them require additional effort in order to be implemented correctly. It is up to project managers (or whoever is in charge of choosing a specific contract type) to assess this trade-off, and to evaluate whether the practice is applicable in the specific project context.

5.1   Bias and Limitations

Although we followed a rigorous research process there are obvious limitations to our study. The major restriction is the limited amount of participants. We based our data on a workshop conducted with eight participants and five semi-structured interviews. Our sample might be difficult to reproduce and is not representative. To address external validity we support our preliminary model with findings available in agile as well as in traditional project management literature. To address construct validity we conducted several reality checks with experts and revised the final paper and preliminary model with IT lawyers. We believe that the quotes and extracted code categories put into perspective with already available individual case studies, provide a good overview of relevant themes and a solid ground for a further quantitative research.

6   Conclusions

In this paper we discuss contracting practices for Agile software development projects. First, we review common contracting types as discussed in Agile and traditional project management literature, and present our empirical evaluation of these contracting types applied in practice. Second, we analyze and divide contracting types into four categories of contracting practices (basis, incentive, risk mitigation and governance) and affecting factors (project content, institutional context and people). Finally, based on our analysis and empirical evidence, we give concrete recommendations to practitioners.

Based on our study the categories of contract practices presented in Table 2 contribute to the understanding of different configurations of contracts. In that sense we can only provide examples of such configurations and their advantages and disadvantages in practice. Their tailoring for a project needs to be carefully considered by the involved parties. To what extent such arrangements can differ is illustrated in the following examples:

1. *Small size web development project: fixed-price contract with a statement of hours and scope, and a collaboration agreement.*
2. *Medium size projects, with an intermediate risk level but opportunities for value creation with preliminary functionality delivered (e.g. e-Commerce or infrastructure): payment-per-sprint contract with a collaboration agreement*
3. *Large enterprise-wide implementation projects, with high risk of making inaccurate cost estimates and difficulty to elicit clear requirements from the customer: Multi-phase contract, with fixed-price in the first phase, where the planning is made, and a Collaborative Agile Contract in the next phases. Payments are made after each delivered increment of the system.*
4. *Large governmental R&D system development project, with high level of uncertainty (comparable to large Agile software projects): Two-phase contract with collaboration agreement. Target-price in first phase (concept definition), T&M in second phase (system development and demonstration)*

To scholars our findings contribute a better understanding of contracting practices in context. To practitioners we provide a preliminary framework to understand basic contracting types, their elements, and choose them according to a respective project context. We would like to help building a shared understanding and trust across project teams and legal consultants to help making better contracting arrangements in the future. As such this paper contributes to managerial and governance aspects of Agile organizations and how collaborations across such can be formed.

6.1 Recommendations for Research and Practice

To get a better understanding of the interdisciplinary possibilities and challenges, especially to understand procurement in the public sector, further interviews with jurists, public administrators and economists should prove beneficial. Further, the preliminary framework presented in Table 2 provides good opportunities to be elaborated and strengthened in a more quantitative research setting.

Acknowledgments. This research project has been supported by the Living Lab The Hague project co-funded with support from the European Regional Development Fund of the European Union. We thank all participants for generously contributing to this study.

References

1. Dybå, T., Dingsøyr, T.: Empirical studies of agile software development: A systematic review. Information Software Technology 50(9-10), 833–859 (2008)
2. Boehm, B., Turner, R.: Management challenges to implementing agile processes in traditional development organizations. IEEE Software 22(5), 30–39 (2005)
3. Book, M., Gruhn, V., Striemer, R.: adVANTAGE: A fair pricing model for agile software development contracting. In: Wohlin, C. (ed.) XP 2012. LNBIP, vol. 111, pp. 193–200. Springer, Heidelberg (2012)
4. Hoda, R., Noble, J., Marshall, S.: Negotiating contracts for agile projects: A practical perspective. In: Abrahamsson, P., Marchesi, M., Maurer, F. (eds.) XP 2009. LNBIP, vol. 31, pp. 186–191. Springer, Heidelberg (2009)
5. Kerzner, H.R.: Project Management: A Systems Approach to Planning, Scheduling, and Controlling. Wiley (2009)
6. Molokken-Ostvold, K., Furulund, K.M.: The relationship between customer collaboration and software project overruns. In: Agile Conference (AGILE), pp. 72–83. IEEE (2007)
7. Steven, P.: 10 contracts for your next agile software project (2009), http://agilesoftwaredevelopment.com/blog/peterstev/10-agile-contracts (accessed: April 14, 2013)
8. Hofbauer, J., Sanders, G.: Defense industrial initiatives current issues: Cost-plus contracts (2008), http://csis.org/files/media/csis/pubs/081016_diig_cost_plus.pdf (accessed: November 14, 2013)
9. Opelt, A., Gloger, B., Pfarl, W., Mittermayr, R.: Agile Contracts: Creating and Managing Successful Projects with Scrum. Wiley (2013)
10. Arbogast, T., Larman, C., Vodde, B.: Agile contracts primer (2012), http://www.agilecontracts.org/agile_contracts_primer.pdf   (accessed: November 20, 2013)
11. Thorup, L., Jensen, B.: Collaborative agile contracts. In: Agile Conference, AGILE 2009, pp. 195–200. IEEE (2009)
12. Concha, M., Visconti, M., Astudillo, H.: Agile commitments: Enhancing business risk management in agile development projects, pp. 149–152 (2007)
13. Yin, R.K.: Case Study Research: Design and Methods (Applied Social Research Methods), 4th edn. Sage Publications (2009)
14. Runeson, P., Höst, M.: Guidelines for conducting and reporting case study research in software engineering. Empirical Software Engineering 14(2), 131–164 (2009)
15. Glaser, B.G., Strauss, A.L.: The discovery of grounded theory: Strategies for qualitative research. Transaction Books (2009)
16. Krebs, J.: Agile Portfolio Management. Microsoft Press (2008)
17. Hoda, R., Kruchten, P., Noble, J., Marshall, S.: Agility in context. In: Proceedings of the ACM International Conference on Object Oriented Programming Systems Languages and Applications, OOPSLA 2010, pp. 74–88. ACM, NY (2010)
18. McLeod, L., MacDonell, S.G.: Factors that affect software systems development project outcomes: A survey of research. ACM Computing Surveys (CSUR) 43(4), 24 (2011)
19. Stettina, C.J., Kroon, E.: Is there an agile handover? an empirical study of documentation and project handover practices across agile software teams. In: 19th ICE & IEEE-ITMC International Conference, The Hague, Netherlands (2013)

Maturing in Agile: What Is It About?

Rafaela Mantovani Fontana[1,2], Sheila Reinehr[1], and Andreia Malucelli[1]

[1] Pontifícia Universidade Católica do Paraná (PUCPR)
1155 Imaculada Conceição st, Curitiba, PR, Brazil
[2] Universidade Federal do Paraná (UFPR)
1225 Dr. Alcides Vieira Arcoverde st, Curitiba, PR, Brazil
rafaela.fontana@ufpr.br, sheila.reinehr@pucpr.br, malu@ppgia.pucpr.br

Abstract. Maturity in agile software development is a subject still in definition. Although a number of models have been proposed, they usually adapt agile practices to CMMI-DEV requirements or differ among authors. The objective of this study was to identify how agile practitioners define a road map to maturity. We conducted a survey with Brazilian agilists and analyzed data using statistical Chi-square method. Our findings suggest that practitioners' opinion is that a prescribed model to agile maturity would not be useful – we propose, then, an initial guide for maturity. This guide defines some essential practices, but space should be left for teams to do the job as they please.

Keywords: maturity, agile software development, software process improvement.

1 Introduction

Maturity in agile software development has been discussed in literature under two main approaches. On the one hand, adopters of traditional software process improvement methods combine agile methods with prescriptive process definition and control, as defined by Capability Maturity Model Integration – Development (CMMI-DEV) ([26], [4], [6], [9], [16], [11], [32], [20]) or ISO/IEC 15504 ([38]). On the other hand, agilists define models to get mature by other means than increasing processes control: the focus is on keeping agile practices and agile values ([24], [30], [27], [25]).

The issue with the first approach is that higher maturity levels hampers keeping agility – the detailed processes coding and controlling naturally slows down the pacing ([26], [20]). The second approach does not shift the focus of agile methods, sustaining agility. The issue here, however, is that models are still initial ([7]), few approaches have been scientifically tested ([28]) and there are some evidences that agile practitioners do not realize benefits in having prescriptive maturity models ([30], [28], [17]).

As agile community still lacks a clear definition on how a team could get mature with agile methods, we conducted this study to identify how practitioners define the road map to maturity in agile software development. This

G. Cantone and M. Marchesi (Eds.): XP 2014, LNBIP 179, pp. 94–109, 2014.
© Springer International Publishing Switzerland 2014

research was based on a survey in an agile conference in Brazil and data were statistically analyzed. The findings interest practitioners and researchers as they complement current agile maturity models and go further suggesting new issues to be addressed.

2 Related Work

A number of maturity and adoption models for agile methods have been proposed in the last years. Apart from the initiatives to adapt agile methods to fit CMMI-DEV assessment requirements ([26], [4], [6], [9], [16], [11], [32], [20]), the agile maturity models focus on developing agile values and practices by means of stages or levels.

The Packlick's empirical model describes a goal oriented approach with 5 levels to reach maturity ([24]). Nottonson and DeLong model, developed based on the experience of a single company, is based on 3 steps of agile adoption ([23]). More structured approaches have been proposed by Sidky and colleagues ([30]), Qumer and Henderson-Sellers ([27]) and Patel and Ramachandran ([25]).

Sidky and colleagues ([30]) propose a model where each level comprises a number of practices that address principles from the agile manifesto. Agile adoption is done on a four-stage process: 1) identify discontinuing factors; 2) project level assessment; 3) organizational assessment; and 4) reconciliation. The maturity levels are, from lowest to highest, the "Collaborative", where the focus is on communication and collaboration between stakeholders; the "Evolutionary", where the focus is on continuous delivery of software; the "Effective", where the focus is on adopting engineering practices; the "Adaptive", where the focus is on responding to change; and "Encompassing", where the focus is on sustaining agility.

The model presented by Qumer and Henderson-Sellers ([27]) is part of a framework (Agile Software Solution Framework) that allows measuring agility and integrating it to governance. The maturity levels are 1) Agile Infancy, characterized by speed, flexibility and responsiveness; 2) Agile Initial, which is communication oriented; 3) Agile Realization, which focus on executable artifacts; 4) Agile Value, when the team is people oriented; 5) Agile Smart, when the focus is on learning; and 6) Agile Progress, characterized by lean production and keeping agile.

The structure proposed by Patel and Ramachandran ([25]) is similar to CMMI-DEV model as maturity is gained through the implementation of key process areas. The maturity levels are five, starting with the "Initial", when environment is unstable. Next, comes the "Explored", focused on project planning and requirements; the third is "Defined", where the team works on customer satisfaction and improvements in communication; then the "Improved" level, implementing risk management; and, last, "Sustained", which focus is on customer and developer satisfaction and collecting metrics.

Beyond these, other purposes are available from industry practice, but not scientifically tested yet ([28]) and the standard for a maturity model in agile software development is still on the way ([7]). What should be realized is that agile community has been trying to build a concept for maturity that leaves aside the increasing process definition and control stated by the traditional CMMI-DEV.

Other approaches to measure agility have also been proposed, not specifically related to maturity gaining. These approaches intent to measure how agile a team is ([19], [35]), to evaluate agility comparatively ([36]), to relate agile practices to project success ([1]), to define practices to assess maturity ([7]), to assess the adequacy of an agile method ([31]), or to identify if agile practices match the organization strategy ([17]).

To build a theoretical basis for this research, we consolidated the practices suggested by these studies using mind mapping and grouped them according to Software Engineering Body of Knowledge (SWEBOK) areas ([2]). This was done using a mind mapping tool: we created a map grouping the practices by nodes that identified their author. Then, with the help of the tool, we iteratively reviewed the practices and dragged them to new nodes that grouped them according to SWEBOK areas. Identifying each author with a particular color, we kept the reference to the source. Some agile practices did not fit any area and were classified as "Customer" and "Environment". Table 2 presents the resulting group of practices for each area.

Table 1. Agile practices related to the items in the survey

Area	Practices	Survey Statement
Software Requirements	Product Backlog, Minimal big requirements and design up front, Evolutionary Requirements, Story formation, Requirements, Technical design, Emergence, Level of detail, Communication focus, Light requirements, Traditional analysis, Metaphor	Focus on agile requirements
Software Design	Simple Design, Architecture and configuration, Architecture modeling	Focus on software architecture
Software Construction	Collective code ownership, Build process, Refactoring, Pair programming, Code standards, Database practice, Continuous Integration	Focus on agile coding
Software Configuration Management	Software Configuration Management, Source code management	
Software Testing	Automated Unit Tests, Customer Acceptance Tests, Test driven development, Test Metrics	Focus on agile testing

Software Engineering Management / Software Project Planning	Planning Game, Planning levels, When do we plan, Timeboxes, Iteration Length, Iterative and incremental development, Short Releases, Continuous Delivery, Agile Project Estimation, Planning for critical variables, Sources of dates and estimates	Focus on agile planning
Software Engineering Management / Review and Evaluation	Sustainable Pace, Daily Progress Tracking meetings, Retrospective meetings, Iteration progress tracking and reporting	Focus on agile project monitoring
Software Engineering Tools and Methods	Response to stress, Focus, Communication, Team learning, Collaboration, Simplicity, Management style, Shared responsibility, Just in Time, Self-Organizing Teams, Continuous Feedback, Agile Documentation, Appropriate distribution of expertise	Focus on agile values on team
Software Quality	Revision and light tests, Traditional quality assurance, Code analysis and inspection, Agile quality assurance, Inspection Frequency	Focus on agile quality assurance
Environment	Infrastructure, People, Geographical distribution, Organization distribution, Organizational complexity, Regulatory compliance, Physical setup reflecting agile philosophy, Team composition, Team member location, Title and salary alignment, Domain complexity, Technical complexity, Enterprise discipline	Focus on defining an agile physical environment
Customer	Communication Customer involvement, Responsiveness to business, Client-driven iterations, Onsite Customer	Focus on involved customer
Software Engineering Process	Process / governance, Assurance / governance	Focus on metrics, Focus on defining processes, Focus on controlling processes

The consolidated list presented in Table 1 reports how agility has been assessed in literature. It allows to securely build a set of activities performed by an agile team and, for that reason, they provided the basis to the questionnaire used in this study to identify a road map to maturity in agile methods. Thus, the third column shows how they were presented to practitioners analysis, as explained in the next section.

3   Research Design

We conducted a survey with Brazilian agile practitioners during the Agile Trends 2013 event in São Paulo, Brazil. The purpose was to quickly inquire event participants about their opinion on how would be a road map for an agile team to get mature. We used a printed questionnaire that occupied half a page for simplicity and agility on answering.

The set of practices used by different authors to assess agility was translated to empirical domain ([15]) and grouped in issues where an agile team could emphasize work to develop maturity. For example, "Software Requirements" has practices for eliciting agile requirements, thus, we called them "Focus on agile requirements". "Software Design" has agile design practices, so we grouped them in "Focus on agile architecture", and the remaining were classified as shown in Table 1. For "Software Engineering Process" area, the focus was divided separately in metrics, defining and controlling processes, to ease respondent evaluation. For now on, we will call each of these "focuses" simply as *practices*.

The resulting group of 13 practices were listed and respondents had to number them, from 1 to 13, thinking about an incremental sequence of implementation of practices to get mature. Respondents were free to leave practices blank (which meant they though it was not relevant), place more than one practice at the same numbering, or include other practices not listed. Respondents were also asked about the usefulness of having a model to assist teams to become mature in agile software development. There was a space to explain their responses.

We got 87 respondents, from 10 different cities in Brazil. The average experience in software development was 10 years and the average experience in agile software development was 3.6 years. 31 respondents declared to have more than 3 years of experience in agile methods and 39 to have up to 3 years. From the total, 70 agreed to number the practices and the other 17 questionnaires were left blank, numbered equally or with other comments.

The first analysis was done on the question about the usefulness of an agile maturity model and on the open space where respondents gave their opinion. Next, for each numbered practice, we conducted three Chi-Square tests *for each practice*. The first verified if the practice was considered relevant in a road map to maturity. The second, if there was a trend for it to be implemented in the beginning, in the middle, or in the end of the road map to maturity. And, the third, verified if experienced (more than 3 years) and non-experienced (up to 3 years) practitioners had the same opinion on practices numbering. These tests are described in the next subsections.

3.1   Relevance Test

For each practice, we verified if practitioners think it is relevant in a path to maturity. For that, the following null hypothesis was defined:

Hypothesis 1. *The probability to consider the practice relevant (to number it) is equals to the probability to consider the practice not relevant (to leave it blank).*

3.2   Implementation Sequence test

To identify if practitioners place practices in some significant sequence, or if this sequence is not relevant, for each practice, the following null hypotheses was tested:

Hypothesis 2. *All numberings (1 to 13) have the same probability to be chosen by respondents (there is no preference for a particular classification).*

Once identified there is a numbering trend, we grouped the numbering gave by respondents to each practice in 3 classifications:

- when numbered as 1, 2 or 3, it was classified to an *essential* level;
- when numbered as 4, 5, 6, 7, 8, or 9, it was classified to an *intermediate* level; and
- when numbered as 10, 11, 12 or 13, it was classified to a *desirable* level.

For each classification (essential, intermediate or desirable), the average percentage of responses given to inner practices was calculated. Thus, for example, when an specific practice was numbered by 5% of respondents as 1, by 7% of respondents as 2 and by 10% of respondents as 3, its average percentage in essential level is 7.30%. Analyzing the average percentage of each classification we were able to realize where most respondents concentrate each practice (in the beginning, in the middle or in the end of maturing process).

3.3   Differences between Experienced and Non-experienced Practitioners

As respondents had different experience levels with agile methods, we tested if non-experienced practitioners had the same opinion on numbering the practices as experienced practitioners. Then, for each practice, the null hypothesis tested was:

Hypothesis 3. *There is the same distribution of numberings for experienced practitioners and for non-experienced practitioners.*

3.4   Threats to Validity

We chose this research approach because participants in a corporate agile event usually have a good practical experience. When argued, they could provide their perception on how they have seen companies improving their work with agile methods. However, it limits our conclusions to the *perceived* road map to maturity in agile software development. In addition to that, although we have included in the survey practitioners from all over the country, the small sample size makes our findings initial and subject to future validation.

Next section presents resulting data for the usefulness of an agile maturity model and the results for the three hypothesis tests.

4   Data Analysis

This section shows the responses analysis in three subsections. The first shows if respondents think an agile maturity model would be useful; the second presents individual practices analysis (results for Hypothesis 1 and 2 tests) and the third identifies the differences between the opinion of experienced and non-experienced practitioners (result for Hypothesis 3 test).

4.1   The Usefulness of an Agile Maturity Model

When argued if a model would be useful to help teams to get mature in agile software development, 60 (69%) respondents answered that yes, it would be useful; and 24 (28%) respondents said it would not be useful. Three left it blank.

From the ones that think that, yes, it would be useful, the main comments on it is that a model would help organizations to recognize the implementation of agile methods, to help as a guide, to define agility, and to help in the beginning of agile adoption. Respondents also pointed out that a model limits the team, but as a guide it would be helpful.

From the respondents that do not think it would be useful, the comments are that maturity is too much dependent on the context, that there is not a model that could fit all organizations. They said that a model would make processes rigid, limiting the application of agile values, of creativity. For them, a model would help only in the beginning of maturing process: to get mature, a team has to experiment and learn.

4.2   The Relevant Practices to Maturity

Table 2 shows the resulting data for Hypothesis 1 and 2 considering all practitioners responses.

For all responses, the test on Hypothesis 1 was refused for all practices. It means that all of them are relevant in the road map to gain maturity. Even though, it is important to notice the percentage of respondents that left the practice blank, as non relevant. In general, the least associated with the essential

Table 2. Relevance and average percentage of responses in each classification level (essential, intermediate or desirable), considering ALL participants. P>0.05 (practices highlighted in gray, for Hypothesis 2 test) mean that the practice was not statistically related to a specific level. **Boldface** emphasizes where highest percentage is for each practice.

Focus on	Perception of irrelevance	Essential	Intermediate	Desirable	p
Agile values in team	4.30%	**28.86%**	1.49%	1.12%	<0.001
Involved customer	8.60%	**18.23%**	5.21%	3.52%	<0.001
Agile planning	8.60%	**15.10%**	8.85%	0.39%	<0.001
Agile requirements	10.00%	**11.64%**	9.79%	1.59%	<0.001
Agile testing	12.90%	**9.84%**	9.56%	3.28%	0.011
Agile coding	15.90%	9.77%	**10.06%**	2.59%	0.003
Defining an agile physical env.	21.40%	9.70%	7.58%	6.36%	0.503
Defining processes	31.40%	7.64%	4.86%	**11.98%**	0.022
Agile quality assurance	17.10%	7.47%	8.33%	6.90%	0.824
Software architecture	20.30%	6.06%	**11.21%**	3.64%	0.005
Agile project monitoring	22.90%	5.56%	8.64%	7.87%	0.509
Metrics	28.60%	3.33%	7.67%	**11.00%**	0.038
Controlling processes	32.90%	2.84%	5.32%	**14.89%**	<0.001

classification, the least relevant, also. There were practices, for example, that around 30% of respondents think they are not relevant to maturity (e. g. defining processes and controlling processes).

On testing Hypothesis 2, the practices highlighted in gray are the ones where p>0.05, meaning that the hypothesis of no preference for a particular classification (essential, intermediate or desirable) is not rejected. Thus, the practices "defining an agile environment", "agile quality assurance" and "agile project monitoring" could be implemented at any time, there is no specific sequence.

The practices where p<0.05 are the ones where it was possible to identify a trend of implementation sequence. The highest percentage number for each practice appears in boldface, placing it in an essential, intermediate or desirable classification. Thus, according to data, in the road map to maturity, a team should focus in (1) Agile values on team; (2) Involved customer; (3) Agile planning; (4) Agile requirements; (5) Agile testing; (6) Agile coding; (7) Software architecture; (8) Metrics; (9) Defining processes and (10) Controlling processes. For agile testing, we understand it is in the frontier from essential to intermediate level as values have a difference of less than 0.5%.

A different scenario is uncovered when testing hypothesis for the experienced practitioners responses. Table 3 shows the data. Here, when testing Hypothesis 1, some practices presented p>0.05, meaning it was not possible to reject it. Thus, these practices may not be relevant in the road map to maturity. They are underlined in Table 3. P values for them were 0.369 to "Defining processes", 0.106 to "Metrics" and 0.590 to "Controlling processes".

When tested for Hypothesis 2, experienced practitioners responses did not reject it for more practices. The lines highlighted in gray in Table 3 are those where it was not possible to identify a trend in numbering meaning, thus, there is no specific sequence for implementation. These are the "Defining an agile environment", "Software architecture", "Agile project monitoring" and "Agile quality assurance".

The other practices had numbering distributions on classification levels that enabled the rejection of Hypothesis 2 ($p<0.05$), which allows the inference of an sequence of implementation. Highest average percentage values appear in bold-face for each practice in Table 3. From the most essential to the least essential, the sequence of practices was (1) Agile values in team, (2) Involved customer, (3) Agile requirements, (4) Agile coding, (5) Agile planning, and (6) Agile testing.

Table 3. Data considering EXPERIENCED participants. Underlined practices mean they are not relevant, when tested for Hypothesis 1. $P>0.05$ (highlighted in gray, for Hypothesis 2 test) mean it is not possible to place the practice in a specific level. **Boldface** emphasizes highest percentage for each practice.

Focus on	Per-ception of irrel-evance	Essen-tial	Interme-diate	Desi-rable	p
Agile values in team	0.00%	**31.18%**	0.54%	0.81%	<0.001
Involved customer	9.70%	**20.24%**	4.76%	2.68%	<0.001
Agile requirements	11.80%	**16.67%**	8.33%	0.00%	<0.001
Agile coding	23.30%	**14.49%**	9.42%	0.00%	0.003
Agile planning	9.70%	**14.29%**	9.52%	0.00%	0.001
Defining an agile physical env.	29.00%	12.12%	7.58%	4.55%	0.244
Agile testing	19.40%	**12.00%**	10.67%	0.00%	0.004
Software architecture	30.00%	11.11%	8.73%	3.57%	0.224
Defining processes	41.90%	9.26%	3.70%	12.50%	0.102
Agile project monitoring	29.00%	9.09%	8.33%	5.68%	0.704
Agile quality assurance	19.40%	6.67%	10.67%	4.00%	0.165
Metrics	35.50%	6.67%	7.50%	8.75%	0.903
Controlling processes	45.20%	5.88%	3.92%	14.71%	0.040

Filtering responses from practitioners with up to 3 years of experience in agile software development, for Hypothesis 1, all practices were rejected, meaning they are all relevant to non-experienced practitioners. For Hypothesis 2, Table 4 shows in gray the practices where $p>0.05$, meaning that, for these, it is not possible to infer a sequence of implementation. They could be implemented at any time. They were "Agile testing", "Defining an agile environment", "Agile quality assurance", "Agile coding", "Defining process" and "Agile project monitoring".

For the practices where Hypothesis 2 test resulted in $p<0.05$, there is a possibility to infer the sequence, from the most essential, to intermediate and, then, desirable practices. The highest average percentages for each practice is highlighted with boldface in Table 4 and indicate when practices should be implemented to

Table 4. Data for NON-EXPERIENCED practitioners. P>0.05 (highlighted in gray, for Hypothesis 2 test) mean the practice cannot be related to a specific level. **Boldface** emphasizes the highest percentage for each practice.

Focus on	Perception of irrelevance	Essential	Intermediate	Desirable	p
Agile values in team	7.70%	**26.85%**	2.31%	1.39%	<0.001
Involved customer	7.70%	**16.67%**	5.56%	4.17%	0.001
Agile planning	7.70%	**15.74%**	8.33%	0.69%	<0.001
Agile testing	7.70%	8.33%	8.80%	5.56%	0.534
Defining an agile physical env.	15.40%	8.08%	7.58%	7.58%	0.987
Agile quality assurance	15.40%	8.08%	6.57%	9.09%	0.711
Agile requirements	8.30%	7.07%	**11.11%**	3.03%	0.034
Agile coding	10.30%	6.67%	10.48%	4.29%	0.112
Defining processes	23.10%	6.67%	5.56%	11.67%	0.161
Agile project monitoring	17.90%	3.13%	8.85%	9.38%	0.182
Software architecture	12.80%	2.94%	**12.75%**	3.68%	0.002
Metrics	23.10%	1.11%	7.78%	**12.50%**	0.013
Controlling processes	23.10%	1.11%	6.11%	**15.00%**	0.001

gain maturity. The implementation sequence, for non-experienced, would be (1) Agile values in team, (2) Involved customer, (3) Agile planning, (4) Agile requirements, (5) Software architecture; (6) Metrics and (7) Controlling processes.

There was an open space on questionnaire for respondents to mention other practices they found relevant for agile maturity. Most practitioners have mentioned specific agile values (as adapting to changes, continuous delivery, focus on people, team work, customer in the team), which were already part of the given 13 practices. But, it is important to mention two other practices that were cited by more than one practitioner: the focus on learning and the focus on delivering value to business.

4.3 The Differences between Practitioners Opinion

There were differences on the responses of experienced and non-experienced practitioners. Table 5 shows these practices where the test to Hypothesis 3 resulted in p<0.05, meaning that practitioners disagreed on the implementation sequence.

The "Agile requirements", for experienced practitioners should be implemented in essential (50%) or intermediate levels (50%). For non-experienced, majority placed it in intermediate level (66.7%), then came essential level (21.2%) and, some considered implementing it at desirable level (12.1%).

For the practice "Software architecture", experienced practitioners placed it among the three levels: essential (33.3%), intermediate (52.4%) and desirable (14.3%). The non-experienced placed it mostly on intermediate level (76.5%), then on desirable (14.7%) and a few on essential (8.8%).

Table 5. Practices where opinion diverged among experienced and non-experienced practitioners (p<0.05)

Focus on	p
Agile requirements	0.017
Software architecture	0.029
Agile coding	0.020
Agile testing	0.025

Practitioners also disagreed on the implementation of agile coding practices. Among experienced, 43.5% placed it as essential, 56.5% as intermediate and non (0%) as desirable. Among non-experienced, a different scenario: 20% on essential, 62.9% on intermediate and 17.1% on desirable.

For the "Agile testing", 36% of experienced practitioners placed it as essential, while 25% of non-experienced did the same. As intermediate, 64% of experienced placed as intermediate, while 52.8% of non-experienced. And no experienced practitioner said it is desirable (0%), while 22.2% of non-experienced said so.

For the other 9 practices, as p>0.05, it is argued that experienced and non-experienced agree on the placement of practices among essential, intermediate and desirable classifications.

5   Discussion

We found that the opinion of practitioners is that maturing in agile is not about following a predefined and detailed path to maturity. Firstly, as a relevant amount of practitioners pointed out that an agile maturity model is not useful because organizations are too different in context, we propose that there is a need for a *guide* to maturity, and not for a model. Second, we still can identify some *essential practices* that may provide the basis to maturity, but space should be left for teams to do the job as they please.

On respect to the usefulness of a model, studies on traditional software process improvement endeavors report that small companies usually do not accomplish the benefits ([34]). Actually, on day-to-day basis, people focus on having the job done ([3]), and codified processes tend to be abandoned to stabilize in a "minimum process" ([12]). Organizational management literature shows that companies that work in high velocity markets and need to be fast – as agile software development teams – cannot work with detailed codified process. Rules have to be simple to enable people to create novelty, to innovate ([14]). When teams are recognized as complex adaptive systems ([33]) it is understood that the behavior is emergent – the self-organization – and trials to command and control overcome its potential ([22]). For agile teams, the trend to tailor methods according to context is already established ([29], [5], [10], [12], [18], [8]) and it suggests that agile practitioners prefer to do the job as their context demands, with no commitment to predefined and detailed processes or rules.

On respect to the road map to maturity, our findings suggest that agile methods cannot focus on traditional CMMI-DEV increasing process control and definition – experienced practitioners do not even think it is important to agile maturity. Based mainly on experienced practitioners opinion, we could identify a group of practices that should be implemented as a basis (e.g. agile values, involved customer, agile planning and agile requirements), others to be implemented as intermediate (e.g. agile testing and agile coding) and some that could be implemented at any time (e. g. software architecture, agile physical environment, agile quality assurance and agile project monitoring).

These results corroborate with findings from the extensive Brazilian study from Melo and colleagues ([37]), which have realized that agile teams with 3 to 5 years of experience focus on planning practices and more experienced teams (more than 5 years) focus on practices related to coding and testing. According to their study, as experience grows, more agile practices are adopted. And, interestingly, they have reported that experienced companies sometimes abandon some planning practices, like estimation techniques, which is another evidence of tailoring in agile methods.

We found evidence that there is a group of essential practices and it is important to implement them before the remaining to create an essential foundation to agile maturity. Although organizations have their particular way to improve, there are a group of practices, the so-called, "best practices" that need to be implemented ([14]) to provide the basis to the emergence of the context-specific maturity. Experienced practitioners actually agree on these essential best practices and non-experienced practitioners still do not realize them exactly the same way.

The process-related practices – metrics, defining processes and controlling processes – were mainly classified as desirable on our survey. For experienced practitioners, they were not directly related to agile maturity. As we recognize the importance of having a software process, even not being the main focus, we believe they are optional to gain maturity in agile software development. After all essential and intermediate practices are established, metrics, process definition and control could be placed to improve this agile basis, and not to overcome it. Based on these outcomes, Fig. 1 proposes an initial guide to agile software development maturity.

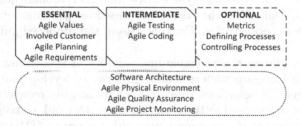

Fig. 1. An initial guide to agile software development maturity

The main contribution of this study is that experienced practitioners find that maturity in agile software development should be built over agile values, and, for that, exact codification of the road map is probably not possible. It raises the important issue on how assessments could be performed without this codification.

Organizational maturity has been mainly expressed as the adherence to a structured process, but other perspectives have also been purposed, as the emphasis on people and the emphasis on learning ([21]). The different perspectives for assessing maturity point out that this assessment may be more subjective than we are used to ([21]).

Our purpose to address this issue is following the clues of some studies that have already been proposing the evaluation or description of software processes based on how efficient it is to reach objectives ([24], [18],[17]). This goals-based approach would leave space for teams to do the job as they please. Recent studies from Sidky and colleagues ([30]) and Kettunen ([17]) support this approach reporting exactly this need to describe – and not prescribe – the road map to maturity.

The findings of this study go beyond current studies that have been implementing agile and CMMI-DEV simultaneously. These initiatives build maturity over traditional processes definition and control. We are consonant to some current agile maturity models, in the sense that maturity has to be built over agile values, but we complement them in the sense that there is evidence that agile practitioners do not believe in a prescriptive road map to get mature.

6   Conclusions

We conducted a survey with agile practitioners to find out how would be a road map to mature in agile software development. Our findings show that agile practitioners disagree with the need for a maturity model because the way teams implement agility is too context-dependent. The purpose, then, is to have a guide to maturity. This guide points somewhat predefined sequence of practices, but there are also practices that could be implemented at any time and some that are recognized as optional.

This study was made exclusively with Brazilian practitioners quickly inquired during an event, and, thus, the results are based on practitioners report, and not on real projects observation. For this reason, the proposed guide intends to be initial.

We want to argue on the probable impossibility of predefining this path to maturity and to instigate some research on how to develop maturity leaving space to emergency of behaviors. Researchers have already recognized that agile methods have revolutionized software engineering ([13]) and, to keep it, maturity needs also to be rethought in some more subjective ways ([21]) to allow agile teams to get mature without leaving its values aside.

This work was part of an exploratory stage of a PhD thesis that now intends to deepen this guide definition and to find out the mechanisms teams apply to gain this context-specific agile maturity.

Acknowledgments. We are thankful to Agile Trends 2013 organization committee, in special to Dairton Bassi and Prof. Dr. Tiago Silva da Silva, who supported the application of the survey during the event.

References

1. Abbas, N., Gravell, A.M., Wills, G.B.: Using Factor Analysis to Generate Clusters of Agile Practices – A guide for agile process improvement. In: Agile Conference (2010)
2. Abran, A., Moore, J.W.: SWEBOK - guide to the software engineering body of knowledge. IEEE CS Professional Practices Committee (2004)
3. Adolph, S., Krutchen, P., Hall, W.: Reconciling perspectives: A grounded theory of how people manage the process of software development. J. Syst. Softw. 85, 1269–1286 (2012)
4. Anderson, D.J.: Stretching Agile to fit CMMI Level 3 the story of creating MSF for CMMI Process Improvement at Microsoft Corporation. In: Proceedings of the Agile Conference, ADC 2005 (2005)
5. Armbrust, O., Rombach, D.: The right process for each context: objective evidence needed. In: ICSSP 2011: Proceedings of the 2011 International Conference on Software and Systems Process, pp. 237–241 (2011)
6. Baker, S.W.: Formalizing Agility, Part 2: How an Agile Organization Embraced the CMMI. In: Proceedings of the AGILE 2006 Conference (2006)
7. Buglione, L.: Light Maturity Models (LMM): an Agile application. In: Profes 2011: Proceedings of the 12th International Conference on Product Focused Software Development and Process Improvement (2011)
8. Bustard, D., Wilkie, G., Greer, D.: The Maturation of Agile Software Development Principles and Practice: Observations on Successive Industrial Studies in 2010 and 2012. In: 20th Annual IEEE International Conference and Workshops on the Engineering of Computer Based Systems, ECBS (2013), doi:10.1109/ECBS.2013.11
9. Caffery, F.M., Pikkarainen, M., Richardson, I.: AHAA Agile, Hybrid Assessment Method for Automotive, Safety Critical SMEs. In: ICSE 2008: Proceedings of the 30th International Conference on Software Engineering (2008)
10. de Cesare, S., Lycett, M., Macredie, R.D., Patel, C., Paul, R.: Examining Perceptions of Agility in Software Development Practice. Commun. ACM 53 (2010)
11. Cohan, S., Glazer, H.: An Agile Development Teams Quest for CMMI Maturity Level 5. In: Agile Conference (2009)
12. Coleman, G., O'Connor, R.: Investigating software process in practice: A grounded theory perspective. J. Syst. Softw. 81, 772–784 (2008)
13. Dingsöyr, T., Nerur, S., Balijepally, V., Moe, N.B.: A decade of agile methodologies: Towards explaining agile software development. J. Syst. Softw. 85, 1213–1221 (2012)

14. Eisenhardt, K.M., Martin, J.A.: Dynamic Capabilities: What are they? Strat. Mgmt. J. 21, 1105–1121 (2000)
15. Forza, C.: Survey research in operations management: a process-based perspective. Int. J. Oper. Prod. Manag. 22(2), 152–194 (2002)
16. Jakobsen, C.R., Johnson, K.A.: Mature Agile with a Twist of CMMI. In: Agile Conference (2008), doi:10.1109/Agile.2008.10
17. Kettunen, P.: Systematizing Software Development Agility: Towards an Enterprise Capability Improvement Framework. Journal of Enterprise Transformation 2(2), 81–104 (2012)
18. Kirk, D., Tempero, E.: A lightweight framework for describing software practices. J. Syst. Softw. 85, 582–595 (2012)
19. Layman, L., Williams, L., Cunningham, L.: Motivations and Measurements in an Agile Case Study. In: Proceedings of the 2004 Workshop on Quantitative Techniques for Software Agile Process, pp. 14–24 (2004)
20. Lukasiewicz, K., Miler, J.: Improving agility and discipline of software development with the Scrum and CMMI. IET Software 6, 416–422 (2012), doi:10.1049/iet-sen.2011.0193
21. Maier, A.M., Moutrie, J., Clarkson, J.: Assessing Organizational Capabilities: Reviewing and Guiding the Development of Maturity Grids. IEEE Transactions on Engineering Management 59 (2012)
22. McDaniel Jr., R.R.: Management Strategies for Complex Adaptive Systems. Performance Improvement Quarterly 20(2), 21–42 (2007)
23. Nottonson, K., DeLong, K.: Crawl, Walk, Run: 4 Years of Agile Adoption at Baby-Center.com. In: Agile 2008 Conference (2008)
24. Packlick, J.: The Agility Maturity Map a Goal Oriented Approach to Agile Improvement. In: Agile 2007 (2007)
25. Patel, C., Ramachandran, M.: Agile Maturity Model (AMM): A Software Process Improvement framework for Agile Software Development Practices. Int. J. Softw. Eng. 2 (2009)
26. Paulk, M.: Extreme Programming from a CMM Perspective. IEEE Software (2001)
27. Qumer, A., Henderson-Sellers, B.: A framework to support the evaluation, adoption and improvement of agile methods in practice. J. Syst. Softw. 81, 1899–1919 (2008)
28. Schweigert, T., Nevalainen, R., Vohwinkel, D., Korsaa, M., Biro, M.: Agile Maturity Model: Oxymoron or the Next Level of Understanding. In: Mas, A., Mesquida, A., Rout, T., O'Connor, R.V., Dorling, A. (eds.) SPICE 2012. CCIS, vol. 290, pp. 289–294. Springer, Heidelberg (2012)
29. Sheffield, J., Lemétayer, J.: Factor associated with the software development agility of successful projects. Int. J. Proj. Manag. (2012), doi: 10.1016/j.ijproman.2012.09.011
30. Sidky, A., Arthur, J., Bohner, S.: A disciplined approach to adopting agile practices: the agile adoption framework. Innovations Syst. Softw. Eng. 3, 203–216 (2007), doi:10.1007/s11334-007-0026-z
31. Soundararajan, S., Arthur, J.D., Balci, O.: A Methodology for Assessing Agile Software Development Methods. In: Agile Conference (2012)
32. Spoelstra, W., Iacob, M., Van Sinderen, M.: Software Reuse in Agile Development Organizations A Conceptual Management Tool. In: SAC 2011: Proceedings of the 2011 ACM Symposium on Applied Computing (2011)
33. Stacey, R.: Complexity and Creativity in Organizations. Berret-Koehler Publishers, San Francisco (1996)

34. Staples, M., Niazi, M., Jeffery, R., Abrahams, A., Byatt, P., Murphy, R.: An exploratory study of why organizations do not adopt CMMI. J. Syst. Softw. 80, 883–895 (2007)
35. Williams, L., Krebs, W., Layman, L., Antón, A.: Toward a Framework for Evaluating Extreme Programming. In: 8th International Conference on Empirical Assessment in Software Engineering (EASE 2004), pp. 11–20 (2004)
36. Williams, L., Rubin, K., Cohn, M.: Driving Process Improvement Via Comparative Agility Assessment. In: Agile Conference (2010)
37. Melo, C.O., Santos, V., Katayama, E., Corbucci, H., Prikladnicki, R., Goldman, A., Kon, F.: The evolution of agile software development in Brazil. J. Braz. Comput. Soc. 19, 523–552 (2013), doi:10.1007/s13173-013-0114-x
38. Lami, G., Falcini, F.: Is ISO/IEC 15504 Applicable to Agile Methods? In: Abrahamsson, P., Marchesi, M., Maurer, F. (eds.) XP 2009. LNBIP, vol. 31, pp. 130–135. Springer, Heidelberg (2009)

Why We Need a Granularity Concept for User Stories

Olga Liskin, Raphael Pham, Stephan Kiesling, and Kurt Schneider

Software Engineering Group, Leibniz Universität Hannover, Germany
{olga.liskin,raphael.pham,stephan.kiesling,
kurt.schneider}@inf.uni-hannover.de

Abstract. User stories are a widespread instrument for representing requirements. They describe small user-oriented parts of the system and guide the daily work of developers. Often however, user stories are too coarse, so that misunderstandings or dependencies remain unforeseeable. Granularity of user stories needs to be investigated more, but at the same time is a hard-to-grasp concept.

This paper investigates *Expected Implementation Duration (EID)* of a user story as a characteristic of granularity. We want to find out, whether it is suitable as a quality aspect and can help software teams improve their user stories.

We have conducted a study with software engineering practitioners. There, many user stories had a relatively high EID of four or more days. Many developers state to have experienced certain problems to occur more often with such coarse user stories. Our findings emphasize the importance to reflect on granularity when working with user stories.

Keywords: user stories, user requirements, requirements quality.

1 Introduction

Communication plays a crucial role in software development [3]. Collaboration of a group of developers demands for an effective way of exchanging information and coordination. Communication is especially important with regard to software requirements. Inadequate communication between team members can lead to team members misunderstanding core requirements [6] and subsequently to the development of undesired software - thus jeopardizing the project's success.

User stories, as one form of requirements, have the potential to divide a complex system into small user oriented pieces, which can be implemented independently. At the same time, such user stories have a great influence on the daily work of all involved team members. The quality of user stories impacts communication and coordination in a project and therefore plays an important role. When trying to understand, how user stories impact the daily work of a software team, their granularity is an interesting aspect.

The granularity of a user story can heavily impact its quality: A user story with otherwise good quality features (such as a clear priority and attached acceptance tests)

G. Cantone and M. Marchesi (Eds.): XP 2014, LNBIP 179, pp. 110–125, 2014.
© Springer International Publishing Switzerland 2014

could still be disastrously underestimated by developers, if it is too coarsely grained. The reason behind this is that a flawed granularity indicates a number of problems with a user story. A coarsely grained user story could be formulated unclearly and pose difficulties for estimating the associated effort. This can also point to inter-team and customer-related communication gaps.

Granularity of a user story has many facets. It can be understood in terms of:

- *Clarity/vagueness.* If a user story leaves out a lot of information, it is written vaguely.
- *Concreteness/abstraction.* A user story can describe the desired functionality as an abstract concept or already sketch a concrete manifestation of this concept.
- *Scope.* This represents the scope of the system functionality that is described *or meant* by the information given in a user story. A user story that implies a lot of system functionality (and according implementation work) would have a large scope.

While all three aspects are important for the quality of a user story, we focus on granularity in the sense of scope size. In order to change the scope of a user story, the desired functionality must be changed. For example, in order to reduce implementation work, some of the desired functionality must be removed or the story must be split into smaller ones. In contrast, the clarity or abstractness of a user story is varied by providing different information about the desired functionality that the customer has in mind, while the functionality remains the same.

The three aspects are orthogonal. For example, a user story can be clear and have a high scope size (imply a lot of implementation work), while another story can have the same scope size, but be vague. However, there is a chance that reducing the scope of a user story by splitting it into multiple smaller stories can improve its clarity and help make it more concrete. This aspect needs further research though.

In practice, some scope-related aspects like effort or complexity of user stories are estimated in order to characterize user stories [5]. For this, abstract scales, like t-shirt sizes or Fibonacci numbers are used, so that, again, individual values mean different things to different teams.

Therefore, we see the need for a more tangible and comparable concept in order to be able to investigate granularity of user stories. We define the *Expected Implementation Duration (EID)* of a user story as a viable concept for quantifying the scope of a user story. Then, we demonstrate why it is a good quality aspect for user stories and why it should be taken into account when working with user stories.

We picked user stories for our study because we think that differences in the understandings of what a user story is are smaller for user stories than for other requirements concepts. Further, user stories are known to take a relatively small amount of time to be implemented [4]. However, we think that our findings are applicable to other requirements concepts as well.

The paper is structured as follows: In the next section, we present related literature. Section 3 shows the research questions we have based our study upon. In Section 4 the study design is sketched, followed by the study results in Section 5. Section 6 discusses Threats to Validity. We conclude with a discussion and outlook.

2   Related Work

In agile software development, user stories and story cards are a widely practiced form of documenting requirements. The activity of estimating user stories has been in the focus of recent literature [5]. Miranda et al. [10] focus on improving these estimation strategies as well as improving the estimations. Haugen, Mahnič et al. and Tamrakar et al. [7][9][13] examine whether introduction of planning poker improves the team's ability to estimate user stories. Furthermore, Imaz and Benyon [8] describe a way to enhance traceability between user stories as pre-requirements and semi-formal requirements such as use cases. Cohn [5] specifies how to split up user stories. However, Patel and Ramachandran [11] describe the lack of clear guidelines or rules for aspects of a *good* user story and motivate research in this area.

According to Cohn [5], the *ideal* days measurement is as good as *story points* – as long as the organizational overhead is ignored. He proposes to estimate user stories in *ideal* days and emphasizes to not rely on *elapsed* days as a measurement. EID is related to Cohn's notion of ideal days. This study is a first step to understand how this measure is perceived and handled by practitioners.

Wake [14] suggests with INVEST[1] six quality criteria for a good user story. One of these says that a user story should be *small*. With our work, we try to further concretize this criterion. First, EID is a possible means to determine whether a user story is *small*. Further, it is not known yet, whether it is easy to measure and act on story size in practice. Second, so far publications only explain theoretically why a small story is good. We want to substantiate this with real data and experiences from practice.

Many studies have been conducted in the field of agile requirements engineering in order to understand the practitioners' perspectives. Cao and Ramesh [2] revealed agile RE practices in an empirical study. Bjarnason et al. [1] examine overscoping and therewith bring up a topic that is also related to planning with requirements. With a user study on user story implementation duration we try to complement these works to help understand how agile requirements are handled in industry.

3   Expected Implementation Duration as a Quality Aspect for User Stories

In our context, the term granularity represents the scope of the system functionality that is described or meant by the information given in a user story. Expected implementation duration is a way of quantifying the scope size of a user story.

---

[1] Independent, Negotiable, Valuable, Estimable, Small, Testable.

By *Expected Implementation Duration* we mean the estimated time (in days) that a developer or pair will need to implement a user story. Implementation of a user story includes coding as well as all other tasks that the developer performs to deliver a user story, such as designing or testing. Like Cohn's concept of ideal days [5], EID ignores tasks that are not related to a user story but are done in-between its implementation.

Expected implementation duration has the potential to add new value to the characterization of user stories. This can generally improve the development timetable. If the estimation of implementation time for a user story exceeds a certain threshold (for example, one week or more), chances are high that it becomes more inaccurate. Humans are better at grasping events when they are in the near future. When thinking about events that cover a long period of time, it is easy to forget an event or to misestimate one of these events. If implementation time takes a week or more, a seemingly simple user story with low complexity can still be underestimated in terms of when it will actually be finished. Likewise, a user story that is described in much detail, might still be missing information if its expected implementation duration is too long.

However, the expected implementation duration is still an estimation. And, as with other metrics, estimated values can be wrong. In this context, we are not aiming at hourly precision. Literature suggests that a user story should not take more than one or two days to be implemented [12]. The reality of implementation durations of user stories often looks different. In the study presented by this paper, 50% of the participants have stated that 30% or more of their user stories require more than four days to be implemented. We want to raise awareness to this quality aspect, so that in the future, user stories are shrunk to an implementation time of no more than one day.

In order to show that Expected Implementation Duration is a valid aspect, we propose the following **research questions**:

RQ1: Is Expected Implementation Duration easy to measure?
A quality aspect is only applicable, if the user is able to measure it and is able to obtain meaningful values. We investigate if practitioners are able to express the EID of a user story. Furthermore, we inquired how practitioners measure other aspects of a user story, such as its complexity.

RQ2: Which actual Expected Implementation Duration values do user stories in current software projects have?
In order to understand how teams handle their user stories with respect to Expected Implementation Duration, it is also meaningful to get a picture of current EID values in real projects. It is especially interesting to see, how big differences are among projects as well as among user stories within the same project.

RQ3: Is it possible to control Expected Implementation Duration for user stories by splitting them?
Obtaining the current EID characteristics for a user story is beneficial. However, users should also be able to influence it. We investigate what opinion practitioners have of splitting user stories and at what size user stories should be split. We are interested in

experiences they have made when splitting user stories and which problems arise when doing so.

RQ4: Is Expected Implementation Duration a relevant factor for user stories?
We want to clarify whether the EID is worth investigating by investigating its relevance. If other quality aspects, such as a clear priority, are more important for a workable user story than its EID, developers will not need to focus on it.

We found that EID or related aspects are perceived as easy to assess. The participants used different strategies for this, but had problems with under-/overestimation (RQ1, Section 5.1). The actual EID values stated in the study vary among most projects. User stories that take four days or longer have a relatively high portion of 32% (RQ2, Section 5.2). The participants believed that it is possible to split user stories in many cases, especially when they take longer than four days. However, we found various challenges with splitting user stories (RQ3, Section 5.3). Further, we found that the scope size of a user story controls many relevant aspects such as communication, planning, and detection of dependencies (RQ4, Section 5.4).

4   Survey

To gain a first understanding of how practitioners handle user requirements with regard to its "size", we conducted a two-staged study using two separate online questionnaires. Our target population were practitioners with experience in industrial software projects. The GitHub Archive[2] records any user activity (forking, pull requesting, commenting) on the social coding site GitHub[3]. We queried the GitHub Archive for users who had specified a company name (non-empty string) in their GitHub profile and had been active on GitHub at the beginning of September 2013.

In a preliminary study, we invited 400 GitHub users to participate in a questionnaire and received 68 answers (response rate 17%). We encouraged the user to share experiences from an industrial project, but let her answer for a private project if needed. This first questionnaire covered three topics: Which form did the participant's requirements take (user stories, use cases, UML models, plain text), what factors made a good requirement and what challenges did the participant have when handling these requirements. This first round of broad questions and answers enabled us to focus our efforts on more specific challenges: Challenges regarding inter-team communication seemed to be less prominent than others and were subsequently not investigated further. Furthermore, the number of different forms of requirements documentation (user stories, use cases, UML models, etc.) left us with only a vague understanding of how the practitioners handled their requirements in particular.

Hence, for the main questionnaire in mid-September 2013, we concretely focused on user stories. We invited 600 GitHub users to partake in this second questionnaire and received 72 answers (12% answer rate). This questionnaire enquired more deeply

---

[2] http://www.githubarchive.org/
[3] http://github.com

how the questionees judged the implementation time of a user story and whether this estimation would work as a well-defined concept (see Section Results).

5   Results

Of the 72 answers from the main questionnaire, 27 (38%) participants stated to have no experience with user stories. The answers of these participants were removed from the final set of answers since the invitation directly addressed users with experience in using user stories. Of the remaining 45, 33 (73%) participants enlisted to report on experiences with user stories in industrial software projects. However, 4 of those were not able to estimate the expected implementation time of a user story. As this is an important foundation of our questions, we removed these participants' answers from the final set of answers as well. 11 participants reported on private projects. One participant did not state her project's origin – we counted her answers towards private projects. Eventually, we counted 41 participants from industrial projects and 12 participants from private projects, resulting in a total of 53 usable answers. The project sizes for this population are shown in Fig.1. We asked the participants, in how many projects they have worked with user stories. This gave us a better understanding of the participants' general experience with user stories.

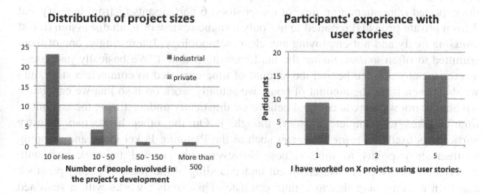

Fig. 1. Population characterization

5.1   Measurability of Expected Implementation Duration (RQ 1)

Can developers estimate the expected time for implementation?
We asked the participants, whether or not they take the estimated time to implement a user story into consideration when rating the effort of a user story. 49% (26 participants) stated that time estimation was a factor for rating a user story (see Fig. 2), while 9% (5) saw no connection. Seven participants generally did not rate their story cards, but did not comment further on the matter. We also asked the questionees whether or not they were able to estimate a story card's expected time to implement. 15% (8) of the participants reported to be able do so and that they always work with

user stories that were estimated according to the expected implementation time. Additionally, 55% (29) of participants claimed to be able to do so, if necessary, but did not do this on a daily basis. 3 participants did not answer this question.

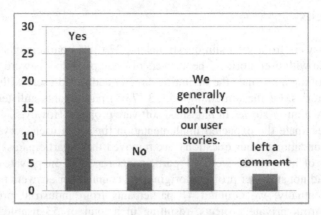

Fig. 2. Consideration of time to implement when rating a user story

Methods for estimating the expected implementation time of a user story
We inquired further and asked the developers to specify their strategy for estimating the expected implementation time of a user story. 6 participants (3 from industry and 3 from private projects) reported to use only a vague review or team discussion or just *guessing* freely and not employing any clear methodology. Interestingly, one of them admitted to often *underestimate* the implementation time ("We basically just guess. There isn't any science behind the amount of time expected to complete a story, and we don't even track the amount of hours we actually work on it so that we can gauge whether or not we were accurate. I believe we drastically underestimate the amount of time it takes to complete a story, though."). On the other hand, two industry participants used *elaborate strategies* such as the Planning Poker game and mapping abstract story points to time values. However, this seemed to work best with experienced developers ("Based on our understanding of the value of a story point we can then directly map this to a time estimate. This *only* works with a seasoned team."). Participants reported more generally on estimation strategies for user stories, which involved time estimation. These started by a *clarification phase* in which the developers tried to gain a thorough understanding of the given user story. When estimating the implementation time, developers often relied on their *general experience* and based their estimates on *similar, existing systems*. Often, user stories would be *compared to another*, using the simplest user story as a *well-known baseline*. Participants tried to *eliminate unknown technologies* and unknown risks and would *refuse* user stories that did not comply their requirements ("... I refuse to estimate implementation time if they involve technologies that are foreign to me. Foreign technologies have no place in implementation user stories as they introduce numerous unknowns. Such issues have to be figured out before the implementation phase."). User story estimation sometimes involved *skill assessment* of the current

team. Developers would also try to *analyze* the user story's *impact* on existing components of the *system, its test suite* or *legacy systems* ("Breakdown of tasks, evaluation of the code quality of the legacy (any existing code is legacy in this sense) code that the new functionality needs to integrate with"). Eventually, most developers tried to *split user stories up*. Some participants used abstract *measures* ("as-simple-as-possible"), others had found hard time values to work best ("16 hours", "around a day", "Make sure the story is a good size (a week of work max IMO)").

Problems when estimating the expected implementation time

We enquired what kind of problems were experienced, when estimating the time of implementation for a user story. Firstly, we wanted to know, whether over- or underestimation was a problem and proposed each an over- and underestimation option. Secondly, we intended to gain further insights into other problems and added a third, user-editable option. All three choices could apply in any combination [checkboxes]. Of the final data set of 53 usable participants, none had left the answer to this question blank. Seven participants added their own answer, which we will explain further below, and we counted these seven answers against over- or underestimation. Table 1 shows the distribution of answers in detail. 12 participants found over- and underestimation to be problematic and we counted these answers both towards over- and underestimation. In Table 1, we see that underestimation of implementation time seems to be more problematic for developers than constant overestimation. One could argue that overestimation does not seem as problematic to a developer – she has finished her work before deadline after all – and, thus, overestimation is underrepresented here. However, no such comment or indication was given by our questionees.

Two participants deemed the expected implementation time to be unreliable, especially when handling unknown technologies ("When utilizing unfamiliar technologies I've noticed that story estimates are mostly inaccurate."). Two other participants found user stories to inaccurately state user intentions and thus being hard to estimate time wise ("The user stories in general rarely reflect what the actual user will use the software for causing unforeseen changes during the scrumlike iterative feedback process"). Another two participants seemed to have no problems with a little over- or underestimation and also linked this to the complexity or novelty of the user story ("Sometimes over, sometimes under, but for simplest or repetitive stories the estimates are quite precise.").

Table 1. Number of participants who have experienced over- and underestimation. 'Com.' stands for 'Comments'.

		underestimation		
		yes	no	
over-estimation	yes	12	5	**17**
	no	17	Com.: 7	
		29		

5.2 Characterization of Expected Implementation Duration of User Stories (RQ2)

We asked the participants which expected implementation durations user stories they work with typically have. We presented 5 options – a few hours, one day, 1-3 days, 4-5 days, and more than one week - and asked the participants to distribute 100 percent points to reflect the distribution of the different durations for their user stories.

34 participants have answered this question. In total, they have distributed 3400 points. Figure 3 depicts how the 3400 points were distributed to the different EID options in total. 43% of the total quantity of points was assigned to user stories that last only one day or less (answers for option "one day" and "a few hours" aggregated). Thus, 57% of all rated user stories in this study take longer than one day. More specifically, 13% even take longer than one week.

Fig. 3 also distinguishes the distribution of points for industrial (2500 points assigned) and private projects (900 points assigned). Here, some peculiarities can be seen. In both groups, short under-one-day user stories make up for about half of the user stories. However, in private projects, a greater part (30%) of that amount falls into the "a few hours"-category. In industry, these hours-long user stories only add up to 16%. On the other hand, one-day user stories are more present in industrial projects (26%) than in private projects (18%). Then again, user stories that take more than one week are more prominent in private projects (21% vs. 11%).

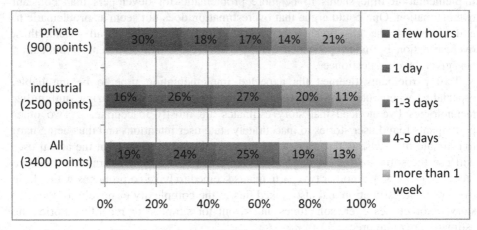

Fig. 3. Distribution of different user story durations

In Table 2, we aggregated the distributed points. First, we aggregated the different possible durations. For example, the column "more than 4 days" contains information about user stories with an EID of 4-5 days and user stories with an EID of more than 1 week. Further, we differentiated, how many users have allocated a number of percent points that is higher than a certain threshold (left column) to each of the aggregated groups. From this table, we can see that more than half of the respondents (53%) have assigned 30 or more of 100 points to user stories that take more than 4 days to complete. This means, for more than half of the respondents about one third of their user stories take more than 4 days. Furthermore, 58% of the respondents have stated that about two thirds (60%) of their user stories last more than one day.

Table 2. Percent of the questionees who have allocated x or more points to user stories of the according sizes

Allocated Points	One day or more	more than 1 day	more than 4 days	more than 1 week
>=0	100	100	100	100
>=10	97,06	97,06	88,24	58,82
>=20	97,06	94,12	70,59	29,41
>=30	97,06	85,29	52,94	11,76
>=40	97,06	73,53	38,24	11,76
>=50	97,06	67,65	29,41	5,88
>=60	88,24	58,82	17,65	2,94
>=70	85,29	35,29	8,82	2,94
>=80	67,65	26,47	2,94	2,94
>=90	50	11,76	0	0

5.3   Controlling Expected Implementation Duration (RQ3)

Experience in splitting user stories
Of the 39 people who answered this part of the questionnaire, 90% stated to have split up a user story before while 10% had no experience with splitting a user story.

Possibility to split user stories
We proposed different durations for expected implementation time (1 day, 1 to 3 days, 4 to 5 days) for one user story and asked the participants whether they thought that they could split such a user story. The results are depicted in Fig. 4. For 1-day-long user stories most participants stated that such a story can be split sometimes. Four participants even said that such a user story always should be split into smaller parts. For a user story which is expected to take 4-5 days, most participants thought that it should always be split into smaller user stories. Only three participants stated that a user story of 4-5 days could only sometimes be split into smaller pieces.

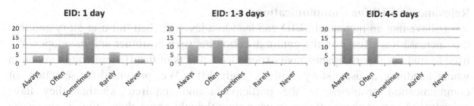

Fig. 4. Could a user story with the given expected implementation duration (EID) be split into smaller stories? (n= 39)

Challenges with splitting user stories
We asked the participants to describe problems they have encountered, when trying to split a user story. In total, 14 participants have mentioned problems. The most prominent problem was regarding *dependencies*. Six of the participants mentioned dependencies in their replies. Four respondents noted that user stories were sometimes *lacking in clarity* and therefore *additional communication with the customer* was required for splitting these user stories. This is an interesting aspect: The process of splitting a user story might reveal a user story that needs clarification. Further, one participant mentioned that a user story which gets too small, is *not very valuable* without other user stories.

5.4   Relevance of Expected Implementation Duration (RQ4)

Problems occurring when granularity is wrong
We wanted to know whether a long or a short EID caused specific problems. In total, 24 users commented to having experienced problems with stories that had a long EID, while seven users declined. Four participants found *hidden additional effort needs* problematic: This was the case, when requirements were unclear and additional effort was needed for clarification. Also, longer user stories were associated with a higher probability of encountering problems. Four participants mentioned *problems brought by change*, both for customer-initiated change or inter-team driven change.

Three users suggested different strategies to avoid these problems a priori. For example, the user story with the longest EID would be given the lowest priority by the customer or removed altogether.

When asked whether they have encountered problems with user stories with a short EID, 13 participants affirmed while 20 participants stated to not have had any problems. The 13 comments about problems with short user stories all came from industrial projects. Again, one person stated *hidden additional effort* as a problem, referring to a case when important functionality had simply been forgotten to specify. The most dominant problem, brought up by five participants, was the *difficulty to stick to the estimation*. In their experience, small user stories had been under- as well as overestimated. This was caused, for example, by wrong expectations of third party libraries.

While changes were stated as a problem with long user stories, nobody had brought up this problem for short user stories.

Relevance of EID for Communication
We believe that an increase in EID can lead to a less sketched-out user story and that this increase has effects on the communication between customer and developer. We tried to find out if participants have experienced effects of insufficient communication when handling a user story with a high EID. We presented a selection of communication problems to the participants and inquired whether they have experienced any of these effects or what they thought about them. Fig. 5 shows the suggested problems and the respective distributions among the participants.

Noticeably, most participants have experienced clarification problems when handling big user stories: either the number of post-development changes increased ("one has to change more details afterwards") or details were not clearly sketched out, causing unnecessary development ("more probable that one develops more than what was expected"). Also, bigger user stories influence the customer-developer feedback cycle. A significant number of users reported to have to wait longer for gathering feedback for a user story ("it takes longer until one can gather feedback about this story").

This finding is very important and underlines the important role of a valid concept for EID when handling user stories: short and effective feedback cycles with the customer are the basis of any serious agile software development. Without a useful guideline for estimating the implementation duration correctly, the developer is at risk of misjudging the EID considerably. In this situation, the developer will ultimately have to deal with user stories that take longer than expected – and the aforementioned effects follow: the crucial customer feedback cycle is disturbed and the number of change requests rises.

Additionally, some practitioners have experienced that it is harder to deliver exactly what the customer wanted when a user story is large ("it is harder to meet the customer's requirements"). This statement, however, had the least affirmation. Many participants also disagreed or had experienced the contrary.

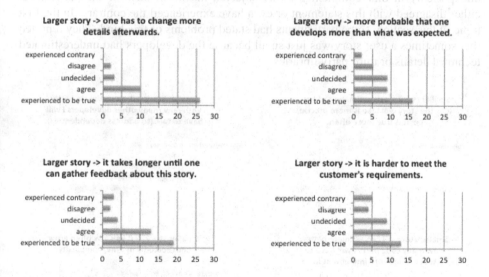

Fig. 5. Degrees of agreement on suggested communication problems (n=41)

Relevance of EID for Tangibility for Implementation

The other aspect we wanted to investigate with respect to EID relevance is the tangibility of a user story. The better a developer can picture all necessary actions for implementing a user story, the more likely it is that she will notice dependencies and risks. User stories that are too coarse can carry the risk to grow unexpectedly, for example due to underestimated dependencies. In this part, we describe whether our participants have experienced a better tangibility with smaller user stories. Again, we presented a selection of ideas - benefits that smaller user stories can have - and inquired about the participants' experiences. Fig. 6 shows the suggested benefits and the respective experiences of the participants.

The two most prominent statements are that smaller user stories allow more precise duration estimations and estimations about which actions within the code will be necessary ("our estimation of how long a user story will take is more precise i.e. it is true more often" and "I can estimate better how many code parts I will have to touch in order to implement it"). Here, more than 65% of the participants were able to confirm the statements from their own experience. This indicates that smaller user stories are indeed perceived to be more tangible. Further, the participants confirmed that they could better estimate which dependencies a user story has when it is smaller ("I can estimate better with how many other

Again, these findings underline the importance of a useful concept for EID: When practitioners assessed an EID for a user story to be small, this estimation turned out to be precise more often and thus enabling the developer to correctly judge this user story's implementation duration. This way, the developer can try to avoid user stories that will take longer and create risks of communication (see previous paragraph).

The claim that a smaller user story will less often grow ("it will less often grow unexpectedly in time/complexity") was objected the most. 30% of the participants either disagreed with this statement or even have experienced the contrary. In the first topic of this section, some participants had stated problems of this kind. They reported that sometimes a user story was just small because the developers had underestimated technical details or third party libraries.

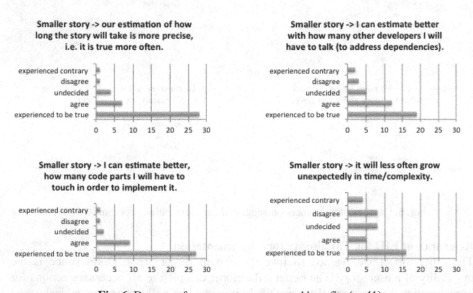

Fig. 6. Degrees of agreement on suggested benefits (n=41)

6   Threats to Validity

This study is a first step into recognizing the granularity of user stories. Our study resulted in 41 usable practitioner answers and 12 answers from private developers (results of the second, more focused questionnaire). Although we presented a fair amount of data points, we refrained from a more sophisticated statistical analysis. However, our study focuses on practitioner's opinions and real experiences and mostly deals with qualitative data. In this sense our study presents a trend analysis.

We are aware that the voluntary nature of our study is a threat to *internal validity*. Our population sample is self-chosen: we did not offer any kind of compensation and practitioners and private users participated voluntarily. This leaves the questionees' motivation to participate undefined.

This study introduces a new aspect of requirements quality, the expected implementation duration. Questioning the practitioner online and not in a personal interview could potentially lead to a different understanding of concepts like user story and user requirements. We tried to mitigate this threat to *construct validity* by explaining our understanding of such concepts in the questionnaire where necessary. Furthermore, our dataset and questionees' comments do not indicate an underlying misunderstanding.

Our study design only distinguishes between private and industrial users of user stories, regardless of the actual implementation of such user stories practiced or the requirements process. This is a threat to both *construct validity* and *external validity*. However, this study should serve as a first understanding of the EID-related issues of user stories and requirements. We believe that the presented concept of EID can be applied to most of the currently practiced variants of user stories. A follow-up study could analyze this more thoroughly.

We used a non-empty string in the company-tag of GitHub profiles to find practitioners in the sense of developers that develop software for a living. However, a non-empty company name string does not automatically ensure that this person currently works in a software company. We mitigated this *threat to construct validity* by specifically asking the participant to state whether she will report experiences about an industrial or private project.

7   Discussion and Outlook

We have presented Expected Implementation Duration as a concept to grasp the granularity of user stories. In a study with 72 participants we have seen that EID is a measurable and influenceable concept. A peek into real projects reveals that user story sizes (in the sense of EID) vary widely between different projects but also among single projects. More than half of the participants have stated to work in projects where more than 30% of user stories take four days or more. At the same time the practitioners state certain problems they have with large as well as small user stories.

We have seen that working with small user stories cannot prevent a project from unexpected surprises. Small user stories still can grow unexpectedly in time or complexity. Nevertheless, keeping an eye on EID can help developers get more manageable requirements. Concretely, smaller user stories are perceived as more tangible and predictable, they help keeping feedback-cycles short, and they entail less post-development changes.

We do not present a perfect duration for user stories. The perfect duration probably does not exist, since different story granularities are well-suited for different tasks. However, this paper emphasizes the importance of EID as an aspect of user stories.

Using EID as a metric could influence the estimations. Developers could make smaller estimations because they want to look better and have smaller stories. We do not want to encourage developers to kid themselves. We also do not see the necessity for this as long as there are alternative ways to influence EID, such as splitting a user story. However, there are risks and it would be interesting to see the effects of introducing EID as a quality metric for user stories in a real project.

After revealing requirements granularity as an important factor in requirements engineering, we see many interesting directions for more research. The developers' views on user story granularity and its effects should be complemented by the *customers' or product owners' perspectives*. It is especially likely that having very small user stories, and therefore many of them, can be a burden for product owners. In this case, having different views with different granularities on the same set of user requirements can be an interesting solution.

Further, we believe that the concept of EID can also be transferred to *other types of requirements*. Here, as we have seen, measuring the EID of a user requirement introduces interesting challenges, because there are so many different understandings of what a user requirement is.

Many participants of our first questionnaire have stated to split user requirements into more technical work packages and then actually work on these. The *relation between a user requirement and a work package* would also be an interesting aspect arising from our study.

References

1. Bjarnason, E., Wnuk, K., Regnell, B.: Are you biting off more than you can chew? A case study on causes and effects of overscoping in large-scale software engineering. Information & Software Technology 54(10), 1107–1124 (2012)
2. Cao, L., Ramesh, B.: Agile requirements engineering practices: An empirical study. IEEE Software 25, 60–67 (2008)
3. Cockburn, A., Highsmith, J.: Agile software development, the people factor. IEEE Computer 34(11), 131–133 (2001)
4. Cohn, M.: User Stories Applied: For Agile Software Development. Prentice Hall (2004)
5. Cohn, M.: Agile Estimating and Planning. Pearson Education (2005)
6. Coughlan, J., Macredie, R.D.: Effective communication in requirements elicitation: A comparison of methodologies. Requirements Engineering 7(2), 47–60 (2002)
7. Haugen, N.C.: An empirical study of using planning poker for user story estimation. In: Agile Conference 2006, pp. 9–34 (2006)
8. Imaz, M., Benyon, D.: How stories capture interaction. In: INTERACT 1999, IFIP TC.13, pp. 321–328. IOS Press (1999)

9. Mahnič, V., Hovelja, T.: On using planning poker for estimating user stories. Journal of Systems and Software 85(9), 2086–2095 (2012)
10. Miranda, E., Bourque, P., Abran, A.: Sizing user stories using paired comparisons. Information and Software Technology 51(9), 1327–1337 (2009)
11. Patel, C., Ramachandran, M.: Story card based agile software development. International Journal of Hybrid Information Technology 2(2), 125–140 (2009)
12. Schwaber, K., Beedle, M.: Agile Software Development with Scrum. Prentice Hall (2002)
13. Tamrakar, R., Jørgensen, M.: Does the use of Fibonacci numbers in Planning Poker affect effort estimates? In: Proceedings of the 16th International Conference on Evaluation & Assessment in Software Engineering (EASE 2012), pp. 228–232 (2012)
14. Wake, W.C.: INVEST in Good Stories, and SMART Tasks. XP123 (2003), http://xp123.com/articles/invest-in-good-stories-and-smart-tasks/

Self-organized Learning in Software Factory: Experiences and Lessons Learned

Xiaofeng Wang[1], Ilaria Lunesu[2], Juha Rikkila[1],
Martina Matta[2], and Pekka Abrahamsson[1]

[1] Free University of Bozen-Bolzano, Bolzano, Italy
{xiaofeng.wang,juha.rikkila,pekka.abrahamsson}@unibz.it
[2] University of Cagliari, Cagliari, Italy
{ilaria.lunesu,martina.matta}@diee.unica.it

Abstract. Self-organization is one of the key agile principles. How it can be applied in an educational context is not explored extensively. In this paper we draw on relevant educational literature as the theoretical basis to investigate the self-organized learning that happens in Software Factory, an experimental, shared educational platform between several universities. Based on a comparative case study of two Software Factories we identified a set of themes that can potentially explain self-organization from the learning viewpoint. These themes include self-decided learning goals and personalized learning outcomes, peer teaching through active collaboration, diversity is the key and the personal attitude towards the learning matters. We also reported how students perceive the necessary infrastructure and the role of traditional lecturing and teachers in the Software Factory context. The study contributes to a better offering of learning experience in software engineering education by making most out of the self-organized learning approach.

Keywords: Self-organization, self-organized learning, Software Factory, agile approaches, software engineering education, diversity.

1   Introduction

One serious challenge faced by software engineering education is that software engineering cannot be taught exclusively in the classroom, because it is a competence and not just a body of knowledge [1]. To address the challenge, many educators resort to agile approaches as one key source of inspiration to improve software engineering education, and have introduced an increasing percentage of practice and hands-on experience in software engineering courses (e.g. [2], [3], [4]). However, traditional teaching/lecturing always plays a key part of the game.

What happens if we were to give up this element and leave the learning completely to the students themselves? Self-organization is one of the key agile principles and has been actively advocated for software development teams. Is it equally applicable in an educational context where students rather than teachers are made primarily

G. Cantone and M. Marchesi (Eds.): XP 2014, LNBIP 179, pp. 126–142, 2014.

responsible to meet their educational needs? In fact self-organized learning has been discussed in the education literature for different educational purposes and in various settings [5]. However, it is seldom discussed in the context of software engineering education.

Software Factory [6] is a shared educational platform for universities to hold courses where students are engaged in a real-world project developing software jointly or separately. Software Factory relies on self-organization as its primary way of organizing the work. Earlier studies in the Software Factory context [7], [8] have shown how self-organization in software development teams is enabled. However, self-organization has not been examined from the learning viewpoint.

In this paper we report the case study findings of two Software Factory courses held in two different universities, to better understand the self-organized learning approach in software engineering education. We have conducted 27 interviews with the students from both software factories. The analysis of interview data and other related case materials reveal that self-organized learning can be an effective approach for learning if certain pre-conditions and enabling factors are in place. Consequently the role of traditional teaching will be bound to change if we want to continue meeting the needs of the software industry.

The rest of the paper is organized as follows. In the next section we review a set of studies focusing on the agile approaches in software engineering education and the education literature on self-organized learning. Section 3 contains the research approach that explains how we conducted the case study and analysed the collected data, and provides the key information on the two Software Factory courses. The empirical findings are presented in Section 4. The following section carries the findings further and discusses about their implications. The last section concludes the paper with the outlook of future work.

2   Literature Review

2.1   Agile Approaches for Software Engineering Education

Since the start of agile software movement marked by the Agile Manifesto in 2001, different agile approaches have been introduced in software engineering education. Monett [4] argues that agile approaches play the double roles, both as subjects and means of education. Not only the agile theory and practice are taught and experienced in class, also the teaching itself, and consequently the learning, should be adapted to changing requirements and priorities in each edition of the course. In this study we focus on agile approaches as means to deliver learning in software engineering education. Since we set out to understand the self-organized learning approach, we arrange the related work in the order of the increased focus on the active role of students in their own learning experience and decreased reliance on external teaching.

Several early studies were focused on applying agile approaches to improve teaching techniques. Bergin et al. [9] investigate the tools and techniques of XP that can be used to enhance teaching processes. They claim that many of the agile ideas are more broadly applicable. The emphasis on individuals and interactions can provide students with an incentive to reflect on and adjust the process, rather than blindly following it. Alfonso and Botia [2] propose an iterative and agile process model in a software engineering undergraduate course. The proposed model serves both as an educational technique (for teachers) and as a subject of learning (for students). Drawn upon the analogy of project management, the model prescribes the sequence of tasks for teaching the topics of any discipline. Wondering how to find what are the requirements for a robust methodology for teaching software engineering, Mann and Smith [3] have attempted for several years to expose students to "real world" situations, while maintaining a positive and constructive learning environment. An agile framework that incorporates agile development approaches in a structured manner is proposed for teaching software engineering. Werner et al. [10] guide their students through the process of developing software using an industrial modification of Scrum, which is called Three-Sprint Scrum. They also ask students to periodically reflect on the use of the processes.

Other studies emphasize more on practice-based, hands-on learning experience as a necessary complement of teaching. Student projects or lab exercises are the forms commonly used to acquire it. Reichlmayr [11] offers a vision that the educational objective of a program should be to provide a solid foundation for a student's life-long professional growth. Based on this vision, a team-based project is run in the introductory software engineering course that attempts to address the challenges using agile development techniques. Layman et al. [12] also contend that the overall goal of a software engineering course is to teach students practical techniques and tools that they will encounter in professional software development. Their teaching approach is focused on tools and techniques rather than lecture-based concepts, which involves a weekly lab component that takes the place of the third lecture. Rico and Sayani [13] introduce hands-on experience into their software engineering course utilizing agile methods. They ask institutional researchers who had been experimenting with agile methods and publishing their results to adapt agile methods and design the lesson plan for the capstone course. The students can use the agile method of their choice, such as Scrum, Extreme Programming, etc. Each student team will develop a general-purpose business-to-consumer (B2C) website for buying and selling digital media products. Mahnic [14] describes a capstone course in which students are asked to work as Scrum teams, responsible for the implementation of a set of user stories. The study shows the achievement of teaching goals and provides empirical evaluation of students' progress in estimation and planning skills. With a focus on teaching human interaction and work-life balance, Schroeder and Klarl [15] allow the students to experience a full agile product development cycle in the risk-free academic environment. They take the approach of teaching by example and specifically rely on agile processes and the state-of-the-art tooling support implemented in the lab course. All students have taken part in a programming lab that focused on programming activities.

It is worth noting that *Software Factory* term has been used by Chao and Randles [16], which is different from Software Factory introduced in this paper. The authors introduce a teaching and learning strategy that integrates meaningful community service with instruction and reflection to enrich the learning experience, teach students civic responsibility, and strengthen communities. The *Software Factory* provides the service-learning experience through a controlled classroom and laboratory environment with instruction on various software engineering tools and methodologies that are commonplace in industry. The students are exposed to the real-world problems associated with software engineering and gain valuable experiences in situations that they will be faced in industry.

In summary, despite the abundant literature and different proposals of applying agile approaches to software engineering courses, self-organized learning as a potentially effective education approach has received far less attention in this context.

2.2   Self-organized Learning in Education

Broadly speaking, almost all teaching-learning interactions can be classified as one of the following types, as suggested by Mitra [17]:

1) Those where the teacher or external resource determines the learning content and methodology,
2) Those where the teacher or external resource determines the learning, in consultation with the learners, and
3) Those where the learners determine their own learning outcomes and how they will go about it.

Further, it is argued that any curriculum can be divided into three parts in order for learners to acquire the necessary competence [18]:

1) A part that needs a human teacher who is conversant with the subject matter and teaching methodology,
2) A part that needs an assistant who is somewhat more knowledgeable than the learner, and
3) A part that needs resources and a peer group alone.

The distribution of curricula into the three parts would depend on the nature of the subject. For the third type of education/learning course, a model called MIE (Minimally Invasive Education) is proposed [17], [19]. It involves exposing the learner to the learning environment without any instruction. The concept of MIE has been evolved into SOLE (Self-Organized Learning Environment) over the recent years [20], [21].

A list of benefits that students can gain from a self-organized learning approach include having fun, increased motivation to learn about more subjects and ideas, taking ownership of their own learning experience, developing habits to become a lifelong learner, improved creativity and problem-solving abilities, and strengthened interpersonal skills [22].

However, self-organized learning has its limits [21]. In unsupervised environments, different students do what they like doing and therefore tend to excel in their particular areas of interest. Not everybody learns something about everything. Some individuals may benefit; others may not. With the presence of a friendly mediator who provides supervision but exercises minimal intervention (encouraging rather than teaching), these issues are less likely to be a problem.

The experiments based on which the self-organized learning approach has been developed were conducted with young-aged kids for the purpose of computer literacy using Internet. Would this approach apply in other settings such as software engineering education at the higher education level? Our study aspires to shed some lights on the understanding of self-organized learning in this setting.

3   Research Approach

The overall research approach employed in our study is multiple-case study. Each case is a Software Factory course. As described earlier in Introduction, Software Factory is considered an ideal setting to study self-organized learning. We studied two Software Factory courses, one at Free University of Bozen-Bolzano, the other at University of Cagliari. Both sessions were held in the Spring semester of 2013. More details are presented in Table 1.

Table 1. The profiles of the two Software Factory sessions

Software Factory Name	Bolzano SF	Cagliari SF
Starting date	04/03/2013	18/03/2013
Duration	11 weeks	9 weeks
Study level	Undergraduate/post-graduate	Undergraduate/post-graduate/PhD
Credit Points	8	4 for undergraduate/post-graduate, 8 for PhD
No. of students involved	21	9
No. of official teaching staff	2	None
No. of projects hosted	3	1
Max. Team size	14 (further divided into smaller sub-teams)	8
Students participation	No working time defined	8 hours per day, twice per week

Apart from collecting related contextual information, such as the setups of the factories, the projects implemented, etc., we conducted a set of 27 interviews with almost all the students who participated in the courses. The students were individually interviewed and all the interviews were audio recorded and transcribed verbatim later on. The data analysis followed the within-case analysis and cross-case comparison steps that are suggested in [23]. We coded the interview data following an open coding process, which allowed the codes to emerge from the data.

Before the case study findings are reported, the detailed contextual information on the two Software Factory courses is provided in the following sub-sections.

3.1   Bolzano SF

The Bolzano SF course started in early March 2013 and lasted 11 weeks. This is the second Software Factory session held in the university. The course is an 8 credit-point course offered to both post-graduate and undergraduate students. One teacher and one teaching assistant were officially assigned to the course.

In total 21 students have participated. 15 of them are master students, 13 from the Computer Science Faculty, one from the management discipline and another having design background. Six are undergraduate students, among them three are Computer Science students and another three are from the Art and Design Faculty. These students have highly diversified cultural backgrounds. The nationalities include Italian, Croatian, German, Polish, Indian, American, Vietnamese and Nigerian.

Three projects have been developed at and owned by Bolzano SF: Memoree, Glasshub and RaspberryPi Cloud. Memoree was based on the business idea of a local entrepreneur who needed to develop a prototype to prove his idea. The intended software solution packed personal photos, videos and audios into a memory package and shared it among friends. The entrepreneur played the customer role for the Memoree project and made himself available all through the course. The Glasshub project was to build a knowledge and information-sharing portal for the Software Factory network, and the two teaching staff played the role of the customer. The third project, RaspberryPi Cloud, was a hardware/software project which built a computing cluster based on hundreds of low-cost RaspberryPi mini computers. The purpose was to provide cost effective cloud infrastructure to the university students and faculty members for educational purposes. The technology and programming skills required by each project were different from one to another. The students with computer science and management background chose to work on one of the three projects according to their own interests, and the design students were rotated among the projects.

Two introductory lectures were held in the beginning of the course, one introducing the nature of Software Factory, the other on agile methods and practices. There was no teaching scheduled, only the weekly demos of the project progresses. There was no obligation for the students to be present at the factory except for the demo sessions. The students met with their team members at their own time, either in or outside the factory.

The course ended with a public event where the students presented their projects to the university and local communities. The students were evaluated jointly by the customers, the team members and the course instructors based on the results of the projects and their performance during the course.

3.2   Cagliari SF

The Cagliari SF course started on March 18th 2013 and finished on May 15th 2013. Similarly this is the second session at University of Cagliari. The course is available to the students at all levels of university study. It counts 4 credit points for post-graduate and undergraduate students but 8 credit points for PhD students.

There were nine students participated in the course, including three master students, four undergraduates and two PhD students. Eight were from the Faculty of Electronic Engineering and Computer Science and one undergraduate student from linguistics background. Different from the students at Bolzano SF that are international, the students at Cagliari SF are all Italians.

There were no official teachers involved in Cagliari SF. One of the PhD students with a complete knowledge of the project and all the relevant technologies played the role of coordinator/coach of the team.

Apart from one student who participated in the Glasshub project of Bolzano SF remotely, the other eight students all worked on the Matchall2 project. Matchall2 created a personal communication engine based on innovative principles and functionalities, with a web implementation and diffusion strategy. The final product intended to provide a labeling facility (precisely a bookmarklet) that allowed one to classify and categorize pictures and videos in a customized manner using tags. A local entrepreneur played the role of the product owner.

No formal lectures were held at Cagliari SF. Pair programming was adopted and pairs were freely formed. The only requirement was an expert student should pair with a less experienced one. The students were free to choose the tasks according to their own interests. They came to the factory twice per week to work on the project. The working day was established as 8 hours. During a working day the students worked in a professional manner.

At the end of the course each student was asked to produce a report on the work they have done in the factory, and was evaluated based on it and the "passion and devotion" each one dedicated to achieve the results.

4   Findings

When the interviewed students commented on the experience they had in their respective Software Factories, "*positive*", "*interesting*", "*stimulating*", "*optimal*" are the words they used. The practical, real-life experience of interacting with customers and developing software is very much appreciated, as one student in Bolzano SF who is an exchange student from USA commented:

"If I really have to select the primary things that I benefited, I would say, a practical environment, an actual environment for developing software, whereas with a lot of other courses I've taken, even like those which were ended 'software engineering' it's really theoretical, highly theoretical, not practically applying the skills actually building software".

It is echoed by the comments from the Cagliari SF students. One student commented that the Software Factory environment can be easily related to a real office setting and provides the feeling of working in a real company.

At both Software Factories, teamwork, various technical knowledge, and the way of managing work were the significant learning outcomes frequently mentioned by the interviewed students.

Main themes regarding self-organized learning emerged from the data analysis of the two cases are reported in the following sub-sections.

4.1   Self-decided Learning Goals and Personalized Learning Outcome

The overall prescribed learning objectives of the Software Factory sessions were for students to experience and learn agile software development and the way of working in highly uncertain situations. However, what each individual student would and could learn varied greatly. The learning goals were essentially set up by the students themselves, as one student at Bolzano SF commented:

"The course is not like pre-defined, sort of the same 'you take from this course X, Y and Z'. It is really you commit to it and ... [get] whatever you could make of it".

The students had the possibility to collaborate on real projects where they could decide technologies, architecture and so on. Different students worked on different projects or different parts of a project, therefore the technical knowledge and skills they had to learn were greatly different. This huge difference made traditional teaching difficult and inefficient and favored more a self-organized learning style. The freedom of setting up own learning goals was also considered by the students *"a fun way"* of learning. One Bolzano SF student recalled his experience of exploring a cloud storage solution for the Memoree project:

"I thought this is really interesting, and I could do it because nobody knows it, and let's do it, I mean let's take some risk, let's take a chance".

It is interesting to note that, even though Bolzano SF did not set the minimal effort needed from the students, they would put significant effort voluntarily nevertheless. Several students claimed that they worked hard on this course, as shown by the following quote from one Bolzano SF student:

"I don't think I spent less time on this course than what I spent on other courses definitely, because it's difficult. If you have a class you know it's like 2[pm] to 4[pm] and that's it. But this is like you can't say you are leaving it because work is not done".

At Cagliari SF, even though a working day was established as 8-hour long, the students often remained longer than required to work on the project. In general they got into the working mode immediately when they came into the factory and worked with passion.

Personalized learning outcomes were achieved through pursuing self-decided learning goals. The students who did not have any working experience emphasized that they learnt how to work in a team and the way to manage work. Less technically competent students put more focuses on their improvement of technical knowledge and skills. The designers who were specialized on product designs acquired competence in user interface and web design. Experienced working students learnt more on how to teach others and interact with people from different disciplines. The two Software Factories allowed their students to learn by doing in a friendly and risk-free environment.

4.2   Peer Teaching through Active Collaboration

Self-organized learning does not mean self-teaching. In effect, in both Software Factories, it took the form of peer teaching: *"we have all been learning from each other"*, and *"it is 'give and take'"*, as the Bolzano SF students explained.

Peer teaching happened naturally through active collaboration on projects, which creates opportunities for one to learn certain knowledge or skills one does not have from others who know better. One Cagliari SF student recalled that:

> *"Surely the fact of open space and working closely with a partner help both to communicate and collaborate and above all to share knowledge between us, then ultimately to improve our learning experience".*

Peer teaching through collaboration could also take away the pressure from the students and bring a relaxing learning experience. At Cagliari SF, due to the implementation of pair programming, less experienced or skilled students were constantly supervised by those who are more experienced or skilled, even if just by a little bit. The result has been positive from both the point of view of work and learning perspective. One feels free to ask any kind of doubt or uncertainty.

Meanwhile, peer teaching has been a learning process for both involved. The students learnt how to answer questions when being asked. They also learnt to appreciate the difficulties faced by others that were often different from those encountered themselves personally. As a Cagliari SF student put it eloquently:

> *"[Peer teaching] contributed to the growth of both. In fact the student with no experience learned to make 'something'. And the expert student consolidated his ideas and learned to mentor another person, which is anyway part of the expertise needed to acquire for his own career".*

When such peer teaching happened through active collaboration, the students found that the Software Factory environments were *"stimulating"*, and it was true for both the students who had no working experience beforehand and those who had various working or company internship experience.

4.3   Diversity Is the Key

Diversity was one of the key factors that both Software Factory students associated with their self-organized learning experience. Diversity had several facets in the two Software Factory settings. The first important facet was the competence diversity. This was especially evident at Cagliari SF. The students had very different technical skills and knowledge. One knew well Java, HTML, Javascript, etc. Another had good knowledge of semantic web and foreign languages. There was a student with no experience in software development and another expert student who had skills in PHP, Java, C scripting, VisualBasic, HTML, HTML5, CSS, Javascript, Postgresq, and knowledge about agile methods. The consequence of competence diversity was evident and positive. It led to active interaction and exchange of knowledge among the students.

Diverse skillset in problem solving approaches also enabled the mutual learning, even in the case where the students had skills in the same domain and at the similar level. For example, two Bolzano SF students worked on the Android solution for the Memoree project. Both had strong Android knowledge and Java programming skills. Nonetheless the learning was happening between them. As the Cagliari SF students argued, because each person had a different method to solve problems compared with that of others, each one could learn from others. In this way there was continuous collaboration for finding more efficient solutions that are difficult for each single person to find out.

Diversity in disciplines was another facet that contributed to the positive learning experience at both Software Factories. The students at Bolzano SF came from computer science, design and management disciplines. Similarly the students at Cagliari SF came from engineering and linguistics backgrounds. This diversity enlarged the pool of competences that the two factories could offer for learning. The students learnt to look at software development through the perspectives of other disciplines. For many of them this was the first time they were actually able to do so. A computer science student at Bolzano SF gave an example of how he and the designers looked at a login page differently:

> "I just look at it, like 'oh I need to create a page and add text and fields of user name and password. They [the designers] look at it in a different way, in the sense of 'oh the color theme should be appropriate, we should put customized images here and there'. It's just different ways of thinking about it".

The consequence of this diversity was so positive that a working student at Bolzano SF who has computer science background commented that he would repeat this type of experiment of collaborating with designers in his company.

Meanwhile, the design students involved in Bolzano SF also found that to work with computer science students allowed them to talk "with someone which has the same objective but respecting each other in the different fields". Similarly, the linguistics student at Cagliari SF commented:

> "I came from a linguistics background. The fact that I found myself working with people who have completely different skills from mine was very exciting, also from the point of view of deepening my own knowledge and improving the work".

Culture diversity was a facet present in Bolzano SF but not in Cagliari SF. Several Bolzano SF students did comment on this diversity but how it influenced the self-organized learning experience was not obvious in the Bolzano SF case.

4.4   Personal Attitude Matters

Self-organized learning may not happen even if the condition of diversity is satisfied. The students need to be motivated to interact with each other and willing to learn from each other. A design student at Bolzano SF was working with the Memoree team. She observed that the team was very motivated. They were using Google+ actively and looking forward to meeting up and to sharing. Based on this observation she commented that:

> *"The attitude matters a lot. If people are not interested, they are not looking forward to meet up. They just want to know what they should do. That's all".*

The motivation should be self-generated, since *"when you motivate yourself, you learn, and encourage yourself to do it"*, as explained by a Bolzano SF student. There can be different self-motivating factors. For example, curiosity played as a self-motivating factor for a design student at Bolzano SF. When being asked how learning happened to him, he explained that he was driven by his curiosity to understand what others were doing. Helping others can be another self-motivating factory, as a Cagliari student put it: *"there is happiness in helping other fellow students".*

With such positive attitudes in minds, the students would offer learning experience to others voluntarily and proactively. When all the students were motivated, positive learning experience was created, as a Bolzano SF student observed:

> *"Everybody gives its contribution and then both try to enrich the process with their thoughts and proposals and so on… Everybody is contributing".*

4.5   Minimal Infrastructure

At Bolzano SF there are five rooms in the Faculty building dedicated to the factory, which are connected by a long corridor. The rooms are of the similar size and none is spacious enough to hold a team of more than seven people to work, but sufficient for meeting purposes. The furniture in the factory is limited to large-sized tables and chairs. White boards and flip charts are available in every room. There is no other IT equipment apart from one desktop and attached audio/video devices that were intended for the weekly demo. Wi-Fi connection is provided by the university. An electronic kanban board is used to track the progress of the projects.

Similarly Cagliari SF is also equipped with minimal infrastructure. It is located in a big room in an old palace very close to Cagliari city center. The room is bright, wide and clean. It is equipped with independent comfortable tables and swivel chairs. There are 4 big screens to show the code or documentation. On the wall, visible to all, there is a white board that the team can use to explain ideas, the architecture of the project and so on. A physical kanban board is present in the room to manage the development process. The Internet connection, the camera and microphone for audio/video meetings are available.

Most students from both software factories believed that the environments and the infrastructure provided were *"cool"* and sufficient for the purpose of the course. Some commented that they found the environments comfortable which put them at ease. It seems that the minimal infrastructure provided at both software factories was not constraining the self-organized learning from happening.

4.6   The Changing Role of Teachers

There were no regular lectures scheduled in either of the Software Factory courses. When being asked if they missed lecturing experience, almost all the students at both factories answered with a firm "no". Since the types of knowledge acquired at the factories were highly practical, e.g., teamwork, technical know-hows, the students believed that learning by doing was the only effective way, as a Cagliari SF student argued adequately:

"In my opinion the team worked exactly because of the reciprocal collaboration among students without any person dictating the path to follow, and because of the fact that the students had opportunities to try by themselves how to solve various problems and choose the most effective solution".

Instead of the teacher role, many students commented on the usefulness of an expert role that could offer help and consultancy in complex and difficult situations, without being involved in the work of the students directly. As the suggestion from a Cagliari SF student shows:

"What helps, more than anything else, is a guide or a reference person for students. Apart from that, the students are able to self-manage the activities. It's important to have a reference person who is able to bring the development process back to the right track at the moments needed. For the rest, give students enough freedom to learn how to manage themselves".

In Cagliari SF, a couple of senior students played such a role, and it was highly appreciated by the students. These senior students were considered competent and had an overview of the problems. They were able and available to explain the problems and provide supports when needed, even though they do not belong to any specific project. In contrast, such a role did not exist evidently in Bolzano SF. Indeed some students expressed the wish to have it *"because sometimes it's good to have expert to check everything or show us better point of the direction we should go".*

If an expert role was in place, the very existence of the teacher role may be seen as the *"threat"* to the other, as one Cagliari SF student suggested. Then is there still a place for a teacher and traditional lecturing if students are self-organized to learn in a practice-oriented course? If yes, what are the functions of a teacher?

At Bolzano SF, a couple of introductory lectures on what Software Factory was, how the course was organized, and an introduction to agile software development were held in the beginning of the session. Several students commented on the usefulness of these lessons but warned that there should not have too many.

Meanwhile, the interviewed students emphasized on the importance of having fixed, regular meetings where all the students could meet together to get feedback from their fellow students, even if they were not working on the same project. No fixed meetings were scheduled in Cagliari SF, and students expressed the wish of having it, as evidenced by the following quote:

"One suggestion would be to have a meeting at least once a week to check the situation and put together the work of each team, as each team works on

a different task. The work that has been done was positive, but just a small meeting of only 5 minutes to better integrate [would be good], even if the level of interaction [at our Software Factory] was great".

Instead at Bolzano SF weekly demo sessions were scheduled to show the progress of the projects. However, since the presence at those sessions was not obligatory, there were always students missing at each meeting. As a result the meeting was found not so beneficial from the learning perspective as they should have been. Some students believed that maybe it was *"too flexible"* for the students without obligatory presence.

In this case the role of a teacher could be useful to ensure the presence of the students at regular meetings or weekly demos, as suggested by the Bolzano SF students. It was an official role and assumed a sort of *"authority"* for the students from a ceremonial perspective.

5   Discussion

It can be seen from the analysis of the two Software Factory courses at two universities that self-organized learning can be an effective way for students to acquire knowledge and competences on software engineering topics. It is also a fun way of learning, more interesting and exciting than the classroom-based, teaching-dominant approaches. Students can decide themselves what their learning goals should be and consequently what learning outcomes they could obtain. Greater autonomy is generally associated with greater responsibility as well. In a self-organized learning environment, making learning happen is the main responsibility of students themselves, not of teachers whom are generally held responsible for how well students learn in a classroom-based learning environment.

Based on our case study findings, it is worth clarifying that self-organized learning is not the same thing as self-learning. Self-learning happens in the Software Factory context as it does in normal classroom settings. But it is not the main form of learning in Software Factory. The main form of learning is peer teaching through active collaboration. Therefore in a self-organized learning environment students are not left on their own devices to pursue their respective learning goals, no matter how different one's goals are from those of another person. Our study shows that a few introductory courses early on, such as the agile lecture in Bolzano SF in the beginning, and certain ceremonies, such as weekly demo sessions, when students can get together in an organized manner, can facilitate self-organized learning to happen. In line with the understanding in agile literature that self-organizing teams does not mean there is no management but it takes a different form [24], self-organized learning does not mean lectures or other education forms do not exist. They can happen in a self-organized learning environment to complement the learning experience of students.

Our case study findings also suggest that self-organized learning does not happen automatically by putting students to work together. Some basic elements and pre-conditions have to be in place to make it happen. The two factory cases indicate that diversity is a key driving factor that makes self-organized learning possible. Diversity has many facets, including competency diversity, diversity in cognitive abilities such as problem solving and diversity in study disciplines. This finding can be better understood by drawing upon the complexity studies on self-organization. According to the complexity theory, self-organization of a system is an emergent property that cannot be manipulated but only facilitated by diversity, interaction and interdependence among parts [25]. Therefore, to maximize the possibility of self-organized learning, students should have diversified competences, backgrounds and profiles. Of course in many cases the degree of diversity is not in the control of the educators since it is not possible to decide who can attend the courses beforehand. Nonetheless it is important to be aware that diversity is to be preserved, not controlled or suppressed.

Self-motivation is another factor that plays a key role in self-organized learning. Our study reveals that intrinsic motivating factors, such as curiosity and altruism, enable a positive and proactive attitude towards interaction and collaboration among students, which in turn can facilitate the happening of peer teaching. Similarly, educators may have very limited influence on self-motivation and intrinsic motivating factors that each student may possess. Again nonetheless it is the responsibility of educators to preserve the existence of self-motivation through building a positive learning environment.

With regard to the roles of traditional classroom teaching and teachers, they are not completely obsolete but minimized in a self-organized learning environment. Ceremony keeper and environment preserver are the new functions of a teacher who is considered an official figure of a course. However, it needs to be cautioned that the official nature of a teacher may compromise the self-organized learning experience of students by being a potential "threat" to more knowledgeable and senior students and experts. Ideally the teacher is an expert in all the learning subjects of a course, which can reduce the cost of having external experts or support to students. The key issue to consider is how to balance the different roles concurrently and it can become an additional challenge for the teacher. Students who have done the Software Factory course in the past could also be hired as mentors for the future courses as employed e.g. in University of Helsinki's Software Factory context [8].

Finally it needs to be emphasized that self-organized learning may not be an effective approach for every type of educational program. The Software Factory courses are focused on practical knowledge in software engineering education, Students work in an organization without history, established rules or routines. They self-develop these to meet the needs of the given context. The Software Factory approach therefore falls into the category of an educational curriculum in which learners determine their own learning outcomes and which only needs resources and a team of peers, as suggested by Mitra [17, 18]. Therefore, educators need to analyze and understand better the nature of a curriculum they offer before embarking on the self-organized learning approach. Other aspects to consider are the duration of a course and the number of participating students. The experience in our Software Factories show that self-organized learning can be effective for short courses of 7 to 12 weeks and the class size of 10 to 20 people. It is yet to understand better whether it is an applicable approach to larger classes and longer courses.

There are limitations in our study that can potentially threat the validity of the findings reported in the paper. First of all we have drawn on two Software Factory cases only. The generalizability of the findings to other Software Factory settings or to other educational context, e.g., in non-IT disciplines, where self-organized learning is utilized, is yet to be verified. Another limitation is that we relied on the opinions of the students only in the study. The perspectives of other stakeholders, such as teachers, external customers, experts, etc., were not included in the current research design. As a result the findings reflected only the perspective of students, and may not depict a whole and comprehensive picture of self-organized learning. Last but not least, we have relied on the self-explanation of students regarding the effectiveness of self-organized learning. We did not measure it using objective instruments due to the exploratory and qualitative nature of the study. In another Software Factory setting the learning outcomes as well as relevant factors have been studied quantitatively [26]. The evaluation approach can be incorporated in our future study to provide more refined and accurate understanding of self-organized learning.

6   Conclusion

Our study is one of the first ones to investigate the self-organized learning approach in software engineering education. Drawing upon two Software Factory courses held in two different universities and the interviews with 27 students who have participated in the courses, we were able to provide a better understanding of the self-organized learning phenomenon. The emerging themes include self-decided learning goals and personalized learning outcomes, peer teaching through active collaboration, diversity is the key and personal attitude towards learning matters. A better understanding of the necessary infrastructure and the role of teaching and teachers in a self-organized learning environment is also offered. The implications of the findings for practice are discussed in the previous section.

Our study opened several avenues for future research on self-organized learning in educational settings. Multiple perspectives on self-organized learning, including both students, teachers and other stakeholders, will allow a more comprehensive understanding of the phenomenon, and thus enable more grounded and holistic reflection on traditional education versus new approaches such as self-organized learning. Systematic evaluation of the advantages and disadvantages of the approach is also necessary. Another potential research direction is to examine the potential linkage and synergy between self-organized learning and other approaches implemented in software engineering education, such as problem-based learning, studio approach, and software internship, to derive new and better educational approaches for the software engineering discipline.

Acknowledgments. We thank the students who participated in both Software Factory courses in Bolzano and Cagliari, Italy. The students cordially gave us consents to interview them and collaborated on this study. This research is supported by Regione Autonoma della Sardegna (RAS), Regional Law No. 7-2007, project CRP-17938 LEAN 2.0.

References

1. Jazayeri, M.: The education of a software engineer. In: Conference on Automated Software Engineering, pp. 1–10 (2004)
2. Alfonso, M., Botia, A.: An iterative and agile process model for teaching software engineering. In: 18th Conf. Softw. Eng. Educ. Train., pp. 9–16 (2005)
3. Mann, S., Smith, L.: Arriving at an agile framework for teaching software engineering. In: Annu. Conf. Natl. Advis. Comm....., pp. 183–190 (2006)
4. Monett, D.: Agile Project-Based Teaching and Learning. world-comp.org (2013)
5. Mitra, S.: Self organising systems for mass computer literacy: Findings from the "hole in the wall" experiments. Int. J. Dev. Issues 4, 71–81 (2005)
6. Abrahamsson, P., Kettunen, P., Fagerholm, F.: The set-up of a software engineering research infrastructure of the 2010s. In: Proceedings of the 11th International Conference on Product Focused Software, PROFES 2010, pp. 112–114. ACM Press, New York (2010)
7. Karhatsu, H., Ikonen, M., Kettunen, P., Fagerholm, F., Abrahamsson, P.: Building Blocks for Self-Organizing Software Development Teams: A Framework Model and Empirical Pilot Study. In: ICSTE 2010, pp. 1–8 (2010)
8. Fagerholm, F., Oza, N., Munch, J.: A platform for teaching applied distributed software development: The ongoing journey of the Helsinki software factory. In: CTGDSD 2013, pp. 1–5 (2013)
9. Bergin, J., Kussmaul, C., Reichlmayr, T., Caristi, J., Pollice, G.: Agile development in computer science education. In: Proceedings of the 36th SIGCSE Technical Symposium on Computer Science Education -SIGCSE 2005, pp. 130–131. ACM Press, New York (2005)
10. Werner, L., Arcamone, D., Ross, B.: Using Scrum in a quarter-length undergraduate software engineering course. J. Comput. Sci. Coll. 27, 140–150 (2012)
11. Reichlmayr, T.: The agile approach in an undergraduate software engineering course project. In: 33rd Annual Frontiers in Education, FIE 2003, pp. S2C_13–S2C_18. IEEE (2003)
12. Layman, L., Cornwell, T., Williams, L.: Personality types, learning styles, and an agile approach to software engineering education. In: Proc. 37th SIGCSE Tech. Symp. Comput. Sci. Educ. - SIGCSE 2006, p. 428 (2006)
13. Rico, D.F., Sayani, H.H.: Use of Agile Methods in Software Engineering Education. In: 2009 Agile Conference, pp. 174–179. IEEE (2009)
14. Mahnic, V.: A Capstone Course on Agile Software Development Using Scrum. IEEE Trans. Educ. 55, 99–106 (2012)
15. Schroeder, A., Klarl, A.: Teaching agile software development through lab courses. In: EDUCON 2012 IEEE (2012)
16. Chao, J., Randles, M.: Agile Software Factory for Student Service Learning. In: 2009 22nd Conference on Software Engineering Education and Training, pp. 34–40. IEEE (2009)
17. Mitra, S.: Minimally invasive education for mass computer literacy. In: CRIDALA 2000, Hong Kong, pp. 1–22 (2000)
18. Mitra, S.: Minimally invasive education: a progress report on the "hole-in-the-wall" experiments. Br. J. Educ. Technol. 34, 367–371 (2003)
19. Dangwal, R., Jha, S., Kapur, P.: Impact of Minimally Invasive Education on children: an Indian perspective. Br. J. Educ. Technol. 37, 295–298 (2006)

20. Mitra, S.: Self organising systems for mass computer literacy: Findings from the "hole in the wall" experiments. Int. J. Dev. Issues. 4, 71–81 (2005)
21. Mitra, S., Dangwal, R.: Limits to self-organising systems of learning-the Kalikuppam experiment. Br. J. Educ. Technol. 41, 672–688 (2010)
22. Mitra, S.: How to Bring Self-Organized Learning Environments to Your Community (2013), http://www.ted.com/pages/sole_toolkit
23. Yin, R.K.: Case Study Research: Design and Methods. Sage Publications, Inc. (2003)
24. Vidgen, R., Wang, X.: Coevolving Systems and the Organization of Agile Software Development. Inf. Syst. Res. 20, 355–376 (2009)
25. Lichtenstein, B.B., Plowman, D.A.: The leadership of emergence: A complex systems leadership theory of emergence at successive organizational levels (2009)
26. Ovais, A.M., Liukkunen, K., Markkula, J.: Student perceptions and attitudes towards the software factory as a learning environment. In: EDUCON (2014)

Using Agile Methods to Implement a Laboratory for Software Product Quality Evaluation

Javier Verdugo[1], Moisés Rodríguez[1], and Mario Piattini[1,2]

[1] Alarcos Quality Center, Paseo de la Universidad 4, 13071, Ciudad Real, Spain
{javier.verdugo,moises.rodriguez,
mario.piattini}@alarcosqualitycenter.com
[2] Institute of Information Technologies and Systems, University of Castilla–La Mancha,
Camino de Moledores s/n, 13051, Ciudad Real, Spain
Mario.Piattini@uclm.es

Abstract. In this paper we discuss how we at Alarcos Quality Center implemented AQCLab, the first laboratory in the world to be accredited as meeting ISO/IEC 17025 for software product quality evaluation based on the ISO/IEC 25000 series of standards. We implemented AQC Lab following agile principles by means of an adaptation of the Scrum methodology. This work method helped us to progress in a challenging context which had several similarities to software development, where the requirements were uncertain from the start.

Keywords: Software, quality evaluation, ISO/IEC 25000, SQuaRE, agile implementation, accredited laboratory, ISO/IEC 17025.

1   Introduction

Alarcos Quality Center (from now on referred to as AQC) is a Spanish company that was spun off from the Alarcos Research Group at the University of Castilla-La Mancha in 2008. It was founded with the goal of providing its customers (software factories and development departments, as well as software acquirers) with software quality assurance services. Though AQC is relatively young, we have over fifteen years of experience in software quality research that has already been carried out by the Alarcos Research Group.

After several projects that involved software process improvement, we realized that, though good development processes are of great help in the effort, they do not always lead to quality software; we became aware that the best way to evaluate quality in software products is by measuring and evaluating their own characteristics, not those of the processes followed.

That is why we decided to focus our work on developing a new service in an area that was not as well-known and widespread as others in the software industry: Indeed it is still not so widely-recognized, even now; we are talking about software product evaluation.

G. Cantone and M. Marchesi (Eds.): XP 2014, LNBIP 179, pp. 143–156, 2014.

By 2010, the new series of International Standards ISO/IEC 25000 [1] (known as Software product Quality Requirements and Evaluation - SQuaRE) was still in an early stage of development. We decided to take ISO/IEC 25000 as the basis for our software quality evaluations, even though the main standards in the series – the quality model and the evaluation process – were still under development. Four years later, SQuaRE is still being developed, though it has matured considerably and most of the main standards of the series have already been released. These include the quality model –presented in ISO/IEC 25010 [2] - and the evaluation process –defined in ISO/IEC 25040 [3].

At the beginning, there was a fair amount of uncertainty about how to deal with the implementation process, as it was a rather complex task in a not very well-known ground that involved a lot of research and experimentation. Right at that point, we knew we would have to:

- Develop a quality model. Starting from the quality model defined in ISO/IEC 25010, which specifies only top-level quality characteristics and their sub-characteristics, it would be essential for us to identify metrics and define how to aggregate their values to evaluate the top-level elements of the model.
- Implement an evaluation framework. We would have to identify tools that provide measurements for the metrics defined in the quality model. We would also need to develop a tool that takes those measurements and aggregates them according to our criteria so that we can obtain quality assessments for the top-level elements of the model.
- Define the evaluation process. Based on the evaluation process defined in ISO/IEC 25040, we would have to decide how to adapt that process to our circumstances.

The specific requirements to implement those three main work products were not totally clear from the start, given that it was difficult to define the scope of that endeavor completely. We thus realized that we would have to identify those requirements and deal with potential change along the way.

At that time, agile methods and techniques for software development had been around for a few years, and after a slow but steady rise and spread they were starting to become really popular in the industry. One of the most popular agile methods, Scrum [4], was a great exponent of the impact that the agile trend was having on the industry.

Seeing that agile principles addressed the same problems we had (dealing with uncertainty via evolutionary development, as well as providing a flexible response to change), though in a different context (software development), we decided to study which of those practices could be applicable and useful to our case. For this purpose, we took several training courses and workshops on Scrum that helped us to understand it better and get a better vision of the framework as a whole. Once we had a better knowledge of Scrum, we decided to adopt some of its practices and adapt them to our own objectives.

One month after we started to work on our software product quality evaluation service, and while researching other standards related to evaluation, we found out about ISO/IEC 17025 [5]. This standard specifies the general requirements for laboratories to carry out tests and/or calibrations competently. To meet those requirements, laboratories have to implement a management system for their quality, administrative and technical operations.

Accreditation complying with ISO/IEC 17025 means the formal recognition by an accreditation body of the technical competency of the laboratory and its capability to provide correct and trustable results. In this regard, accreditation to ISO/IEC 17025 differs from certification to ISO 9001, which solely confirms that a company adheres to, and operates under, a documented quality system. To that end, accreditation bodies perform a thorough evaluation of laboratories, confirming that they:

- Count on qualified and experienced staff.
- Have the necessary equipment and infrastructure for suitable performance of their activities.
- Employ suitable and validated work methods and procedures.
- Perform techniques for quality evaluation of results.
- Inform their clients about test results in a suitable manner, providing clear and precise reports.
- Adhere to, and operate under, a quality system.

We considered that we would be making a valuable contribution in implementing a laboratory that would carry out tests consisting in the evaluation of software product quality; that is how AQC Lab emerged. We decided to pursue laboratory accreditation for several reasons:

- It would guarantee the integrity and competence of AQC Lab in its performance of software product quality evaluations.
- It would be a distinguishing feature and a key factor in keeping an edge over competition.
- Laboratory accreditation would result in an internationally-recognized service, as ISO/IEC 17025 is the best-known and most generally-accepted international standard for laboratory evaluation. In addition, accreditation bodies from different countries co-operate under multilateral agreements.

Implementing a laboratory that complied with ISO/IEC 17025 resulted in a whole new set of requirements, in addition to those we had already identified in relation to developing our software quality evaluation service. To meet the requirements of the laboratory accreditation scheme, we had to implement and document many different processes (both technical and administrative), produce formats, and keep records that documented and showed how those processes were carried out.

After a period of a year and a half of implementing, testing and validating our evaluation method, we carried out the first software quality evaluations for customers. Six months later, in 2012, AQC Lab became the first laboratory in the world to be given accreditation to perform software quality evaluation tests under ISO/IEC 17025.

The rest of the paper is organized as follows: in section 2 we discuss the two approaches to the adoption of Agile methodologies, which are either following them strictly or adapting them to fit the context of each project. In section 3 we describe how we adapted Scrum to implement AQC Lab. Section 4 presents the conclusions of the paper, describing what we found most useful in our adaptation of Scrum.

2   Adapting Agile Methods

Since the emergence of Agile methods, there has been dispute among Agile advocates over the issue of whether to adopt methods "by the book", or rather to adapt them to serve the specific context of each company or development team. Even though nowadays this dispute has been overcome for the most part, there are still some practitioners that hold opposing views regarding this matter.

On the one hand, there are Agile advocates, commonly known as evangelists, who encourage all projects to follow every single practice of the Agile method in question to the letter. They argue that adopting the method as a whole is the only way to take full advantage of it, and any deviation from what is established by their authors would result in not realizing its full benefits. A quote from Kent Beck about XP practices [6] sums this reasoning up: "No single practice works well by itself; each needs the other practices to keep them in balance".

One of the fathers of Scrum, Ken Schwaber, coined a term for any deviation from the rules, roles and time boxes established in Scrum: "ScrumBut" (a term that gained popularity; some people later turned this into the more humorous "ScrumButt"). A ScrumBut can therefore be considered as an inappropriate variation of Scrum that hampers the team from getting the most out of it. Schwaber explains that ScrumButs follow the pattern (*ScrumBut*) (*reason* or *excuse*) (*workaround*). An example of this would be "(We use Scrum, but) (having a daily scrum every day is too much overhead,) (so we only have one per week.)". This example shows a kind of adaptation that negates the advantages of Scrum. In this case, the tailoring leads to not knowing the real progress of the sprint at the right time, in the right way; that in turn, leads to the possibility that the goals established for that sprint may not be met.

On many occasions, ScrumButs have their origins in a dysfunction in the development team and its inability to fix it. This results in the modification of the method, not because that is what is intended, but because the bad habits in the team do not let them find the way to adopt the method correctly.

On the other hand, an increasing number of practitioners and researchers, as stated in [7], argue that Agile development methods and practices should be adapted to fit the context in which they are adopted. These authors contend that, as with any other kind of adaptation, a tailored method may indeed not represent a reasonable adaptation of the original method. The "wrongdoing", however, is not in the act of adaptation itself, but rather in the nature or scope of the adaptation when it is not done suitably. They consider that being restrictive in adapting Agile methods is a kind of a paradox, because, as Conboy and Fitzgerald conclude in [8], "the very name "agile" suggests that the method should be easily adjusted to suit its environment".

This approach to Agility is based on the idea that a project cannot be viewed as an independent part of its surrounding context. Rather, the method followed to manage the project is affected by the interaction of the development team and their organizational culture. It is difficult to keep any element that is external to the method from not affecting it in one way or another. Because of this, the practitioners that follow this approach stand for understanding how Agility can be adapted in context and take advantage of that situation. In this case, the main focus is on adapting the methods in a way that makes sense and improves the performance of the development team. This can only be done by understanding really well the purpose of the practices that will be adapted, introducing only the changes needed to make them work better in the context of each specific project or development team. Otherwise these adaptations, in the case of Scrum, would become negative Scrumbuts; the kind that make a team's performance worse.

There are practitioners and researchers, and we count ourselves among them, who believe that some of the Agile methodologies can even be adapted to other environments outside software development. A good example of this would be Scrum. This framework can be, and actually has been, adapted to different contexts other than software development, due to its strong focus on project management and its independence of specific technical practices.

For example, in [9], the authors present Score, an adaptation of Scrum to manage the mentoring of students in the context of an academic research group. The authors claim that ever since they have been carrying out some of the practices of Scrum, especially the daily scrum, the mentoring has been more efficient, and both the mentors and the students have benefitted from this new approach. For mentors, it is now easier to keep up-to-date with their students' progress, and when students are struggling, it takes less time to address what is not going right. Authors assert that students say they are more productive, more enthusiastic about research, and have better interactions with other students and with their adviser, feeling there is a real sense of community in the group since they began to use Score.

In [10], the author discusses how they applied an agile methodology in an academic environment, and provides insights for non-software industries on how agile is not a set of rigid rules, but a philosophy that can be applied to get maximally effective results with a mindset for continued change.

The authors of [11], among whom is Jeff Sutherland –co-creator of Scrum, together with Ken Schwaber -, describe how Scrum has been adopted in the sales and account management teams at the company iSense in the effort to take more control over the sales process they carry out. They conclude that implementing Scrum has led to escalating revenue and a sustainable competitive advantage.

On reading [12], we see how the author describes the experiences with Agile methods in a marketing department, as well as the series of adjustments they had to make to overcome some problems they had during the first months of adoption.

On a more exotic note, [13] describes how an Italian company producing luxury bathtubs and showers adopted Agile and Lean methods in many departments of the company, explaining how they adapted them to a non-software context.

The growing importance of Agile methods in project management is also reflected by the fact that the Project Management Institute (PMI) has developed a certification for project management practitioners who are adopting Agile approaches in their projects. This certification, known as PMI Agile Certified Practitioner (PMI-ACP), recognizes an individual's expertise in using agile practices in their projects, while demonstrating their increased professional versatility through agile tools and techniques.

In the next sub-section we set out how we adapted Scrum in the implementation of our laboratory for software product quality evaluation tests; this is an endeavor that not only involved software development, but also process implementation, as well as a great deal of research.

3   Implementing AQC Lab

Although Scrum was conceived as a software development framework, it centers on management practices. Being involved in the software industry, though not developing software ourselves, we at AQC saw that Scrum could be applied in contexts other than software development. In our case, we saw Scrum would be suited to our purpose of putting a software quality evaluation service into operation, which would later expand and turn into implementation of a laboratory, AQC Lab, accredited as complying with ISO/IEC 17025 for conducting software quality evaluation tests.

Implementing AQC Lab involved different high-level tasks that would in turn encompass more specific tasks:

- Defining a quality model based on ISO/IEC 25010. As the standard only defines the high-level elements of the model (quality characteristics and its sub-characteristics), we would have to define which metrics affect the characteristics and sub-characteristics. We would also need to specify how to aggregate and combine their values so as to obtain a reasonable indicator of the quality of the software evaluated. For this purpose, we would define a hierarchical model and the methods or functions for obtaining values of higher-level element from the values of the elements on lower levels. Initially, we centered on the characteristic of Maintainability and its five subcharacteristics.
- Defining an evaluation process based on ISO/IEC 25040. We would have to define the steps to take, along with the specific way to carry out the activities of the evaluation process described in ISO/IEC 25040.
- Developing an automated evaluation framework. Once we had decided which metrics would be part of the quality model, we would need to look for tools that allowed us to get their values from the products analyzed. It would also be necessary to develop a software system that took the values of the metrics and carried out their aggregation, thereby obtaining quality values for the high-level elements in the model. This system would consist of three parts: a "core" that performed the aggregations and stored the results of the evaluation in a database, a Maven plugin that allowed the automated execution of the "core", together with a web tool that showed the results of the evaluation in a helpful, attractive and practical way.
- Defining, documenting and establishing the Quality Management System of the laboratory. The QMS would consist of a Quality Manual, along with

administration and technical processes, technical instructions, records and formats. For example, some of the administration processes involved internal auditing, personnel training and qualification, documentation control, control of non-conformities, corrective and preventive actions, and management reviews. Some examples of the technical processes carried out are: result quality assurance, validation of the quality model, validation of the software analysis tools used in evaluations, report elaboration and test item manipulation. Some examples of technical instructions are the ones that define how to configure the execution of the different analysis tools in the context of the evaluation framework, as well as their installation and deployment.

Seeing that the scope of the matter at hand was quite vast and our team size was very small (three people), we saw fit to use an iterative and incremental approach. In addition, the scope of some of the tasks was uncertain initially, and we knew some of the requirements might change during the implementation; (for example, when we started the definition of our quality model and evaluation process, the ISO/IEC 25010 and ISO/IEC 25040 standards were still draft versions that might have changed once the final version was released).

Even though Scrum was developed with software development in mind, we found similarities between software development and what we had to do, as both are unique creative efforts that require the development of different components and demand knowledge in diverse areas. Nevertheless, our endeavor also entailed software development, since we had to develop the evaluation framework. For that task we were also able to take full advantage of Scrum.

All of these circumstances led us to choose Scrum as the best approach for managing the implementation of AQC Lab.

Of course, we knew there were also differences between implementing AQC Lab and developing software. For instance, the extent of research, experimentation and validation involved was larger in our case than what you typically have in a software development project. The particular circumstances of our context made it necessary to adapt some of the practices of Scrum, while at the same time ignoring some of the rules.

Below is a description of the adapted Scrum process that we followed:

- We kept the three roles described in Scrum. In our case there was no external client; because of that, the role of Product Owner was assigned to our CTO, as he had the appropriate characteristics: product vision and leadership. As we were a small team of just three people, the role of Scrum Master was shared by the same person as above, since he also had the best characteristics to fill this particular role; he possessed the capacity to facilitate the process, resolve impediments, enforce time boxes and promote improvement. The other two people made up the Development Team, although in the implementation of a few of the elements of the Product Backlog, the person holding the Product Owner/Scrum Master roles also took a small part in the Development Team. Having one person that plays both the roles of Scrum Master and Product Owner is considered among most practitioners to have potential for a conflict of interests, due to the fact that the same person is responsible for supporting and protecting the team, as well as for "pushing" the team to get more business value out of the product being developed. Even thought the potential for conflict exists, it does not necessarily have to materialize if the person playing both roles finds the right balance between the interests related to each of them. In a very small team without external client, the dual role solution is perfectly viable as long as the Scrum Master/Product Owner is able to support the team while ensuring they keep a sustainable development pace. In this case, time constraints may be the main problem to deal with, as performing the tasks related to both roles can be quite time-consuming.

- We kept all of the elements to implement in the Product Backlog (PB), and made it accessible for everyone via Google Docs (now Google Drive). The items in the PB were prioritized by the Product Owner. The PB was a living artifact, dividing the top-priority items into more specific and granular ones when we had enough knowledge to do so. Occasionally, implementing some items led to the discovery of new requirements, as well as to a change of scope; this was subsequently reflected in the PB. The whole team took part in estimating the effort that PB items would take.

- The effort required for the elements in the PB was not always as small as recommended by Scrum experts. Due to some of the items requiring a lot of research and trial and error, it was impossible to break them down into smaller items. For this same reason, some of the items did not fit a sprint, which meant that we broke one of the rules of Scrum.

- We had a Sprint Backlog (SB) for each Sprint. An example of the structure of the SB is given in Table 1. The items in the Sprint Backlog were extracted from the top-priority items in the PB. We kept the status of each item ("pending" – "done") in the SB, along with an estimate of the remaining time to be completed. This estimate was updated by the Development Team every day after the Daily Scrum. We also used Sprint burn-down charts to monitor the progress of the Sprint and the remaining effort, since the SB always had the information of the remaining effort updated to present estimates (Fig. 2 shows an example). The SB, like the PB, was accessible via Google Docs. We did not find it necessary to have a physical board to keep the information about the tasks, as we found it more useful to keep it centralized in the SB.

- We started each Sprint with a Sprint planning meeting where the whole team took part. The first point in this meeting was to establish the duration of the Sprint. At first, the Sprints were three weeks long, but we later decided to make them four weeks long, since the nature of the tasks (longer than what is usual in software development) made it feel more consistent to have longer Sprints. The main advantage of a shorter sprint is allowing the team to detect earlier if the product being developed does not meet the needs of the client. This way, the risk of developing the wrong product is reduced. In our case, this potential risk was not a problem, since the Product Owner attended the Daily Scrums and was completely aware of the progress being made during the Sprint. More information about the Sprints is given in Table 2. Once the duration of the Sprint was established, the team revised the PB and decided as a group which set of PB items would be implemented. The set was decided based on the priorities assigned by the Product Owner, as well as the effort estimation made by the whole team. Based on this information, the team would decide which set of items would be achievable in the time box established for the Sprint. Once the items were chosen, the whole team debated which tasks each item would entail and in which order they should be performed. The list of tasks to perform for each item was also included in the SB. The recommendation to have tasks that require one day or less of work was often difficult to fulfill, due to what has been explained above –the degree of research and experimentation involved. The planning meeting usually took us about an hour.

Table 1. Structure of the Sprint Backlog and example of part of its content during Sprint #9

PB Item	Remaining effort	Status	Tasks
Visualization module: AQC Lab-web	12	Pending	Pending: - Include Line chart for evolution of Characteristic values for selected project in Historic page - Include Line chart for evolution of Subharacteristic values for selected project in Historic page Done: - Include TreeMap chart with info from all projects in Home Page - Include Kiviat chart of selected project in Characteristic page - Include Kiviat chart of selected project in Subcharacteristic page ...
Validation of the test method	0	Done	Pending: Done: - Research and select software products to use in validation - Download source code of selected products - Evaluate selected products - Extract information from bug tracking systems
...	...	...	...

- In each Sprint, the team performed the different tasks for the PB items that had been committed to in a collaborative way. For the PB items that involved software development, the recommendations of Scrum were followed: the team focused on producing, within the Sprint, software that had been tested and which, at the end of the Sprint, actually worked. For other PB items, like documents or forms, we also tried to always have a revised version at the end of the Sprint.

Sprint #1 Burndown chart

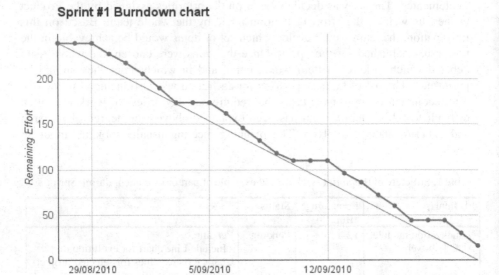

Fig. 1. Burn-down chart for Sprint #1. The line with dots shows the estimated remaining effort, which was updated after the Daily Scrum. The straight thin line represents the ideal trend. As we can see in this figure, the initial estimations were too optimistic and the team could not keep the velocity necessary to complete all the committed PB items.

- We conducted a Sprint review and retrospective meeting after every Sprint. We usually had the review meeting first, which took us about an hour; right afterwards, we had the planning meeting for the next Sprint. The whole team took part in the review, and the Product Owner led the discussion about which committed PB items had been done and which had not been carried out. The experimental nature of some of the tasks made them rather unpredictable as regards the effort they would take. Because of that, in the first Sprints our estimates were quite off target and usually there would be many unfinished items at the end of each Sprint. Nonetheless, as we gained experience, our estimates of the effort required for the PB items and related tasks got better, which led us to choose a more adequate amount of tasks to perform in later Sprints. After reviewing the work completed, the group then discussed what problems they had had during the Sprint, outlining how they were solved. We then had a live demonstration of the work products that involved software development (some elements of the evaluation framework). For other work products, we did not usually have a live demonstration of what had been done during the Sprint, because it was often the case that there was not a product to show *per se*. The result of a task would often be a document or a section of a document, and these results were reviewed as they were produced, not at the end of the Sprint. After the review, we would usually have a quick retrospective meeting to look back on and discuss the process. It usually took only a short time, as the whole team was comfortable with the process and we all felt few adjustments were necessary.

Table 2. Details of some Sprints in the implementation of AQC Lab

Sprint #	Dates	Main goals
01	27/08/10 - 21/09/10	Research and define Metrics for Maintainability. Research tools that provide values for the metrics in the Maintainability model.
02	21/09/10 – 15/10/10	Define functions to aggregate metric values and obtain values for high-level elements of the Maintainability model. Set thresholds for metric values.
03	18/10/10 – 12/11/10	Design the architecture of the evaluation framework. Document the Maintainability model. Produce the QMS Quality Manual. Refine metrics (filter rules from static source code analyzers).
04	15/11/10 – 03/12/10	Develop business domain and data layer of the evaluation framework. Document administrative procedures (documentation control, organization, and personnel). Document technical procedures (tool configuration).
05	03/12/10 – 24/12/10	Develop the evaluation engine of the evaluation framework (tool result integration and aggregation of values). Create personnel records (training, authorizations, etc.).
06	10/01/11 – 31/01/11	Develop the evaluation engine of the evaluation framework (tool result integration and aggregation of values). Define and document evaluation process (test method). Document administrative procedures (internal audits, management reviews).
07	31/01/11 – 18/02/11	Develop automation module of the evaluation framework (plugin for Maven). Document technical procedures (threshold revision). Create forms and records related to administrative procedures (document control, internal audits, etc.)
08	21/02/11 – 11/03/11	Develop visualization module of the evaluation framework (data visualization). Improve core of evaluation framework: improve multi-module product evaluation. Define procedure for validation of the test method.
...	...	...
22	02/05/12 – 01/06/12	Perform the internal audit. Carry out evaluation of product AAA for client BBB.
23	04/06/12 – 06/07/12	Define and implement corrective actions for non-conformities detected in internal audit. Carry out evaluation of product XXX for client YYY.
24	16/07/12 – 10/08/12	Receive accreditation audit. Produce documentation requested by accreditation body auditors. Define and implement corrective actions for non-conformities detected in accreditation audit.

- We conducted Daily Scrums; the whole team, including the Product Owner, took part in these. In these quick meetings each team member reported on what had been done the previous day, the problems he had faced, and what he would do that day. The Daily Scrums were usually kept to no more than fifteen minutes, though there were days on which discussing some topics (like how to tackle the problems the team members faced) would prolong the meeting. However, we sometimes found it useful to go beyond the fifteen minute time-box, since this gave us a good opportunity to share the vision of the Product Owner about topics that mattered to the development team.

4   Conclusions and Future Work

Methodologies and process frameworks, such as Scrum, are supported by a lot of effort and empirical research whose goal is to test how the practices they define interrelate and work together to attain their intended benefits. Each one of their components and practices serves a specific purpose and is essential to the successful usage of the methodology or process framework. In a nutshell, they are not part of the methodology simply because of some whim; teams have to take that into account when they adapt a methodology to their own circumstances.

Nonetheless, we advocate for a contextual approach to Agile methods, adapting the elements to suit the context in which they are adopted. It seems paradoxical to affirm that an Agile method cannot be adapted and that it must be followed strictly.

Even though it is a software development framework, we found Scrum really useful for our purpose of implementing a software evaluation laboratory. We believe, moreover, that it can be easily adapted to other contexts outside the realm of software development, since it focuses mainly on project management. We do concur that method adaptations have to be done carefully, though. You have to be perfectly clear about the purpose of each element of the method that you are changing, as well as how that change affects what really matters, i.e., the performance of the team.

We found Scrum to be really well-crafted for project management. It enabled us to get different levels of zoom on the information required to monitor the progress of the project:

- The Product Backlog provided us with a general snapshot of what has to be done, with the advantage that it was not a static snapshot, since it was updated constantly to reflect newly-discovered scope throughout the project. Moreover, this snapshot provided closer detail about what was most important at each point in time, via the priorities specified for its items.
- The Sprint Backlog provided a sharper focus on what was important within the time box of a month (or less). It allowed us to concentrate on the most urgent items, taking an incremental approach that made implementation easier.
- The Daily Scrum allowed us to know how we were progressing on a day-by-day basis. We found the Daily Scrum to be the most useful practice in Scrum, as it improved our decision-making by keeping the whole team involved. It made for

better performance; since everybody in the team knew what the others were doing, each individual could lend a hand to other members when they had issues to solve.

Achieving the accreditation may be considered a major milestone in the implementation of AQC Lab. However, that did not mean that we had reached the end of the road. Since the accreditation, we have been working on expanding the scope of the evaluations carried out by the laboratory; we are defining evaluation models for other quality characteristics, like Functional Suitability and Usability, or researching and developing tools to measure the metrics related to those characteristics; we are also researching tools to evaluate Maintainability on software products developed with other programming languages not supported initially, like Groovy and Objective C, etc. We are still using Scrum to manage all this work.

In addition, maintaining accreditation requires the continual improvement of the QMS that governs the activity of the laboratory. This correct operation and improvement is monitored by the accreditation body via follow-up audits. We have just received our first follow-up audit and we have had very positive feedback from the audit team. The effectiveness of our QMS is a consequence of the fact that we also use Scrum to manage the operation of AQC Lab, which involves carrying out software quality evaluation tests and performing administrative and technical activities, as well as implementing improvement actions.

Acknowledgements. This work has been funded by the GEODAS-BC project (Ministerio de Economía y Competitividad and Fondo Europeo de Desarrollo Regional FEDER, TIN2012-37493-C03-01) and by the ECU: Evaluación y Certificación de la fUncionalidad del Producto Software project (Consejería de Empleo y Economía y Fondo Europeo de Desarrollo Regional FEDER, 1313CALT0056).

References

1. SO/IEC 25000:2005 - Software Engineering – Software product Quality Requirements and Evaluation (SQuaRE) – Guide to SQuaRE. International Organization for Standardization, Geneva, Switzerland (2005)
2. ISO/IEC 25010:2011 - Software Engineering – Software product Quality Requirements and Evaluation (SQuaRE) – System and software quality models. International Organization for Standardization, Geneva, Switzerland (2005)
3. ISO/IEC 25040:2011 - Software Engineering – Software product Quality Requirements and Evaluation (SQuaRE) – Evaluation process. International Organization for Standardization, Geneva, Switzerland (2005)
4. Schwaber, K.: Scrum Development Process. In: Business Object Design and Implementation, pp. 117–134. Springer, London (1997)
5. ISO/IEC 17025:2005 - General requirements for the competence of testing and calibration laboratories. International Organization for Standardization, Geneva, Switzerland (2005)
6. Beck, K.: Extreme Programming Explained: Embrace Change. Addison-Wesley, Boston (2000)

7. Hoda, R., Kruchten, P., Noble, J., Marshall, S.: Agility in Context. In: Proceedings of the ACM International Conference on Object Oriented Programming Systems, Languages, and Applications (OOPSLA 2010), pp. 74–88. ACM, New York (2010)
8. Conboy, K., Fitzgerald, B.: The Views of Experts on the Current State of Agile Method Tailoring. In: McMaster, T., Wastell, D., Ferneley, E., DeGross, J.I. (eds.) Organizational Dynamics of Technology-Based Innovation: Diversifying the Research Agenda. IFIP International Federation for Information Processing, vol. 235, pp. 217–234. Springer, Heidelberg (2007)
9. Hicks, M., Foster, J.S.: Adapting Scrum to Managing a Research Group. Technical Report CS-TR-4966, University of Maryland, Department of Computer Science (2010)
10. Willeke, M.H.H.: Agile in Academics: Applying Agile to Instructional Design. In: Proceedings of the 2011 Agile Conference (AGILE 2011), pp. 246–251. IEEE Computer Society, Washington (2011)
11. van Solingen, R., Sutherland, J., de Waard, D.: Scrum in Sales: How to Improve Account Management and Sales Processes. In: Proceedings of the 2011 Agile Conference (AGILE 2011), pp. 284–288. IEEE Computer Society, Washington (2011)
12. DeFauw, R.: Can Marketing Go Agile? In: Proceedings of the 2012 Agile Conference (AGILE 2012), pp. 136–140. IEEE Computer Society (2012)
13. Mazzanti, G.: Agile in the Bathtub: Developing and Producing Bathtubs the Agile Way. In: Proceedings of the 2012 Agile Conference (AGILE 2012), pp. 197–203. IEEE Computer Society (2012)

Software Metrics in Agile Software: An Empirical Study

Giuseppe Destefanis[1], Steve Counsell[2], Giulio Concas[1], and Roberto Tonelli[1]

[1] DIEE, University of Cagliari, Italy
{giuseppe.destefanis,concas,roberto.tonelli}@diee.unica.it
[2] Brunel University, Kingston Lane, Uxbridge, UK
steve.counsell@brunel.ac.uk

Abstract. This paper presents a software metrics analysis of eight object-oriented systems. Five systems had been developed using Agile methodologies and three using plan-driven methodologies; three systems were written in Python and five in Java. For each system, we considered 10 traditional metrics such as LOC and the Chidamber and Kemerer metrics. These metrics were computed at class level. In our study we present empirical results considering systems developed with Agile methodologies and we compare them with previous results for non Agile systems. In particular, we verify that the distributions of software metrics in a software system developed using Agile methodologies does not differ from the distribution in systems developed using plan-driven methodologies.

Keywords: agile, software metrics, data mining, object-oriented programming.

1   Introduction

Software engineers have been trying to measure software to gain quantitative insights into its properties and quality since its inception. IEEE defines Software Engineering as the application of a "systematic, disciplined, quantifiable approach to the development, operation and maintenance of software." With the advent of the object-oriented (OO) approach, specific measures have been introduced to evaluate the quality of software systems. The rationale behind OO metrics is that a good design must keep complexity low, and this can be accomplished by minimising coupling and increasing cohesion. The first attempt in this direction was Chidamber and Kemerer's metrics suite (CK), and these have became the most popular OO metrics suite and the process of defining new measures is still a vibrant research area; that said, theoretical reasons supporting the adoption of specific metrics is not enough. Software engineers need to have empirical evidence that these metrics are actually related to software quality. Unfortunately, "software quality" is an elusive concept, software being an immaterial entity that cannot be physically measured in traditional ways. In general software quality has many different meanings, it is associated with practices that lead to software products that are accurate, effective, delivered on time and within budget.

G. Cantone and M. Marchesi (Eds.): XP 2014, LNBIP 179, pp. 157–170, 2014.
© Springer International Publishing Switzerland 2014

It is still difficult to relate software metrics to the phenomena we want to improve and to reduce the complexity of software, new development methodologies and tools are being introduced.In particular, to our knowledge, there are no studies investigating the distribution of traditional metrics in software developed using Agile methodologies. [19].

In this paper, we attempt to present the results about software metrics distributions on 8 open source software system, (5 developed using Agile methodologies, 3 developed using plan-driven methodologies, 5 developed using Java, 3 developed using Python) in order to study possible differences due to Agile methodologies. We considered the following systems:

- **FlossAR** [4]: a program to manage the Register of Research of universities and research institutes. floss-AR was developed with a full OO approach and released with GPL v.2 open source license.
- **jAPS (Java Agile Portal System)** [5] is a Web application, implemented through a specialization of an open source software project that is a Java framework for Web portal creation. This system is certified as a software developed using Agile methodologies.
- **OpenErp** [7]: OpenERP is an open-source enterprise resource planning (ERP) software actively programmed, supported, and organized by OpenERP s.a. OpenERP similar to many open source projects where customized programming, support and other services are also provided by an active global community and partner network. OpenERP is developed using agile software development and test-driven development methodologies.
- **OpenBravo** [6]: Openbravo ERP is a web-based ERP business solution for small and medium sized companies released under the Openbravo Public License, the program is among the top ten most active projects of Sourceforge as of January 2008. OpenBravo is also known as Openbravo Agile Erp.
- **Zope** [8]: Zope is a community project concerned with free and open-source, OO web application server written in the Python programming language. Zope stands for "Z Object Publishing Environment" and was the first system using the now common object publishing methodology for the Web. Zope has been recognized as a Python killer app, an application that helped put Python in the spotlight. The Zope project pioneered the practice of sprints for open source software development. Sprints are intensive development sessions when programmers, often from different countries, gather in one room and work together for a couple of days or even several weeks. During the sprints, various practices drawn from agile software development are used, such as pair programming and test-driven development
- **Ant** [1]: Apache Ant is a software tool for automating software build processes. It is similar to Make but is implemented using the Java language, requires the Java platform and is best suited to building Java projects.
- **Weka (Waikato Environment for Knowledge Analysis)** [3] is a popular suite of machine learning software written in Java, developed at the University of Waikato, New Zealand. Weka is free software available under the GNU General Public License.

- **Blender** [2]: Blender is a free and open-source 3D computer graphics software product used for creating animated films, visual effects, art, 3D printed models, interactive 3D applications and video games.

OpenERP and OpenBravo are both ERP systems developed using Agile methodologies but written using different languages: OpenERP in Python, OpenBravo in Java (information about the use of Agile methodologies are available on their respective websites [7], [6]). This fact is interesting for evaluating differences between programming languages. For Japs and Zope it is possible to check information about Agile methodologies during development phases on respective websites. Regarding to floss-AR system, according to further discussions with the developers team, the following Agile practices have been applied:

- Pair programming
- Stand Up Meeting
- Refactoring
- On Site Customer

Pair Programming is an Agile Software development technique in which two developers work together at one workstation. The driver writes code while the observer reviews each line of code. A Stand Up Meeting is a daily team meeting held to provide a status update to the team members. Refactoring is the process of restructuring an existing body of code altering its internal structure without changing its external behavior. On Site Customer describes the need to have on-site access to people who have the authority and ability to provide information pertaining to the system being developed and to make pertinent and timely decisions regarding the requiriments. Results presented in this paper are not conclusive because we have analyzed only open source software; the link between open source development and the Agile methodology is under-researched - Adams et al. [10] studied gaps between Agile development and open source development. This work is a starting point and clearly, further research is needed to prove and validate differences between metrics distributions generated by Agile methodologies and those generated by plan-driven methodologies, especially considering proprietary software developed by companies.

In this paper, we answer the following research questions:

- **RQ1:** Is it possible to recognize the use of Agile methodologies through the analysis of software metrics?
- **RQ2:** Metrics distributions generated from software developed using Agile methodologies are similar to metrics distributions generated from software developed using plan-driven methodologies?
- **RQ3:** It is possible to assert that metric distributions generated from Agile methodologies are related to better quality software?

All data considered in this paper are available online at http://agile.diee.unica.it/xp2014.

2   Related Work

Several studies have analyzed software metric distributions with regard to study software quality and to define a methodology for guiding the softare process development, but to our knowledge no studies have tried to analyze the relationship between software metrics and software development methodologies as Agile processes. Therefore many empirical studies have been performed to validate empirically the CK suite from these two aspects, showing an acceptable correlation between CK metrics values and software fault-proneness and difficulty of maintenance [11], [12], [13], [14]. Other OO metrics suites have also been proposed, MOOD [17] and by Lorenz and Kidd [18], but the CK suite is by far the most popular.

In Adams et al. [9] it is argued that the impact of certain Agile practices (in this case, specifically sprinting) on a Free Software project can be partially assessed through analysis of code repository logs, using average commits per day as a metric. In the paper, sprints from two Free Software projects (Plone and KDE PIM) are assessed and two hypotheses are formulated: do sprints increase productivity? Are Free Software projects more productive after sprints compared with before? The primary contribution of the paper is to show how sprinting creates a large increase in productivity both during the event and immediately after the event itself: this argues for more in-depth studies focussing on the nature of sprinting.

Adams et al. in [10] argue that it is possible to quantify the level of agility displayed by Open Source projects. An indicator of agility, the Mean Developer Engagement (MDE) metric is introduced and tested through the analysis of public project data. Projects sampled from two repositories (KDE and SourceForge) are studied and a hypothesis is formulated: projects from the two samples display a similar level of MDE. The paper provides two main contributions: first, the MDE metric is shown to vary significantly between the KDE and SourceForge projects. Second, by combining MDE with a project's lifespan, it is also shown that SourceForge projects have insufficient uptake of new developers resulting in more active, shorter, initial activity and in a quicker "burning out" of the projects.

Concas et al. [15] present an extensive analysis of software metrics for 111 OO systems written in Java. For each system, authors considered 18 traditional metrics such as LOC and CK metrics, as well as metrics derived from complex network theory and social network analysis; they also considered two metrics at system level, namely the total number of classes and interfaces and the fractal dimension. They discuss the distribution of these metrics and their correlation both at class and system level. They found that most metrics followed a leptokurtotic distribution. Only a couple of metrics have patent normal behaviour while three others are very irregular and even bimodal.

In Concas et al. [16] the authors present a comprehensive study of an implementation of the Smalltalk OO system, one of the first and purest OO programming environment, searching for scaling laws in its properties. They studied ten system properties, including the distributions of variable and method names, inheritance hierarchies, class and method sizes, system architecture graph. They systematically found Pareto or log-normal distributions in these properties. Programming activity, even when modelled from a statistical perspective, can not be modelled as a random addition of independent increments with finite variance; it exhibits strong organic dependencies on what has been already developed. There is a comparison of the results with similar results obtained for large Java systems. The work shows how the Yule process is able to stochastically model the generation of several of the power-laws found, identifying the process parameters and comparing theoretical and empirical tail indexes. The authors discuss how the distributions found are related to existing OO metrics such as CK's and how they could provide a starting point for measuring the quality of a whole system, versus that of single classes. In fact, the usual evaluation of systems based on mean and standard deviation of metrics can be misleading.

3   Methodology

The aim of this paper is to investigate possible relationship between software metrics obtained from software developed using Agile methodologies and software developed using plan-driven methodologies. Our corpus includes: OpenERP, OpenBravo, Zope, Japs, Ant, Weka, FlossAR, Japs.

We built the software graph of each project analyzing the source code, where the nodes of the graph are associated to the classes of the system. Using this graph, we computed 10 metrics on each node of the graph. We designed and wrote all the code for building the software graph and for computing on it all the considered metrics. The statistical analysis on the results were performed using R.

- IFANIN: Number of immediate base classes;
- NOC: Number of Children (CK): number of directed subclasses of the class;
- NIM: Number of instance methods, methods defined in a class that are only accessible through an object of that class;
- NIV: Number of instance variables, variables defined in a class that are only accessable through an object of that class;
- WMC: Weigthed methods per class (CK), a weighted sum of all the methods defined in a class.
- RFC: Response For a Class (CK): the sum of the number of methods defined in the class and the cardinality of the set of methods called by them and belonging to external classes.
- LOC: Lines of code of the class, excluding blank lines and comments.
- CLOC: Lines of comments of the class.
- NOfS: number of declared statement;
- DIT: Depth of Inheritance Tree (CK), length of longest path from a given class to the root class in the inheritance hierarchy.

For each metric, we computed five statistics on all the classes of a system, aimed at giving a global measure of the value of the metrics for all the classes of the system. These statistics are:

- Mean: the mean of the metric;
- Median: the median of the metric;
- First Quartile: lower quartile = 25th percentile (splits off the lowest 25% of data from the highest 75%);
- Third Quartile: upper quartile = 75th percentile (splits off the highest 25% of data from the lowest 75%);
- Standard deviation of the metric.

We calculated the complementary cumulative distribution function (CCDF) for each metric to assess the distribution type. All CCDF representations of metrics considered in this paper are available at http://agile.diee.unica.it/xp2014. We have reported the most interesting in the results section.

4 Results

Table 1, shows caratheristics of our corpus in terms of development language, Agile methodologies (Yes if used, No if not used), number of classes. In the high part of the table there are systems developed using plan-driven methodologies, in the lower part of the table are systems developed using Agile methodologies (we mantain this convention in the other tables of the paper).

Table 1. Corpus description

System	Language	Agile	# of Classes
Ant	Java	No	1670
Blender	Python	No	2276
Weka	Java	No	1934
FlossAR	Java	Yes	1441
Japs	Java	Yes	456
OpenBravo	Java	Yes	1513
OpenERP	Python	Yes	1741
Zope	Python	Yes	6852

The corpus is homogeneus enough considering the size (number of classes) of analyzed systems, except for Japs and Zope. The first has 456 classes and the latter 6852 classes. This is a desired work set in order to test hypothesis considering two outliers. As may be seen below (tabs. 2,4,5,6) there is no evident relationship between number of classes and the average value of metrics considered. The first result is related to metrics differences between systems developed in Java and systems developed in Python. Python is a general-purpose, high-level OO programming language. Its design philosophy emphasizes code readability and its syntax allows programmers to express concepts in fewer lines of code than would be possible in languages such as Java. The language provides constructs intended to enable clear programs on both a small and large scale.

Table 2 shows LOC statistics from the analyzed systems and the average LOC (per class) of systems developed using Python are significantly lower than systems developed in Java (regardless of the development methodology used). It is well known that the LOC metric is well related with code defects [23], and the Python language allows the developer to mantain a low level of LOC. Blender has 38.14 as average LOC value against 80.87 of Ant and 130,9 of Weka. Considering the use of Agile methodologies tab. 2 shows that there is no influence: FlossAR has 122.1 (higher than Ant), OpenBravo 137.5, and OpenERP 67.14 (higher than Blender). OpenERP and OpenBravo are ERP systems (management systems) and there are several large classes (in terms of lines of code) related to database writing and reading operations.

Table 2. Lines of Code

System	Min	1st Qu	Median	Mean	3rd Qu	Max	Sd
Ant	0	12	34	80.87	90	1586	137.52
Blender	1	9	18	38.14	37	1892	80.91
Weka	2	8	35	130.9	147	4078	247.27
FlossAR	2	41	96	122.1	142	6198	204.8
Japs	0	27.75	54.5	78.78	102.2	595	78.82
OpenBravo	1	24	65	137.5	156	3330	229.7
OpenERP	1	12	29	67.14	70	3686	143.15
Zope	1	4	11	33.57	33	1227	72.4

From Tab.3 we considered the number of lines related to code comments. Tab.3 shows that systems developed using Python have a low average value of CLOC (Blender 3.32, OpenERP 4.4, Zope 3.04) and one tentative proposal might be that the design philosophy of Python language emphasizes code readability reducing comments.

Table 3. Comment line of code

System	Min	1st Qu	Median	Mean	3rd Qu	Max	Sd
Ant	0	1	13	45.45	47	1319	94.92
Blender	0	0	0	3.32	2	289	13.16
Weka	0	0	12	65.82	83.75	1141	115.77
FlossAR	0	4	23	36.14	47	1342	57.47
Japs	0	0	5	13.05	18	122	19.55
OpenBravo	0	0	3	21.98	18	870	59.7
OpenERP	0	0	0	4.4	2	384	17.85
Zope	0	0	0	3.04	1	303	11.94

The second result is that systems developed using Agile methodologies are less commented than systems developed using plan-driven methodologies. Support for this interpretation comes from fast development and frequent releases

Table 4. DIT

System	Min	1st Qu	Median	Mean	3rd Qu	Max	Sd
Ant	0	1	2	2.29	3	7	1.23
Blender	0	1	1	1.03	1	6	0.61
Weka	1	1	1	1.89	2	7	1.38
FlossAR	1	1	1	1.71	2	5	0.87
Japs	1	2	3	2.55	3	6	1.08
OpenBravo	0	1	2	2.38	4	5	1.3
OpenERP	0	1	1	1.47	2	5	0.89
Zope	0	1	1	1.66	2	10	1.43

Table 5. RFC

System	Min	1st Qu	Median	Mean	3rd Qu	Max	Sd
Ant	2	17	29	42.37	58	663	34.44
Blender	0	1	2	3.57	3	119	6.78
Weka	13	14	21	95.26	51.75	890	200.8
FlossAR	13	21	25	27.53	30	112	11.92
Japs	13	22	30	36.21	44	114	20.02
OpenBravo	1	18	33	47.01	93	135	32.73
OpenERP	0	1	3	13.33	12	150	26.47
Zope	0	1	4	11.77	12	251	23.64

Table 6. WMC

System	Min	1st Qu	Median	Mean	3rd Qu	Max	Sd
Ant	0	2	4	8.08	10	125	10.82
Blender	0	1	2	2.39	2	84	4.41
Weka	0	1	3	8.63	11	127	12.5
FlossAR	0	4	9	10.85	13	99	10.2
Japs	0	3	6	8.74	12	55	7.72
OpenBravo	0	2	4	7.2	8	122	10.44
OpenERP	0	1	2	3.83	4	106	6.93
Zope	0	0	2	3.42	4	207	6.65

characterizing Agile methodologies. Data from Tab.4 shows that also considering the DIT metric it is not possible to highlight the use of Agile methodologies. As tab.4 shows, there is not a significant difference (Mean column) between the two groups. Differences exist between software developed in Python and software developed in Java.

Tabs.5 and 6 show that for the RFC and WMC metrics it is not possible to distinguish the use of Agile methodologies. No significant differences were found between the non-Agile set and Agile set. Also in this case, differences exists between software developed in Python and software developed in Java. Figs. 1, 2, 3, present the CCDF ditributions considering LOC, RFC and WMC. It is

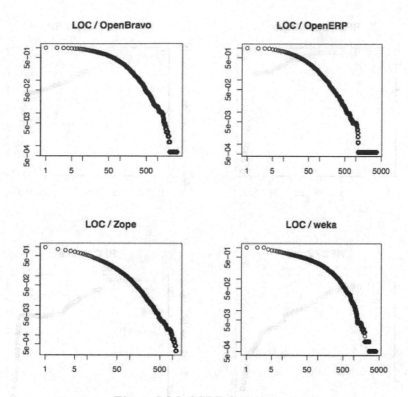

Fig. 1. LOC CCDF distributions

apparent from these figures that there are not differences (in terms of CCDF) between software developed using Agile methodologies and software developed using plan-driven methodologies. Considering Fig.6 that contains CCDF distributions of the WMC metric, there is an evident difference between Blender and the others systems. The difference is due to the language; Blender is developed using Python and as can be seen from Tab.6, the mean value of WMC for systems developed in Python (Blender, Zope, OpenERP) is lower than the mean value for systems developed using Java.

4.1   Discussion

According to these results, we can now answer to the research questions:
RQ1: Is it possible to recognize the use of Agile methodologies during the software devolopment process analyzing software metrics?
The answer to this research question is negative. According to Tabs 2, 5, 6, 4 and considering Figs. 1,2,3 the metrics distributions of classes across systems are approximately the same. These empirical results suggest that the use of Agile methodologies and programming practices does not influence the distribution of metrics in the classes.

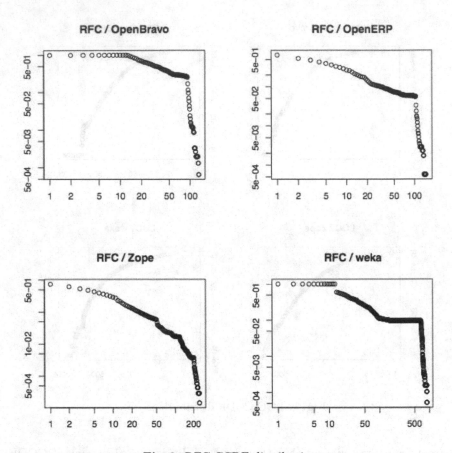

Fig. 2. RFC CCDF distributions

RQ2: Metrics distributions generated from software developed using Agile methodologies are similar to metrics distributions generated from software developed using plan-driven methodologies?

The answer is yes, as it is possible to see in Figs. 1,2, 3, the CCDF ditributions are the same. Small differences exist in the RFC ditribution of Zope, but considering our data it is not possible to assert that there differences due to use of Agile methodologies.

RQ3: It is possible to assert that metrics distribution generated from Agile methodologies are related to better quality of software?

The answer is negative; metrics distributions are practically the same. In systems developed using Agile methodologies, the LOC distribution does not demonstrate major differences. Considering the average values for each software project under consideration, we obtain similar values. Even in systems developed in Python, which still requires fewer lines of code to express a concept (compared to Java), the LOC distribution is similar to LOC distribution obtained from system developed using Java.

In conclusion, the development methodology does not seem to affect metric distributions.

5   Threats to Validity

Threats to construct validity are related to the Agile methodologies not used during the system's development (like TDD and continuous integration). This may influence our conclusion that the use of agile methodologies may improve software quality, given that Agile development has been adopted partially. Threats to external validity are related to generalization of our conclusions. With regard to the system studied in this work we considered only open source systems written in Java and Python and this could affect the generality of the study; our results are not meant to representative of all environments or programming languages. Commercial software is typically developed using different platforms and technologies, with strict deadlines and cost limitation and by developers with different experiences.

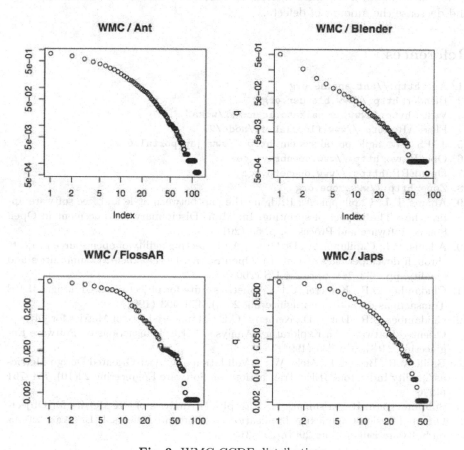

Fig. 3. WMC CCDF distributions

6   Conclusions

In this paper, we presented an analysis of a set of software metrics, performed on 8 number of open source Systems (3 written in Python, 5 written in Java, 5 developed using Agile methodologies, 3 developed using plan-driven methodologies). The size, in classes, of the analyzed projects ranges from 456 to 6852. Overall, we analyzed 17882 classes. The motivation of this work was to understand metric distributions in Agile open source software and to highlight potentially interesting features of software metrics. Our analysis shows that the metrics distribution among systems remains roughly the same as that found in non Agile systems. Thus, the adoption of Agile methodologies does not influence such distribution.

We can conclude that software metrics may be helpful in evaluating the quality of an Agile software project during the development process. A tool like the one used in the present work could be used in order to monitor the different stages of development and possibly to control the temporal evolution of each category of metrics. Considering the natural adaptiveness of Agile development, it could be useful to monitor software metrics in order to increase the software quality and decrease the amount of defects.

References

1. Ant: http://ant.apache.org
2. Blender: http://www.blender.org/
3. Weka: http://www.cs.waikato.ac.nz/ml/weka/
4. Floss-AR: http://www.flosslab.it/node/20
5. JAPS: Java agile portal system, http://www.japsportal.org
6. OpenBravo: http://www.openbravo.com
7. OpenERP: https://www.openerp.com
8. Zope: http://www.zope.org
9. Adams, P.J., Capiluppi, A.: Bridging the gap between agile and free software approaches: The impact of sprinting. In: Multi-Disciplinary Advancement in Open Source Software and Processes, p. 54 (2011)
10. Adams, P.J., Capiluppi, A., De Groot, A.: Detecting agility of open source projects through developer engagement. In: Open Source Development, Communities and Quality, pp. 333–341. Springer US (2008)
11. Chidamber, S.R., Kemerer, C.F.: A metrics suite for object oriented design. IEEE Transactions on Software Engineering 20(6), 476–493 (1994)
12. Chidamber, S.R., Darcy, D., Kemerer, C.F.: Managerial Use of Metrics for Object-Oriented Software: An Exploratory Analysis. IEEE Transactions on Software Engineering 24(8), 629–639 (1998)
13. Basili, V.R., Briand, L., Melo, W.: A Validation of Object-Oriented Design Metrics as Quality Indicators. IEEE Transactions on Software Engineering 22(10), 751–761 (1996)
14. Subramanyam, R., Krishnan, M.S.: Empirical Analysis of CK Metrics for Object-Oriented Design Complexity: Implications for Software Defects. IEEE Transactions on Software Engineering 29(4), 297–310 (2003)

15. Concas, G., Marchesi, M., Murgia, A., Pinna, S., Tonelli, R.: Assessing traditional and new metrics for object-oriented systems. In: Proceedings of the 2010 ICSE Workshop on Emerging Trends in Software Metrics, pp. 24–31. ACM (2010)
16. Concas, G., Marchesi, M., Pinna, S., Serra, N.: Power-laws in a large object-oriented software system. IEEE Transactions on Software Engineering 33(10), 687–708 (2007)
17. Brito e Abreu: The MOOD Metrics Set. In: Proc. ECOOP 1995 Workshop on Metrics (1995)
18. Lorenz, M., Kidd, J.: Object-oriented software metrics: a practical guide. Prentice-Hall, Inc., Upper Saddle River (1994)
19. Agile Manifesto, http://www.agilemanifesto.org
20. Mohammad, A., Li, W.: An empirical study of system design instability metric and design evolution in an agile software process. Journal of Systems and Software 74(3), 269–274 (2005)
21. Alshayeb, M., Li, W.: An empirical validation of object-oriented metrics in two different iterative software processes. IEEE Transactions on Software Engineering 29(11), 1043–1049 (2003)
22. Olague, H.M., et al.: Empirical validation of three software metrics suites to predict fault-proneness of object-oriented classes developed using highly iterative or agile software development processes. IEEE Transactions on Software Engineering 33(6), 402–419 (2007)
23. Zhang, H.: An investigation of the relationships between lines of code and defects. In: IEEE International Conference on Software Maintenance, ICSM 2009. IEEE (2009)
24. Dorairaj, S., Noble, J., Malik, P.: Understanding Team Dynamics in Distributed Agile Software Development. In: Wohlin, C. (ed.) XP 2012. LNBIP, vol. 111, pp. 47–61. Springer, Heidelberg (2012)
25. Bachmann, A., Bernstein, A.: Software process data quality and characteristics: a historical view on open and closed source projects. In: IWPSE-Evol 2009 Proceedings of the Joint International and Annual ERCIM Workshops on Principles of Software Evolution (IWPSE) and Software Evolution (Evol) Workshops. ACM (2009)
26. Dybå, T., Dingsyr, T.: Empirical studies of agile software development: A systematic review. Information and Software Technology 50(9), 833–859 (2008)
27. Concas, G., Marchesi, M., Destefanis, G., Tonelli, R.: An empirical study of software metrics for assessing the phases of an agile project. International Journal of Software Engineering and Knowledge Engineering 22, 525–548 (2012)
28. Tasharofi, S., Ramsin, R.: Process Patterns for Agile Methodologies. In: Ralyté, J., Brinkkemper, S., Henderson-Sellers, B. (eds.) Proceeding of: Situational Method Engineering: Fundamentals and Experiences, Geneva, Switzerland, September 12-14. IFIP – The International Federation for Information Processing, vol. 244, pp. 222–237. Springer, Boston (2007)
29. Martin, R.: Agile Software Development: Principles, Patterns, and Practices. Prentice Hall PTR, Upper Saddle River (2003)
30. Hoda, R., Noble, J., Marshall, S.: How much is just enough?: some documentation patterns on Agile projects. In: Proceedings of the 15th European Conference on Pattern Languages of Programs (EuroPLoP 2010), Article 13, 13 pages. ACM, New York (2010)

31. Martinez, J., Diaz, J., Perez, J., Garbajosa, J.: Software Product Line Engineering Approach for Enhancing Agile Methodologies. In: Abrahamsson, P., Marchesi, M., Maurer, F. (eds.) XP 2009. LNBIP, vol. 31, pp. 247–248. Springer, Heidelberg (2009)

32. Olague, H.M., et al.: An empirical validation of objectoriented class complexity metrics and their ability to predict errorprone classes in highly iterative, or agile, software: a case study. Journal of Software Maintenance and Evolution: Research and Practice 20(3), 171–197 (2008)

33. Hartmann, D., Dymond, R.: Appropriate agile measurement: Using metrics and diagnostics to deliver business value. In: Agile Conference 2006. IEEE (2006)

34. Frank, M., Martel, S.: On the productivity of agile software practices: An industrial case study (2002) (retrieved september 20, 2004)

35. Concas, G., Destefanis, G., Marchesi, M., Ortu, M., Tonelli, R.: Micro Patterns in Agile Software. In: Baumeister, H., Weber, B. (eds.) XP 2013. LNBIP, vol. 149, pp. 210–222. Springer, Heidelberg (2013)

36. Olague, Hector, M., et al.: An empirical validation of objectoriented class complexity metrics and their ability to predict errorprone classes in highly iterative, or agile, software: a case study. Journal of Software Maintenance and Evolution: Research and Practice 20(3), 171–197 (2008)

Visualizing Testing Activities to Support Continuous Integration: A Multiple Case Study

Agneta Nilsson, Jan Bosch, and Christian Berger

Software Engineering Division, Dpmt of Computer Science and Engineering, Chalmers University of Technology, University of Gothenburg, Gothenburg, Sweden

Abstract. While efficient testing arrangements are the key for software companies that are striving for continuous integration, most companies struggle with arranging these highly complex and interconnected testing activities. There is often a lack of an adequate overview of companies' end-to-end testing activities, which tend to lead to problems such as double work, slow feedback loops, too many issues found during post-development, disconnected organizations, and unpredictable release schedules. We report from a multiple-case study in which we explore current testing arrangements at five different software development sites. The outcome of the study is a visualization technique of the testing activities involved from unit and component level to product and release level that support the identification of improvement areas. This model for visualizing the end-to-end testing activities for a system has been used to visualize these five cases and has been validated empirically.

Keywords: continuous integration, software testing, and visualization.

1 Introduction

Software development companies are increasingly striving towards continuous integration in their efforts to deliver high quality software faster and faster. Continuous integration is an agile development practice, which has become increasingly popular with the growing agile movement [1], [2]. The agile movement advocates flexibility, efficiency, and speed to meet the ever-changing customer requirements and market needs. Continuous integration is about *integrating* software parts in order to assembling a complete system *continuously*, i.e. frequently, and throughout all phases in the development cycle [3].

The anticipated benefits of continuous integration are e.g. to improve release frequency and predictability, increase developer productivity, and improve communication [4]. However, there is currently no consensus on continuous integration as a single homogeneous practice, and there are great differences of experienced benefits in both literature and practice [4]. Many software development companies are struggling to achieve continuous integration and the benefits they were expecting.

G. Cantone and M. Marchesi (Eds.): XP 2014, LNBIP 179, pp. 171–186, 2014.

One common and well-known bottleneck when introducing continuous integration is testing [1], particularly for large and complex software with many dependencies such as software intensive embedded systems. Efficient testing arrangements are the key for achieving continuous integration, and arranging these are highly complex. The complexity faced by developers and test engineers often leads to problems such as double work, slow feedback-loops, too many issues still present in the post-development, disconnected organizations, and unpredictable release schedules due to issues identified lately. In this multiple case study, we explore current testing arrangements at five different software development sites (four companies). We aim to improve our understanding of how testing activities are arranged, and how to support companies in their efforts towards continuous integration by providing right communications means about test efforts throughout the process.

The rest of the paper is structured as follows: In Section 2, related work is discussed; Section 3 describes the approach, which we have followed to realize our case study with five different development sites; Section 4 summarizes the challenges in testing, with which the companies that we have investigated are faced; Section 5 introduces our "CIViT" Continuous Integration Visualization Technique that helps companies to describe intuitively their testing efforts. Section 6 validates our CIViT model before our article closes with a conclusion and an outlook for future work.

2   Background and Related Work

Continuous integration is the consequent continuation of applying unit tests and automated regression testing as quality assurance during the software development. In its most agile variant, teams evolve towards test-driven (TDD) or even test-first development, where new code is only added to fulfill the previously added test cases, which formally describe the function to be realized [5]. Large companies even of the size of Google are nowadays not only able to implement the concept of test-driven development for a large variety of products ranging from "software only" up to "software/hardware" products"; they are also able to coach and improve their product development teams towards a better project hygiene and better and faster ways of testing [6].

The goal for this paper is to make the currently applied testing activities explicit to all involved stakeholders. Therefore, a suitable visualization technique is the basis for the communication between these different parties. To evaluate existing visualization techniques, we addressed the following research question: Which visualization techniques for testing activities are available that (criterion 1) focus on the entire product deployment/release process, (criterion 2) are proven to be successfully applicable in industrial contexts, and (criterion 3) considered to be the important decision support methodology to improve the overarching testing processes towards continuous integration?

We re-evaluated the results from the systematic literature review [4], performed by one of the co-authors together with another researcher, to address the aforementioned research question. Holck and Jørgensen [3] analyze the continuous integration process on the example of open source software (OSS) FreeBSD (operating system) and Mozilla (web browser suite). Due to the different nature of OSS, which – as they state – is "focusing on stability and performance" in their examples, a comparison to business-value driven commercial products is difficult. Therefore, the aforementioned three criteria are not applicable to their examples. Furthermore, their work does not suggest a taxonomy for describing and visualizing the dependencies and drawbacks of the currently applied software quality assurance process.

A number of studies report on various ways to communicate build status. In the work from Sturdevant [7], the adaptation of the freely available tool CruiseControl is outlined with the focus of the support for test process itself. Concerning the aforementioned criteria, the author focuses on end-to-end testing (criterion 1) applied at Jet Propulsion Labs (criterion 2) mainly considering cost-efficiency of testing (criterion 3). However, in contrast to our work, no specific visualization technique is suggested or applied with different dimensions to outline deficiencies of the surrounding test process.

Downs et al. [8] provide guidelines for build monitoring systems in their work. They focus on how problems from broken builds or defects committed to a centralized repository are utilized within a software development team. Concerning our research question, they investigate only communication among developers and testers (criterion 1) by conducting interviews with software developers and testers (criterion 2) to derive guidelines how communication channels between developers and testers should be utilized (criterion 3). In contrast to our work, they do not focus on visualization of inefficiencies of the overall test process.

Stolberg presents in his work a technical description of a continuous integration framework [9] by following Fowler's checklist of 10 practices for continuous integration. Thus, he was able to visualize the status quo of the quality assurance process before and after implementing a continuous integration environment. Thus, his work focuses on the entire test and deployment process (criterion 1) using an experience report within an industrial setting (criterion 2). As results, continuous integration improved the quality assurance (criterion 3), however in contrast to our work, he did not propose a visualization scheme to unveil testing process bottlenecks.

Kim et al. present in their works [10], [11] a technical description of a test automation framework by applying the tool CruiseControl. They mainly focus on the test automation technology (criterion 1) applied to an industrial context (criterion 2) to improve the communication between involved stakeholders (criterion 3). However, they do not visualize the test process and its inefficiencies at large as we propose in our work.

Hoffman et al. [12] describe in their work how the tool chain cmake/ctest/cdash/cpack has been applied to a research lab of the Department of Defense. This work was mainly driven by employees of the supporting company of the aforementioned tools and thus, should be considered as an experience report. With respect to our research question, they focus on all aspects of the test and deployment process but from the tool support perspective (criterion 1) in the context of a research lab for high-performance computing (criterion 2). They conclude that the proposed tool chain is effective (criterion 3), however, they do not describe how to visualize the current status of the test process at large to derive improvement initiatives.

Ablett et al. [13] present "BuildBot" as a means to enforce the fixing of broken builds. With respect to our research question, they focus only on results from a continuous integration server (criterion 1) evaluated among a group of students (criterion 2). Thus, no evidence is given for industrial benefits (criterion 3). In comparison to our work, they do not focus on the overall test process and a subsequent visualization of its dependencies and deficiencies.

Yuksel et al. [14] present a technical description of a test automation framework. Regarding the aforementioned criteria, they are partly focusing on the entire process, which still includes some manual tasks (criterion 1), to ensure the quality of multi-platform control system (criterion 2); they achieve an improved quality of the code but they do not visualize interdependencies or deficiencies of the overall test process. However, they summarize the status of automation and periodicity in a tabular representation, which includes similar dimensions as we propose for our visualization technique. In contrast to our technique however, they do not describe the test process in a comparable granularity including dependencies to derive actions for the responsible management for improving the test process.

Lacoste describes in his work the introduction of continuous integration for the tool "LaunchPad", which is used by several open source software projects [15]. Concerning our research question, his work focuses to run test-suites before integrating newly added features (criterion 1) by applying them to the widely used software "LaunchPad" (criterion 2). As a result, the testing process could improve its efficiency (criterion 3) but in contrast to our work, no visualization of interdependencies and bottlenecks is provided.

Goodman and Elbaz provide an experience report [16] focusing on the entire deployment/release process (criterion 1) for an industrial project (criterion 2). Their work confirms the need of an adequate visualization scheme for the test process to make inefficiencies in the infrastructure explicit to the management e.g. to take action on improvement initiatives (criterion 3). However, they do not propose a visualization methodology as we do in our work.

Downs et al. analyze the impact of ambient systems to notify about the build status [17]. They primarily focus on the influence of notification means like lighting devices on the quality of commits from developers, i.e. if the number of failed builds decreases while the total number of all commits is still similar. With respect to our research question, they focus only on build status notification (criterion 1) by evaluating their hypotheses among team members of an agile team in an industrial setting (criterion 2) to investigate the impact of these ambient devices within a software development process (criterion 3). However, a visualization scheme as proposed by our work is neither outlined nor addressed.

To summarize our findings on the aforementioned research question, continuous integration as the fundamental principle of the software development, testing, and deployment process in agile teams is implemented increasingly. However, we are not aware of any work, which proposed a structured and easily applicable test process description and classification scheme, which unveils interdependencies and bottlenecks of the overarching test process to derive test process improvement initiatives. Furthermore, no other work exists that evaluates such a taxonomy systematically in a multiple case study.

3   Research Approach

In this paper, we report from a multiple case study [18] involving five software development sites from four companies that are striving towards continuous deployment of software. The four companies are large, developing complex software intensive embedded systems. The companies range in size from around 10.000 to 115.000 employees of which the number or R&D staff ranges from a few thousand to close to 25.000. Depending on the company, from 30% to more than 80% of the R&D staff work with software. As most of the existing research and industrial practice related to continuous integration is concerned with, typically, smaller companies in the SaaS and Web 2.0 domain, we believe that studying continuous integration at embedded systems companies is particularly relevant.

In our study, we have focused on specific sites within these companies with demarcated products and projects. Two companies are within the automotive industry, one company is within the defense industry, and one company is within the telecom industry. The first three companies can be described as largely doing traditional development with various degrees of agile practices established and moving towards continuous integration. The fourth company can be described as a company with some degree of established practices for continuous integration. The companies' existing testing infrastructure, tools, and ways of working did not sufficiently support a transition to continuous integration.

This research is conducted within the Software Center[1], a research center for collaboration between Chalmers University of Technology, the University of Gothenburg, Malmö University and seven software-intensive companies in the Nordics with the aim to conduct research projects together.

The research question we focused on was: *How can we visualize end-to-end testing activities in order to support the transformation towards continuous integration?* With end-to-end testing, we refer to all code, from code written by individual engineers to product release. The aim of this research is to gain insights into how to support the transition towards continuous deployment in the software development industry. The transition from traditional software development to continuous deployment is dependent on and intertwined in complex organizational structures and processes, which makes it particularly suited for a case study approach [18], [19].

Data collection was conducted through group-interviews, workshops, and complementing email correspondence to ensure triangulation of data [18], [20]. We conducted group interviews [21] at each company site, using a semi-structured interview guide, each lasting approximately 2 hours, which has been recorded and transcribed afterwards. Each group comprised of 5-6 people, and we conducted the interviews with both questions answered in a round-robin-style to make sure that all participants were heard, as well as facilitating ample free discussions as needed. The members of each group were working together and knew each other well in order to be sufficiently comfortable to discussing freely together. We covered questions on what testing activities each site were conducting, the frequency of these and how long

---

[1] www.software-center.se

the feedback loop for each testing activity was, and their experiences of challenges and enablers during their processes.

We arranged two joint workshops with representatives from the various research sites to jointly share and discuss the tentative results from the ongoing research, as well as to further discuss their situations, reflections, and ideas of how to proceed. Each workshop lasted approximately three hours, and the involved researchers took careful notes of these discussions.

In the data analysis, we focused on synthesizing the data from the different sites by identifying common denominators in their descriptions of their current testing activities. The two dimensions *scope*, and *periodicity* emerged during the group interviews as a common way of discussing the sites' testing activities. Each site described their testing activities starting from their lowest level, continuing with the subsequent levels until the released product level. We also focused on understanding how frequently these testing activities were conducted and how long time their feedback loops took. In the analysis, we translated the local labels used at the different sites to more general levels of scope (referred to as component, subsystem, partial product, full product, release, customer), and similarly a more general periodicity (referred to as immediate/minutes, hour, day, week, month, once/release), to create the CIViT model as presented in this paper that captures and reflects the overview of each site. Having identified the two dimensions and the various labels for these dimensions, we iteratively tried out various ways to illustrate the current testing activities at a site. Eventually a box with four squares emerged to represent the different testing activities (referred to as functional, quality, legacy, edge). In order to illustrate coverage of these testing activities, we introduced a color scheme, and a similar color scheme was introduced to illustrate the level of automation.

As a first validation of the model, we interpreted the data from each company and created a CIViT model of their current testing activities. These models were then shared with each company site and confirmed as an accurate representation of their current testing activities. Some minor adjustments were made based on discussions with some of the sites about the interpretations of some of testing activities, mainly regarding interpretation of data such as the level of coverage or regarding the scope whether it would be regarded as subsystem or partial product in their context.

A second validation was conducted when each company used their CIViT model to identify a box to focus on for improvement. Each site found the model helpful as a basis for discussions about the current situation, and to decide what area to target and in what way, e.g. increase periodicity, increase scope, increase coverage in any of the testing areas, or increase the level of automation. The selected improvement initiative was followed-up and again the model was used to identify the intended initiative and the outcome of the initiative.

4   Problem Statement

Verification and validation of software systems through testing of software is a widespread activity that has been studied extensively over the last decades [22].

Traditionally, in the waterfall model of development, the testing activities were performed at the end of the development process, after the implementation of the software had been completed and the organization would move on to testing and fault fixing. With the increasing popularity of agile development methods, industrial practice, and consequently research, has moved towards more frequent testing during the development cycle as the ambition is to being able to deliver at the end of each agile sprint, i.e. every 2-4 weeks. Some companies have even adopted approaches where every check-in of code results in the release of software, resulting in dozens of releases of the software per day [23].

The companies studied in this paper, which predominantly operate in the software intensive embedded systems industry, have had similar developments towards agile practices over the last decade. Some testing efforts are performed more frequently and in a more automated fashion. However, due to the complexity and size of the systems developed by these companies, it became clear that several challenges around the verification and validation of the systems produced by these companies remained. These challenges can be summarized as follows:

No End-to-end Overview of Testing in Companies: During the interviews at the companies, it became abundantly clear that very few people, if anyone in the company, had a holistic, complete overview of all the testing activities going on in the development process, ranging from the individual developer checking in code to the release of a system to customers. Everyone involved in the verification process understood their own part really well and, by and large, knew who they received software assets from, whom to deliver these assets after completing their task and how to report issues. However, there was very limited understanding of the end-to-end process. This problem resulted in several additional problems.

Significant Duplicate Testing Efforts: Due to the lack of understanding of the type and quality of testing performed by others and the ambition to minimize the number of faults that slip through, every activity in the testing process repeated significant amounts of testing already performed by others. This caused both longer testing cycles and a reduction of focus on the areas of testing best performed in the current step in the end-to-end verification process.

Slow Feedback Loops: In all interviews, the challenge of long feedback loops was raised as a key challenge. Even though virtually all companies employ forms of unit testing by individual engineers that give feedback within minutes, receiving feedback on the quality of the code from all perspectives, i.e. correct functionality, not breaking any legacy functionality and achieving the desired quality requirements, would typically take several weeks if not months. As an illustrative anecdote, one engineer received testing results about a month after returning from a six-month paternity leave on code that he had written before his leave.

Late Testing of Quality Attributes: A common challenge at the interviewed case study companies is that testing of quality attributes of the system, e.g. performance, robustness, upgradability, etc., took place late in the development cycle and that identified issues, e.g. significantly degraded performance, caused unpredictable development efforts late in the process at a time when the organization can least afford it.

Ad-hoc, Tactical Improvement Efforts: In the case study companies, the verification activity was viewed as a challenge that required improvement efforts. However, the improvement efforts that were presented tended to be mostly tactical in nature, driven in a bottom-up fashion by a team responsible for one step in the process and based on limited understanding of the end-to-end nature of the verification process and the key issues.

When analyzing the data from the interviews at the case study companies for root causes, we realized that the problems that were identified share a common root cause that, if addressed, alleviates these problems significantly: the lack of a holistic, end-to-end understanding of the testing activities and their periodicity, i.e. the frequency of executing the testing activities. Once the organization has a solid understanding of these issues, changing when and how testing activities are performed becomes significantly easier as well as it allows for much easier understanding of the implications of changes.

Based on our analysis of root causes, in the next section we present our solution for addressing the lack of holistic, end-to-end understanding. The model has been validated with the case study companies and currently used to drive strategic improvement activities in testing.

5   Continuous Integration Visualization Technique (CIViT)

Customers expect quality from the products that they receive from the manufacturer or system provider. Verification has been part of the development of software intensive systems for as long as we have written code and interestingly the practices around testing have evolved only slowly. In the case study companies, we have identified that many testing activities take place in different organizations with different coverage of the requirements of the system. In response to this, we have developed a visualization technique called CIViT to show all testing activities performed around a product or product platform. The visualization technique is used by the companies to address the challenges that were discussed in the previous section.

Table 1 presents the different testing activities and their frequency at each participating site. The suggested dimensions "product granularity" and "periodicity" evolved during our workshops with the industrial partners. Based on the companies' feedback and reports, we could cluster their technical and organizational approaches into these two dimensions. Afterwards, we could also validate these dimensions with the work from Yuksel et al. [14], who are using a similar classification scheme but only in tabular form.

Next, we first introduce the types of testing that are visualized. Subsequently, we describe the scopes of the testing activities. Then, the periodicity of the testing activities is discussed. The section is concluded with an illustrative example of a CIViT model from one of the case study companies followed by a summary.

Table 1. Research sites and their key testing activities

Research Site	Testing activities, frequency, and time for feedback loop
Site 1	V1 (SW, minutes)
	V2 (SW, minutes)
	V3 (SW + HW, 2 weeks, 8 weeks)
	V4 (SW + HW, 8 weeks)
	V5 (System, 10 weeks)
	V6 (Real product)
Site 2	Design (unit/component/system level, seconds, 30m minutes, 8 hours)
	Function (system level, 8 -12 hours, 20 hours)
	System (system level, 4 hours, 1 week, x weeks)
	Integration (network, weeks)
	Solution ()
	Customer ()
Site 3	Individual (unit/component, seconds)
	Team (unit/component/function/load, 10 min)
	Logical product (unit/component/function/full legacy, minutes; 2 hours, 3-30 days)
	Real product (feature/integration, daily, weekly, 12-14 weeks)
	Release (acceptance, year, once, 10 days)
	Customer ()
Site 4	Unit (seconds, minutes, daily)
	Lab (function,
	Subsystem (integration/verification, weeks, months)
	System (integration, weeks, months)
	Release (acceptance, two times)
Site 5	Unit (seconds, minutes)
	Subsystem (months)
	System (six months)
	Release (six months)

5.1   Types of Testing

CIViT is concerned with four types of testing: new functionality, legacy functionality, quality attributes, and edge cases. These types of testing are described in more detail below.

New functionality testing is concerned with testing the functionality that is currently under development. As agile methods typically encourage or demand test-driven development, the test cases resulting from TDD fall into this category.

The second category of testing is concerned with legacy functionality, i.e. functionality that has already been built and operates according to its specification. The importance of testing legacy functionality is driven from the desire to have expansion in the functionality that the system provides without relapses. This requires frequent testing of legacy functionality to ensure that ongoing development efforts have not caused unwanted side-effects where new functionality works but legacy functionality now fails to function.

Quality attributes constitute the third category of testing. Quality attributes such as performance, reliability, safety, and security are affected by ongoing development and it is important to ensure that these quality attributes do not start to deteriorate below the minimal acceptable level. Similar to the case of legacy functionality, the intent of frequent testing of quality attributes is to guarantee that the system continues to satisfy the quality requirements and to avoid a situation where late in a development cycle significant effort has to be dedicated to improving deteriorated quality attribute levels.

Finally, there is a category that is not often mentioned in the literature, but that, based on the interviews at the case study companies, we have experienced as important: edge cases. Edge case testing is concerned with testing really unlikely or weird situations that, often, originate from faults that slipped through to customers and that were discovered after significant investigative effort. The company obviously wants to avoid similar situations in the future and consequently adds test cases to test for these specific exceptional situations.

In Fig. 1, we show the four squares forming a bigger square. The "F" stands for new functionality and the "L" for legacy functionality. The "Q" represents quality attributes and "E" edge cases. Each smaller square can have one of five colors, ranging from red to green. The color of the square refers to the level of coverage of all test cases in the specific square. In the figure, the mapping between coverage and color-coding is shown in the upper right.

Furthermore, the line around the four squares can have one of three colors, again ranging from red to green, which indicates the level of automation of the testing. The lower right part of the figure shows the mapping between colors and level of automation.

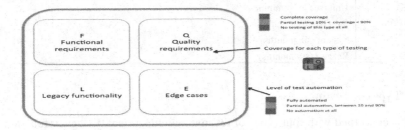

Fig. 1. The four types of testing in the CIViT model with explained color coding and mapping to coverage and automation. Red equals no coverage/no automation, orange equals partial coverage/automation, and green equals complete coverage/fully automated.

5.2   Scope of Testing

The second aspect of CIViT is the scope of testing. Scope, in this case, refers to the segment of the overall system that is tested as well as the level of trust that can be associated with the test results. CIViT is concerned with five main levels, ranging from a component, a subsystem, a partial product, the full product, on-site release testing and, finally, customer-site release testing. Below we describe each scope in more detail:

Component: A component or module is a part of the system that can be the scope of an individual engineers or a small team, in case of pair-wise programming. At this level, typically unit testing takes place.

Subsystem: In the case of component teams, a subsystem is often the scope of responsibility for a team or a small set of teams. At the subsystem level, the types of test cases are broader in the area of covered functionality and less white-box than the previous level.

Partial Product: Especially in the case of embedded systems, system level testing can only take place realistically in case some parts of the mechanics and hardware of the system are available and other parts are simulated. Frequently, companies build test rigs that combine the most important aspects in a structure that allows for testing the primary functional and quality requirements.

Product: No matter how accurate a test rig is in terms of providing a realistic testing environment, there still are significant needs to test the full product with all parts present, including mechanics, hardware and all software. The challenge with product-level testing is that the cost of providing the full product often is quite high and not all teams can have full and continuous access to the product. Also, in cases where the hardware and mechanics are developed in parallel with the software, the full product typically becomes available only late in the development process.

Release: Organizations are keen to minimize the number of issues that reach the customer and in response often create a separate release organization that tests the full product for all aspects that are of importance to the customer. The release organization is concerned with completeness of testing, including edge cases and quality attributes of secondary priority. Typically, the focus of release testing is on completeness and ensuring the expected functionality and quality at the customer site.

Customer: Finally, in the case of lower volumes, but highly priced embedded systems, the company often installs the system or product at the customer site and performs testing activities to ensure the correct operation of the system in the context of the customer.

Finally, it is important to recognize that the levels describing the scope of testing are not mutually exclusive, but rather the contrary. In practice, there are significant testing activities at each or at least at most levels.

5.3   Periodicity of Testing

Finally, CIViT is concerned with the periodicity of testing, which we define as a combination of the frequency of a testing activity and the time between the start of the testing activity and the availability of feedback from that testing activity. Again, we identify three levels of periodicity, i.e. "in the development workflow" (minutes and hours), "disrupting the development workflow" (days and weeks) and finally "outside the development workflow" (months and once per release).

Although the case study companies were quite pleased with giving feedback within days or one or a few weeks, the fact is that this is experienced as disruptive to the development workflow. In this case, the team working on a feature typically has moved on to other tasks and errors that are returned after days or weeks require the team to return to work that had already been completed. At this point, the engineers that originally implemented the feature need to stop working on what they were concerned with, make a context switch, make the change, submit the updated code and return to the task that they were working on now.

The even longer periodicity, i.e. months or once per release, often results in high-level, more complicated system errors that cannot be allocated to a team that did the original implementation. Hence, these tasks are assigned to dedicated teams or randomly to the development teams. Focusing on these errors is outside the normal development workflow in that the teams are not temporarily disrupted from development, but rather perform error fixing for a period of time without other tasks in the pipeline.

Finally, rather than providing exact feedback loop length, CIViT is concerned with indicating the order of magnitude of the feedback loop. For instance, the point "hours" indicates from one to a small number of hours, but clearly less than a day.

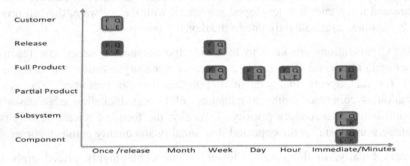

Fig. 2. An example instantiation of the CIViT model from one of the participating companies

5.4   Illustrative Example

To illustrate the CIViT model, below we show an example from one of the case study companies in Fig. 2. One can derive significant information from this chart, including the following:

- The organization uses automated unit testing for some parts of the functionality at the component level.
- At the subsystem level, automated testing of part of the functional, legacy and quality requirements takes place.

- The company does not employ partial product testing, but rather performs testing at the full product. Different tests take place every couple of hours, every day or days and every week or small number of weeks.
- Manual testing of all requirements and edge cases takes place once per release.
- Finally, at the customer site a subset of the requirements is tested to guarantee correct "in situ" operation of the system.

5.5 Summary

The CIViT model aims to visualize the testing activities that an organization deploys to achieve the desired quality levels during the development of a product or system. The model was developed in response to the observation that many researchers and, sometimes, even practitioners assume that the validation of a system or product occurs in a single location in the timeline of development as well as in the organization. In practice, this is obviously more complicated and the CIViT model visualizes this complexity while providing a simple overview that can be used for selection and prioritization of improvement activities.

6   Validation

In this study, we aim to improve our understanding of how testing activities are arranged, and how to support companies in their efforts towards continuous integration. We identified a number of challenges that remain around the verification and validation of the systems produced by the companies involved in this study. We developed the CIViT as a solution for addressing these challenges:

No End-to-end Overview of Testing in Companies: The CIViT model has been validated in a two-step process by all five cases in this multiple case study. As a first validation step, the data from each company were carefully analyzed and translated into the CIViT model for each company. Each company has reviewed and confirmed their model as a fair reflection of their end-to-end testing activities at the studied site. The feedback from the companies was positive that the model provides a useful overview of their end-to-end testing activities. The model helps to gain a clear overview and understanding of the end-to-end process of testing activities. As a second validation step we used the model for each company to identify what testing activities in their model that they would like to focus on to improve. Each company considered the model helpful as a basis for discussion about the current situation, and to decide what area to target on and in what way, e.g. increase periodicity, increase scope, increase coverage in any of the testing areas, or increase the level of automation. Each company selected a specific box in their model and explicated in what way they aimed to improve the selected testing activities, for example by increasing periodicity from e.g. month to week, or by increasing scope from e.g. subsystem to partial product. We followed-up the improvement initiative again using the model to discuss the intended initiative and the outcome of the initiative, and again the model proved useful as a basis for these discussions.

Significant Duplicate Testing Efforts: The overview provided by the CIViT model enables useful discussions that reveal what type and quality of testing that are performed within the settings. The study shows that this is helpful to identify unintended and undesired duplicate testing efforts, as well as to ensure that sufficient testing efforts are in place at the various levels of the end-to-end process.

Slow Feedback Loops: In a similar way, the CIViT model both visualizes directly the periodicity of the involved testing activities and consequently reveal their feedback loops in the settings, and enables useful discussions about what would be reasonable and desired times of feedback loops within the end-to-end process of testing activities.

Late Testing of Quality Attributes: The CIViT model also directly visualizes what different types of testing that are dealt with in the involved testing activities. For example, the study shows that this helps to reveal to what extent the testing of quality attributes, e.g. performance and robustness, takes place and when. As this is commonly dealt with late in the development cycle, the companies find the CIViT model useful to visualize the current end-to-end process of the various testing activities and that it serves as a useful basis for discussing reasonable and desired ambitions regarding the testing of quality attributes.

Ad-hoc, Tactical Improvement Efforts: Based on the overview that the CIViT model provides, it also enables useful discussions of the testing activities that are performed within the settings regarding what areas would be suitable to improve and how. This helps the companies to move away from the typical ad-hoc approach towards improvement efforts and have a better understanding of the end-to-end verification process and the key issues when they make decisions about what to do and how.

7   Conclusions and Future Work

In this work, we have collaborated with five software development sites from four companies affiliated with the Software Center. We have unveiled weaknesses and hurdles in the companies' evolution towards continuous integration to meet their customers and markets' needs.

Based on our findings, we have developed our holistic Continuous Integration Visualization Technique CIViT to provide a useful overview of end-to-end testing activities. Thus, engineers, testers, and managers have been enabled for the first time according to our studies on related work to see, understand, and act accordingly on an integrated and overarching test process.

The validation of the CIViT model carried out the involved companies confirms that the model serves as a solution to the lack of a holistic, end-to-end understanding of the testing activities and their periodicity. It also confirms that by enabling the organization a solid understanding of the end-to-end testing activities, it enables the organizations to identify how to best change their testing activities and to understanding the implications of changes. Companies that participated, as well as additional companies, have been using the model after the completion of the study and claim that the model is particularly useful as a basis for discussion, which help to identify problems and to reason about suitable measures.

While CIViT is our first step towards a simple and intuitive yet powerful visualization and test process improvement techniques, further aspects need to be addressed and investigated. As immediate next steps, we want to further analyze the motivations behind a selected test process improvement initiative. Furthermore, we need to understand commonalities and differences in the charts from the involved companies to derive guidelines where to focus on improvements and how to organize them.

Acknowledgments. This study would not have been possible without the help of the involved partners from the Software Center. Thus, we would like to thank all engineers, testers, and managers who participated in our study.

References

1. Fowler, M.: Continuous integration (2007), http://martinfowler.com/articles/continuousIntegration.html
2. Beck, K., Beedle, M., van Bennekum, A., Cockburn, A., Cunningham, W., Fowler, M., Grenning, J., Highsmith, J., Hunt, A., Jeffries, R., Kern, J., Marick, B., Martin, R.C., Mellor, S., Schwaber, K., Sutherland, J., Thomas, D.: Manifesto for the Agile Software Development (2001)
3. Holck, J., Jørgensen, N.: Continuous Integration and Quality Assurance: A Case Study of Two Open Source Projects. Australian Journal of Information Systems 11(1), 40–53 (2004)
4. Ståhl, D., Bosch, J.: Modeling continuous integration practice differences in industry software development. Journal of Systems and Software 87, 48–59 (2014)
5. Beck, K.: Test Driven Development: By Example. Addison-Wesley Professional (2002)
6. Whittaker, J.A., Arbon, C., Carollo, J.: How Google Tests Software. Addison-Wesley Professional (2012)
7. Sturdevant, K.: Cruisin' and Chillin': Testing the Java-Based Distributed Ground Data System 'Chill' with CruiseControl. In: Aerospace Conference 2007, pp. 1–8 (2007)
8. Downs, J., Hosking, J., Plimmer, B.: Status Communication in Agile Software Teams: A Case Study. In: Proceedings of the Fifth International Conference on Software Engineering Advances, pp. 82–87 (2010)
9. Stolberg, S.: Enabling Agile Testing through Continuous Integration. In: Proceedings of the Agile Conference, pp. 369–374 (2009)
10. Kim, E.H., Na, J.C., Ryoo, S.M.: Implementing an Effective Test Automation Framework. In: Proceedings of the 33rd Annual IEEE International Computer Software and Applications Conference, pp. 534–538 (2009)
11. Kim, E.H., Na, J.C., Ryoo, S.M.: Test Automation Framework for Implementing Continuous Integration. In: Proceedings of the Sixth International Conference on Information Technology: New Generations, pp. 784–789 (2009)

12. Hoffman, B., Cole, D., Vines, J.: Software Process for Rapid Development of HPC Software Using CMake. In: Proceedings of the DoD High Performance Computing Modernization Program Users Group Conference, pp. 378–382 (2009)
13. Ablett, R., Sharlin, E., Maurer, F., Denzinger, J., Schock, C.: BuildBot: Robotic Monitoring of Agile Software Development Teams. In: Proceedings of the 16th IEEE International Symposium on Robot and Human Interactive Communication, pp. 931–936 (2007)
14. Yuksel, H.M., Tuzun, E., Gelirli, E., Biyikli, E., Baykal, B.: Using Continuous Integration and Automated Test Techniques for a Robust C4ISR System. In: Proceedings of the 24th International Symposium on Computer and Information Sciences, pp. 734–748 (2009)
15. Lacoste, F.: Killing the Gatekeeper: Introducing a Continuous Integration System. In: Proceedings of the Agile Conference, pp. 387–392 (2009)
16. Goodman, D., Elbaz, M.: 'It's not the pants, it's the people in the pants' Learnings from The Gap Agile Transformation. In: Proceedings of the Agile Conference, pp. 112–115 (2008)
17. Downs, J., Plimmer, B., Hosking, J.: Ambient Awareness of Build Status in Collocated Software Teams. In: Proceedings of the 34th International Conference on Software Engineering (ICSE), pp. 507–517 (2012)
18. Yin, R.K.: Case study research: design and methods. Sage-Publications, Newbury Park (1994)
19. Runeson, P., Höst, M.: Guidelines for conducting and reporting case study research in software engineering. Empirical Software Engineering 14(2), 131–164 (2009)
20. Patton, M.Q.: How to Use Qualitative Methods in Evaluation. Sage Publications, Newbury Park (1987)
21. Myers, M.D., Newman, M.: The qualitative interview in IS research: Examining the craft. Information and Organization 17, 2–26 (2007)
22. Bertolino, A.: Software testing research: Achievements, challenges, dreams. In: Proceedings of Future of Software Engineering (2007)
23. Ries, E.: The Lean Startup: How Constant Innovation Creates Radically Successful Businesses. Portfolio Penguin (2011)

Comparing a Hybrid Testing Process with Scripted and Exploratory Testing: An Experimental Study with Practitioners

Syed Muhammad Ali Shah, Usman Sattar Alvi,
Cigdem Gencel, and Kai Petersen

Politecnico di Torino, 24 10129 Torino, Italy
Seamless AB, Stockholm, Sweden
Free University of Bolzano-Bozen, 39100 Bolzano (Bozen), Italy
Blekinge Institute of Technology, Karlskrona, Sweden
syed.shah@polito.it, usman.alvi@seamless.se, cigdem.gencel@unibz.it,
kai.petersen@bth.se

Abstract. This study presents an experimental study comparing the testing quality of a Hybrid Testing (HT) process with the commonly used approaches in industry: Scripted Testing (ST) and Exploratory Testing (ET). The study was conducted in an international IT service company in Sweden with the involvement of six experienced testers. Two measures were used for comparison: 1) defect detection effectiveness (DDE) and 2) functionality coverage (FC). The results indicated that HT performed better in terms of DDE than ST and worse than ET. In terms of FC, HT performed better than ET, while no significant differences were observed between the HT and ST. Furthermore, HT performed best for experienced testers, but worse with less experienced testers.

Keywords: Exploratory Testing, Scripted Testing, Hybrid Testing, Experiment, Industrial.

1 Introduction

The common testing process in industry is scripted testing (ST) (also referred to as prescriptive or test case based testing [1]). ST is a plan-driven testing process where test cases are designed prior to test execution in order to structure and to guide the testing tasks. This approach provides several benefits such as test awareness, test coverage, repeatability, and tracking [2],[3].

However, some recent studies indicate that the use of rigorous and well-documented ST is not very common [4],[5],[6]. One reason stated by Itkonen [7] was that documenting every scenario in a test case being very time consuming and hence testers requiring more time in writing test cases as compared to actually executing them. Furthermore, Andersson and Runeson [2] mentioned that testers do not often rely on the test cases while actually executing them.

Furthermore, Itkonen [7] mentioned that the actual effectiveness and importance of these pre-designed test cases in terms of defect detection efficiency is

G. Cantone and M. Marchesi (Eds.): XP 2014, LNBIP 179, pp. 187–202, 2014.

also unknown. Agruss et al. [2] and Andersson et al. [5] claimed that if all the pre designed test cases pass in the first execution, chances of finding any new bugs by executing the same test set again are nominal. Kaner [8] described another limitation of using predesigned test cases as the need to redesign the test cases for every new version of the software.

Exploratory testing (ET) is another testing approach, which has also become popular particularly in the agile world [9],[10]. In ET, tests are not planned and defined in advance, but are dynamically designed, executed, and modified [11]. As defined by [12] *"Exploratory testing is simultaneous learning, test design, and test execution"*. Therefore, ET embraces similar values as agile development and combines learning, test design, and test execution into one test approach [9]. Following this approach, testers can freely explore an application by utilizing human intuition and experience [13],[14]. As it is not explicit how testers make this exploration, ET is often referred to as 'ad hoc' testing [2]. Recently, the term 'exploratory' was introduced by a group of testing experts instead of 'ad hoc' [12] to avoid wrong perception of this approach.

A few studies such as [15],[16],[3] mentioned that ET makes better use of testers creativity and skills to discover the bugs that ST may not uncover because of its mechanical nature. On the other hand, some shortcomings of the ET approach have been also reported such as; the difficulty in assessing whether all features are tested, unavailability of oracles, and invisibility of the quality of testing [16],[3],[6]. Furthermore, Agruss et al. [2] stated that ET is not suitable while performing acceptance testing.

In our previous study [17], we made a comprehensive review of the strengths and weaknesses of ST and ET by performing a systematic literature review and conducting interviews with testing experts in industry. One of the significant findings of our study was that the performance of ST and ET with respect to testing quality depend on a number of conditions. For example, quality of testing when using ST depends on the test case design, which depends on the skills, experience, and domain knowledge of the test designers as well as the previous documents from which the product requirements are inherited. On the other hand, the quality of the testing when using ET depends on skills, experience, and domain knowledge of the testers who execute the tests.

Therefore, a number of researchers and practitioners [2],[15],[3] highlighted that organisations can benefit more if they use ET in addition to ST, as they are in fact complementary approaches. In general, there is a general interest in industry for a hybrid testing (HT) approach unifying the two approaches, which is, for example, visible in lively discussions in industry oriented blogs. Therefore, in our previous study [17], we designed a hybrid testing (HT) process incorporating the different aspects of ST and ET to mitigate the weaknesses of one by leveraging on the benefits of the other.

In this study, we empirically evaluated the test design and test execution phases of the HT process through an experimental study in a software company. Our research question was formulated as "How does a hybrid testing process affect testing quality as compared to ST and ET?"

This paper is organised as follows. In Section 2, we provide a short description of the HT process that this study is based on. In Section 3, we present our research methodology. The results are presented and discussed in Section 4. The conclusions are given in Section 5.

2 Background

This section provides background information on the HT process [17] (Figure 1), which we evaluated in the experimental study in terms of testing quality. Here, we do not discuss the whole process defined, but only provide background on test design and implementation and test execution sub-processes. The other sub-processes were not in the scope of the experimental study. A detailed account of the overall process and the differences between them is given in [17], which forms the foundation for this work.

Test Design & Implementation: In HT test design, Requirement Based Test Cases (RBTC) [18] and test missions are introduced to enable both high functionality coverage and defect detection effectiveness in addition to cost effectiveness through reducing the test bed size. RBTC specify those test cases that are defined only from the requirements specification. The "test mission" is a concrete instruction for testing and the problem being looked for.

Test Execution: The test execution part is highly flexible. Both RBTCs and the test missions are executed, which were designed in test design phase. First, a tester has given the freedom to freely explore the application in order to learn and get knowledge about it. After that, RBTCs and then the test missions are executed and the execution artifacts are recorded. A session is an uninterrupted block of test time slot assigned to a specific test mission in which test mission has to be executed.

3 Method

We evaluated the test design and test execution phases of the HT process in terms of testing quality (defect detection effectiveness and functionality coverage) through an experimental study. The aim of the evaluation was to test the introduction of HT under a realistic scenario from an industrial standpoint where practitioners first use ST and then migrate to ET and thereafter to HT where different versions of the same software are tested, each version having different defects. Our main research question (RQ) was as follows: *RQ: How does a hybrid process affect the testing quality (DDE, FC) in comparison to ST and ET?*

Overall, by using the template of Goal Question Metric paradigm [19], the intend of the experimental study can be summarized as:

- Analyze the *introduction of ET and HT in an organization originally using ST* for the purpose of *evaluation and proposition generation*
- With respect to *defect detection effectiveness (DDE) and functionality coverage (FC)*

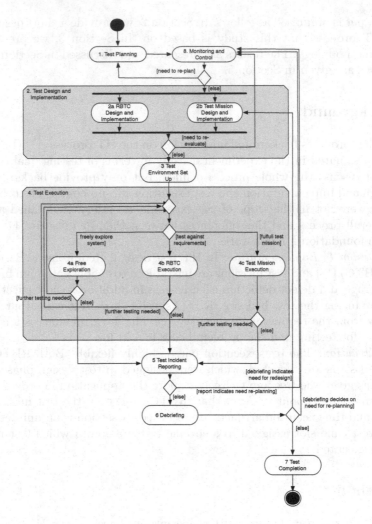

Fig. 1. HT Process

- From the point of view of the *researcher*
- In the context of *experienced industry practitioners (at least 3 years of experience) using the testing approaches from a black box testing perspective on different versions of a calculator software with different bugs seeded.*

With respect to testing techniques this means that no white-box approaches were applied, such as covering statements, branches, or decisions. From a black-box perspectives the practitioners freely explored the application using ET, no techniques were prescribed for that. The same applies to HT where test mission statements were used. Test coverage was hence measured in terms of *functionality coverage.*

The null and alternative hypotheses for the experiment were as follows:

- Detect Detection Effectiveness (DDE)
  - $H1_0$: There is no significant difference between HT, ST and ET
  - $H1_1$: DDE by HT (DDE_{HT}) is higher than by ST (DDE_{ST})
  - $H1_2$: DDE by HT (DDE_{HT}) is higher than by ET (DDE_{ET})
- Functionality Coverage (FC)
  - $H2_0$: There is no significant difference between HT, ST and ET
  - $H2_1$: FC by HT (FC_{HT}) is higher than by ST (FC_{ST})
  - $H2_2$: FC by HT (FC_{HT}) is higher than by ET (FC_{ET})

Experimental Planning and Design: This experimental study was conducted at Logica AB in Sweden (Logica is currently owned by CGI). Logica AB was an international IT service company that creates value by integrating people, business and IT. It had around 39,000 employees, 5,200 of who work in Sweden. The company provided business-consulting, systems integration, development, testing and outsourcing services to all around the world.

We designed the experiment as a "One factor with more than two treatments" [20]. The factor here is the testing approach used with three treatments: ST, ET and HT. The main differences between the three treatments are described in Table 1.

Table 1. Treatment characterization and examples

Treatment	Characterization	Example Instructions
ST	The test cases used are the formal detailed level test cases, describing every procedure and condition required for testing with inputs and expected outcomes. That is, they also contained the test data.	*Test case:* Addition of two numbers *Steps:* First, go to the application. Perform the addition of two numbers, i.e. 2+2. *Expected outcome:* Correct operation and correct answer given (i.e. 4). *Test status:* Pass or Fail.
ET	No test cases are provided, testers can freely explore the application.	No information due to free exploration
HT	During HT, RBTCs and test missions were provided allowing the practitioners to utilize the process. The RBTCs, which are the functional requirement based test cases, were used to assure that high priority requirements went under test first (no test data). The test missions are the particular scenarios for the testing tasks specifying what specific test problems the tester is required to look on.	*RBTC:* Perform the operations to check the addition functionality working accordingly. *Expected output:* The addition functionality should work accordingly. *Test status:* Pass or Fail.

Application: The case application was a calculator application with 11 functions developed by the first two authors of this paper. One application with three versions was developed with the same functionality, but was seeded with different defects for each of the experiment sessions. That is, if in one version (e.g. seed 1) division is working without defects, this might not be the case in another version (e.g. seed 2 or seed 3). In total, 25 defects were seeded into each version of the application. The defects were not the same per application, but were of similar types. That is, the testers would not benefit by figuring out a defect once and then could easily discover the same defect with a different testing process. A colleague not involved in the experiment to avoid biasing the results did the seeding of defects. The only information provided to that person was that different types of defects should be seeded, e.g. cosmetic, quality requirements such as response time, functional defects, etc.

The application was tested using ST, ET, and HT, consecutively. This application was chosen to ensure that the practitioners were familiar with the application domain so that there would not be learning effect when they tested the application first with ST, secondly with ET, and finally with HT. In other words, they were as familiar with the application in the beginning as in the end.

Furthermore, for practical reasons, the choice of a calculator application means that the testers would test a small set of functions of an application they are familiar with and have domain knowledge about within a limited amount of time available in the company. However, the alternative, i.e. choosing a version of the systems developed at the company, would not have been feasible due to the lack of experimental control, e.g. with respect to defect population and other factors that would influence/bias the testers in their testing. Therefore, we suggest using the results of this study as an input for proposition generation when conducting future studies (for example in the form of a case study) to learn more about the longitudinal effects of introducing HT into practice.

Test cases: For ST implementation, the designed test cases were provided to the testers. The test cases were written before seeding the defects. That way we avoided writing test cases biased towards the seeded defects. The test cases were documented in the form of test scenarios stating pre-conditions, scenario steps, and post conditions. An example for a scenario step is to conduct a calculation with mixed operations (e.g. multiplication and addition). According to our pre-study and without time limitation the test cases, provided to the subjects for ST and HT, would have identified most of the defects in each seed.

Subjects: The subjects of the experiment were selected from the same company. Giving the potential experiment subjects a questionnaire; we identified 6 subjects considering their experience: T1 (5 years); T2 & T4 (more than 5 years); T3 & T5 (test managers with more than 10 years) and T6 (more than 3 years). The same subjects having similar backgrounds participated in the experiment for each treatment to reduce measurement error due to subject heterogeneity, and thus to increase statistical power when sample size is small [21].

Observed Outcome Metrics: In order to be able to compare the testing quality of HT to ST and ET, we chose to use two metrics: (1) 'defect detection effectiveness (DDE)', and (2) 'functionality coverage (FC)'. Both metrics are in ratio scale and, therefore could be used in further statistical tests. Here, DDE corresponds to total number of detected defects out of all seeded defects. We talk about defect detection *effectiveness* instead of *efficiency* as time has not been considered as a factor in comparing the outcome.

FC corresponds to total number of incorrectly implemented or missing functions detected out of all functions implemented in the software. However for the experiment, all functions of the application were seeded with some defects. Therefore, in this case, FC is the number of detected functions with defects out of the total defective functions. For example, if 6 functionalities are identified to have defects out of 11 functions implemented, this means that the testers achieved 55% functionality coverage. We should note that, we did not need to normalize these values against the number of total seeded defects and total number of functions, as these were the same for all versions of the Calculator application. Therefore, for DDE, we only report the total number of defects detected whereas for FC, the total number of incorrectly implemented or missing functions detected.

Experiment Execution: Before the experiment date, we gave an initial presentation about the experiment and general guidelines for how to perform the tests using each testing approach. All three versions of the test application were deployed to the laptops of the subjects as well. As the subjects had no access to the source code of the application, this ensured that testers conducted a black-box test of the application.

The experiment was held in two sessions (training and test execution) and totally took two hours. During the first session, we gave detailed instructions for each test approach. Then we provided the subjects with templates for bug investigation report, session sheet and RBTC forms, which were designed to collect experiment related data such as bugs, types of bugs and functionality tested, etc. The first session lasted for 15 minutes and extra 15 minutes were given for additional questions in order to clarify any ambiguities. The subjects were requested not to communicate during the experiment with other testers and concentrate only on the experiment.

The second session was the actual experiment execution session. Maximum 30 minutes was allocated to execute tests using each testing approach. In this session, first, Calculator application with seed 1 was tested using ST. The pre-designed test cases were provided to the subjects. It was explicitly mentioned to strictly follow the test steps in the test cases and in case they felt a need to divert from the test steps they were asked to state so in the bug report with the reasons and any related outcomes.

Then, Calculator application with seed 2 was tested using ET. No test cases were provided to the subjects. Therefore, they had to perform free testing and they were not bound to follow any test cases or test steps. They only needed to log the identified bugs in the bug sheet. Bug report template was also given to the subjects in order to log the identified bugs.

Finally, Calculator application with seed 3 was tested using HT. The RBTCs and test missions were provided to the subjects. They executed the test missions after completely performing the RBTC. While performing a test mission, subjects were told that they should look into the specified area as mentioned on the test sheet but they can use their ideas and follow whatever steps they want to. At the same time they should also write down some high-level test steps, which they performed during a session. Upon completion, all relevant material including the test cases, RBTCs, test sessions and bug sheets were collected.

Validity Threats: For the experimental study the following validity threats have to be considered. The application, which was used for the experiment was a simple calculator with eleven functionalities. We do not know how the results would have been influenced if this had been a larger and more complex application. Therefore, the conclusions of this experiment are limited, but were useful for formulating propositions for future studies. However, as pointed out earlier the application reduced the threat of learning effect as how a calculator works is common knowledge. Hence, there was a trade-off to be made between a complex application and learning effect.

On the other hand, even though we controlled the learning effect with respect to the application to some extent, there still exist a learning effect for how to test the application. In order to evaluate an as realistic scenario as possible from an industrial standpoint (a company developing a software using ST adopts ET and later on evolves it to HT with the software having changes in defect population over time) the learning effect could only partially be controlled. That is, in the first run testers had test cases given to the subjects, and with that had ideas what inputs they could use. Hence, they could utilize this knowledge during their testing in the next step (free exploration). Furthermore, if they are finding new interesting tests, this knowledge could again be used to improve. Overall, this is a threat to control the learning effect, while in practice the situation would be similar, where when adopting a new practice, the testers would carry on the knowledge to the new practice. Hence, this is a threat to theoretical validity, while it strengthens external validity.

Another validity threat is the limitation of the FC measure used in relation to extent of testing. As many functions have more than one defect, it is possible that the function was marked as covered by identifying only one defect and other defects in that function might have remained undetected. Such scenario is possible but we think that this should not cause too much impact on the experiment outcomes as the seeded defects were of similar types and related to functionality of a function. Therefore, there is a limited chance that one might find a defect related to functionality and missed the other similar defect related to same functionality.

Another threat to validity is the sample size used. Three treatments, each having six subjects were tested. The small number of subjects in each group could be a potential threat from two perspectives: a practical perspective and a statistical perspective. In order to increase the statistical power, we first reduced the subject heterogeneity by having a background check and using subjects from only one company. Furthermore, we used a powerful statistical test. Our power calculations showed both large effect size and power for the significant differences observed.

However, we should note that a threat from a practical perspective still exists as, if the subjects were not completely homogenous, the effect of the difference between them could not be ruled out given that the sample is not representative for a larger population of testers. Furthermore, no novice testers were part of the experiment. That is, more data points would reduce the risk of lack of heterogeneity.

Finally, the experimental study was scoped to testing quality (defect detection effectiveness and functionality coverage). However, cost effectiveness, customer satisfaction and some other aspects of the nature of processes (such as risk management etc.) are important outcome variables as well. Hence, they need to be evaluated in further case studies to observe, for example, how much effort is required to test a sufficiently large system in a real world setting, as this would provide rich information on cost or the impacts of HT on customer satisfaction and risk management etc.

Overall, the results hence provide indications that later on can be used as hypotheses in the forthcoming empirical studies (for example, validation studies in the form of controlled experiments or evaluation studies in the form of case studies) in different contexts and further studies. We also would like to emphasize that our analysis provides input to meta-analysis that later allows to aggregate experiments (hence we presented the statistics in detail to allow for that), which with every additional experiment would add an important piece to the overall evidence.

4   Results and Discussion

We analyzed the collected data by first evaluating it using descriptive statistics and then performing hypothesis testing.

Defect Detection Effectiveness (DDE): In total, 25 defects were seeded into each version of the application. The numbers of detected defects, found by each subject against each alternative treatment are presented in Table 2.

Table 2. Defect Detection Effectiveness (The number of detected defects)

Subject	ST	ET	HT
T1	6	12	10
T2	7	13	11
T3	6	15	12
T4	8	12	10
T5	9	16	13
T6	6	11	8

The descriptive statistics of the three treatments, including median, mean, standard deviation, skewness and kurtosis are given in Table 3 and the box plots for the number of detected defects are shown in Figure 2.

As this experimental study was designed to have 3 treatments to compare (i.e., ET and ST to HT), we first used Analysis of variance (ANOVA), which enables detecting significant differences between the treatments as a whole instead of separate t-tests comparing each treatment with another. We chose this analysis technique as it is reliable when being applied to small samples [22].

An important assumption underlying the ANOVA is that all treatments have similar variance. Therefore, we checked the data for "homogeneity of variance".

Table 3. Descriptive statistics for the number of detected defects for three treatments

Approach	Median	Mean	Std. Dev.	Skewness	Kurtosis
ST	6.5	7	1.26	0.592	1.56
ET	12.5	13.16	1.94	0.425	1.43
HT	10.5	10.67	1.75	-0.165	1.78

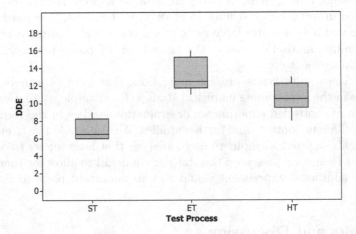

Fig. 2. Box plots of number of detected defects for three treatments

We looked up the table for F_{max} [22] for the number of treatments in our data and the degrees of freedom (number of replicates per treatment -1). The variance ratio, F was found to be 2.2. As this is smaller than F_{max} which is 10.8 for 3 treatments and 5 degrees of freedom at p-value = 0.05, there was no need to transform the data (cf [22]).

Table 4 shows the ANOVA results for DDE, where u = number of treatments and v = number of replicates (The total "Degree of freedom" (df) is one less than the total no of data entries).

Table 4. ANOVA Summary for DDE

Source of variance	Sum of squares (SS)	Degrees of freedom (df)	Mean square ($=SS/df$)
Between groups (bg)	115.44	$u-1=2$	57.72
Within groups (wg)	42.17	$u(v-1)=15$	2.81
Total	157.61	$(uv)-1=17$	

The tabulated value for the variance ratio for $p=0.05$ was found as $F=3.7$. The variance ratio for the experiment ($F=20.53$) exceeds this and even exceeds the tabulated F value for $p = 0.001$ ($F=11.3$). This shows that there is a significant difference between treatments and hence $H1_0$ was rejected.

We further tested the alternative hypotheses by assuming that the calculations of ANOVA are the same as that of a t-test.

First, the least significance difference (LSD) between any of the means is calculated for $p=0.05$ (the level of probability chosen for the t value) using the following formula: $LSD = t - value \times \sigma_d$, where $\sigma_d^2 = \frac{2 \times SS/df}{n}$. Hence, we obtained LSD as 2.92 for t-value ($t=2.13$) and σ_d: 1.37

Table 5 shows the differences between the means of treatments for DDE as well as LSD ($p=0.05$). Two means would be significantly different from one another if they differ by more than LSD. The results showed that HT provided higher DDE than ST (i.e., $H1_1$ is accepted) whereas HT provided lower DDE than ET (i.e., $H1_2$ is rejected).

Table 5. The Differences between the Means of Treatments for DDE

Treatment pairs	$\overline{X_1} - \overline{X_2}$	$LSD = t \times (\sigma_d)$
$DDE_{ET} - DDE_{ST}$	6.17	2.92
$DDE_{ET} - DDE_{HT}$	2.50	
$DDE_{HT} - DDE_{ST}$	3.67	

After having performed the ANOVA analysis, we made statistical power analysis [23] (t-test for the difference between two independent means), retrospectively (see Table 6).

Table 6. Power analysis results for the differences between the means of ST, ET and HT treatments for DDE (sample sizes for group 1 and group 2 = 6, $\alpha=0.05$, $DF=10$, and Critical $t=1.81$)

Pair of treatment	Effect size (d)	Power (1-β)
ET versus ST	3.77	0.99
HT versus ET	1.35	0.70
HT versus ST	2.41	0.99

So, we conclude that our results are significant as both the effect size values and the statistical power are larger than the conventional values [21] (that is Power=0.80 and effect size=0.2(small), 0.5 (medium) or 0.80 (large)) despite the small sample size used in this experimental study.

Functionality coverage: The functionality covered by each experiment subjects against each treatment is presented in Table 7.

Table 7. Functionality Coverage (Total number of incorrectly implemented or missing functionalities detected)

Subject	ST	ET	HT
T1	7	5	7
T2	9	6	8
T3	8	9	11
T4	7	7	9
T5	8	6	10
T6	8	7	8

The descriptive statistics of the three treatments, including median, standard deviation, skewness and kurtosis are given in Table 8 and the box plots for the number of detected defects are shown in Figure 3.

Table 8. Descriptive statistics for functionality coverage of three treatments

Approach	Median	Mean	Std. Dev.	Skewness	Kurtosis
ST	8	7.83	0.75	0.208	1.76
ET	6.5	6.67	1,37	0.593	2.17
HT	8.5	8.83	1.47	0.279	1.54

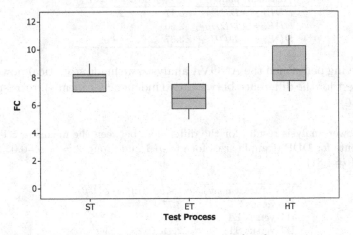

Fig. 3. Box plot of functionality coverage for three treatments

As we did for DDE, we checked the data for FC for "homogeneity of variance". The variance ratio, F was found to be 3.87. As this is smaller than F_{max} which is 10.8 for 3 treatments and 5 degrees of freedom at $P = 0.05$, there was no need to transform the data.

A single t-test was performed to see if there are differences between the means at a chosen probability level ($p-value = 0.05$). Table 9 shows the values of sum of squares for FC.

Table 9. ANOVA Summary for FC

Source of variance	Sum of squares (SS)	Degrees of freedom (df)	Mean square ($=SS/df$)
Between groups (bg)	14.11	u-1=2	7.06
Within groups (wg)	23	$u(v-1)$=15	1.53
Total	37.11	$(uv)-1$=17	

The tabulated value of F ($p = 0.05$) was found as 3.7 . Our calculated F value ($F = 4.6$) is higher than this limit, meaning that there is a significant difference between the treatments. Therefore, the null hypotheses $H2_0$ was rejected.

We further tested the alternative hypotheses by calculated the least significance difference (LSD) between the two means and comparing this value to the differences between the means of two treatments. Table 10 shows the differences between the means of treatments for FC as well as LSD (p=0.05).

Table 10. The Differences between the Means of Treatments for FC

Treatment pairs	$\overline{x_1} - \overline{x_2}$	$LSD = t \times (\sigma_d)$
$FC_{ET} - FC_{ST}$	1.16	2.15
$FC_{HT} - FC_{ST}$	1	
$FC_{HT} - FC_{ET}$	2.16	

The results showed that only the difference between the means of HT and ET (at p=0.05) is slightly greater than 2.15. Therefore, we conclude that HT provided higher FC than ET (i.e., $H2_2$ is accepted)). No significant differences were observed between the means of HT and ST (i.e., $H2_1$ is rejected).

After having performed the ANOVA analysis, we again made a post hoc (retrospective) statistical power analysis. The results are shown in Table 11.

So, we conclude that our result for the difference between HT and ET is significant as both the effect size value and the statistical power are larger than the conventional values [21]. As for the differences between HT and ST as well as ST and ET, no significance was observed between the means, which might be due to low statistical power values associated with the tests and, therefore should be further investigated.

Table 11. Power analysis results for the differences between the means of ST, ET and HT treatments for FC (sample sizes for group 1 and group 2 = 6, α=0.05, DF=10, and Critical t=1.81)

Pair of treatment	Effect size(d)	Power($1-\beta$)
ET versus ST	1.05	0.52
HT versus ET	1.52	0.80
HT versus ST	0.86	0.40

As a summary, our alternative hypothesis tests showed that in terms of defect detection effectiveness, HT performed better than ST and worse than ET. In terms of functionality coverage, HT performed better than ET.

Experience: When different subjects are compared with respect to their performance considering their experience levels:

- All subjects were more successful in terms of DDE when they implemented ET. Testers T3 and T5 who hold the maximum level of testing experience (more than ten years) performed better than other subjects when they used either ET or HT. Interestingly, tester T3 was not very effective in terms of DDE when he used ST and in terms of FC when he used ET. However, both T3 and T5 outperformed in terms of FC when they implemented HT.
- Testers T1, T2 and T4, who hold same level of experience (five years), were also similar in detecting defects when they used the same approach. They all found higher number of defects implementing ET as compared to HT

and ST. For FC, these subjects on the average covered the same number of functionalities implementing the ST and HT. However, they were not as successful in terms of FC when they implemented ET.
– Tester T6 who holds the less experience among all, detected more defects in comparison to ST when implemented ET and HT, but still less than the other subjects. For FC on the other hand, this subject performed similarly as the other moderate level experienced subjects.

From the box-plots in combination with the observations mentioned above some interesting propositions can be derived that should be checked in larger, controlled experiments and industrial case studies. Note that these observations were made in a situation where limited amount of time is available for testing, and that no novice testers participated in the experiment.

– FC: Figure 5 and Table 17 show descriptive statistics for all three treatments. The median values for ST and HT are very close whereas HT shows much higher standard deviation. Highly experienced testers (T3 and T5 with more than 10 years of experience) perform best in terms of FC when using HT. With a moderate level of experience (3-5 years) ST and HT seem to perform similar. When comparing ET and HT we could see that each tester achieves higher test coverage with HT than ET (see Table 7).
– DDE: Figure 4 and Table 12 show that ET outperforms ST and HT. For each of the testers we could see that they perform better with ET and HT than with ST. Furthermore, every tester performed better with ET than with HT. The standard deviation shows that experienced testers benefit more from having freedom in exploring.

5   Conclusion

In this research we conducted a experimental study comparing a hybrid testing process incorporating scripted and exploratory testing. The study was conducted with industry practitioners.

The results indicate that HT is more effective in defect detection than ST and less effective than ET. In terms of functionality coverage, HT performs better than ET. As the statistical power results showed both large effect size and power, we conclude that our results are significant. On the other hand, for FC, no significant differences between the means of HT and ST as well as ST and ET were observed. This might also be due to low statistical power which should be tested in future studies. These results indicate that the HT process provides a compromise solution for testing quality.

Implications Related to Experience: Looking at the individual data points in the results, some interesting patterns were also brought into light, which led to the following proposition: If one aims at high DDE then ET process should be chosen, especially for experienced testers. However, if FC is important at the same time, HT performed best for experienced testers, but not worse with less experienced testers. Hence the optimum solution for high DDE and FC would be to choose

HT. Only using ST is not recommended as after the experiment testers reported that they did not like to use ST as it limits their creativity and does not allow them to bring in their experience and competence, which was also reflected in the poor results ST achieved in comparison to ET and HT with respect to DDE. Given the limitations of the experimental study (see validity threats), these statements only provide indications that need to be further evaluated in future studies.

Furthermore, which process to choose seems to depend also on the experience level (or may be skills) of the tester. Our final observations revealed HT to perform best for experienced testers, but worse with less experienced testers. Therefore, the skills, experience and domain knowledge of testers should also be taken into account for future studies. For example, Itkonen et al. [16] and Juristo et al. [24] found that different testers have varying test case designs even though they follow the same test case design strategy. That is, there are indications that the outcome of the test case design varies with individual experience and skill. A survey of literature related to comparisons between novices and experts has shown that experience has positive effects on various parameters. For example, Sim et al. [25] reported that experience has a positive effect with respect to domain knowledge, speed of completing tasks, ability to identify meaningful patterns, superior recall because experts organize short-term and long-term memory more efficiently, etc.

Our study contributes to highlight the importance of experience. In future work experiments should focus on exploring the role of experience further.

HT and Agile: It was observed that with time-boxed iterations there is limited time for testing, in particular fitting enough testing in an iteration is perceived a challenge [26]. Hence, even though not widely considered an agile practice, the flexibility that HT provides (in particular for experienced testers) merits further investigations to understand how to integrate HT as an agile practice into the set of agile practices, and how it can be beneficial when combined with other agile practices (such as time-boxing).

References

1. ISO/IEC: 29119-2: Test processes, international software testing standard. Technical report (2013)
2. Agruss, C., Johnson, B.: Ad hoc software testing, a perspective on exploration and improvisation. Technical report, Florida Institute of Technology, USA (April 2000)
3. Itkonen, J., Mäntylä, M., Lassenius, C.: How do testers do it? an exploratory study on manual testing practices. In: Proceedings of the Third International Symposium on Empirical Software Engineering and Measurement (ESEM 2009), pp. 494–497 (2009)
4. Ahonen, J.J., Junttila, T., Sakkinen, M.: Impacts of the organizational model on testing: Three industrial cases. Empirical Software Engineering 9(4), 275–296 (2004)
5. Andersson, C., Runeson, P.: Verification and validation in industry – a qualitative survey on the state of practice. In: International Symposium on Empirical Software Engineering (ISESE 2002), pp. 37–47 (2002)
6. Itkonen, J., Rautiainen, K.: Exploratory testing: a multiple case study. In: International Symposium on Empirical Software Engineering (ISESE 2005), pp. 84–93 (2005)

7. Itkonen, J.: Do test cases really matter? An experiment comparing test case based and exploratory testing. PhD thesis, Helsinki University of Technology, Finland (2008)

8. Kaner, C., Falk, J., Nguyen, H.Q.: Testing computer software, 2nd edn. Van Nostrand Reinhold, New York (1993)

9. Crispin, L., Gregory, J.: Agile Testing: A Practical Guide for Testers and Agile Teams. Addison-Wesley (2009)

10. Itkonen, J., Rautiainen, K., Lassenius, C.: Toward an understanding of quality assurance in agile software development. International Journal of Agile Manufacturing 8(2), 39–49 (2005)

11. Bourque, P., Dupuis, R.: Guide to the software engineering body of knowledge (swebok). Technical report. IEEE Computer Society, Los Alamitos, California (2004)

12. Bach, J.: Exploratory testing. In: Veenendal, E.V. (ed.) The Testing Practitioner. UTN Publishers (2005)

13. Bach, J.: Session-based test management. Software Testing and Quality Engineering Magazine 2 (2000)

14. Shoaib, L., Nadeem, A., Akbar, A.: An empirical evaluation of the influence of human personality on exploratory software testing. In: Proceedings of the IEEE 13th International Multitopic Conference (INMIC 2009), pp. 1–6 (2009)

15. Copeland, L.: A practitioner's guide to software test design. Artech House, Boston (2004)

16. Itkonen, J., Mäntylä, M., Lassenius, C.: Defect detection efficiency: Test case based vs. exploratory testing. In: Proceedings of the First International Symposium on Empirical Software Engineering and Measurement (ESEM 2007), pp. 61–70 (2007)

17. Shah, S.M.A., Gencel, C., Alvi, U.S., Petersen, K.: Towards a hybrid testing process unifying exploratory testing and scripted testing. Journal of Software Maintenance and Evolution: Research and Practice (2013)

18. Tahat, L.H., Bader, A., Vaysburg, B., Korel, B.: Requirement-based automated black-box test generation. In: Proceedings of the 25th International Computer Software and Applications Conference (COMPSAC 2001), pp. 489–495 (2001)

19. Basili, V.R., Caldiera, G., Rombach, H.D.: The goal question metric approach. Encyclopedia of Software Engineering 2, 528–532 (1994)

20. Wohlin, C.: Experimentation in software engineering: an introduction. Kluwer, Boston (2000)

21. Dybå, T., Kampenes, V.B., Sjøberg, D.I.K.: A systematic review of statistical power in software engineering experiments. Information & Software Technology 48(8), 745–755 (2006)

22. David, H.A.: Upper 5 and 1% points of the maximum f-ratio. Biometrika 39(3), 422–424 (1952)

23. Cohen, J.: Statistical power analysis for the behavioral sciences, 2nd edn. L. Erlbaum Associates, Hillsdale (1988)

24. Juristo, N., Moreno, A.M., Vegas, S.: Reviewing 25 years of testing technique experiments. Empirical Software Engineering 9(1-2), 7–44 (2004)

25. Sim, S.E., Ratanotayanon, S., Aiyelokun, O., Morris, E.: An initial study to develop an empirical test for software engineering expertise. Institute for Software Research, University of California, Irvine, CA, USA, Technical Report# UCI-ISR-06-6 (2006)

26. Petersen, K., Wohlin, C.: A comparison of issues and advantages in agile and incremental development between state of the art and an industrial case. Journal of Systems and Software 82(9), 1479–1490 (2009)

Impediments to Flow: Rethinking the Lean Concept of 'Waste' in Modern Software Development

Ken Power and Kieran Conboy

[1] Cisco Systems, Galway, Ireland
ken.power@gmail.com
[2] National University of Ireland, Galway, Ireland
kieran.conboy@nuigalway.ie

Abstract. Eliminating waste is a core principle of lean thinking. Despite the emergence of literature that applies lean in the software domain, an underlying analysis of this literature reveals the fundamental interpretation of waste has remained largely unchanged since its origins in manufacturing. Lean defines waste as any activity that does not directly add value as perceived by the customer. Software development is a creative design activity, not a production activity, and agile teams and organizations are more akin to complex adaptive self-organizing systems than repetitive production lines. Waste has different meaning in such systems. This paper reframes the lean concept of waste as impediments to flow in complex human systems. Drawing from ongoing research, this paper presents an updated categorization to describe the impediments faced by teams and organizations. The categories are extra features, delays, handovers, failure demand, work in progress, context switching, unnecessary motion, extra processes, and unmet human potential. These categories provide a foundation for helping teams and organizations to see, measure and reduce impediments to flow in their systems.

Keywords: agile, lean, waste, impediment, flow, value, complexity, human systems dynamics, extra features, delays, handovers, failure demand, work in progress, context switching, unnecessary motion, extra processes, unmet human potential.

1 Introduction

The first step in creating a lean organization is learning to see and manage waste [1, 2]. Lean defines waste as any activity that does not directly add value as perceived by the customer [1]. However, the waste metaphor does not translate comfortably from its origins in automobile manufacturing to modern knowledge work [3]. End-to-end flow of work through the system is still a valuable goal for teams and organizations, yet smooth flow remains difficult or unachievable for many. Teams and organizations attempting to achieve flow face many impediments. Removing impediments to flow is critical to improving a team's or organization's process [4]. The translations of the lean concept of waste in the agile literature to date have

G. Cantone and M. Marchesi (Eds.): XP 2014, LNBIP 179, pp. 203–217, 2014.

focused on an almost literal translation of the wastes of manufacturing production. These translations are inconsistent and lack a coherent presentation in the context of modern knowledge work, including software development. This paper proposes that a more appropriate perspective on the lean concept of waste for the complexity of 21st century teams and organizations of knowledge workers is to reframe waste as impediments to flow. Its not that we simply use the terms interchangeably; they are different but related concepts. Waste still exists in software development. However, this paper argues that a focus on impediments to flow is more appropriate. There are cases where waste leads to impediments, and impediments lead to waste. There are cases where the lens of impediments is a more useful perspective than the lens of waste.

2   Background

The original waste categories were created in the 1940s to address problems and promote a focus on cost reduction in the automobile-manufacturing domain. There are several definitions of waste in the literature. Ohno originally identified seven categories of waste in business and manufacturing processes [2]. Ohno originally described seven categories of waste in manufacturing, explaining the number seven comes from an old Japanese expression "*He without bad habits has seven*", which Ohno used to reinforce the point that "*even if you think there's no waste you will find at least seven types.*" [5]. Liker added an eighth waste to give what have become known as the eight wastes of the Toyota Production System [6]. Definitions of waste vary, and include defining waste as those elements of production that increase cost without adding value [2], or activities that do not contribute to operations [7]. The lean production literature defines waste as "*any human activity that consumes resources but creates no value*" [8]. Definitions of waste in software development have largely just reused the TPS and lean production definitions, emphasizing waste as anything that does not add value from the perspective of the customer [1], or that consume time and effort, therefore creating costs, without adding value [9] [10] [11] [4]. Lean Startup simply restates the TPS definition [12] [13]. Other bodies of work in manufacturing and product development use between seven and ten categories of waste [14].

Among the few authors who have written about the dissonance that comes from applying the concept of waste from the manufacturing domain to modern product development are Reinertsen [15], Shalloway [4] and Anderson [3, 16]. Anderson refers to "wasteful" activities in economic terms as costs, and describes three types of cost [3]. Transaction costs are the setup and teardown costs incurred by software projects. Coordination costs are any activities that involve communication and scheduling. The third cost, Failure load, is what Anderson defines as demand generated by customers "*that might have been avoided through higher quality delivered earlier*" [3].

Although there is much the software industry can learn from the manufacturing domain, agile teams and organizations are better understood as complex adaptive systems (CAS) that are self-organizing and have emergent properties. Dooley notes that *"the prevailing paradigm of a given era's management theories has historically mimicked the prevailing paradigm of that era's scientific theories"* [17]. The complexity sciences have emerged as one of the prevailing paradigms for modern management thinking in general [18, 19], and agile management in particular [20]. Stacey has shown that *"all organisations are complex adaptive systems in which groups and individuals are the agents"* [21]. Waste has different meanings in such systems. Acknowledging nature of modern software development, the Scrum framework is specifically designed to deal with complex adaptive problems. Sutherland and Schwaber write that Scrum is a framework *"within which people can address complex adaptive problems, while productively and creatively delivering products of the highest possible value"* [22].

3   Impediments to Flow

This research has found that discussing *'waste'* is an emotive topic in teams and organizations. It is not easy for people to see that the activities they are engaged in, which can vary from wasteful tasks to the core of their job description, are actually waste from a holistic systems perspective. Anderson writes that *"a focus on flow, rather than a focus on waste elimination, is proving a better catalyst for continuous improvement within knowledge work activities such as software development"* [16].

It has proven relatively easier to talk to people, teams and organizations about what slows them down, what impacts the flow of work through their organization. This research has also found that coming from the perspective of impediments reveals much more about what is happening within the system. By taking a purely waste-focused perspective, people tend to focus on efficiencies and costs. By taking an impediment-focused perspective, people tend to focus more on effectiveness and optimizing the flow of value.

Frameworks such as Scrum place an explicit focus on removing impediments, though without defining what impediments are, or providing guidance on learning to see, understand or manage impediments [22]. This research has found that people have difficulty understanding what an impediment is, how to see them, how to measure and quantify their impact, and how to reduce them. Using the definition and categories presented in this can paper help teams and organizations to see impediments, and give them a foundation for understanding, measuring and reducing the impediments so that work flows more smoothly through their system. While this research addresses all these areas, the scope of this paper is to provide a foundation for defining impediments and present a set of impediment categories that are used to develop the habit of spotting patterns in human systems.

Part of the challenge relates to the balance between efficiency and effectiveness. As DeMarco notes *"you're efficient when you do something with minimum waste. And you're effective when you're doing the right something"* [23]. A focus purely on waste leads to a focus on efficiency, possibly at the expense of effectiveness. A focus on impediments, on the other hand, balances the discussion with an emphasis on effectiveness. Research by Wang has shown that *"agility requires waste to be eliminated but only to the extent where its* [the organization's] *ability to respond to change is not hindered. This does not remove the need to be economical, only lowers its priority"* [24]. Removing waste is a valuable goal in a production process, and a useful metaphor for the parts of software development that are a production activity. Removing impediments is a more useful metaphor for the creative work that is the design activity (including architecture, design, coding, testing) of software development.

Another example of where the perspective of impediments is more useful than that of waste comes into play when considering variability. TPS emphasizes removing variability from the manufacturing process through eliminating waste [5]. Variability in product development, on the other hand, is something to be embraced [15]. In agile software development, a perspective that emphasizes removing impediments to innovation is more useful than one that seeks to eliminate variability.

3.1   Definitions of Value, Flow and Impediment

The Merriam-Webster dictionary defines value as *"usefulness or importance"* [25]. According to Liker, what defines value is the answer to the question *"What does the customer want from this process?"* [6]. In other words, is what the team or organization doing delivering value for the customer? Value Stream Maps are one technique for visualizing the process that delivers customer value. According to Beck, XP team members do only what is needed to create value for the customer [26]. Scrum is designed to reveal the efficacy of the product management and development practices used to deliver value so that teams and organizations can improve [22]. Value has more than direct financial connotations. For the purposes of this research, *value is anything the customer wants, and any activity that is useful or important in the context of providing value to customers.*

Beck defines flow as one of the core principles of XP: *"Flow in software development is delivering a steady flow of valuable software by engaging in all the activities of development simultaneously"* [26]. When creating XP, Beck chose practices that are "biased towards a continuous flow of activities rather than discrete phases".

The Merriam-Webster dictionary defines an impediment as *"something that makes it difficult to do or complete something; something that interferes with movement or progress"* [27]. Synonyms include obstacle, hindrance, obstruction, interference and encumbrance. From a CAS perspective, an impediment is anything that inhibits the system from achieving its purpose or goal. From a lean perspective, one purpose of an organization is to deliver value to its customers, and balance the needs of its wider community of stakeholders. Combining these two perspectives gives this definition:

An **impediment** *is anything that obstructs the smooth flow of work through the system and/or interferes with the system achieving its goals.*

So, determining if something is an impediment, can be based on the answer to two questions; (1) is this thing obstructing or preventing the work from flowing smoothly through the system? (2) Is this thing preventing the system from achieving its goals? If the answer is 'yes' to either or both of these questions, it is an impediment to flow.

There is a relationship between wastes and impediments. From the earlier definition of waste, it can be seen that the definition of impediments includes waste, but broadens the perspective. In other words, *a waste is an impediment* if it obstructs the smooth flow of work through the system, or interferes with the fitness of the system. A *waste causes an impediment* if it results in something that obstructs the smooth flow of work through the system, or interferes with the fitness of the system. This multi-dimensional perspective gives us a more reasoned way to assess waste in the context of impediments.

4   Impediments in Complex Adaptive Human Systems

Wang and Conboy express a concern about whether CAS is appropriate to the study of human organizations, given its origins in the natural sciences and suggest *"a combination of CAS theory with appropriate social theories might be a promising avenue"* [28]. Recognizing that concern, this research uses a particular field of CAS study called Human Systems Dynamics, or HSD [29]. Self-organization is widely acknowledged as a key property of successful agile teams [30]. HSD provides a model for understanding self-organization in human systems.

HSD defines a CAS as a *"collection of individual agents who have the freedom to act in unpredictable ways, and whose actions are interconnected such that they produce system-wide patterns"* [31, 32]. HSD uses three core elements to describe systems: containers, differences and exchanges (CDE). Containers are boundaries within which self-organization of human systems occurs. This is accomplished through focusing and constraining the interactions among the agents in the system. Examples include teams and organizations. Differences establish the potential for change in a human system, creating the possibility for the system to self-organize to a new state. Exchanges, also known as *Transforming Exchanges*, are interactions between the agents (people, teams, etc.) in a Container, and are *"a necessary condition for self-organizing processes to occur"* [29].

In software development, and lean in general, flow is a system goal. Impediments to flow show up in the system-wide patterns that emerge as the agents interact to achieve flow. The diagram in Fig. 1 illustrates this. As the agents interact, patterns emerge in the system. Impediments influence the patterns that emerge, and create a tension in the system that in turn influences the behavior of the agents.

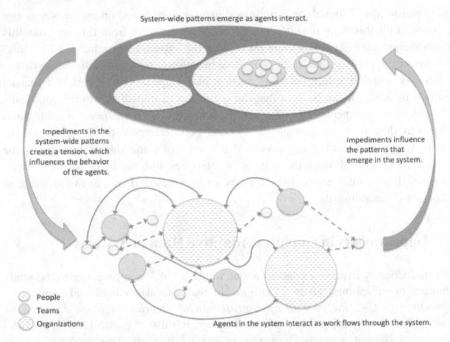

Fig. 1. Impediments influence the system-wide patterns in a CAS

5   Nine Categories of Impediments to Flow

This paper presents a framework of nine impediment categories that is built on the literature from manufacturing [2], lean production [33], lean thinking [8], lean software development [1, 11, 34, 35], product development flow [15], construction [36, 37] and healthcare [38, 39] and other sources [40].

The 9 categories of impediments to flow in software development, as identified in this research, are:

1. Extra Features
2. Delays
3. Handovers
4. Failure Demand
5. Work In Progress

6. Context Switching
7. Unnecessary Motion
8. Extra Processes
9. Unmet Human Potential

Each of these impediments is present in human systems. As with waste, having a set of categories helps reinforce the habit of seeing impediments in human systems [34]. In CAS terms, these impediments show up as patterns in human systems, as discussed in section 4 above. For the purposes of this research, and attempting to see and understand impediments, categories give a useful frame of reference and help form the habit of seeing these patterns. The nine impediments are described in turn in the following sub-sections, and summarized in section 5.10 below. These are explored fully in a separate work [40].

5.1   Extra Features

Extra Features are those features that are added without either a proven need or valid hypothesis. Extra features impede the flow of valuable work through the system by consuming time and effort that could otherwise be spent on more value-adding work. They later prove to add no value for customers, or delay the delivery of more valuable features.

Liker refers to *overproduction* [6]. Beck notes software development "*is full of the waste of overproduction*", including "*elaborate architectures that are never used*" and "*documentation no one reads until it is irrelevant or misleading*" [26].

A Standish group report shows that approximately 45% of features in a typical system are never used, with 19% rarely used [1]. Extra features can be architecture features as well as business features.

Adding extra features significantly slows down feedback and revenue generation, as the product could be release sooner with fewer features. Many organizations do not consider the hidden economic costs of adding features that customers don't want, or for which there is not a sufficient demand. Beyond the initial costs to develop the feature, these hidden costs include:

- Time invested in maintaining the feature, possibly in multiple branches.
- Time invested in Failure Demand related to the feature, e.g., fixing defects, refactoring, or managing technical debt.
- The motivation of the team that developed the feature.

The opportunity costs associated with time lost on these other costs means the company could have been investing the time and money in something more valuable.

5.2   Delays

A delay is a situation in which something happens later than it should, and implies a holding back, usually by interference, from completion or arrival. [41]. Delays impede the flow of work through the system by adding to the overall lead time from request or idea to delivered product or service.

This impediment is also called *waiting* or *time on hand* [6]. The Poppendiecks note that "*one of the biggest wastes in software development is usually waiting for things to happen*" [1].

Delays can take many forms in teams and organizations. There is the delay that results from waiting for an activity to start or end. There is delayed learning. There is delay in information flow, resulting in the people who need the information to do their jobs do not get it in a timely fashion. This either causes them to wait, or to fill in the missing information with guesses.

Delays prevent the organization from delivering value to the customer as quickly as possible [1]. The ability of a team or organization to respond to an idea or request is directly related to the delays in the system. Reinertsen asserts that 85% of product development organizations do not understand the cost of delay associated with their projects or features [15]. He argues that understanding delay is so critical that, if organizations were to quantify just one thing, they should quantify the cost of delay, which he codifies as *"The Principle of Quantified Cost of Delay"*. Brooks noted the *"severe financial, as well as psychological, repercussions"* of delays discovered late in a project [26]. Delays can have a cumulative effect. Brooks notes the secondary costs incurred by other projects waiting on the delayed project can far outweigh all other costs.

5.3   Handovers

Handovers occur whenever incomplete work must be handed over from one person or group to another. Handovers impede the flow of work through the system by adding delays, requiring more people, or losing knowledge as work is handed over from one person or group to another. Handovers are also referred to in the literature as hand-offs.

Ward argues that handovers are the most fundamental waste in companies because they separate knowledge, responsibility, action and feedback [42]. The Poppendiecks describe a case study from Ericsson that illustrates the cost of handovers [35]: *"handovers of information between functions tended to be inefficient; both knowledge and time were lost in every handover. As the number of handovers increased, the problems tended to escalate nonlinearly. Furthermore, workers in each function were assigned to multiple projects, causing severe multitasking that increased inefficiencies. The inefficiencies of handovers and multitasking showed up as decreased speed, and therefore slower time to market."*

5.4   Failure Demand

Failure demand refers to the demand placed on systems (including teams and organizations) and is *"demand caused by a failure to do something or do something right for the customer"* [43]. It is the opposite of value demand, where the demand on systems is driven by value-adding work. [11] defines it as *"the demand on the resources of an organization caused by its own failures"*. It impedes flow by consuming time and effort that could be spent on value-adding work.

Failure Demand includes what TPS calls rework [2], and is an example of *Type Two muda* [8]. Anderson calls it *"Failure Load"* [3].

Examples include defects, forced rework, technical debt, incomplete features, incorrect features, poor customer service, poor design, and poor or insufficient documentation. The Poppendiecks describe *relearning*, e.g., failing to remember what was learned at least once already [34]. Impediments occur when a support team places demands on a development team. Products that are difficult to integrate, deploy, or configure all create large amounts of failure demand. If the software *"gives operations and support organizations problems, both you and they are wasting valuable time."* [11].

Eliminating failure demand has a large economic benefit. In the financial services sector failure demand can vary from 20% to 45% of demand [43]. Seddon also shows that in police forces, telecommunications and local authorities failure demand can be as high as 50% to 80%. Removing failure demand can lead to enormous productivity improvements.

5.5   Work in Progress

Work in progress is analogous to inventory in software development. It is work that is not yet complete, and, therefore, does not yet provide any value to the business or the customer. Too much work in progress impedes the flow of work through the system by slowing down the flow of work for individual work items, and delaying the point at which value can be realized.

The Poppendieck's first book translated the TPS waste of "inventory" to "partially done work" [1]. It is also referred to as work in *process*, but that term is overloaded in software development.

Teams and organizations often get into trouble by having too much work in progress. Lots of WIP is often mistakenly taken as a measure of progress. Beck gives examples of waste resulting from excess work in progress, including *"requirements documents that rapidly grow obsolete"*, and *"code that goes months without being integrated, tested, and executed in a production environment"* [44].

Example impacts include starting lots of projects or work items, but taking a long time to finish anything. Measuring progress in terms of perceived activity rather than delivered value.

5.6   Context Switching

Context switching occurs when people or teams divide their attention between more than one activity at a time [15]. Context switching impedes the flow of work through the system by adding to the overall lead time from request or idea to delivered product or service, and by causing failure demand and relearning. Context switching is sometimes necessary; the advice from this research is to use it consciously, deliberately and carefully. Unplanned context switching is generally worse than planned context switching, though poorly planned context switching is also harmful.

Context switching is often called task switching in the literature [1]. Much of the lean literature describes task switching as *working* on more than one thing at a time. However, as the wider research represented by this paper shows, context switching in knowledge work such as software development is caused by more than contending with multiple work items or tasks.

Example impediments include a developer working on more than one user story at a time. A tester working on more than one project at time. An engineer interrupted while working on a design. A team tasked with working towards delivering two or more projects at the same time. Meetings scheduled at times that guarantee interruptions.

Impediments occur when people switch their focus from one context to another. The cost includes more than lost time. Context switching is a root cause of some instances of estimation problems. Developers often do not predict unplanned context switches, deal with unplanned context switches effectively, or plan effectively for known context switches. This leads to work taking significantly longer than estimated.

In human systems the time that gets wasted is significant, but there are other costs associated with context switching. These include the opportunity cost associated with the interruption, as well as motivational costs. People have reported dissatisfaction with repeated context switching because it does not allow them to properly engage with the work, prevents them from contributing their best work, prevents them from developing mastery of their skills, and contributes to feelings of guilt because they feel they are letting down team members by not completing tasks or taking longer than they committed.

5.7   Unnecessary Motion

Unnecessary motion is any movement of people, work or knowledge that is avoidable, that impedes the smooth flow of work, or that creates additional inefficiencies. A classic example in software is the unnecessary motion caused by not having team members sitting together. Unnecessary motion impedes the flow of work through the system by adding overhead and causing delays in information or decision-making. TPS refers to the waste of unnecessary movement [6]. Authors translating from TPS to software translate *motion* to '*task switching*' ([1, 34] and [9]), but this research more accurately reflects task switching under the wider heading of *context switching* in 5.6 above.

5.8   Extra Processes

Extra processes generate extra work that consumes time and effort without adding value. Extra processes impede the flow of work through the system by adding additional steps, barriers, documentation, reviews, or other activities.

Extra processes is also referred to as *overprocessing* or *incorrect processing* [6]. In their first book the Poppendiecks translate "Extra Processing" to "Extra Processes" [1], and in a later book to "*Relearning*" – the waste often caused by long feedback loops [34]. A simple example is the relearning that developers must do to reacquaint themselves with code for a feature they worked on 6 months ago. For this research, "*relearning*" is more appropriately categorized as "Failure Demand". Another reason this research does not use the term "relearning" is that it can cause confusion. Learning is obviously a good thing in software development. Participants in focus groups have also expressed confusion about the terms. Hibbs et al translate overprocessing to "unneeded processes [9]".

Examples include paperwork and documentation that add no value. Pursuing a standard of quality that is higher than necessary. Time spent chasing an unreasonable level of certainty in estimating projects or features. Manual tasks that could be automated [9]. Forced conformance to centralized process checklists of "quality" tasks [10].

Extra processes have a demotivating impact on people who are forced to comply with non-value adding processes. Inefficiencies caused by poor tools or poor design can lead to defects (failure demand).

5.9   Unmet Human Potential

Unmet human potential is the waste of not using or fostering people's skills and abilities to their full potential. Unmet human potential impedes the flow of work through the system in many ways, though generally there is an opportunity cost through failing to reach the potential capability of the system. The flow of work, and the associated value created, is neither as effective nor efficient as it could be.

This is an expanded perspective on the waste of unused employee creativity [6]. This research categorizes this as "*unmet human potential*" because it goes beyond lack of engagement or not using employee creativity. The Poppendiecks describe the serious problem of not engaging people in the development process [34]. However, they describe this in the context of "*relearning*", which this research has framed more appropriately as *failure demand* (section 5.4). Not engaging people is more appropriately categorized under unmet human potential because it is a failure to take advantage of people's knowledge and creativity, removes ownership over their process, and removes opportunities for learning and improvement.

Deming wrote the "*greatest waste in America is failure to use the ability of people. Money and time spent for training will be ineffective unless inhibitors to good work are removed*" [45].

It impedes the potential of the individual, the team and the organization. Research into motivation has shown that engagement through sense of purpose, combined with the opportunity to develop one's skills and abilities, are vital ingredients in fostering intrinsic motivation [46].

5.10   Summary of the Nine Impediments to Flow

Table 1 summarizes the definitions of each of the impediment categories, and how they generally impede the flow of work through a system.

Table 1. Summary of Impediment Categories

Category	Definition	How it Impedes Flow
Extra Features	Extra Features are those features that are added without either a proven need or valid hypothesis.	Extra features impede the flow of valuable work through the system by consuming time and effort that could otherwise be spent on more value-adding work. They later prove to add no value for customers, or delay the delivery of more valuable features.
Delays	A delay is a situation in which something happens later than it should, and implies a holding back, usually by interference, from completion or arrival.	Delays impede the flow of work through the system by adding to the overall lead time from request or idea to delivered product or service.
Handovers	Handovers occur whenever incomplete work must be handed over from one person or group to another.	Handovers impede the flow of work through the system by adding delays, requiring more people, or losing knowledge as work is handed over from one person or group to another.
Failure Demand	Failure demand refers to the demand placed on systems (including teams and organizations) and is "demand caused by a failure to do something or do something right for the customer"	It impedes flow by consuming time and effort that could be spent on value-adding work.
Work In Progress	Work in progress is analogous to inventory in software development. It is work that is not yet complete, and, therefore, does not yet provide any value to the business or the customer.	Too much work in progress impedes the flow of work through the system by slowing down the flow of work for individual work items, and delaying the point at which value can be realized.
Context Switching	Context switching occurs when people or teams divide their attention between more than one activity at a time	Context switching impedes the flow of work through the system by adding to the overall lead time from request or idea to delivered product or service, and by causing failure demand and relearning.
Unnecessary Motion	Unnecessary motion is any movement of people, work or knowledge that is avoidable, that impedes the smooth flow of work, or that creates additional inefficiencies	Unnecessary motion impedes the flow of work through the system by adding overhead and causing delays in information or decision-making
Extra Processes	Extra processes generate extra work that consumes time and effort without adding value	Extra processes impede the flow of work through the system by adding additional or incorrect/unsuitable activities
Unmet Human Potential	Unmet human potential is the waste of not using or fostering people's skills and abilities to their full potential	Generally there is an opportunity cost through failing to reach the potential capability of the system. The flow of work, and the associated value, is neither as effective nor efficient as it could be.

6   Conclusions

This paper presented an updated framework for categorizing impediments in agile software development teams and organizations. The paper draws from ongoing research by the authors, and provided examples from both the research results and literature. The perspectives presented in this paper are compatible with, rather than competing with, other work that seeks alternative views to the traditional metaphor of waste from the manufacturing domain, in particular Anderson's cost perspective [3] and Reinertsen's economic framework [15].

The research presented in this paper is part of an ongoing program of research work by the authors. This paper provides the terminology and categories for impediments to flow. Other work by the authors provides an analysis of the causes of impediments, a detailed analysis of the impacts of the impediments, how to assess the impact, and how to reduce impediments.

Using a management paradigm grounded in the complexity sciences helps to better deal with the multi-dimensional nature of problems in software development. This research views organizations, teams, and the entire value stream as Complex Adaptive Systems, and uses Human Systems Dynamics (HSD) as a lens through which to better understand such systems. The HSD lens also helps us understand how to influence those systems to make improvements, such as removing impediments.

This paper provides the following:

- Reframe the lean concept of waste as impediments to flow.
- A set of nine categories of impediments to flow to help people see impediments.
- How each type of impediment impacts the flow of work.
- Examples of each type of impediment.
- Frame impediments to flow in the context of modern knowledge work, viewing teams and organizations as complex adaptive human systems.

Using the categories presented in this paper, researchers and practitioners can identify impediments to the flow of work in the patterns that emerge in the systems occupied by teams and organizations.

References

1. Poppendieck, M., Poppendieck, T.: Lean Software Development: An Agile Toolkit. Addison-Wesley, Bostan (2003)
2. Ohno, T.: Toyota production system: beyond large-scale production. Productivity Press, Cambridge (1988)
3. Anderson, D.J.: Kanban: Successful Evolutionary Change for Your Technology Business. Blue Hole Press, Sequim (2010)
4. Shalloway, A., Beaver, G., Trott, J.: Lean-agile software development: achieving enterprise agility. Addison-Wesley, Upper Saddle River (2010)
5. Ohno, T.: Taiichi Ohno's Workplace Management, Special 100th Birthday Edition. McGraw-Hill, New York (2013)

6. Liker, J.K.: The Toyota way: 14 management principles from the world's greatest manufacturer. McGraw-Hill, New York (2004)
7. Shingo, S.: A Study of the Toyota Production System. Productivity Press, New York (1989)
8. Womack, J.P., Jones, D.T.: Lean Thinking: Banish Waste and Create Wealth in Your Corporation. Simon and Schuster (2003)
9. Hibbs, C., Jewett, S., Sullivan, M.: The Art of Lean Software Development. O'Reilly Media, Inc. (2009)
10. Larman, C., Vodde, B.: Scaling lean & agile development: thinking and organizational tools for large-scale Scrum. Addison-Wesley, Boston (2009)
11. Poppendieck, M., Poppendieck, T.: Leading lean software development: results are not the point. Addison-Wesley, Upper Saddle River (2010)
12. Ries, E.: The Lean Startup: How Constant Innovation Creates Radically Successful Businesses. Penguin (2011)
13. Maurya, A.: Running Lean: Iterate from Plan A to a Plan That Works, 2nd edn. O'Reilly Media, Inc. (2012)
14. Pessôa, M.V.P., Seering, W., Rebentisch, E., Bauch, C.: Understanding the Waste Net: A Method for Waste Elimination Prioritization in Product Development. In: Global Perspective for Competitive Enterprise, Economy and Ecology, pp. 233–242 (2009)
15. Reinertsen, D.G.: The principles of product development flow: second generation lean product development. Celeritas, Redondo Beach (2009)
16. Anderson, D.J.: Lean Software Development. Lean Kanban University (LKU), Seattle (2013)
17. Dooley, K.J.: A Complex Adaptive Systems Model of Organization Change. Nonlinear Dynamics, Psychology and Life Sciences 1, 69–97 (1997)
18. Snowden, D.J., Boone, M.E.: A Leader's Framework for Decision Making. Harvard Business Review (2007)
19. Vasconcelos, F.C., Ramirez, R.: Complexity in business environments. Journal of Business Research 64, 236–241 (2011)
20. Appelo, J.: Management 3.0: leading Agile developers, developing Agile leaders. Addison-Wesley, Upper Saddle River (2011)
21. Stacey, R.: Emerging Strategies for a Chaotic Environment. Long Range Planning 29, 182–189 (1996)
22. Sutherland, J., Schwaber, K.: The Scrum Guide. The Definitive Guide to Scrum: The Rules of the Game. Scrum.org (2013)
23. DeMarco, T.: Slack: getting past burnout, busywork, and the myth of total efficiency. Broadway Books, New York (2001)
24. Wang, X.: Organizing to be Adaptive: a Complex Adaptive Systems based Framework for Software Development Processes. School of Management, PhD. University of Bath (2007)
25. Merriam-Webster, http://www.merriam-webster.com/dictionary/value
26. Beck, K., Andres, C.: Extreme Programming Explained: Embrace Change, 2nd edn. Addison-Wesley, Boston (2005)
27. Merriam-Webster, http://www.merriam-webster.com/dictionary/impediment
28. Wang, X., Conboy, K.: Understanding Agility in Software Development from a Complex Adaptive Systems Perspective. In: 17th European Conference on Information Systems (ECIS), Verona, Italy (2009)
29. Eoyang, G.H.: Conditions for Self-Organizing in Human Systems. Doctor of Philosophy. The Union Institute and University (2001)

30. Cohn, M.: Succeeding with Agile: Software Development Using Scrum. Addison-Wesley, Upper Saddle River (2010)
31. Eoyang, G.H.: Human Systems Dynamics Professional Certification Training Manual. HSD Institute, Cohort 32 - Roffey Park, UK (2013)
32. Eoyang, G.H., Holladay, R.J.: Adaptive Action: Leveraging Uncertainty in Your Organization. Stanford University Press, Stanford (2013)
33. Womack, J.P., Jones, D.T., Roos, D.: The machine that changed the world: the story of lean production - Toyota's secret weapon in the global car wars that is revolutionizing world industry. Simon & Schuster, London (2007)
34. Poppendieck, M., Poppendieck, T.: Implementing lean software development: from concept to cash. Addison-Wesley, London (2007)
35. Poppendieck, M., Poppendieck, T.: The Lean Mindset: Ask the Right Questions. Addison-Wesley, Upper Saddle River (2013)
36. Mossman, A.: Creating value: a sufficient way to eliminate waste in lean design and lean production. Lean Construction Journal 2009, 13–23 (2009)
37. Sadreddini, A.: Time for the UK construction industry to become Lean. Proceedings of the Institution of Civil Engineers Civil Engineering Special Issue 165, 28–33 (2012)
38. Dickson, E.W., Anguelov, Z., Vetterick, D., Eller, A., Singh, S.: Use of Lean in the Emergency Department: A Case Series of 4 Hospitals. Annals of Emergency Medicine 54, 504–510 (2009)
39. Jimmerson, C.L.: A3 problem solving for healthcare: a practical method for eliminating waste. Healthcare Performance Press, New York (2007)
40. Power, K.: Impediments to Flow: Understanding the Lean Concept of 'Waste' in Self-Organizing Human Systems. PhD. National University of Ireland, Galway, Ireland (in Porgress)
41. Merriam-Webster, http://www.merriam-webster.com/dictionary/delay
42. Ward, A.C.: Lean Product and Process Development. The Lean Enterprise Institute Inc., Cambridge (2007)
43. Seddon, J.: Freedom from command & control: rethinking management for lean service. Productivity Press, New York (2005)
44. Beck, K., Andres, C.: Extreme programming explained: embrace change. Addison-Wesley, Boston (2005)
45. Deming, W.E.: Out of the Crisis. The MIT Press, Cambridge (1986)
46. Pink, D.H.: Drive: The Surprising Truth about what Motivates Us (2010)

Examining the Structure of Lean and Agile Values among Software Developers

Fabian Fagerholm and Max Pagels

Department of Computer Science, University of Helsinki
P.O. Box 68, FI-00014 University of Helsinki, Finland
fabian.fagerholm@helsinki.fi, max.pagels@cs.helsinki.fi

Abstract. Gaining maximum benefit of Lean and Agile methods requires a thorough understanding of their assumptions regarding culture, mindset, and values. This paper examines the value system structure of experienced developers working with Lean and Agile methods, and compares it to universal human values and individual personality. We developed and deployed an online survey on Lean and Agile values, with embedded measures for universal values and personality. The resulting data set, with 61 respondents, was analysed using agglomerative hierarchical clustering and multidimensional scaling. A value structure containing 11 Lean and Agile values was uncovered, yielding insight into how Lean and Agile developers experience values in their work. The analysis shows that Lean and Agile values are connected, but not equal, to universal values and personality. The proposed model can help practitioners understand the ethos of Lean and Agile methodologies and to assess their organisational culture. It may also help researchers to study models of software developer experience and value systems.

Keywords: values, Agile software development, Lean software development, survey, quantitative study, developer experience, human factors.

1   Introduction

In contemporary organisations, software teams often consist of people with varied cultural backgrounds and different personal characteristics. While diversity in knowledge and expertise can improve team performance, diversity in personal values can lead to conflict and lower performance [1]. Several studies indicate that diversity enhances performance by broadening the perspectives of work groups [2]. A shared professional culture can help individuals overcome differences in personal values and perform better. Culture and values have been considered important in software development for several reasons. In an essay on the history of the Agile Manifesto, Jim Highsmith, one of the founders of the Agile movement, notes [3]:

> At the core, I believe Agile Methodologists are really about "mushy" stuff – about delivering good products to customers by operating in an environment

G. Cantone and M. Marchesi (Eds.): XP 2014, LNBIP 179, pp. 218–233, 2014.

that does more than talk about "people as our most important asset" but actually "acts" as if people were the most important, and lose the word "asset". So in the final analysis, the meteoric rise of interest in – and sometimes tremendous criticism of – Agile Methodologies is about the mushy stuff of values and culture.

Integrating culture and value concerns into the software development process is a promising way to enhance developer experience [4]. While the importance of these issues is easy to understand, values themselves are very difficult to grasp. There is a lack of research illuminating the structure of values among software developers working with Lean and Agile methodologies. Many previous studies attempting to grasp the level of "agility" or "leanness" resort to checklists of methodological procedures. An improved understanding of the values that form the basis of individual reasoning and action, and their relationship to normative values in the Lean and Agile software development philosophies, would allow a discourse that goes beyond the practices that have been documented to date. In this paper, we report on a quantitative survey study which examines the structure of the Lean/Agile value system among professional software developers.

The rest of this paper is structured as follows. In Section 2, we first examine theories of human values; belief systems that influence evaluation of events and choice of action in broad and general terms. We then examine literature on Lean and Agile approaches in both software engineering and other fields, in order to gain a picture of possible value dimensions. In Section 3, we describe the research design: the research questions, survey design, sampling, survey deployment, and methods of analysis. In Section 4, we report the results of the study in detail. In Section 5, we discuss the findings and limitations of the study. Finally, in Section 6, we summarise the findings and outline some possible future directions.

2   Related Work

Software engineers' motivation has received much systematic attention [5,6,7]. Motivation is moderated by complex socio-cognitive factors, including the cultural context with its value system and individual personal characteristics [6]. Values form an important component in motivation [8], and, thus influence performance and overall work experience. An understanding of values is therefore vital for improving many outcomes, including motivation and developer experience [4].

2.1   Theories of Human Values

Human values are deeply rooted, abstract motivations that guide, justify, or explain attitudes, norms, opinions, and actions [9]. Values constitute concepts or beliefs that serve as standards for desirable end-states or behaviours. They are deeply linked to affect and the self-concept [10]: when a value is activated in an individual, a corresponding feeling also occurs. Values prime attitudes and guide the selection of behaviours and events [10,11,12,13]. They are ordered by relative importance, forming a system of priorities to guide action [9]. Values are sometimes divided into *terminal* and *instrumental* values (e.g. [10]). Terminal values represent desirable end-states of existence – the goals that a person would like to achieve during their lifetime. Instrumental values represent preferable modes of behaviour – the means of achieving the terminal values. Values have practical consequences in many everyday situations. They are the most abstract type of social cognition used to guide general responses to classes of stimuli [14]. Values can guide the selection of behaviours and evaluation of events [13], and they impact organisational outcomes [15], business ethics [16,17], and managerial behaviour [18]. It should be noted that values do not focus on specific objects or situations [10,8]. They explain behavioural patterns over longer periods of time rather than specific behaviours in particular situations [19].

Values are thought to stem from three universal requirements for human existence: individual biological needs; the preconditions for coordinated social action; and the survival and welfare needs of groups [13,12]. Values are influenced by the cultures in which humans live. Hofstede's extensive work on values found four basic dimensions on which national cultures differ: Power Distance (the degree of inequality considered normal), Uncertainty Avoidance (preference for structured situations), Individualism (preference to act as an individual rather than as a group), and Masculinity (valuing things, power, and assertiveness more than people, quality of life, and nurturance) [20].

Fig. 1. Theoretical circumplex structure of relations among motivational types of values in the Schwartz model. (Adapted from Bilsky & Schwartz [21].)

The Schwartz [9,12,13] model of individual value differences has been widely used in social and cross-cultural psychology. The theory has been extensively verified in numerous countries, and postulates that values form a circumplex of related motivations, so that adjacent values in the model are mutually compatible (Figure 1). For example, the shared motivational emphasis in the combination stimulation – self-direction is an intrinsic motivation for mastery and openness to change, while the combination stimulation – hedonism represents a desire for affectively pleasant arousal [9].

2.2   Values in Lean and Agile Software Development Methodologies

Values play a special role in software development methodologies. Lean and Agile concepts have become commonplace in today's software development landscape. Both approaches have a core set of values that establish their fundamental philosophies, forming a base for more practical rules and methods.

Lean Values. The term Lean Software Development was introduced in 2003 through the book "Lean Software Development: An Agile Toolkit" [22]. This treatment of Lean is positioned in relation to Agile software development. However, the roots of Lean thinking extends further back in history. Lean, or Toyota Production Systems (TPS), are just-in-time manufacturing systems initially developed at Toyota during 1948–1975 [23,24]. This approach concerns not only manufacturing procedures, but is a comprehensive management philosophy – a foundation for competitive strength that relies on a deeply ingrained corporate culture [25]. In 2004, Jeffrey Liker published "The Toyota Way", introducing Toyota's corporate culture and the TPS to a large audience and popularising the Lean manufacturing philosophy [26].

The Toyota Way is the foundation of TPS [25,26]. It is a summary of the managerial convictions and value systems inherited within Toyota as tacit knowledge; a code of conduct for its employees at all levels [25]. Numerous companies have attempted to emulate the structural parts of Lean, but have not succeeded in introducing the accompanying organisational culture and mindset [27]. Several authors have argued that Lean cannot be implemented effectively without also implementing the underlying value system [25,27,26,28,29,23]. Liker attributes the difficulties in introducing Lean to a disregard for the Toyota Way [26,25]. Liker points out that managerial understanding of the Toyota Way, and the ability to instil this thinking into the minds of workers, is essential in order to raise the level of lean companies [26].

Several authors have summarised essential Lean thinking. According to Womack and Jones [30] and Liker [26], Lean focuses on identifying customer value and delivering it by letting the product flow uninterrupted through a series of value-adding processes. Thus waste becomes visible and can be eliminated. Liker lists 14 Lean principles, including emphasising "a long-term philosophy, even at the expense of short-term financial goals"; levelling workload to work "like the tortoise, not the hare", building "a culture of stopping to fix problems, to get quality right the first time", "[growing] leaders who thoroughly understand the work, live the philosophy, and teach it to others", making decisions "slowly by consensus, [...] considering all options", and "[becoming] a learning organization through relentless reflection and continuous improvement" [26].

Agile Values. In manufacturing, Agile is often considered the next step after Lean, but the two may also be viewed as complementary [31]. Agile software development was a response to perceived difficulties stemming from a turbulent business environment [32,33]. Though the term Agile software development was introduced in its namesake manifesto in 2001 [34], few of its ideas are new. Larman and Basili note that incremental and iterative development was in use as

early as 1957 [35], making the approach several decades old. The initial driving
force behind Agile software development consisted of practitioners and consultants [36]. Combined with a lack of rigorous conceptual studies, the result is a
fragmented understanding of Agile, unclear definitions and even direct contradic-
tions. Meanwhile, a unique characteristic of Agile software development is that
it was founded on a set of core values [34]:

1. Individuals and interactions over processes and tools.
2. Working software over comprehensive documentation.
3. Customer collaboration over contract negotiation.
4. Responding to change over following a plan.

However, the perception and understanding of these values among practitioners is not necessarily literal. A critical analysis [37] examined the discourse
of key methodological contributors using Lasswell's value framework [38], and
found strong expressions of enlightenment – valuing knowledge and insight – and
power – valuing possibly coercive influence to affect policies. Wealth and skill
were present to a lesser degree; rectitude, respect, affection, and well-being were
only weakly expressed. The study claims that this is a legitimisation strategy
to improve diffusion and industry adoption of Agile [37]. There is thus room to
consider whether the true values of Lean and Agile practitioners are different.
As practical enactments are often a combination of Lean and Agile, it is justified
to examine the value structure of both methodologies as a single expanded set.
While Lean and Agile can be considered complementary and partially overlapping, it is not clear how the combination of their underlying value systems are
understood by practitioners, a gap that this study aims to address.

3   Research Design and Execution

We took a quantitative survey approach to examine the structure of Lean and
Agile values among software developers. We sought to expand the understanding
of this construct by addressing the following research questions:

RQ1 What is the structure of the Lean and Agile value system among software
developers?
RQ2 What is the relationship between the Lean and Agile value system and
the general human value system?
RQ3 What is the relationship between the Lean and Agile value system and
individual personality?

3.1   Survey Design

We designed a survey with inventories on human values, personality, and
Lean/Agile values. The survey was piloted twice with a small number of students to adjust length, improve item wording, and remove low-quality items. We
used the Schwartz Portrait Values Questionnaire (PVQ) [12] to obtain a measure of human values for each respondent. The PVQ measures the ten basic value

orientations shown in Figure 1. It consists of 21 short verbal descriptions, portraits, of different people, each implying an orientation towards a single value type. For each, respondents must answer the question "How much like you is this person?" on a six-point scale. We used the Ten-Item Personality Inventory (TIPI) [39], a short instrument for assessing personality according to the Big Five personality model. While being short, the TIPI correlates well with established instruments such as the BFI, NEO-FFI, and NEO-PI-R, and although it does not allow assessment of individual sub-scales, it is suitable for research purposes when personality is not the main topic of research [39]. To assess Lean/Agile values, we devised a set of value statement items. These were derived from multiple literature sources, including research articles and books aimed for practitioners. Respondents were asked to indicate their agreement with each statement on a seven-point Likert scale. We included several different wordings of items, and items that were not explicitly given by any single source, but were implied. The survey included a total of 94 items, available as supplementary material [40].

3.2 Sample and Survey Deployment

Our main focus at this stage of research was Finnish software developers who work with Lean and/or Agile software development methods. However, we also allowed respondents from other countries to participate. We deployed the survey online during February to June 2013, and recruited participants from several sources where we knew experienced software development professionals could be reached. We directly contacted three companies in Finland; each agreed to let one of their teams participate in the survey. In addition, we obtained a number of respondents through social media discussion forums on relevant topics. Finally, we ran a Google AdWords campaign, promoting the survey to people who searched for related topics. Respondents were also recruited at scientific conferences with industry participants.

3.3 Analysis Methods

We used agglomerative hierarchical clustering and nonmetric multidimensional scaling to examine the structure of the responses. Agglomerative hierarchical clustering is a statistical data analysis method [41]. In our case, each survey response can be characterised as a point in a value space where Lean/Agile value items constitute the spatial dimensions. The clustering initially considers each point as an individual cluster, working bottom-up to iteratively join them based on similarity, i.e. closeness in the multidimensional space. The resulting tree structure reveals (dis)similarities in the data. We used cluster averages for agglomeration, and correlation as the distance metric.

Multidimensional scaling (MDS) is a technique for reducing the dimensionality of a data set while retaining its discriminative properties [42]. MDS can collapse a data set into a two-dimensional representation, allowing an accessible visual representation of the data for interpretation. While value structures have previously been examined using theory-based MDS, where value dimensions are assigned initial locations, we chose not to use such an approach. The reasons for this are twofold. First, our aim at this stage is not to confirm an articulated hypothesis on Lean/Agile value structures but to explore the construct. Second, current literature is too fragmented to support a single theory-based hypothesis. This is contrary to the situation in, e.g., research on general human values, where such theoretical support does exist (see e.g. [21]).

4 Analysis and Results

Of 61 received responses, 57 were retained after cleaning the data. Unfortunately, due to several avenues used to contact potential respondents, the response rate of the survey could not be determined. The respondents were between 22 and 62 years of age, with a median age of 35 years. 47 respondents were male, 7 female, and 3 did not disclose their gender. Respondents' country of birth was Finland (65%), Germany (7%), Sweden (7%), Turkey (4%) and USA (4%); other countries (United Kingdom, Bangladesh, The Netherlands, Italy, Russia, Israel and China) formed the remaining 13%. 72% of respondents currently lived in Finland, and 63% were of Finnish nationality. 14% had completed high school or vocational education, 31% had a Bachelor's degree, and 46% a Master's degree. 86% were currently employed. The median years of work experience was 12. Respondents reported working in a wide range of positions, including software development, testing, architecture, and coaching, product management, and consulting. A small number of company owners and top management members responded to the survey. Organisations ranged from small (less than 10 employees) to large (more than 1000 employees), with the mean size being between 100 and 499 employees. The demographics match the intended population, with a relevant background and level of professional experience.

4.1 Structure of Lean and Agile Values

Figure 2 shows the hierarchical clustering of the Lean/Agile values data. Ten clusters, highlighted with a solid surrounding box, have a confidence level of $p \geq 0.9$, indicating a large degree of support. An additional cluster and three expanded clusters, indicated by dashed lines, have somewhat weaker confidence levels ($p \geq 0.8$ or higher) but are theoretically motivated. We examine the contents of these clusters from left to right.

Valuing a Narrow Work Focus. The items in the first cluster represents the view that software developers should focus on their technical work and not deal with stakeholders or management of work: "Programmers are supposed to write code, and it's not their responsibility if tasks overlap or are unclear" (v80), "User needs might be important, but software developers should focus on the implementation details" (v22), "The main thing is just to get the work done, it's not my job to figure out work processes" (v65). This is contrary to ideas of self-organisation, process ownership, continuous self-improvement, and inclusion of the customer in the development process – notions that are valued in Agile development.

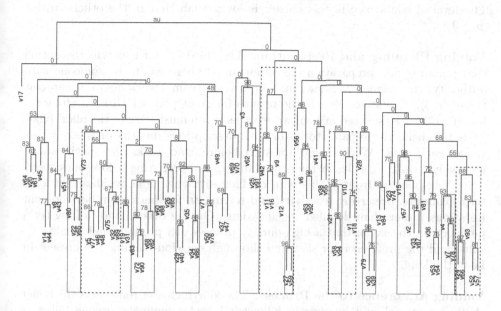

Fig. 2. Hierarchical clustering dendrogram of Lean/Agile values data. Variables are shown as leaves in the tree. The numbers in the branch junctions indicate the p-value of the corresponding subtree. The value (AU) is the "approximately unbiased" p-value [43]. Clusters with $p \geq 0.9$ (AU) are marked with a solid box; theoretically motivated clusters are marked with a dashed-line box.

Valuing Flexibility in Task Execution and Leadership. The second cluster includes beliefs concerning flexibility. "I try to be flexible and if someone has an important task that is not in the iteration backlog, I do it anyway" (v73), "Working on many things simultaneously makes me more productive" (v5), and "I have no problem switching tasks even though I have already started another task" (v77) (task-level flexibility). "Several product owners is better than one product owner" (v46), and "To get more done in software projects, you must work longer hours" (v48) point to flexibility in work direction and amount. One person working on too many tasks simultaneously is against Agile and Lean principles; working longer hours and having several product owners can be seen as having an adverse effect on the ability to maintain a constant pace of development, something that both Agile and Lean philosophies strive to achieve.

"Asking someone who already knows the answer to a question is always better than figuring out the solution oneself" (v75), "The best software developers are highly specialised and focus on their speciality" (v32), and "Only those with the greatest knowledge and highest expertise in one particular area should make decisions that have to do with that area" (v89) represent information-seeking flexibility, and the view that expertise should lead to decision-making authority. Agreement with these statements represent valuing a strong distinction between leader and follower, and giving up individual control to follow given instructions. The level of confidence in this cluster is lower than that of the other clusters ($p \geq 0.8$).

Valuing Planning and Preparation. The third cluster concerns the notion that planning and preparation are important: "There has to be someone with authority who regularly reviews and approves a team's work before it can continue" (v83), "Great software is the result of a great plan which is carefully followed" (v72), "To succeed in a software project, you must stick to the plan" (v90), "It is beneficial to prepare stories or task descriptions months or weeks in advance" (v68), and "Work should not start before exact tasks and specifications are ready" (v82). This cluster refers to planning and preparing before work starts – the "big plan up front". This is in conflict with the Agile avoidance of long-term planning, preferring reactivity, and relying on feedback from development iterations rather than detailed specifications. On the other hand, a long-term perspective, the belief that a high-quality process will produce high-quality results, and the preference for slow and thorough decision-making, are present in Lean thinking.

Valuing Adherence to the Process. The fourth cluster represents the belief that processes should be strictly followed:"I prefer having everyone follow a process rather than interacting with people to agree on what to do next" (v29), "Even if something is broken in the software under development, the focus has to be on what was planned, not on fixing everything" (v35), "I prefer large software development teams rather than small ones" (v34), and "Great software is the result of carefully applying a great software development process" (v86). This view may be connected to a preference for working in large organisations (v34), where the impact of individual deviation is negligible: "It's ok to make up a feature in order to justify the use of the latest technology" (v40).

Valuing Discipline. The fifth cluster emphasises discipline: "A development process has to be followed strictly and with discipline" (v3), "Team members should be able to justify why they use certain tools" (v62), and "Having no development process leads to chaos and failed projects" (v25). However, the statement "Great software is the result of constant replanning when changes occur" (v91) is also within this cluster, indicating that discipline does not preclude responsiveness to change.

Valuing Reliance on People. The sixth cluster concerns valuing people, represented directly in the Agile Manifesto: "Having the best people in the project is more important than having the best development tools" (v27), and "Having the best people in the project is more important than spending time on managing the process" (v59). However, by including some additional items in this branch (Figure 2; $p \geq 0.87$), we can see a more complicated picture: "People are more important for success than following a development process" (v12), "If something is broken in the software under development, it should be fixed immediately" (v9), "If an ongoing task can be finished very soon, it should always be finished even if there is a more important task pending" (v42), "It is very important for team members to know the contents of the contract(s) made with the paying customer" (v11), and "It is impossible to fully plan a software project" (v16). In this extended cluster, "valuing people" relates to responsiveness and knowledge of contractual obligations, and to the belief that planning a software project is impossible. In other words, this value is instrumental, aiming to increase performance, not necessarily to improve well-being.

Valuing the Freedom to Organise. The seventh cluster concerns self-organisation and responsiveness: "In software development projects, I prefer to just solve problems as they come rather than thinking far ahead" (v21), "The best architectures and designs are created when teams can organise themselves" (v58), and "Software development team members should be allowed to organise themselves in any way they see fit" (v94). Extending the cluster with three additional items ($p \geq 0.85$) yields a more complete picture: "Physically moving around a lot lowers my productivity" (v10), "Software developers should be allowed to freely choose any tools they wish to use" (v1), and "Software development team members should have the authority to choose what they work on" (v18). This cluster seems to be in opposition to the fifth cluster. High agreement here could represent valuing freedom for developers to learn and organise their work.

Valuing a Sense of Purpose. The eighth cluster represents the value of knowing the purpose of one's work and its role for an end goal: "Not knowing who the end user is during a project is a big problem" (v79), "When implementing a feature, it is critical to know who needs it and why" (v30), and "All team members must have a clear understanding of who the software is intended for" (v39).

Valuing Predictability and Justification. The ninth cluster concerns a desire for uncertainty reduction. It is related to the desire to base action on evidence and observation rather than prescribed rules or unjustified orders. "Before implementing a feature, its value should be tested on end users" (v15), "Requirements can change, but it should not be permitted to change requirements during an iteration" (v67), "I want to spend time on identifying and eliminating unnecessary work in software development projects" (v2), "Tasks should always be doable in one iteration" (v33), and "I need to feel sure that the goals set for each development iteration are achievable" (v87). This cluster highlights a preference for specific, justified, and time- or scope-limited commitment.

Valuing Collaboration. The tenth cluster shows another side of valuing people: the desire for close, collaborative work: "I wish pair programming would always be used in the projects I work in" (v4), "When faced with a large problem, everyone in a software development team should stop what they are doing and work together to solve it" (v7), and "It is best to meet in person instead of calling or emailing" (v78). This cluster separates the instrumental people values in cluster four from the benefits of collaborative work, putting emphasis on the value of working together.

Valuing Broad Stakeholder Involvement. The eleventh and final cluster concerns customer involvement: "Great software is the result of the customer constantly monitoring the project" (v24), and "Great software is the result of close collaboration with the paying customer" (v66). In some ways, this is the counterpart to the first cluster. By cluster inclusion criteria ($p \geq 0.88$), we can gain a broader understanding: "Everyone in a team should know what all the others are working on" (v93), "My highest priority is to satisfy the customer by continuously delivering valuable software" (v52), and "Working software is the only right measure of project progress" (v57). Together, these items indicate valuing customer involvement, with the customer and team co-creating the software.

4.2   Relationship to Human Values

In order to answer RQ2, we examined how the Lean/Agile value dimensions obtained through clustering relate to general human values. Figure 3 shows a two-dimensional MDS of both sets of value dimensions. Although there are some relationships between the two, our Lean/Agile value dimensions exhibit a structure that is different from the universal values. On the horizontal axis, human value dimensions are mostly centred, with Lean/Agile dimensions towards either end. The latter can thus be seen as polarised variants of the former. This axis represents a continuum ranging from an open, inclusive, and self-enhancing view to more authoritative, plan-based, and conforming values. This axis can be seen as representing the traditional dichotomy between "bureaucratic" and "people-oriented" views of software development approaches. The two value systems are more mixed on the vertical axis, but human values are present at either end. The

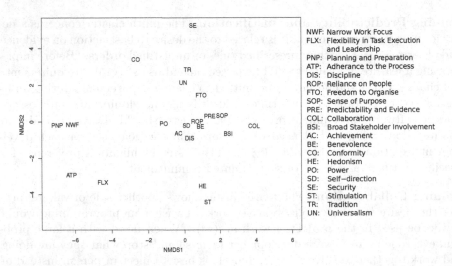

Fig. 3. Two-dimensional MDS of Lean/Agile value dimensions combined with Schwartz value data. The dimensions of the Lean/Agile values data are shown as variable names, and the Schwartz value dimensions are shown as two capital letters.

dimensions in the lower end are related to openness to change, those in the middle are mixed, and conservation values are located in the high end. Lean/Agile values in the lower end can be interpreted as a relaxed attitude towards being led; the ones in the middle reflect a balanced and disciplined view required for collaborative work and group decision-making; the higher end reflects a self-oriented and more individualistic stance. This axis can be seen as a continuum of values regarding decision-making, control, and ambition that ranges from a focus on the self, through a collective view, and ends with carefreeness and flexibility to the degree of giving up control.

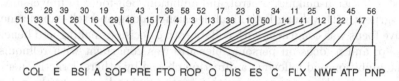

Fig. 4. One-dimensional MDS of Lean/Agile values combined with Big Five personality traits. The numbers represent each respondent, while the letters represent Lean/Agile values and personality traits. ES: Emotional stability, E: Extraversion, O: Openness to experience, A: Agreeableness, C: Conscientiousness.

4.3   Relationship to Personality

Lean/Agile values may be expressions of individual personality. We therefore examine the relationship between Lean/Agile values and personality traits. Figure 4 shows an MDS of the Lean/Agile values with the Big Five personality traits. The data is scaled to a single dimension to gain an overall comparison. The scale can be considered as a continuum ranging from adherence to processes and roles, and submission to leadership, to a more collaborative and social approach to work. Extraversion, and to a slightly lesser extent, Agreeableness, tend towards the latter end of the continuum. Openness to experience is close to Reliance on People, but interestingly, Discipline also falls near this personality trait. The meaning of Discipline in the Lean/Agile values model may not refer to lack of imagination or creativity, but rather to a systematic approach to dealing with work. This corroborates the findings presented earlier (see Section 4.1, Discipline). Emotional Stability and Conscientiousness are closely located. However, they are far from the adherence end of the scale, indicating a stronger relation to the values of professional, systematic openness and creativity.

5   Discussion and Limitations

We are now in a position to answer our research questions. RQ1 concerned the structure of the Lean and Agile value system. Our analysis revealed eleven main dimensions (see Section 4.1), providing a model for the Lean and Agile value system. We can see that this model touches upon several aspects of software development work. The value structure reflects the holistic, practice-oriented approach in both Lean and Agile software development. It consists of a mixture of human aspects on individual and group levels, concerns regarding process adherence and flexibility, and notions of what is essential to meaningful work. The model is a foundation on which further studies can be built, as well a framework within which practitioners can position themselves.

RQ2 concerned the relationship between the value system and the general human value system. The largest differences lie on a continuum ranging from high preference for bureaucratic order to people-orientation, where differences in Lean/Agile values are more pronounced. Similarities exist on a continuum regarding type of decision-making, control, and ambition. Self-focus in universal values was congruent with valuing individual decision-making and self-enhancement; a collective focus was congruent with collaborative decision-making and benefiting the group; and a focus on personal pleasure was congruent with relinquishing personal ambition and following a direction chosen by others. Practitioners may want to consider their placement on this continuum and compare the value system of their local or corporate culture with their perception of Lean and Agile values.

RQ3 concerned the relationship between the Lean/Agile value system and individual personality. Our interpretation is that the two may be weakly linked. A preference for social values relates to the Extroversion/Agreeableness pair, while valuing the systematic, creative, and organisational side is more related to Openness to experience, Emotional stability, and Conscientiousness. However, values pertaining to adherence to processes, roles, and leadership, do not seem connected to personality. Valuing these dimensions may have more to do with company and national culture, schooling, and the business area in which a person works.

The largest threat to validity in this study is the limited sample. It is biased by lack of random selection and reliance on participant self-selection. It may not be representative of a larger Finnish population. However, based on the demographic characteristics of the sample, we argue that our results represent a reasonable starting point for empirically examining the Lean and Agile value construct. A second threat to validity is the possible bias in the survey instrument. We are aware that the instrument may lack some aspects of Lean and Agile thinking. However, the selection made here does represent a large number of aspects in the literature, and we argue that it provides reasonable coverage given the fragmented nature of the field.

6   Conclusions and Future Work

In this paper, we reported on a study that investigated the value structure among Lean/Agile software developers. We found a model with eleven dimensions that structures Lean/Agile values as perceived by practitioners. Our analysis indicates that Lean/Agile values touch upon software development work as a whole rather than being limited to specific sub-areas. Comparing the value system to universal human values indicates that while there are some important links between the two, there are also areas where Lean/Agile values are more specific than universal human values. Some weak links between the Lean/Agile values and individual personality were also found.

The implications of our findings are twofold. First, practitioners can benefit from making implicit values more explicit in their work. Basing software development methodology on values can be beneficial: as values increase adaptive fitness by providing individuals with flexible patterns of behavioural response options [44], steering software development through values can be effective. In other words, rather than specifying actions for specific situations, a values-based approach allows practitioners to react dynamically in new and unforeseen situations. Also, a methodology that is compatible with cultural values has better odds of being accepted by practitioners, thus increasing chances for positive adoption. Being able to articulate the dimensions of the value system, rather than speaking in terms of methodological practices, could facilitate clarity and flexibility, increase opportunities for diversity in the workplace, and improve developer experience. This paper contributes a model which can be used for these purposes in practice.

Second, our findings have implications for future research. The construct validity of the model proposed in this paper should be tested further. With larger and more controlled samples, and by integrating the emerging literature on Lean software development, the combination of Lean and Agile, and the scaling of Lean and Agile methodologies, better validity may be obtained. Larger samples are also needed for other statistical techniques such as factor analysis. Apart from strengthening the results presented here, future research could benefit by examining Lean/Agile approaches from the perspective of culture and values rather than from traditional software engineering constructs such as methodologies or processes. As demonstrated in this paper, the often fuzzy and tacit understanding of Lean/Agile software development held by practitioners in the field can be made explicit by leveraging theory and research methods from social and behavioural sciences. In our own work, we aim to explore the possibilities of an improved sample to increase the breadth and validity of the results presented in this paper. We encourage other researchers to replicate our findings and expand the understanding of software development driven by values.

References

1. Liang, T.P., Liu, C.C., Lin, T.M., Lin, B.: Effect of team diversity on software project performance. Industrial Management and Data Systems 107(5), 636–653 (2007)
2. Patrick, H.A., Kumar, V.R.: Managing Workplace Diversity. SAGE Open (2012)
3. Highsmith, J.: History: The Agile Manifesto (2001) (accessed January 01, 2014)
4. Fagerholm, F., Münch, J.: Developer Experience: Concept and Definition. In: Proceedings of the International Conference on Software and System Process, pp. 73–77 (2012)
5. Beecham, S., Baddoo, N., Hall, T., Robinson, H., Sharp, H.: Motivation in Software Engineering: A systematic literature review. Information and Software Technology 50(9-10), 860–878 (2008)

6. Sharp, H., Baddoo, N., Beecham, S., Hall, T., Robinson, H.: Models of motivation in software engineering. Information and Software Technology 51(1), 219–233 (2009)

7. França, A., Gouveia, T., Santos, P., Santana, C., da Silva, F.: Motivation in software engineering: A systematic review update. In: 15th Annual Conference on Evaluation and Assessment in Software Engineering (EASE 2011), pp. 154–163 (2011)

8. Rokeach, M.: Understanding human values. Free Press, New York (1979)

9. Schwartz, S.: Universals in the content and structure of values: Theoretical advances and empirical tests in 20 countries. Advances in Experimental Social Psychology 25(1), 1–65 (1992)

10. Rokeach, M.: The nature of human values. Free Press, New York (1973)

11. Feather, N.T.: Values, deservingness, and attitudes toward high achievers: Research on tall poppies, pp. 215–251. Lawrence Erlbaum Associates, Inc., Hillsdale (1996)

12. Schwartz, S., Bilsky, W.: Toward a Theory of the Universal Content and Structure of Values: Extensions and Cross-Cultural Replications. Journal of Personality and Social Psychology 58(5), 878–891 (1990)

13. Schwartz, S., Bilsky, W.: Toward A Universal Psychological Structure of Human Values. Journal of Personality and Social Psychology 53(3), 550–562 (1987)

14. Kahle, L.: Social values and consumer behavior: Research from the list of values, pp. 135–151. Lawrence Erlbaum Associates, Inc. (1996)

15. Weeks, W., Kahle, L.: Social values and salespeople's effort. Entrepreneurial versus routine selling. Journal of Business Research 20(2), 183–190 (1990)

16. Feather, N.: Values, Valences, and Choice: The Influence of Values on the Perceived Attractiveness and Choice of Alternatives. Journal of Personality and Social Psychology 68(6), 1135–1151 (1995)

17. Mumford, M., Helton, W., Decker, B., Connelly, M., Doorn, J.V.: Values and Beliefs Related to Ethical Decisions. Teaching Business Ethics 7(2), 139–170 (2003)

18. Smith, P., Peterson, M., Schwartz, S.: Cultural Values, Sources of Guidance, and their Relevance to Managerial Behavior: A 47-Nation Study. Journal of Cross-Cultural Psychology 33(2), 188–208 (2002)

19. Bond, M.H., Kwok, L., Schwartz, S.: Explaining Choices in Procedural and Distributive Justice Across Cultures. International Journal of Psychology 27(2), 211 (1992)

20. Hofstede, G.: Culture's consequences: International differences in work-related values, vol. 5. Sage Publications, Inc. (1984)

21. Bilsky, W., Janik, M., Schwartz, S.: The Structural Organization of Human Values – Evidence from Three Rounds of the European Social Survey (ESS). Journal of Cross-Cultural Psychology 42(5), 759–776 (2011)

22. Poppendieck, M.: Lean Software Development: An Agile Toolkit. Addison-Wesley Professional (2003)

23. Ōno, T.: Toyota production system: beyond large-scale production. Productivity Press (1988)

24. Ward, A.: Lean product and process development. Lean Enterprise Institute (2007)

25. Saruta, M.: Toyota Production Systems: The 'Toyota Way' and Labour-Management Relations. Asian Business & Management 5(4), 487 (2006)

26. Liker, J.: The Toyota Way: 14 Management Principles from the World's Greatest Manufacturer. McGraw-Hill, New York (2004)

27. Hines, P., Holwe, M., Rich, N.: Learning to evolve: A review of contemporary lean thinking. International Journal of Operations & Production Management 24(9), 994–1011 (2004)

28. Holweg, M., Pil, F.: Successful Build-To-Order Strategies Start With the Customer. MIT Sloan Management Review 43(1), 74–83 (2001)
29. Womack, J.P., Jones, D., Roos, D.: The Machine That Changed the World. Simon & Schuster (2007)
30. Womack, J.P., Jones, D.: Banish waste and create wealth in your corporation. Free Press, New York (2003)
31. Naylor, J.B., Naim, M.M., Berry, D.: Leagility: Integrating the lean and agile manufacturing paradigms in the total supply chain. International Journal of Production Economics 62(1-2), 107–118 (1999)
32. Cockburn, A., Highsmith, J.: Agile software development, the people factor. Computer 34(11), 131–133 (2001)
33. Highsmith, J., Cockburn, A.: Agile software development: the business of innovation. Computer 34(9), 120–127 (2001)
34. Alliance, T.A.: The Agile Manifesto (2001), http://www.agilemanifesto.org/ (accessed January 01, 2014)
35. Larman, C., Basili, V.: Iterative and Incremental Development: A Brief History. Computer 36(6), 47–56 (2003)
36. Conboy, K.: Agility from first principles: Reconstructing the concept of agility in information systems development. Information Systems Research 20(3), 329–354 (2009)
37. Lawrence, C., Rodriguez, P.: The Interpretation and Legitimization of Values in Agile's Organizing Vision. In: Proceedings of the European Conference on Information Systems (ECIS), pp. 10–13 (2012)
38. Lasswell, H., Kaplan, A.: Power & Society: a Framework for Political Inquiry. Yale University Press, New Haven (1950)
39. Gosling, S., Rentfrow, P., Swann, J.W.: A very brief measure of the Big-Five personality domains. Journal of Research in Personality 37(6), 504–528 (2003)
40. Fagerholm, F.: Lean and Agile Values Survey 2013. Technical report (2014), http://www.cs.helsinki.fi/people/fabian.fagerholm/agilevalues2013/ (retrieved January 04, 2014)
41. Johnson, S.: Hierarchical clustering schemes. Psychometrika 32(3), 241–254 (1967)
42. Davison, M.: Introduction to Multidimensional Scaling and Its Applications. Applied Psychological Measurement 7(4), 373–379 (1983)
43. Suzuki, R., Shimodaira, H.: pvclust: Hierarchical Clustering with P-Values via Multiscale Bootstrap Resampling, R package version 1.2-2 (2011)
44. Michod, R.E.: Biology and the origin of values, pp. 261–272. Aldine de Gruyter, Hawthorne (1993)

Agile Methodologies in Web Programming: A Survey

Giulio Barabino[1], Daniele Grechi[1], Danilo Tigano[1]
Erika Corona[2], and Giulio Concas[2]

[1] DITEN, University of Genova, Italy
[2] DIEE, University of Cagliari, Italy
{giulio.barabino,daniele.grechi,danilo.tigano}@unige.it,
{erika.corona,concas}@unica.it

Abstract. This paper reports the results from a survey concerning the use of Agile Methodologies (AM), techniques and tools for Web Programming. The survey lasted from October to December 2013, and involved 112 Web application developers from 32 countries. Its main purpose was to assess the usage of AMs, and of specific practices and tools, in the context of Web programming and of related technologies, such as Content Management Systems. The results confirm a broad adoption of AMs among Web developers, and the prevalence of Scrum among AMs.

Keywords: Web programming, Agile Methodologies, CMS.

1 Introduction

Agile Methodologies is a name referring to a set of practices and processes for software development that were created by experienced practitioners. The principles inspiring AMs were formalized in 2001 in the "Agile Manifesto" [1]. The main goal of AMs is to increase the ability to react and respond to changing customer, business and technological needs at all organizational levels [2]. Several software companies are moving to Agile software development to improve quality and productivity and to reduce delivery times.

AMs are commonly reputed to be useful for driving the development of non-critical systems under vague or changing requirements. This is exactly the context of most Web applications. We call "Web application" a system that makes use of Web browsers – possibly running on mobile devices – to interact with the user. So, a Web application spans from simple or complex Web sites to mobile apps, to custom client-server systems built using this approach.

The goal of this work is the study the extent to which, and how, AMs, Agile practices and Agile tools are used by Web programmers. To achieve this goal we investigated not only the specific AMs and practices used, but also the tools, frameworks, databases and languages most commonly used for this type of application.

G. Cantone and M. Marchesi (Eds.): XP 2014, LNBIP 179, pp. 234–241, 2014.

Some surveys on AM usage have already been published, such as ref. [3], or the very detailed survey conducted annually by VersionOne [4]. However, our intent was to create a specific survey to ascertain whether and how AMs are used for Web programming, a sector of software engineering that has become very large in the past years.

The paper is organized as follows: in Section 2 we present the research method, the gathered data and the results. Section 3 presents a discussion and concludes the paper.

2   Research Method and Gathered Data

Our survey includes 12 questions, and it is intended to be answered by personnel involved in Web programming. It gathers information about the type and size of the respondent's company, the possible usage of AMs or Agile practices, and the technologies used during Web application development. It was created with PollDaddy [5] because of its better flexibility compared to similar tools. The data collection lasted for about three months, starting from October 2013 – survey publishing date – to the end of December 2013. The survey was filled on the Web. It was advertised through a call on the main reference sites related to the Agile world and Web programming, through requests directly given at an Italian Agile conference, and through emails sent to fellow researchers, asking them to forward it to the software companies they were in contact with. Clearly, the respondent set cannot be considered an unbiased sample of Web developers.

2.1   Main Features of the Sample

The total number of respondents is 112, divided in 78 "Agile" and 34 "non-Agile" persons (6 respondents, 5.4% of the sample, belonging to the Italian Agile Conference). Figure 1 shows with different levels of green the nations where the respondents live and their relative number. As you can see, the survey was answered by people living all over the world (32 countries). The heterogeneity of the sample is in fact a prerequisite for the external validity of the results.

Country	Nr.	%	Country	Nr.	%	Country	Nr.	%
United States	24	21.4%	Estonia	2	1.8%	Brazil	1	0.9%
Italy	23	20.5%	Panama	1	0.9%	Bangladesh	1	0.9%
Germany	12	10.7%	New Zealand	1	0.9%	Australia	1	0.9%
United Kingdom	7	6.3%	Mexico	1	0.9%	Austria	1	0.9%
Sweden	6	5.4%	Mongolia	1	0.9%	Czech Republic	1	0.9%
France	5	4.5%	Philippines	1	0.9%	Denmark	1	0.9%
Netherlands	3	2.7%	Pakistan	1	0.9%	Indonesia	1	0.9%
India	3	2.7%	South Africa	1	0.9%	Hungary	1	0.9%
Canada	3	2.7%	Turkey	1	0.9%	Hong Kong	1	0.9%
Israel	2	1.8%	Singapore	1	0.9%	Iran, Islamic Rep. of	1	0.9%
Spain	2	1.8%	Moldova, Rep. of	1	0.9%			

Fig. 1. Sample distribution

The first questions of the survey identify the user from a business point of view (job role and type of company), together with the perceived use of Agile practices in her/his working activities. Tables 1, 2 and 3 show the main characteristics of our sample, composed for the greatest part of software developers (42%) belonging to small/medium companies (78%). We compare our results (first column of each figure) to those obtained by the 2013 VersionOne survey [4], where it is possible.

Table 1. Role of the respondents

Q1. What is your job at your company?	% of total	VersionOne [4]
Developer	42%	23%
Product/Project manager	19%	-
Consultant	12%	33%
Other Option	11%	14%
Develop team leader	10%	15%
IT staff	4%	3%
Tester	4%	-

Table 2. Size of the sample

Q2. How many people do work in your company?	% of total
From 11 to 100 people	36%
From 2 to 10 people	27%
Only one	15%
More than 500 people	12%
From 101 to 500 people	10%

Table 3. Percentage of Agilists

Q3. Do you use an Agile approach to software development?	% of total	VersionOne [4]
Yes	69%	88%
No	31%	12%

2.2 Agile Development Practices, Process and Technologies

Respondents who declared to use AMs (*Agile users*) were asked questions about the specific AM and practices used, reported in Tables 4 and 5, respectively. For completeness, non-Agile respondents were asked a question about the kind of software development process they use, reported in Table 6. Other questions were about what language, CMS, DBMS and other tools were used at a basic use and about having attained or not an Agile certification.

The first question asked to Agile users was *"Which of the following Agile Methodologies do you use the most?"*, allowing three answers of decreasing relevance (*most, average, least used*)[1]. The answers confirmed the strong preference in the use of Scrum [6] inside Agile users' projects: we have an overall usage of 65%. In second place there was Extreme Programming [7], with 33% of answers. The respondent had the option to insert other names besides the listed ones, as in most questions of our survey. In this particular case, no further Agile Methodology was reported. The results are shown in Table 4.

---

[1] In the case a respondent used only one or two technologies, we provided the options "*I use one of them / two only*".

Table 4. Diffusion and classification of the Agile Methodologies

Methodology	Most used	Average used	Least used	VersionOne [4]
SCRUM	23	13	5	55%
Extreme Programming	15	6	0	1%
Custom hybrid	5	3	2	10%
Lean	7	4	2	3%
SCRUMBAN	4	5	3	7%
Agile modeling	6	4	5	1%
Lean Kanban	6	5	6	-
None	4	18	31	-

Another question asked to *Agile users* investigated the most used Agile software development practices. To this purpose, each *Agile user* had to specify the usage frequency for each practice, choosing between *sometimes*, *often*, *always* and *not used*. The answers are shown in Table 5, toghether with the percentage of *always* and *often* answers on the total of Agile respondents, and compared to the VersionOne survey [4]. AM usage within the software development area is quite homogeneous; the three most used practices are: "open work area", "daily standup meetings" and "requirements expressed with user stories/features to be developed independently".

Table 5. Agile software development practices

Q4. Which Agile software development practices do you use?	Always	Often	Some-times	Always or Often perc.	VersionOne [4]
Daily standup meetings	31	9	16	51%	85%
Open work area	31	12	9	55%	44%
Requirements expressed with user stories/ features to be developed independently	29	18	16	60%	-
Digital taskboard	27	14	12	53%	45%
Feature - driven, time boxed iterations	27	22	10	63%	-
Unit testing	26	17	13	55%	72%
Continuous integration	25	16	13	53%	58%
Iteration Planning meetings	25	19	11	56%	75%
Team based estimation	24	21	18	58%	69%
Refactoring	21	23	14	56%	47%
Analog taskboard	19	14	20	42%	22%
Burndown chart	19	10	22	37%	69%
Collective code ownership	19	21	15	51%	29%
Continuous customer involvement	17	24	23	53%	-
Continuous Deployment	15	19	17	44%	25%
Test driven development (automated)	15	18	18	42%	38%
Cumulative flow diagram (Kanban)	11	9	25	26%	39%
Work in progress (WIP) limits/kanban board	11	11	24	28%	39%
Automated acceptance testing	8	8	31	21%	22%
Pair programming	6	15	31	27%	30%

Table 6. Software development process used

Q5.Which software development process do you use?	Count	Percentage
In house process	14	30%
Waterfall	8	17%
None	6	13%
Iterative/Incremental	6	13%
RUP	5	11%
Spiral	4	9%
In house certified process (ISO 9000 or CMMI)	3	6%
Other Option	1	2%

We then focused our attention on the usage of Agile tools. The development of a Web project using AM is usually made with the help of one or more tools to plan and develop in a right way. For that reason we proposed the question: *"Which of the following Agile tools do you use the most?"*. There are a number of tools for Agile business planning and we chose those that we thought were the most representative in the category. Table 7 shows that Jira [8] is the most used tool by respondents; the reasons are explained by its ductility and dissemination. In addition, Jira is suitable for Scrum and Lean-Kanban development, and there are many additions that make it a very Agile product. Another tool that is quite used is Bugzilla, which we included in the survey despite it being a bug-tracking tool commonly used also in non-Agile projects. We received some answers about some Agile tools that are not on the list. More than one respondent indicated the following tools: "Excel", "Google Docs", "RedMine" and "Pivotal Tracker". Note also the high number of respondents who answered "None", an answer in line with the opinion of hard-core agilists that it is way better to use tangible artefacts such as cards and boards rather than electronic tools.

Table 7. Diffusion and classification of Agile tools

Tool	Most used	Average used	Least used	VersionOne [4]
Jira	22	7	3	36%
Bugzilla	9	1	4	21%
None	8	23	30	-
MS TFS	5	1	1	26%
Extreme planner	3	5	1	4%
HP	2	0	0	26%
Xplanner	2	1	2	-
CA	1	1	0	1%
IBM Rational	0	1	2	6%
Scrumworks	0	0	2	-
Version One	0	0	2	41%

Finally, we tried to understand what is the most used language in Web programming (server side) by asking the question: "Which of the following languages/technologies for Web programming do you use the most?".

The results are clear and show the predominance of Java and JSP technology over all others (Table 8). More than 50% of the respondents are using one of two technologies among those listed. The result is not surprising, because Java and JSP technologies are known to be the most used in the Web programming world. We also noticed a moderate spread of ASP and ASP.net, in addition to using Php.

Table 8. Diffusion and classification of the programming languages

Language	Most used	Average used	Least used
Java	25	9	10
JSP	14	13	3
ASP.NET	13	4	2
PHP	8	11	6
None	5	15	14
Ruby	5	4	5
ASP	4	2	2
Phyton	2	1	7
Perl	1	2	3
CGI	0	0	1

Another question, whose results we do not report in full for the sake of brevity, was: "*Which language framework (like Spring, Rails, Django, etc) do you use?*". The results show a supremacy of Spring and a great fragmentation of the other framework. Rails, Jsf and Django achieved good results, though. We asked also the question: "*Have you got, or has anyone in your team got, an Agile certification?*", whose results are reported in Table 9.

Table 9. Agile certification

Language	Count	Percentage
None	78	70%
Certified Scrum Master (CSM)	26	23%
Others	8	7%
Kanban Certified Professional (KCP)	0	0

2.3 Use of CMS and Database

A question about the use of Content Management Systems (CMS): "Which CMS Framework, if any, do you use for Web application development?" was directed to the whole sample of respondents. A CMS greatly eases the management of website content, and modern CMS allow also to integrate custom functionalities. The respondents could choose more than one tool among eight, and could report others not included in the list. The three most used CMS are Drupal, Joomla! and Wordpress. We found also that 40% of respondents do not use any CMS. The results are summarized in Table 10.

Table 11 shows the same results, highlighting the kind of user (Agile, non-Agile). Note that only 24% of non-Agile users do not use a CMS in their work, against a 49% of Agile users (Table 11). The most popular CMS among Agile users is Drupal, while for non-Agile users we found Joomla! and Wordpress. In addition, four non-Agile users said they use "Concrete5".

Table 10. Use of CMS

CMS	Number of replies
None	47
Drupal	25
Joomla!	22
Word Press	20
Other Option	16
OpenCms	13
FrontPage	6
WebMatrix	5
Plone	4

Table 11. Use of CMS: comparison between *Agile* and *non-Agile* users

	Agile users		*non-Agile users*	
CMS	Number of replies	Percentage	Number of replies	Percentage
None	39	49%	8	24%
Drupal	20	25%	5	15%
Joomla!	13	16%	9	27%
WordPress	11	14%	9	27%
Other options	6	8%	10	30%
OpenCms	5	6%	8	24%
WebMatrix	4	5%	1	3%
FrontPage	3	4%	3	9%
Plone	2	3%	2	6%

Finally, we investigated also what are the most used DBMS. Respondents could choose one or more among the 15 designated DBMS. As seen in Table 12, the most used DBMS are MySQL, Oracle and PostgreSQL Server. In this case, there is no significant difference in the responses provided by *Agile* and *non-Agile* users. MySQL is the most used by both categories, and only 3 on 112 respondents answered that they do not use any Database.

Table 12. Use of Databases

Database	Number of replies
MySQL	64
Oracle	39
PostgreSQL	35
Microsoft SQL Server	33
SQLite	17
MS Access	16
MongoDB	13
Other Option	9
DB2 (IBM proprietary)	6
Sybase	3
None	3

3   Results and Conclusions

Cross-referencing the answers makes it possible to get some interesting results. Here we just highlight some among the most interesting.

The majority of respondents that declare to use Scrum as the most widely used methodology (60%), prefers to use Jira project management tool. Scrum users also show a large span of preferences regarding the languages used, much broader than for other respondents. Respondents who declared to use Extreme Programming and Lean development tend to adopt technologies in a heterogeneous way, with no particular correlation.

Also the DBMS used by respondents does not seem to be particularly correlated to specific methodologies or tools.

Referring to Jira tool, it is used by 11 "Certified Scrum Masters (CSM)" (on a total of 26). This makes Jira the preferred tool of CSM, with 43% of CSM respondents using it. The use of the other very popular tool, Bugzilla, is not particularly correlated to methodologies or certification. There are other correlations between using a specific methodology in relation to a tool, but their significance level is not enough to be presented here. This is due both to the size of the sample and to the heterogeneity of the answers.

In conclusion, we presented a survey gathering many data about how Web applications are actually developed, from the perspectives of process management, programming language and frameworks, databases, use of Content Management Systems, tools. These data were studied performing correlations between the various answers, to assess if and to which extent specific AM and practices are linked to specific technologies and tools.

We are presently working on extending the number of respondents to the survey, to increase the significance level of our findings, and to complete the correlation analysis of the results.

References

1. Manifesto for Agile Software Development, http://www.agilemanifesto.org/
2. Abrahamsson, P., Warsta, J., Siponen, M.T., Ronkainen, J.: New Directions on AgileMethods: A Comparative Analysis. In: Proceedings of the International Conference on Software Engineering, Portland, Oregon, USA (2003)
3. West, D.: Water-Scrum-Fall is the Reality of Agile for Most Organizations Today (2011)
4. 8th Annual state of Agile Development Survey (2014)
5. Polldaddy, http://polldaddy.com/
6. Schwaber, K., Beedle, M.: Agile Software Development with Scrum. Prentice Hall, Upper Saddle River (2001)
7. Beck, K.: Extreme Programming Explained: Embrace Change. Addison-Wesley (2000)
8. https://www.atlassian.com/software/jira

How Many Eyeballs Does a Bug Need?
An Empirical Validation of Linus' Law

Subhajit Datta[1], Proshanta Sarkar[2], Sutirtha Das[2], Sonu Sreshtha[2],
Prasanth Lade[3], and Subhashis Majumder[2]

[1] Singapore University of Technology and Design
subhajit.datta@acm.org
[2] Heritage Institute of Technology
[3] Arizona State University

Abstract. Linus' Law reflects on a key characteristic of open source software development: developers' tendency to closely work together in the bug resolution process. In this paper we empirically examine Linus' Law using a data-set of 1,000+ Android bugs, owned by 70+ developers. Our results indicate that encouraging developers to work closely with one another has nuanced implications; while one form of contact may help reduce bug resolution time, another form can have quite the opposite effect. We present statistically significant evidence in support of our results and discuss their relevance at the individual and organizational levels.

Keywords: Linus' Law, Android, Connection, Betweenness, Social Network Analysis, Latent Dirichlet Allocation, Regression.

1 Introduction and Research Question

The *agile manifesto* announced in 2001, and the principles behind it emphasized on "individuals and interactions" in large scale software development[1]. Around the same time, Raymond's influential paper invoked the metaphor of the bazaar to highlight how myriad, spontaneous, and local interactions can fulfil global objectives in developing large and complex open source software [1]. In *Cathedral and the Bazaar* Raymond made a bold conjecture based on his observations of Linux development, calling it *Linus' Law*: "Given enough eyeballs, all bugs are shallow"; or more formally: "Given a large enough beta-tester and co-developer base, almost every problem will be characterized quickly and the fix will be obvious to someone" [1].

With the progressively empirical nature of software engineering research, anecdotal evidence needs to be complemented with statistically significant conclusions [2]. As is widely recognized, Linux is more than just an open source operating system; its significance lies in harnessing the agile methodology of software development in a truly novel way [1]. With this background, Linus'

---

[1] http://agilemanifesto.org/

G. Cantone and M. Marchesi (Eds.): XP 2014, LNBIP 179, pp. 242–250, 2014.
© Springer International Publishing Switzerland 2014

Law proclaims an interesting benefit of using agile methodologies by a wide and distributed developer pool. To validate whether Linus' Law captures merely a fortuitous quirk of Linux development, or has wider relevance in large scale agile development, we need to examine the law in a related but different development scenario. Android's[2] wide currency in today's computing milieu is indicated by the level of its usage in mobile computing devices and active developer pool [3]. Derived from the Linux kernel and having a similar development methodology, Android serves as an appropriate system for validating whether the claim of Linus' Law around the benefits of large scale agile practices indeed go beyond Linux. In this paper we present results from examining Linus' Law using Android bug report data.

In earlier examinations of Linus' Law using data from the Red Hat Enterprise Linux 4, the PHP programming language and the Wireshark network protocol analyzer, files with changes from nine or more developers were found to be 16 times more likely to have a vulnerability than files changed by fewer than nine developers [4], [5]. Linus' Law has also been called a "fallacy" due to the lack of supporting evidence [6]. These and similar other studies point to a lack of consensus on the validity as well as applicability of Linus' Law [7].

Our examination of Linus' Law using data from a large and widely used system has implications at several levels. For individual developers, our results can inform the benefits as well as costs of engaging closely with peers in the resolution of bugs. For managers, an understanding of Linus' Law and its limitations can be valuable for resource allocation. At the organizational level, our results can guide decisions on whether and how latest trends like crowdsourcing may help in bug resolution.

On the basis of the statements of Linus' Law mentioned in the previous section, we assume "eyeballs" to be a metaphor for focused developer attention on a bug, and a "shallow" bug is one which is resolved quickly. Thus Linus' Law is taken to propose that *bugs will be resolved faster if more developers attend to them.* The reference to "co-developer base" underscores a key expectation that developers engage in the bug resolution process *beyond* the immediate bugs they own. With this background, we arrive at our **research question**: *Does higher developer attention lead to Android bugs being resolved more quickly?*

For developers, we need to identify attributes that reflect on the level of their attention to resolving bugs. The spirit of agile development processes underlying Linus' Law encourages developers to engage across their peer group, sharing knowledge, expertise, and responsibilities [1]. We posit that for developers, the extent of connection and interpersonal influence in the project ecosystem is related to how quickly bugs are resolved. On the basis of these observations, we refine the research question into the following **hypotheses**:

- *H1: Developers who are more connected resolve their bugs more quickly.*
- *H2: Developers who have higher interpersonal influence resolve their bugs more quickly.*

---

[2] www.android.com

2   Methodology

Collecting Data: The Android bug reports data was accessed from a publicly available online repository [8]. The source XML file was parsed and the data persisted in a specifically designed MySQL database for easy querying. Each bug was identified by a unique bug identifier, and had the following attributes: title, status, owner, date opened, date closed, type, priority, component, stars, reported by, description. Each comment had the following attributes: identifier of the bug commented upon, commenter, date of comment, contents of comments.

Cleaning and Filtering Data: We calculated the *resolution time* for each bug as the number of days between date the bug was opened and the date it was closed. In the context of our study, we filtered the data by only considering bugs which have been commented by more than one developer. From this set we removed bugs with missing attributes or incorrectly recorded attributes (for example the opened date being later in time than the closed date). Finally we only considered bugs which had a resolution time of one year or less. We assume that a bug which has not been resolved for more than a year is unlikely to have attracted notable developer attention. Our final data-set consists of 1,016 bugs, and 73 unique developers who own at least one of these bugs. Each bug in this data-set has a unique owner; when we refer to a developer's bug(s) in subsequent discussion, we mean bug(s) which are owned by that developer.

Defining Developer Networks: We posit that developers can be connected at two levels as they work together to resolve these bugs: by co-commenting on bugs, which reflect shared interests and expertise, and through ownership of bugs which are related to one another. These two levels seek to capture the well recognized association between structure of work products and the structure of communication surrounding the work products [9]. To capture these two levels in our study, we construct the *developer communication network* (DCN) and *developer ownership network* (DON), whose vertices(nodes) are developers. In DCN two developers are connected by an edge (undirected link) if both have commented on at least one bug. For constructing DON we build an intermediate *bug similarity network* (BSN), whose vertices are bugs. In BSN, two bugs are connected by an edge if they are *similar* to one another by the measure explained below. In DON, two developers A and B are connected by an edge if there is at least one pair of bugs $bug_A - bug_B$ (bug_A owned by A and bug_B owned by B) such that bug_A and bug_B are joined by an edge in BSN.

In large software systems involving many developers such as Android, when a bug is raised its title and textual description are used to make a judgement on how similar it is to other bugs that have been addressed earlier [10]. On the basis of this judgement, the ownership of a bug gets decided; a bug is most likely to be assigned to a developer who has resolved similar bugs earlier. Thus a key step in the bug resolution process - assignment of ownership - is most often based on an evaluation of the similarity between bugs. Thus we can assume that developers owning bugs which are similar to one another are linked by a shared context.

Detecting Bug Similarity: To automatically detect similarities between bugs, we used a Latent Dirichlet Allocation (LDA) based approach. LDA considers a document to be a mixture of a limited number of topics and each word in the document can be attributed to one of these topics [11]. Given a corpus of documents, LDA discovers a set of topics, keywords associated with each of the topics and the specific mixture of these topics for each document in the corpus, and expresses these information as probability distributions [12]. In developing the LDA based topic models, we have used the collapsed Gibbs sampling method [12], [13].

Having obtained the probability distribution over topics for each bug, we calculate the similarity between all pairs of bugs in our data-set using the symmetric Kullback Leibler Divergence (KLD) [14]. KLD is a distance measure between two probability distributions. Since we seek to detect the most significant similarity between bugs (thereby reducing false positives to largest possible extent), we only connected two bugs by an edge in BSN if the corresponding KLD value was in the 96 to 100th percentile.

Examining Hypotheses: On the basis of the data-set and the two networks DCN and DON constructed as described above, we develop multiple linear regression models to examine the hypotheses, whose results are presented next.

3 Results and Discussion

We build regression models for the set of developers owning bugs to examine hypotheses H1 and H2. For the models we need to identify the *dependent variable*, the *independent variables*, and the *control variables*. The models will allow us to determine how the independent variables relate to the dependent variable, after accounting for the effects of the control variables.

3.1 Model Development

We now describe the development of the model for developers.

Independent Variables: To validate hypothesis H1, we need to identify a parameter that captures how much a developer is connected to his/her peers in the context of bug resolution. As defined in the Methodology section, DON captures how developers are linked to one another through the ownership of similar bugs. The *degree* of a developer in DON is the number of other developers (s)he is connected to via edges. As an established network metric, the degree of a vertex is a measure of the extent of its connection [15]. Thus we calculate the *Connection* of a developer as his/her degree in DON. For hypotheses H2, we need a measure of a developer's interpersonal influence in the collective enterprise of bug resolution. In social network analysis, the concept of *betweenness* reflects how important a person is as an intermediary in the flow of information between members of a network. Betweenness is measured by the *betweenness centrality* of a vertex, which is the proportion of all geodesics between pairs of other vertices that include this vertex [15]. Individuals of higher betweenness are in stronger positions to broker the interaction of others. In our context, developers of high *Betweenness* in DON are expected to know more about a diverse range of bugs, and hence offer valuable guidance to other developers. On the basis of this background, *Connection* and *Betweenness* are considered as the independent variables in our model.

Dependent Variable: Both hypotheses H1 and H2 are concerned with how developers may resolve their bugs quickly. As a dependent variable in our model, we take the mean of the resolution time for all the bugs owned by a developer, denoted by *ResolutionTime*. The distributions of the resolution times of bugs owned by developers in our data-set have typically low skewness and kurtosis; thus the mean is a reasonably accurate measure of central tendency.

Control Variables: By developing the model, we expect to understand how *Connection* and *Betweenness* relates to *ResolutionTime*. However, to establish the relationship between independent variables and the dependent variable, we need to isolate some of the peripheral effects on the dependent variable. How much a developer can work on a bug to quickly resolve it, is influenced by how many bugs (s)he owns, or the total *Workload*. Additionally, since developers are encouraged to advice one another, a developer's *SpanOfInterest* - given by the number of bugs the developer has commented on - can also be expected to influence how quickly (s)he resolves his/her bugs. As defined in the Methodology section, DCN links developers through the co-commenting of work items. In social network analysis, clustering coefficient(CC)[3] measures how closely an individual is collaborating with others [15]. In our context, *CollaborationLevel* is the extent to which a developer is working with others and is a likely influence on how quickly (s)he resolves her bugs. Finally, we need to have a general sense of how much interest a bug has generated in the Android community. The "stars" field of bug report is "used in order to represent the number of people following a bug" [3]. The mean number of stars across all bugs owned by a developer - *CommunityConcern* - thus gives an indication of how much concern a developer's bugs have generated in the development ecosystem: a parameter that is likely to influence how quickly his/her bugs are resolved. With this background, we include *Workload*, *SpanOfInterest*, *CollaborationLevel*, and *CommunityConcern* as control variables in our model.

Model Assumptions and Variable Transformations: With reference to Table 1, column I gives the parameters of the *base model* which only considers the effects of the control variables, while column II reflects the *attention model* that additionally includes the independent variables. Multiple linear regression has the underlying assumptions of linearity, normality, and homoscedasticity of the residuals, and absence of multicollinearity between the independent variables.

---

[3] In a network, the clustering coefficient (C_v) for a vertex v is defined as follows: If v has a degree of k_v, that is there are k_v vertices directly linked to v, the *maximum* number of edges between these k_v vertices is k_v *choose* 2 or $k_v * (k_v - 1)/2$. If the *actual* number of such edges existing is N_v, then $C_v = 2 * N_v / k_v * (k_v - 1)$ [15].

The residual properties were verified using histogram, Q-Q plot and scatter plot of the standardized residuals. Among the variables, *Workload* and *SpanOfInterest* had a relatively high correlation (around 0.74), which is understandable as developers who own more bugs tend to comment more. Since the Variance Inflation Factors (VIF) of all variables were found to be below the upper limit of 10 in both the base and attention models [16], absence of appreciable multicollinearity was established. With references to the descriptive statistics in Table 1, although a skewness of around 3 for a variable is considered acceptable for including it in a linear regression model, we considered various established transformations for variables with relatively high values of absolute skewness, for making their distributions close to a normal distribution [16]. Accordingly, *Workload* and *CommunityConcern* variables were logarithmically transformed before including in the model. On the basis of the above discussion we concluded that the assumptions of linear multiple regression are valid within permissible limits in our case [16].

Model Description and Validation: In columns I and II of Table 1, the superscripts of the coefficients denote the range of their respective p values, as we specify in the table caption. The p value for each coefficient is calculated using the t-statistic and the Student's t-distribution. In the table's lower section, overview of the models are given: N denotes the number of data points used in building the model, in our case the number of developers who own bugs. R^2 is the coefficient of determination – the ratio of the regression sum of squares to the total sum of squares; it indicates the goodness-of-fit of the regression model in terms of the proportion of variability in the data-set that is accounted for by the model. *df* denotes the degrees of freedom. F is the Fisher F-statistic - the ratio of the variance in the data explained by the linear model divided by the variance unexplained by the model. The p value is calculated using the F-statistic and the F-distribution, and it indicates the overall statistical significance of the model. For the coefficients as well as the overall regression, if $p \leq$ *level of significance*, we conclude the corresponding result is statistically significant, based on null hypothesis significance testing.

From columns I and II of Table 1, we notice that by adding the independent variables, the R^2 value increases considerably between the base and attention models and the F-statistic also increases. Thus the independent variables have enhanced the explanatory power of the model. The standard technique of 10-fold cross validation was carried out by randomly partitioning the data into 10 sub-samples, training the interaction model with 9 sub-samples and validating the model on the 10th sub-sample, and repeating this procedure 10 times. The overall root mean square of prediction error from the cross validation process was found to be 74.53.

3.2   Threats to Validity

We report results from an observational study rather than a controlled experiment; thus in the statistical models developed, correlation does not imply causation. Threats to **construct validity** arise from whether the variables are measured correctly. Although we have used established network metrics in our models, we recognize structures like DCN, BSN, and DON can be defined in other ways. We have used a LDA based approach for text similarity as simpler methods like cosine similarity do not consider clusters of keywords that are likely to occur together. We have also assumed that the elapsed time between bug opening and closure represents the actual time taken to resolve the bug. **Internal validity** ensures a study is free from systemic errors and biases. As the Android data-set is our only source of data, there is no notable threat to this type of validity. **External validity** is concerned with the generalizability of the results. We report results from studying only one data-set and the R^2 values of the models show there may be several other factors whose influence may not have been considered. We plan to address them in our future work. Thus we do not claim our results to be generalizable as yet. **Reliability** of a study is established when the results are reproducible. Given access to the Android bug report data, our results are reproducible.

Table 1. Left: Results of regression for the effects on bug resolution time.(Superscripts '***', '**', '†' denote $p \leq 0.0009$, $p \leq 0.001$, $p \leq 0.05$, respectively) **Right: Descriptive statistics for model variables.**

	I	II	Mean	Stdev	Skew	Kurtosis
	Base model	Attention model				
Dependent variable						
Resolution Time			69.12	75.94	1.48	1.76
Intercept	81.60**	144.03***				
	(24.62)	(30.92)				
Control variables						
Workload	−27.30	27.42	13.92	26.17	3.57	14.87
	(20.24)	(42.35)				
SpanOfInterest	0.12	−0.004	53.44	12.19	2.33	4.18
	(0.01)	(0.11)				
CollaborationLevel	16.68	15.03	0.63	0.35	-0.5	-1.01
	(27.19)	(25.77)				
CommunityConcern	−17.30	−10.54	11.46	23.93	3.51	18.11
	(20.35)	(19.65)				
Independent variables						
Connection		−3.27**	37.51	18.79	0.02	-1.12
		(1.11)				
Betweenness		1.45†	17.67	25.48	1.80	2.92
		(0.86)				
N	73	73				
R^2	0.05	0.17				
df	68	66				
F	0.89	2.3				
p	0.5	< 0.05				

3.3   Observations and Conclusions

On the basis of the details of the attention model in column II of Table 1, we can make a number of observations. The overall attention model as well as the relationship between both the independent variables and the dependent variable is statistically significant. From the sign of the respective coefficients, we notice that higher *Connection* for a developer relates to decreased *Resolution-Time* whereas higher *Betweenness* relates to increased *ResolutionTime*. Quicker resolution of bugs owned by a developer translates to lower *ResolutionTime*. Thus results from the model supports hypothesis H1, but we find evidence to contradict hypothesis H2.

Recalling that *Connection* is measured by the degree of a developer in DON, our results indicate that more connected a developer is to other developers through the ownership of similar bugs, (s)he is likely to be more deeply embedded in the development ecosystem, which is found to facilitate quicker resolution of the bugs owned by that developer. However, the more involved a developer gets in brokering interactions between other developers through his/her position of higher *Betweenness*, it appears that (s)he gets more distracted, which is reflected in the increased *ResolutionTime* of the bugs (s)he owns.

These results have notable implications in the development of large software systems. While developers need to be encouraged to connect directly with one another, the pitfalls of getting too engaged in facilitating interactions between other developers need to be recognized. As more complex software - many of them open source - is being built by larger teams, understanding the nuances of developer attention and its consequences is beneficial for individuals, management, and organizations. We can thus conclude that the broad assertion on more "eyeballs" making bugs "shallow" obscures important subtleties in the relationship between developer attention and how quickly bugs get resolved. While developers need to be encouraged to connect with one another as they collectively work on bug resolution, they also need to be sensitized to the challenges of too much involvement in mediating interactions between other developers.

References

1. Raymond, E.S.: The Cathedral and the Bazaar: Musings on Linux and Open Source by an Accidental Revolutionary. O'Reilly (2001)
2. Shaw, M.: Continuing prospects for an engineering discipline of software. IEEE Software 26, 64–67 (2009)
3. Guana, V., Rocha, F., Hindle, A., Stroulia, E.: Do the stars align? multidimensional analysis of android's layered architecture. In: 2012 9th IEEE Working Conference on Mining Software Repositories (MSR), pp. 124–127 (2012)
4. Meneely, A., Williams, L.: Secure open source collaboration: An empirical study of linus' law. In: Proceedings of the 16th ACM Conference on Computer and Communications Security, pp. 453–462 (2009)
5. Meneely, A., Williams, L.: Strengthening the empirical analysis of the relationship between linus' law and software security. In: Proceedings of the 2010 ACM-IEEE International Symposium on Empirical Software Engineering and Measurement, ESEM 2010, pp. 9:1–9:10. ACM, New York (2010)

6. Glass, R.L.: Facts and Fallacies of Software Engineering. Addison Wesley Professional, Pearson Education [distributor], Boston, Old Tappan (2002)
7. Wang, J., Carroll, J.M.: Behind linus's law: A preliminary analysis of open source software peer review practices in mozilla and python. In: 2011 International Conference on Collaboration Technologies and Systems (CTS), pp. 117–124. IEEE (May 2011)
8. Shihab, E., Kamei, Y., Bhattacharya, P.: Mining challenge 2012: The android platform. In: The 9th Working Conference on Mining Software Repositories (2012)
9. Conway, M.: How do committees invent?. Datamation Journal, 28–31 (April 1968)
10. Jeong, G., Kim, S., Zimmermann, T.: Improving bug triage with bug tossing graphs. In: ESEC/FSE 2009, pp. 111–120. ACM, New York (2009)
11. Blei, D.M., Ng, A.Y., Jordan, M.I.: Latent dirichlet allocation. J. M. L. R. (March 2003)
12. Steyvers, M., Griffiths, T.: Probabilistic topic models. In: Latent Semantic Analysis: A Road to Meaning. Lawrence Erlbaum (2007)
13. Falessi, D., Cantone, G., Canfora, G.: Empirical principles and an industrial case study in retrieving equivalent requirements via natural language processing techniques. IEEE Transactions on Software Engineering 39(1), 18–44 (2013)
14. Kullback, S., Leibler, R.A.: On information and sufficiency. Ann. Math. Statist. 22(1), 79–86 (1951)
15. Albert, R., Barabasi, A.: Statistical mechanics of complex networks. Cond-mat/0106096 (June 2001); Reviews of Modern Physics 74, 47 (2002)
16. Tabachnick, B., Fidell, L.: Using Multivariate Statistics. Pearson Education, Boston (2007)

The Theory and Practice of Randori Coding Dojos

John Rooksby[1], Johanna Hunt[2], and Xiaofeng Wang[3]

[1] University of Glasgow, UK
[2] Eventyr Ltd, UK
[3] Free University of Bozen-Bolzano, Italy
john.rooksby@glasgow.ac.uk, johanna.hunt@eventyr.co.uk,
xiaofeng.wang@unibz.it

Abstract. The coding dojo is a technique for continuous learning and training. Randori is one implementation format. Even though experience and lessons learnt on how coding dojos could be better organized have been reported in agile literature, the theoretical bases behind it have never been investigated. In this paper we propose to use reflective practice as a sense-making device to underpin the investigation and improvement of coding dojo for effective learning. Based on the examination of two dojo sessions we argue that the insights from the reflective practice and related theories can open new and interesting inquiries on coding dojo, and eventually help to better understand the dynamics of coding dojo, and improve the dojo practice accordingly.

Keywords: coding dojo, deliberate practice, reflective practice, reflect-in-action, reflect-on-action, randori, agile methods, learning.

1   Introduction

"If I want to learn Judo, I will enroll at the nearest dojo, and show up for one hour every week for the next two years, at the end of which I may opt for a more assiduous course of study to progress in the art. Years of further training might be rewarded with a black belt, which is merely the sign of ascent to a different stage of learning. No master ever stops learning. If I want to learn object programming... my employer will pack me off to a three-day Java course picked from this year's issue of a big training firm's catalog." [1]

No master, as Bossavit and Gaillot say, ever stops learning [1]. Bossavit and Gaillot's concern is with how professional developers can master their trade. In order to support continuous learning, Bossavit and Gaillot appropriated the dojo format from martial arts. They instigated a coding dojo in Paris, and the format has since been replicated around the world ([2], [3], [4]). The coding dojo is by no means the only available approach for professional developers to continuous learning (see [4] for an overview of how one organisation supports this). But the coding dojo format (specifically the "randori" format) is widely practiced and worthy of serious attention.

G. Cantone and M. Marchesi (Eds.): XP 2014, LNBIP 179, pp. 251–259, 2014.

Although the dojo format has been discussed widely and is advocated in several textbooks (e.g. [5]), few studies of how coding dojos are practiced have been published. Luz et al. [6] have used interviews and questionnaires to find out about people's experience in dojos. They found dojos to be an activity that favours *"participation and collaboration in an inclusive learning environment"*. A survey by Bravo and Goldman [2] found *"as far as participants' perception goes, the coding dojo is a very effective technique for learning agile practices, independently of how much is already known about them."* These studies are of participants' perceptions and enjoyment of dojos. By doing retrospective evaluations (of what people say after the event, rather than during it) these studies have avoided issues of what happens in a dojo. The studies indicate there is value in dojos, but it is not clear where that value is.

We suggest that attention is turned to practice (by which we mean the embodied, situated and practical conduct of the dojo itself). Much has been said about the coding dojo format, but little about practice. We are well aware that coding dojos are rarely rigidly organised, are often run by enthusiasts, and are often oriented more to local needs and contingencies than any rulebook. But rather than dismiss such dojos as falling short of a grand theory, we suggest that examining their practice gives an opportunity to rethink and question the grander ideas. The paper will argue that rather than tighten up conduct in dojos to more readily resemble "deliberate practice"[7], that the theory itself should be rethought. A candidate 'alternative' theory we consider is Schön's "reflective practice" [8]. Schön advocated that learning is done through practicing. He did not see practice as being a means to becoming so proficient that one does not have to think when acting, but as a means of learning to think when acting; becoming a "reflective practitioner". The primary research question that guides our investigation of the coding dojo is: *Does the perspective of reflective practice enable a better understanding of the coding dojo?*

Section two of this paper will further outline the theory of the coding dojo, and explain the papers focus on "randori" dojos. Section three will use examples from two dojo sessions in the UK to consider how randori dojos play out in practice. Section four will discuss the gap between theory and practice, and suggest that rather than dismiss the dojos we observed as "bad practice" they can be better appreciated with reference to an alternative theory of learning. Section five concludes the paper.

2   The Coding Dojo in Theory

The coding dojo, Bossavit and Gaillot [1] explain, has its origins in Thomas' concept of code kata. Kata is a Japanese term meaning (literally) *form*. The term is used in martial arts to refer to choreographed movements that are practiced repeatedly. Dave Thomas brought this idea to coding [9]. Thomas' "code kata" are exercises for developers to repeat over and over, striving for mastery. The purpose of kata, explains Martin [5], is *"to make the perfected movements automatic and instinctive so that they are there when you need them … you repeat the exercise over and over again to train your fingers how to move and react"* (p.90). According to Martin, kata are useful for learning hotkeys and navigation idioms, and techniques such as test driven development and constant integration. Most importantly, explains Martin, they enable you to develop problem-solution pairs.

Inspired by code kata, Bossavit and Gaillot [1] looked further to martial arts training and appropriated the idea of the dojo. Dojo is a Japanese term that means literally *place of the way*. The term is used in martial arts to refer to a place of formal training. As with code kata, the coding dojo was developed to support the development of skill through repetitive practice. Indeed, the coding dojo can incorporate kata. Unlike code kata however, dojos are fundamentally social and cooperative.

Dojos can take one of several formats. At *kata dojos*, kata exercises are practiced in advance and are then performed in front of an audience. Bache [10] describes of a kata dojo workshop that it will comprise *"perhaps 6 kata performances … [who] will be chosen in advance and work in pairs."* Bache explains that the remaining participants will be there to learn from and critique the pairs. The performances last 10 to 30 minutes, and are followed by feedback. Alternatively, *wasa dojos* are two-person kata where the pair can either work cooperatively or spar with each other. Martin [5] describes wasa dojos where developers take turns, the first writing a unit test and the second implementing code to pass that test. Another format, the *kake dojo* is discussed in [4]. Kake dojos are events at which a code with the same functionality is simultaneously developed in two or more languages. A fourth format, the *randori dojo*, is outlined below. The randori format is, in our experience, the most commonly implemented, and constitutes the focus of this paper.

Randori is a term used in martial arts to describe free-style sparing. Martin [5] describes of the randori coding dojo format: *"With the screen projected on the wall, one person writes a test and sits down. The next person makes the test pass, writes another test and then sits down. … This can be done in sequence around the table, or people can simply line up, as they feel so moved. In either case it is a lot of fun."* Aniche et al. [4] describe a slightly different format in which, instead of writing one thing and then sitting down, the pairs work *"in time-boxed rounds (usually 5-7 minutes)."* At the end of each time-box, the driver moves to the audience, the navigator becomes the driver, and an audience member becomes the navigator. Aniche et al. explain that the problems are usually simple and the goal is not to solve them but to share knowledge, to practice and to learn. Martin [5] states: *"It is remarkable how much you can learn from these sessions. You can gain an immense insight into the way other people solve problems. These insights can only serve to broaden your own approach and improve your skill."*

The dojo format has grown from a recognition that deliberate practice over a sustained period is at the heart of developing and improving expertise. "Practice" is not meant here in the sense that the developer must be a practitioner, but that they literally have to practice. The idea is not for on-the-job learning. Mastery from this point of view is not gained solely through experience, but through discipline. The developer should practice in the way a professional musician, and indeed a practitioner of martial arts, must practice. But how exactly does the randori format fit with this? How can taking turns (not just with people who may not agree with you, but with people with different interests and competencies) constitute deliberate practice? Is working in front of an audience on a shared project something that instils discipline in the pair doing the doing, or something that enables the audience to witness and consider discipline or the lack thereof? Or does the randori dojo depart entirely from the idea of deliberate practice?

3   The Coding Dojo in Practice

We have obtained a set of twelve recordings (specifically screen and voice recordings) made at a randori dojo organised in the UK. One of the authors of this paper was the facilitator at these sessions. The other authors were not in attendance. The facilitator gained advice from Bossavit and Gaillot before running the dojo sessions. The advice she received was largely pragmatic. Some points were about organisation *"always meet at the same place and the same time - it helps to build a community and a ritual"*; *"encourage discussions, but on green bar only, don't discuss about the code when it's in an unstable state"*. Other advice was more practical *"don't cram too much into a session"*; *"use kata to introduce a new language"*. Other advice referred to cooperative aspects of the dojo: *"keep a collaborative journal"*; *"make the dojo everybody's responsibility"*. Finally, the organiser was invited to: *"Trust your process ... part of the learning experience is figuring out what is happening. ... Part of building the community is about finding out why you want to meet every week or so as a group. Answers will become clearer as time goes by, provided that everyone feels free to talk and listens to others' opinions."*

The recordings have each been transcribed in full. Of our twelve recordings, half contain independent sessions, and half contain tasks carried across sessions. Participation in the sessions varied in number and mix of experience, with a hard core of regular attendees and others who came and went. For the purposes of this paper we selected two sessions for in-depth, qualitative analysis. Our method of analysis has been very coarse and discursive. Essentially we have sought to understand and characterize what happens in a dojo as the first step of analysis.

The two selected sessions both focus on the same task (one continues from the other) and therefore constitute a pair. The sessions are on the task: *"Write a Text Adventure Game in Java. The game must contain: a house; a cat; a blue necktie; a nodding dog ornament; something orange; a lift"*. The task was originally intended to be for one session, but at the end of the first session the participants elected to continue on it during the next session. Both sessions saw 12 pairs work together in time-boxed rounds of about 5 minutes. Each session had about 10 people in attendance. The task itself was somewhat irreverent, but this is not to say the dojo was not serious. A characteristic of this and other dojos was that the software and, moreover, the interesting aspects of the problem for the participants to work on, were not specified by the facilitator but were emergent in the dojo sessions themselves. The fact that the participants elected to continue for a second session on this task attracted us because it strongly indicates that they found something of value in their progress.

The first pair (a male and female) of the first session began by reading out the task. They then talked about where to start. In their words:

"Is it just something like north, south, east, west, up, down kind of thing? Or are we going to go for something completely weird and strange?"

"Do you think we need to think about that already?"

"Uh, I think we need to have a vague idea of which way we're going."

The pair continued to discuss where to start, and in what level of detail. The male, as driver and thus with control of the keyboard, won out. This was not necessarily through strength of argument but by starting to code, creating a public class "game" within the first minute. The male suggested the best thing to do was implement a hash map to represent locations. The choice was immediately met with questions of clarification from the audience and a discussion of hash maps. Hash maps are data structures that not everyone in the room was familiar or comfortable with, and not something that everyone felt was necessarily the best data structure to use.

For the second round, the female switched to the driver role, and another male joined her as navigator. The second and subsequent rounds largely continued to be concerned with movement and location (and therefore only a subset of the broader issues in implementing the game). Some work is also done on "items" to be found in the game, but by the very end of the second dojo session, the participants built a game in which it was simply possible to move between several arbitrary locations.

The second and subsequent sessions also continued to use hash maps. In fact, the major topic of discussion, deliberation and sometimes argument during both dojo sessions was hash maps: how, when and why should you implement these? For some participants, hashmaps required basic explanation:

"Yes, hashmaps contain keys and values, and so the key gets you the value."

Interestingly, examples are present in the data of people not previously familiar with hashmaps trying to put what is going on into their own words. Sometimes they did so well; sometimes they had to be corrected. The discussions also covered ways of implementing hashing in java:

"There is with hashmap in Java, a rather neat way of doing this ... we can get the key set which will contain north, south, east and west, or what have you, and there's a list, we can ask whether it contains a direction we want to go in."

The person who explained this, later realised that "*it returns a set, not a list*". Even he was learning and discovering, not simply instructing. Elsewhere the discussion turned to consideration of whether and how hashmaps were appropriate in comparison to and in conjunction with other forms of data structure:

"Personally, I don't like the use of vectors, not that vectors are necessarily a bad thing, but they're lists which are designed for a much bigger environment, and I think we should stick to the idea of a hashmap where you can look at a set via a string."

We have said very little so far about how the participants' work conformed to or exemplified good practice. Concerns for agile methods, and good practice more broadly, were present in the sessions but were far less pervasive than the discussions of data structures. Unit tests were not spoken of, let alone implemented until the third round, and it was not until round five that a test-driven development strategy was introduced. The pair in sessions five and six included someone who was clearly passionate and skilled in test-driven development, and he was able to show how this could be done in this situation. Subsequent sessions did not continue with test-driven development but this is not to say that the presence of this was ignored or forgotten, indeed it was appreciated and is referred back to in later sessions as *"inspiring"*. Regarding unit testing generally, there was an ebb and flow to this. Some pairs would have a push on writing tests and testable code, whereas others would ignore the tests. One pair even decided to comment out all the unit tests. Similar issues can be seen in the data regarding refactoring, some would take this seriously and treat it as an important part of their practice, while others did not. Some took their roles in pair programming seriously, whereas others would not.

Each dojo session ended with a reflective discussion. A key consideration at the end of the first session was whether it was a failure that they had not ended with a functioning game. One person expressed dissatisfaction with having spent some much time considering data structures and writing tests:

"We got tests. Tests on data structures!"

But others defended how the session had progressed. When asked whether the *"actual aim"* of the dojo was *"to get something functioning"* or to get *"really nice crisp code that does a little bit"* the majority consensus was the latter. One participant pointed out:

"It's the journey not the destination."

Clearly, the dojo was not a productive way of producing a game, but was it actually valuable as a *"journey"*? What does it mean that the journey did not adhere to best practices but that there was an ebb and flow to these? Some people heavily oriented to test-driven development, refactoring and so on, others were unfamiliar with these, and yet others were frustrated by them. We do not believe the situation we have observed of this dojo is unique. The authors of this paper have experience of running and participating in dojos other than the ones discussed here, and while there has been a diversity of practices in these, never have we experienced a dojo run strictly to agile principles.

4   Discussion

Considering the dojo in practice reveals there is something of a gulf between theory and practice. At least, there seems to be something of a leap from kata to randori dojos. The former is about repeating a good practice until it is perfected, but the latter seems to rely on group dynamics and seems susceptible to what might be considered poor or inexpert practice. With this in mind, we have been taking interest in the work of Schön ([8], [11]).

Schön was concerned that professional work (not specifically programming, but expert work more broadly) was too often misconstrued as the application of technical knowledge to clearly defined problems. He believed this view devalued the importance of skill and artistry in practice. He argued for *"a new epistemology of practice"* and sought to demystify what constituted skill and artistry. This led him to articulate what he called *"reflection-in-action"*. He explained that professionals routinely grapple with *"situations of uncertainty, uniqueness and conflict"* and when doing so, they can be seen to *"reflect-in-action"*. Schön was not referring to a need for taking time out to reflect but was interested in how thinking is intertwined with action. Schön was interested, as Moon [12] puts it, *"thinking on your feet"*.

One of the professions Schön studied was architecture. He recognised that when designing, architects are rarely confronted with a clear problem. Rather architects articulate problems in conjunction with their solution. When architects work on problem-solution pairs, they go through a "web a moves", exploring options without necessarily dismissing others, articulating parallel alternatives, and backtracking from dead ends to other lines. He describes architects' reasoning processes as thoroughly dependent on talking and on sketching. Designing, he argued, is not a linear problem solving but is a material, embodied practice in which alternatives are explored and a problem-solution articulated. His description of designing has been influential, and his ideas used to describe the software design.

Schön went on to question professional education, which he thought concentrated too much on "technical knowledge" and too little on "skill" and "artistry". Not only were graduates leaving education with a lack of skill in their chosen profession, but a lack of the ability to even recognise or articulate what skilful practice is. He developed the idea of *"the practicum"*, a setting in which students could be coached rather than instructed in a practice. This was not a call for students to be given work experience, but to create a setting that approximates the practice world. Schön said the practicum should be *"a virtual world, relatively free of the pressures, distractions, and risks of the real one, to which, nevertheless, it refers"*. This way, he explained, practice happens in a double sense: the students engage, usually in simulated form, in the practice they wish to learn; but the students also practice *"as one practices the piano"*. Schön proposed the practicum should be under the guidance of *"a studio master"* who would from time-to-time do conventional teaching, but would usually function as a coach *"whose main activities are demonstrating, advising, questioning, and criticizing"*. Schön pointed out that as a coach, the teacher does not oversee or instruct each students every move, and that students will often be as important to one another as the coach. In the practicum, the students are not just applying techniques they have been taught in lectures or textbooks, but are developing and learning to recognize skill.

The randori dojo, we suggest, resembles Schön's practicum. Both look beyond 'technical knowledge' and to artistry and skill. Both encourage learning in a virtual world away from real world pressures. Both prioritise interaction among the students over formal teaching, and to a degree the randori dojo allows for coaching. Importantly, we suggest, Schön does not propose that the students in practicums should already be proficient in skilled or best practice, but rather the practicum provides a space in which the students can begin to recognize what skill actually is and to develop these. Of course, there are differences between the dojo and the practicum. Schön's focus was on the training of pre-professionals whereas the dojo is open to people already working as developers. The turn-taking structure and collaborative format of the dojo is also different to Schön's practicum where students would work on individual projects. But on the whole we note some strong similarities.

With reference to Schön's ideas we think it is possible to begin to see value in what was happening in the dojo we reported above. The dojo rarely exemplified good practice, but there were occasions of this and several discussions. With reference to Schön we should consider that this might be characteristic of a group among which there may be some who are skilled, and others who can barely recognize what skill is, let alone understand which certain skills might be beneficial. Schön's work enables us to consider that in order to learn, it may be better that we allow the topics to emerge and be worked out during the course of learning. We should perhaps not be worried if we see that the learners are more interested in data structures than (say) test-driven development. We should perhaps not be critical of the dojo participants for making rash decisions or rejecting good practices (such as commenting out all the tests), but rather understand that this is all part of a learning process - steps on a long road to mastery.

The randori dojo, from this perspective, is unlike kata. It should not be about the coach instructing the participants in a good practice to follow, and should not necessarily see the coach intervene when something untoward happens. We might better see the Randori dojo as allowing mastery to emerge through participants' reflective action.

5   Conclusion

In this paper we have explained and characterised Randori dojos. We argue that these are unlike kata (and kata dojos) and suggest that they are best understood not as demonstrations among a group of best practice, but as cooperative learning where good practice has the opportunity to emerge. We have suggested the work by Schön on reflective practice and practicums offers an appropriate theoretical perspective to consider randori dojos. Our work neither proves nor disproves the value of dojos, and in fact shows that we are some way off being able to evaluate the effectiveness of dojos – we are still deliberating what criteria to judge effectiveness by. The literature on education and learning is expansive (not limited to Schön). It seems opening the door to this raises many more questions than it settles.

References

1. Bossavit, L., Gaillot, E.: The Coder's Dojo – A Different Way to Teach and Learn Programming. In: Baumeister, H., Marchesi, M., Holcombe, M. (eds.) XP 2005. LNCS, vol. 3556, pp. 290–291. Springer, Heidelberg (2005)
2. Bravo, M., Goldman, A.: Reinforcing the Learning of Agile Practices Using Coding Dojos. In: Sillitti, A., Martin, A., Wang, X., Whitworth, E. (eds.) XP 2010. LNBIP, vol. 48, pp. 379–380. Springer, Heidelberg (2010)
3. Sato, D.T., Corbucci, H., Bravo, M.V.: Coding Dojo: An Environment for Learning and Sharing Agile Practices. In: Agile 2008 Conference, pp. 459–464. IEEE (2008)
4. Aniche, M.F., de Azevedo Silveira, G.: Increasing Learning in an Agile Environment: Lessons Learned in an Agile Team. In: 2011 Agil. Conf., pp. 289–295 (2011)

5. Martin, R.: The Clean Coder: A Code of Conduct for Professional Programmers (2011)
6. da Luz, R., Neto, A., Noronha, R.: Teaching TDD, the Coding Dojo Style. In: ICALT 2013, pp. 371–375 (2013)
7. Ericsson, K.A., Krampe, R.T., Tesch-romer, C., Ashworth, C., Carey, G., Grassia, J., Hastie, R., Heizmann, S., Kellogg, R., Levin, R., Lewis, C., Oliver, W., Poison, P., Rehder, R., Schlesinger, K., Schneider, V.: The Role of Deliberate Practice in the Acquisition of Expert Performance 100, 363–406 (1993)
8. Schön, D.A.: The Reflective Practitioner: How Professionals Think in Action. Basic Books (1984)
9. Thomas, D.: Code kata: How to become a better developer, codekata.pragprog.com
10. Bache, E.: Test Driven Development: Performing Art. In: Abrahamsson, P., Marchesi, M., Maurer, F. (eds.) XP 2009. LNBIP, vol. 31, pp. 217–218. Springer, Heidelberg (2009)
11. Schön, D.A.: Educating the Reflective Practitioner: Toward a New Design for Teaching and Learning in the Professions. Jossey-Bass (1990)
12. Moon, J.A.: Reflection in Learning & Professional Development: Theory & Practice (1999)

Locating Expertise in Agile Software Development Projects

Mawarny Md. Rejab, James Noble, and George Allan

School of Engineering and Computer Science,
Victoria University of Wellington,
Wellington, New Zealand
{Mawarny.Md.Rejab,kjx,george.allan}@ecs.vuw.ac.nz

Abstract. Agile software development projects rely on the diversity of team members' expertise. It is vital to develop the meta-knowledge of the available expertise in Agile teams. However, locating the internal expertise in Agile teams is not explicitly reported in the literature. Through a Grounded Theory study involving 16 Agile practitioners based in New Zealand and Australia, we revealed four ways to identify internal expertise in Agile software development projects: communicating frequently, working closely together, declaring self-identified expertise, and using an expertise directory. The outcome of this study will provide significant insight into how Agile team members depend on each other in locating their peers' expertise, as well as quantify the level of expertise.

Keywords: locating expertise, expertise coordination, Agile software development projects, Grounded Theory.

1   Introduction

Software development projects rely on expertise in producing quality software products [16]. Expertise is a critical resource and it is important to ensure the presence of sufficient expertise for the software development team [8]]. The expertise, however, is not adequate on its own [8], and it is important to leverage the available expertise through expertise coordination.

Expertise coordination is defined as *"the management of knowledge and skills dependencies"* [8]. This definition shows how team members should ideally depend on each other in managing and utilizing their expertise resources. Expertise coordination requires a team to recognize who has a particular expertise, when and where they are needed, and how to access the expertise effectively[8]. Hence, locating the source of expertise is a pivotal step in coordinating the expertise.

Knowing *"who knows what"* will determine who has a particular expertise [8] and indirectly leads to developing a meta-knowledge of the available expertise in their team. This is supported by Garrett and her colleagues [9] who claimed that every team member should be aware of others' expertise, particularly the relevant expertise to perform tasks.

G. Cantone and M. Marchesi (Eds.): XP 2014, LNBIP 179, pp. 260–268, 2014.

In the context of Agile software development, Strode et al. [20] posited that *"know who knows what"* will determine who has the sort of expertise in Agile teams. Reasons for locating expertise in Agile teams are depicted in Table 1:

Table 1. Reasons for locating expertise in Agile teams

Reason	Supported by
to bring the right team member with particular expertise to solve a problem in a timely manner	Lee and Xia [13]
to develop a sense of *"who we are"* and a collective awareness of the available expertise	Bielaczyc and Collins [3]
to select tasks by considering the capability other team members' capabilities	Hoda et al. [12]
to pair with the right Agile team member, particularly in a new task	Vanhanen and Kopi [21]

Thus, it is essential for Agile team members to locate who has which sort of expertise, as well as quantify the level of the expertise of their peers. There is a need to facilitate finding knowledge owners or experts in Agile teams [17]. However, locating the internal expertise in Agile teams is not explicitly reported in the literature. This raises a question: How do Agile team members depend on each other in locating expertise in Agile teams? To answer this question, we have used the Grounded Theory methodology and interviewed 16 Agile practitioners from various software companies based in New Zealand and Australia. This paper aims to describe how Agile team members locate a source of internal expertise in Agile teams.

The rest of this paper is structured as follows: the second section describes Grounded Theory; the third section presents the findings of this study; the fourth section presents the discussion; and the last section puts forward conclusions.

2   Research Methodology

Grounded Theory is an inductive research method that aims to infer new theories from observed data [11]. Grounded Theory is suitable for this study since it is applicable to explore human behaviour and social interaction [10]. Grounded Theory is also appropriate to conceptualize and theorize about the underpinnings of expertise coordination on Agile software development perspectives.

2.1   Data Collection

Semi-structured interviews have been carried out with 16 Agile practitioners from different software organizations based in New Zealand and Australia, as depicted in Table 2. Interviews provide reliable data sources because the researcher has direct contact with participants during data collection [4] . This situation enables us to gain a deeper understanding of participants concerns. This study requires a broad range of Agile roles to enable the triangulation of findings. Different roles provide different insights and perspectives toward locating expertise in Agile teams. As an on-going study, we will continue to collect data until theoretical saturation has been reached, when no new data emerges [11].

Table 2. Summary of Research Participants and Agile Project

Person	Location	Agile Role	Agile Methods	Project Domain
P1	New Zealand	Developer	XP and Scrum	Mobile application
P2	New Zealand	Agile Coach	XP, Scrum, Kanban	Not specified
P3	Australia	Agile Consultant	Not specified	Not specified
P4	New Zealand	Agile Coach	Scrum and XP	Education
P5	New Zealand	Software Tester	Not specified	Printing
P6	Australia	Team leader	Not specified	Accounting
P7	New Zealand	Agile Consultant	Scrum and XP	Financial
P8	Australia	Agile Coach	Scrum, XP, Kanban, Lean	Human resources
P9	New Zealand	Business Analyst	Not specified	Insurance
P10	New Zealand	Software Tester	Scrum	Education
P11	New Zealand	Project Manager	Scrum	Education
P12	New Zealand	Agile Coach	Scrum and Kanban	Not specified
P13	New Zealand	Agile Coach	Scrum and Kanban	Government application
P14	New Zealand	Product Owner	Not specified	Not specified
P15	New Zealand	Agile Coach	Scrum and Kanban	Government application
P16	New Zealand	Agile Coach	Scrum and Kanban	Government application

2.2 Data Analysis

The difference between Grounded Theory and other qualitative methods is the continuous interplay between data collection and data analysis [5]. Glaser argues that separating the data collection and data analysis prevents the emergence of theory [11]. Data analysis is done as soon as the first interview has been conducted.

Key point coding is used to analyze the interview transcripts in detail. We collate the key points by examining phrases, words, sentences from the interview transcripts [1]. Then, we construct codes by rephrasing key points with meaningful labels. In order to look for similarities and differences, constant comparison is used to compare every emerging code with the previous codes. Similar codes with common themes are grouped together and emerge as a concept. Many concepts emerge, and constant comparison is repeated until concepts form a category. A category is a group of similar concepts that are used to generate the core category. To date, several categories have been emerged from our data analysis including *"locating expertise"*.

3   Research Findings

The category *"locating expertise"* emerged from the data analysis, to describe how Agile team members identify the relevant expertise in teams. This study revealed four ways to identify expertise in Agile teams: *communicating frequently, working closely together, declaring self-identified expertise*, and *using an expertise directory*.

3.1   Communicating Frequently

A number of participants noted that through frequent and effective communication, they could determine who in a team possesses particular expertise.

> *"Depending on what you need. Is it domain expertise? Is it expertise with leadership and communication? You need to mix all [expertise] to be successful. So, talk to people and you'll find out."*- P6, Team leader.

Agile team members can identify their team members' expertise by enquiring about the team members' backgrounds, including working experiences, educational background, and proficient skills.

> *"In identifying the expertise, just talk to people and ask 'what do you like to do?' or 'what you have learned?' "*. - P7, Agile Consultant.

In certain circumstances, Agile team members can identify who the experts are in a particular area based on recommendations from other team members. Communication among team members provides a space to disseminate the meta-knowledge of the available expertise in Agile teams.

> *"You have people around talking to you, and you ask people, 'which area of code is the best known to whom?' "* - P2, Agile Coach.

A daily stand up meeting provides a communication vehicle for Agile team members to raise issues and obstacles that impeded their progress. As time is limited, the focus should be on the identification of the right person with the necessary expertise and solution. This situation leads to divulging the available expertise in Agile teams.

> *"A daily stand up meeting is not just reporting progress but [it is purposely] for team coordination. The main activity is to coordinate your work with the members of the team. For example, 'I have started with the [user] story but I'm stuck. Can someone help me?' "* - P4, Agile Coach.

The information flowing freely through communication leads Agile team members to get to know who has which sort of expertise. Through working closely together, the identified expertise can be confirmed and quantified by peers.

3.2   Working Closely Together

Working closely together provides opportunities for Agile team members to identify and confirm their peers' expertise when collaborating together.

> *"We can actually work together and then doing programming together. We [work] in pairs, see and notice [the expertise]."*- P2, Agile Coach.

Working closely together enables Agile team members to acquaint themselves with the progress of expertise development of their peers. Collaboration provides a space to assess and quantify the team members' degree of expertise.

> *"The expertise comes in discussion on the [story] size. If someone is less experienced, they might put the size differently from the experienced person."* - P4, Agile Coach.

Agile team members also have ability to identify and quantify their peers' expertise during task selection.

> *"....when the stories come out, they choose stories or works based on their capability."* - P4, Agile Coach.

Most Agile activities and practices encourage Agile team members to work together. There is no doubt that identifying expertise areas and levels can be obtained through effective collaborations in Agile teams.

3.3   Declaring a Self-identified Expertise

A curriculum vitae is used to represent the expertise details for recruitment purposes. In order to succeed in an interview, Agile team members convincingly disclose their self-identified expertise to interviewers. This process provides a clear picture of Agile team members' expertise at the very beginning.

> *"They are telling you what they are good at. For example, 'I'm a great .NET developer'. So, start with that [declaration], put them into the role, and observe them and see what they can do."* - P4, Agile Coach.

After joining an Agile team, Agile team members tend to expand their expertise into other expertise areas. Some team members, however, are not aware of the development of their team members' expertise. This is the point where Agile team members need to declare their expertise, in order to let others know what they can contribute to Agile teams.

> *"We do a stand up meeting...we talk about challenges that we have faced. Someone might know what the issue is about. They just said 'Yup, I know about that. We can talk about it later.' "* - P5, Software Tester.

The main concern is how reliable the self-identification is, as it is basically based on individual judgement. Thus, it is essential to verify the self-identified expertise through communicating frequently and working closely together.

3.4   Using an Expertise Directory

The expertise directory consists of expertise profiles of Agile team members. The main function of expertise directory is to point where the expertise resides. From P2's perspective, communication is more valuable when finding relevant expertise than using an expertise directory. This finding reveals that relying on the expertise directory to find the relevant expertise is not the best option in Agile teams.

> "You need to talk. It is much more effective than go to some expertise repository. How do you know the 'cruft' factor of the expertise repository [sic]." - P2, Agile Coach.

There is a formidable challenge in using the expertise directory to search the relevant expertise in Agile teams. The main issue is the reability of expertise directory in providing the accurate expertise profiles. The expertise directory requires regular maintenance to update the expertise profiles. The updating task needs someone in the Agile team to act as an administrator to maintain the tool and this indirectly increases the workloads of the Agile teams.

> "For example, I'm a beginner in Java programming. Then after 3 months, I continued improving Java programming. So, who is going to update the repository?" - P2, Agile Coach.

Despite the above perspective, participant P11 preferred to have an expertise directory when selecting the right person with the right expertise for upcoming software projects.

> "We do have the skills database. We developed [it] ourselves. Each person is expected to keep his or her profile and can be searched by others. If I want to start a new project and I need X, Y, Z skills, I guarantee that the skills database can provide these skills."- P11, Project Manager.

P11 believed that there is no issue in updating the expertise directory. Every staff member is required to update his or her expertise profiles to enable them to be selected for upcoming projects when their expertise is aligned with the project requirements.

> "They are motivated to update their skills database. So, that means, for the next exciting project, if they have the skills, they have a chance to be called to join the project." - P11, Project Manager.

Our findings revealed that the size of organization is a factor that influences the organization's preference in using the expertise directory. The growth of an organization with an increased number of staff and projects contributes to the high possibility of using the expertise directory.

"We realized that we have many projects coming. So, it is important to get alignment between the project and people. When we started, we had 110 people, and now 200. It becomes harder to keep track of a lot of skills. So, this tool helps me to identify the skills." - P11, Project Manager.

Access to internal experts through an expertise directory tends to speed up the expertise searching. The necessity of expertise directory however relies on the organization's need to locate a source of their staff's expertise.

3.5   Discussion

This study discovered the ways to locate internal expertise in Agile teams. Locating expertise is a prevalent process to enable the expertise dependencies in Agile software development teams [20]. Faraj and Sproull [8] and Shim et al. [19] asserted that knowing expertise is a part of expertise coordination processes in software development projects.

Several studies proposed an expertise directory as a medium to identify the right expertise in software development projects [15]. One surprising point arising from this study is that most Agile team members prefer communication to identify the relevant expertise rather the expertise directory. Through frequent interactions, team members have opportunities to acquire more detailed information about their peers' expertise [6]. The frequency of communication positively influences the awareness of team members' expertise [7].

The expertise directory has been classified as a coordination tool for locating expertise [18]. However, we found most Agile practitioners were reluctant to use the expertise directory because of the difficulties in keeping the expertise profiles up to date. This major drawback aligns with the research finding discovered by Bertoni and Chirumalla [2]. Through technology improvement such as Web 2.0 tools, the expertise directory can be improved particularly in updating the expertise profile [2]. Therefore, the right match between people and project can be gained through the expertise directory[2].

Relying on communication is not adequate for locating the right expertise. Communication enables Agile team members to identify the area of expertise, but it is difficult to confirm and quantify the level of expertise. Integrating communication with collaboration will strengthen the process in finding the right expertise in Agile team. Working closely together enables Agile team members to directly observe others' expertise. Several researchers have revealed that individuals are better at identifying team members' expertise when they spend more time working together [14]. Wegner et al. [22] suggested that expertise can be identified through direct observation, as well as self-disclosure.

Ultimately, our findings revealed that some Agile values, practices, and principles provide spaces and opportunities for Agile team members to identify the internal expertise in their teams. Through this study, Agile team members realize effective ways to locate the source of internal expertise and indirectly increase the awareness of the development of their peers' expertise.

3.6   Conclusion

This paper presents four ways Agile teams locate internal expertise: communicating frequently, working closely together, declaring self-identified expertise, and using an expertise directory. Locating expertise ultimately leads to the development of collective awareness of the expertise available in Agile teams and tends to improve problem solving capabilities. Further data collection and analysis will reveal more ways to locate expertise in Agile teams. In future, we also intend to investigate how Agile team members recognize the need for the identified expertise. There is no point having expertise available if team members fail to recognize when and where the available expertise is needed.

References

1. Allan, G.: A critique of using grounded theory as a research method. Electronic Journal of Business Research Methods 2(1), 1–10 (2003)
2. Bertoni, M., Chirumalla, K.: Leveraging web 2.0 in new product development: Lessons learned from a cross-company study. J. UCS 17(4), 548–564 (2011)
3. Bielaczyc, K., Collins, A.: Learning communities in classrooms: A reconceptualization of educational practice. In: Instructional-design Theories and Models: A New Paradigm of Instructional Theory vol. 2, pp. 269–292 (1999)
4. Charmaz, K.: Constructing grounded theory: A practical guide through qualitative analysis. Sage Publications Limited (2006)
5. Corbin, J.M., Strauss, A.: Grounded theory research: Procedures, canons, and evaluative criteria. Qualitative Sociology 13(1), 3–21 (1990)
6. Dessai, K., Kamat, M.: Application of social media for tracking knowledge in agile software projects. Available at SSRN 2018845 (2012)
7. Ehrlich, K., Chang, K.: Leveraging expertise in global software teams: Going outside boundaries. In: International Conference on Global Software Engineering, ICGSE 2006, pp. 149–158. IEEE (2006)
8. Faraj, S., Sproull, L.: Coordinating expertise in software development teams. Management Science, 1554–1568 (2000)
9. Garrett, S.K., Caldwell, B.S., Collins, S.T.: Supporting expertise coordination in multidisciplinary project teams. In: Proceedings of the Human Factors and Ergonomics Society Annual Meeting, vol. 53, pp. 1008–1012. SAGE Publications (2009)
10. Glaser, B.G.: Emergence vs forcing: Basics of grounded theory analysis. Sociology Press (1992)
11. Glaser, B.G., Strauss, A.L.: The discovery of grounded theory: Strategies for qualitative research. Aldine de Gruyter (1967)
12. Hoda, R.: Self-organizing agile teams: A grounded theory. Phd Thesis, Victoria University of Wellington (2011)
13. Lee, G., Xia, W.: Toward agile: An integrated analysis of quantitative and qualitative field data on software development agility. Mis Quarterly 34(1) (2010)
14. Littlepage, G., Robison, W., Reddington, K.: Effects of task experience and group experience on group performance, member ability, and recognition of expertise. Organizational Behavior and Human Decision Processes 69(2), 133–147 (1997)

15. Mockus, A., Herbsleb, J.: Expertise browser: a quantitative approach to identifying expertise. In: Proceedings of the 24th International Conference on Software Engineering, pp. 503–512. ACM (2002)
16. Ryan, S., O'Connor, R.V.: Social interaction, team tacit knowledge and transactive memory: empirical support for the agile approach
17. Santos, V.A., Goldman, A., Santos, C.D.: Uncovering steady advances for an extreme programming course, vol. 15, p. 2, Centro Latinoamericano de Estudios en Informtica (2012)
18. Sarma, A., Van der Hoek, A., Redmiles, D.: The coordination pyramid: A perspective on the state of the art in coordination technology
19. Shim, J., Sheu, T., Chen, H., Jiang, J., Klein, G.: Coproduction in successful software development projects. Information and Software Technology 52(10), 1062–1068 (2010)
20. Strode, D.E., Huff, S.L.: A taxonomy of dependencies in agile software development. In: ACIS 2012: Location, Location, Location: Proceedings of the 23rd Australasian Conference on Information Systems 2012, pp. 1–10 (2012)
21. Vanhanen, J., Korpi, H.: Experiences of using pair programming in an agile project. In: 40th Annual Hawaii International Conference on System Sciences, HICSS 2007, p. 274b. IEEE (2007)
22. Wegner, D.M.: A computer network model of human transactive memory. Social Cognition 13(3), 319–339 (1995)

Are Refactoring Practices Related
to Clusters in Java Software?

Giulio Concas, Cristina Monni, Matteo Orrù, and Roberto Tonelli

DIEE - Department of Electrical and Electronic Engineering
P.zza D'Armi, Cagliari, Italy
{concas,cristina.monni,matteo.orru}@diee.unica.it,
roberto.tonelli@dsf.unica.it
http://www.diee.unica.it

Abstract. Refactoring is widely used among the practices of Agile software development. In this preliminary work we present an empirical study carried out on several releases of 5 software systems written in Java. We focus our attention on the effect of refactoring activities on the topology of the software network. We find that refactoring activities involve classes linked together into clusters inside the software network and the clusters may be modified in different ways by the refactoring activity. This could lead to significant changes in source code, whose knowledge could be valuable for people involved in software development.

Keywords: Refactoring, Clustering, Software Networks.

1 Introduction

According to Fowler's definition [1] refactoring is aimed at correcting code structure without affecting the external behaviour, consequently improving software design - eliminating, for example, the presence of code smells [2]. It is a topic of acknowledged interest in the field of software engineering, specifically when it comes to Agile Methodologies. To the best of our knowledge, the state-of-the-art approach for retrieving refactoring operations is based on the work of Kim and Prete [3,4,5] and relies on the comparison of two different versions of the same piece of code (e.g. a class) and the use of a template model to detect the specific refactoring. Since refactoring can be applied to densely connected classes, the impact of a refactoring operation could be extended over the single class to involve the other related classes. On the other hand, in recent years there has been an increasing interest in the study of software systems using a software network approach [6,7,8,9,10,11]. To our knowledge, how and to which extent the impact of refactoring can spread over the associated software network has not been thoroughly studied so far.

In this preliminary work we built software networks by looking at relationships between classes (like dependency, inheritance and collaboration). This perspective allows to study software elements in the context of their reciprocal relationships, without neglecting the aspects that could be measured with the traditional

G. Cantone and M. Marchesi (Eds.): XP 2014, LNBIP 179, pp. 269–276, 2014.
© Springer International Publishing Switzerland 2014

metrics [12,13]. We present a study performed combining these two different approaches. We aimed at understanding whether refactoring operations are applied randomly to each class, or if they involve classes that are linked together. If refactoring shows the tendency to spread among linked classes, this information could be helpful for developers to make predictions, to keep track of which classes need to be refactored, or to detect other code smells.

In the following we report the empirical results of the investigation on refactoring activities performed by developers on 29 releases among 5 popular software systems written in Java: Ant, Azureus, Jedit, Jena and Xalan. First we parsed the source code to recover the software networks of classes, then we recovered all the refactorings related to these systems using RefFinder, and associated them to the corresponding classes, or nodes, in the software network. Every release was considered as an independent network. Eventually we performed a series of analyses comparing sets of refactored files to sets of random sampled files, in order to answer to our research question, namely to understand if refactoring affects classes which tend to be linked together or not. In order to validate our hypothesis we checked it against sub-networks extracted randomly from the whole system. The innovative approach is to combine information gained by analyzing source code differences given by RefFinder and a topological analysis on software networks. We believe that the information retrieved by this kind of analysis is valuable for developers for identifying a subset of classes for refactoring that could be worth to consider during software development. This paper is organized as follows. In Section 2 we will briefly illustrate the literature on refactoring analysis, and explain the main issues in this paper. In Section 3 we present the analyzed systems, explain our methodology and define the cluster measure used in this work. Finally we present and discuss our results in Section 4, and end with our conclusions in Section 5.

2   Background

Refactorings are code changes which do not modify the external system behaviour [1]. Usually developers decide to apply refactoring by examining or changing the software code while they are performing other operations [14], such as bug fixing, addition of functionalities, or other code changes.

This process is widely used in Agile Development, where code is maintained and extended repeatedly in order to avoid code decay. Decay can be caused for example by unhealthy dependencies between classes or packages, bad allocation of class responsibilities, too many responsibilities per method or class, duplicate code, or simply confusion in the code. Changing code without refactoring can worsen the decay process, thus refactoring can spare a lot of time and costs in software development, by keeping the code easy to maintain and extend.

Our purpose is to understand the impact of refactoring on the topology and coarse-grained structure of a software network, by studying the connections between classes before and after refactoring. This work can help to understand whether other classes are good candidates for being refactored, once a class has been chosen to be refactored, and this information can be made available for developers who perform refactoring.

To perform our analysis, we build the software networks associated to every release of our software projects and try to identify refactored classes and network connections among them. We will make use of the knowledge and previous works on software network systems, which can be found in [7,9,15,10,16].

The classes affected by refactoring have been retrieved with the use of RefFinder [5], the most commonly used automatic tool for the detection of refactoring operations. The 72 refactorings catalogued by Fowler [1] have been investigated also by other researchers with the purpose of finding other good techniques for automatic detection different from RefFinder [17], [18], [4]. Nevertheless RefFinder currently supports 65 of the 72 Fowler's refactorings, representing the most exhaustive coverage of all existing techniques. This tool compares two different software releases, analyzing the changes occurred from the first to the last, and identifies the refactoring operations according to Fowler's catalogue. The output is the set of all refactored classes with the associated refactorings.

To our knowledge, our work represents the first attempt to analyze clustering properties of refactored classes in a software network, and extends our previous work [19], which was a preliminary analysis on the clustering of classes in two Java systems affected by different corrective and maintenance operations, among which there were also refactorings. Other recent works [20,21] analyzed refactorings in the context of software networks, presenting a relationship between refactorings and node degree, but not analyzing clustering properties.

3   Experimental Setting and Methodology

The systems analyzed belong to the Java Qualitas Corpus [22], [23] , release version 20101126e, which contains 13 systems for a total of 414 versions. We analyzed 5 systems: Ant, Azureus, Jedit, Jena and Xalan. In total, we have analyzed 29 releases, for a dataset of tenths of thousands of classes.

We built the undirected network corresponding to each release by associating nodes to Java classes, and links to relationships among them, like inheritance, composition, dependencies, aggregation, association and so on. These relationships have been obtained by parsing the source code.

We extracted the maximal connected component of the obtained software networks and performed our analysis on them. We then used RefFinder [5] to extract the information about refactoring activities for each release. RefFinder analyzes the differences among the source code of two releases, the source and the target, and identifies the occurred refactoring operations. We analyzed only the refactorings associated by RefFinder to the source release, and we discarded the refactorings associated to the target release. Every refactoring was associated to the corresponding class, and so we were able to understand if classes affected by refactoring are connected or not.

For every release, we performed a comparison between the clusters formed only among refactored classes and the number of clusters formed by the same number of classes selected at random among all system classes.

We define a cluster of nodes at distance d as a set of nodes such that there is at least one path of length d between each pair of nodes in the set. If $d = 1$, every node inside the cluster is connected with at least another node in the same cluster, so the latter is a connected subgraph. Given this definition, the number of clusters formed inside a set of n nodes can be univocally determined, and trivially it can vary from 1, if all the nodes are connected, to n when all the nodes are isolated. Since we consider the links between classes as undirected, the clusters do not depend on the direction of edges. We have found clusters formed by classes affected by refactoring, and compared the number of these clusters with the average number of clusters formed by a random selection of a number of classes equal to the number of refactored classes. In Section 4 we illustrate our results.

4 Results

Our work is aimed at understanding if refactoring activities are related to clustering and connectivity inside a software network.

From every system we extracted the subsets of classes which have been affected by a refactoring operation. We will refer to the size of the network by n and to the size of the subsets of refactored classes by n'.

We selected randomly a subset of the same size n' and computed inside each subset the number of clusters, i.e. the number of connected subgraphs. We repeated this sampling 100 times in order to have significant statistics, and then computed the average number of clusters found for every sampling. Then we also computed the number of clusters (or connected subgraphs) formed by the sets of refactored classes, to be compared with the average number of the random case.

In the plot of Fig. 1 we show the number of clusters formed by refactored classes, and the average number of clusters obtained by selecting at random the same number of classes among all system classes. The plot shows that, given a fixed cluster size, the random selection brings a higher number of clusters compared to refactored classes. This means that refactoring mainly does not affect classes in a random fashion, but if a class needs this operation, there is a certain probability that also another class connected to the first will need to be refactored. This could be of help in software development and maintenance. We also would like to point out the nearly linear growth of the number of clusters along with the number of classes selected, meaning that the random selection forms a number of clusters related and almost equal to the number of classes, as one would expect. These results confirm our previous analysis in [19], and they are valid specifically for refactored classes.

In Fig. 2 we show an example of how refactoring activities could be related to a change in the topology of a software network. The example we show is a comparison between the releases 4.0.0.0 and 4.1.0.2 of the system Azureus. The figure shows the two sets of classes affected by the refactoring *Replace method with method object*. After the refactoring operation, the connectivity among classes

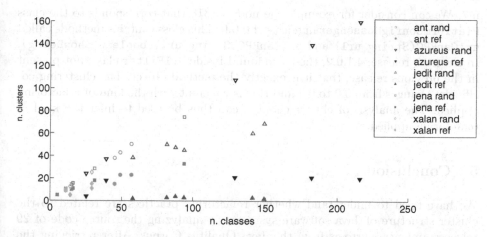

Fig. 1. Comparison between the average number of clusters found by the random selection and the number of clusters formed by refactored classes. The average number of clusters for the random case (empty points of different shapes) is systematically bigger than in case of refactored classes, showing that the latter are more connected with each other.

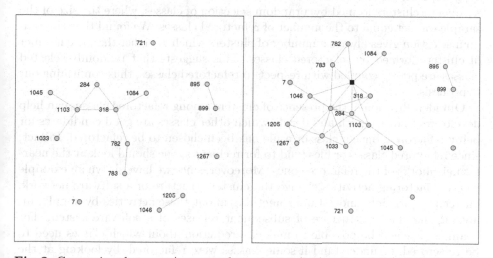

Fig. 2. Comparison between Azureus release 4.0.0.0 (left) and 4.1.0.2 (right). For each release, we report the sets of classes affected by the refactoring named *Replace method with method object*. The node corresponding to `UrlFilter` class has a squared shape and it is black on the right plot.

has changed, since the cluster grows by the addition of new classes. In particular, we can see that in the previous release, 4.0.0.0, the classes involved by this refactoring are 15, while in release 4.1.0.2 there is a bigger cluster, composed of 20 classes, among which there are also the classes which were subject to the same refactoring, but nearly isolated in release 4.0.0.0, such as classes n. 1046 and n.7. We can consider for example the node n. 318 that corresponds to the class `PlatformConfigMessenger` in release 4.0.0.0. This class contains methods called `urlCanRPC(String url)` and `urlCanRPC(String url, boolean showDebug)`. In the next release, 4.1.0.2, these are found inside `UrlFilter` class, not present in the previous release, that it is exactly the method object. The clustering coefficient changes from 0.2 to 0.3 and this is coherent with the kind of refactoring applied. The analysis of cluster changes can thus be used to infer the kind of refactoring applied.

5   Conclusion

We have tried to understand whether refactoring practices are related to the cluster structure of Java software systems, by analyzing the source code of 29 releases among 5 systems from the Java Qualitas Corpus. After retrieving the source code and building the software network for each release of the analyzed systems, we extracted the refactoring operations using RefFinder.

We then analyzed every release of the software systems to understand if classes are more connected with each other after undergoing a refactoring operation. We compared the number of clusters formed by refactored classes to the average number of clusters formed by a random selection of classes, where the size of the sample was set equal to the number of refactored classes. We found that the random selection gives always a number of clusters which is higher than the number of clusters formed by refactored classes. This suggests that randomly selected classes are poorly coupled with respect to refactored classes, thus confirming our hypothesis.

Our identification of the presence of clusters among refactored classes can help developers to distinguish and decide which other classes are good candidates for being refactored, once a class or a file has been chosen to be refactored. In fact, since refactored classes or files tend to form clusters, one should look at the nearest neighbours of the refactored ones. Moreover, since we have shown an example where refactoring activities change the cluster structure of a software network, one can in principle understand something about these activities by simply analyzing the cluster structure of subsequent releases of a software system. For example, it could be possible to make a prediction about which classes need to be refactored, or understand if some classes were refactored, by looking at the cluster structure in the proximity of the involved classes. Our preliminar results could be extended in order to understand if it is possible to make such predictions. Since refactoring generally affects software quality by improving coupling and cohesion, the clustering properties of refactoring activities could be also related to this feature, and then to software quality. For example, we could analyze the topology of such clusters along software evolution to understand if they are related to an improvement of software quality.

Our preliminary analysis involved only Java systems from the Qualitas Corpus, but it could be extended to other systems in order to have a bigger statistics and to better distinguish also among different types of refactoring. Indeed, this analysis can be extended to the other types of refactorings from Fowler's catalogue, to understand also if some types of refactorings tend to form clusters more than others. Our analysis involves different releases over time, and so it can be also viewed as a study of software evolution for what concerns refactoring activities.

Acknowledgments. This research is supported by Regione Autonoma della Sardegna (RAS), Regional Law No. 7-2007, project CRP-17938 "LEAN 2.0".

References

1. Fowler, M.: Refactoring: improving the design of existing code. Addison-Wesley Longman Publishing Co., Inc., Boston (1999)
2. Counsell, S., Hamza, H., Hierons, R.M.: An empirical investigation of code smell 'deception' and research contextualisation through paul's criteria. CIT 18(4) (2010)
3. Kim, M., Gee, M., Loh, A., Rachatasumrit, N.: Ref-finder: A refactoring reconstruction tool based on logic query templates. In: Proceedings of the Eighteenth ACM SIGSOFT International Symposium on Foundations of Software Engineering, FSE 2010, pp. 371–372. ACM, New York (2010)
4. Prete, K., Rachatasumrit, N., Sudan, N., Kim, M.: Template-based reconstruction of complex refactorings. In: Proceedings of the 2010 IEEE International Conference on Software Maintenance, ICSM 2010, pp. 1–10. IEEE Computer Society, Washington, DC (2010)
5. RefFinder, https://webspace.utexas.edu/kp9746/www/reffinder/
6. Albert, R., Barabási, A.L.: Statistical mechanics of complex networks. Reviews of Modern Physics 74, 47–97 (2002)
7. Kohring, G.A.: Complex dependencies in large software systems. Advances in Complex Systems (ACS) 12(06), 565–581 (2009)
8. Li, D., Han, Y., Hu, J.: Complex network thinking in software engineering. In: Proceedings of the 2008 International Conference on Computer Science and Software Engineering, CSSE 2008, vol. 01, pp. 264–268. IEEE Computer Society, Washington, DC (2008)
9. Myers, C.R.: Software systems as complex networks: Structure, function, and evolvability of software collaboration graphs. Phys. Rev. E 68(4), 046116 (2003)
10. Valverde, S., Cancho, R., Sole, V.: Scale free networks from optimal design. Europhysics Letters 60 (2002)
11. Wen, L., Kirk, D., Dromey, R.G.: Software systems as complex networks. In: Proceedings of the 6th IEEE International Conference on Cognitive Informatics, COGINF 2007, pp. 106–115. IEEE Computer Society, Washington, DC (2007)
12. Chidamber, S., Kemerer, C.: A metrics suite for object oriented design. IEEE Trans. Software Eng. 20(6), 476–493 (1994)
13. Lorenz, M., Kidd, J.: Object-Oriented Software Metrics: A Practical Approach. Prentice Hall (1994)
14. Murphy-Hill, E., Parnin, C., Black, A.P.: How we refactor, and how we know it. IEEE Transactions on Software Engineering 38(1), 5–18 (2012)
15. Šubelj, L., Bajec, M.: Community structure of complex software systems: Analysis and applications. Physica A Statistical Mechanics and its Applications 390, 2968–2975 (2011)

16. Watts, D.J., Strogatz, S.H.: Collective dynamics of 'small-world' networks. Nature 393(6684), 440–442 (1998)
17. Advani, D., Hassoun, Y., Counsell, S.: Extracting refactoring trends from open-source software and a possible solution to the 'related refactoring' conundrum. In: Proceedings of the 2006 ACM Symposium on Applied Computing, SAC 2006, pp. 1713–1720. ACM, New York (2006)
18. Arzoky, M., Swift, S., Tucker, A., Cain, J.: Munch: An efficient modularisation strategy to assess the degree of refactoring on sequential source code checkings. In: Proceedings of the 2011 IEEE Fourth International Conference on Software Testing, Verification and Validation Workshops, ICSTW 2011, pp. 422–429. IEEE Computer Society, Washington, DC (2011)
19. Concas, G., Monni, C., Orrù, M., Tonelli, R.: A study of the community structure of a complex software network. In: Proceedings of the 2013 ICSE Workshop on Emerging Trends in Software Metrics, WETSoM 2013, pp. 14–20. ACM, New York (2013), doi:http://doi.acm.org/10.1145/1809223.1809227
20. Murgia, A., Marchesi, M., Concas, G., Tonelli, R., Counsell, S.: Parameter-based refactoring and the relationship with fan-in/fan-out coupling. In: IEEE International Conference on Software Testing Verification and Validation Workshop, pp. 430–436 (2011)
21. Murgia, A., Tonelli, R., Marchesi, M., Concas, G., Counsell, S., McFall, J., Swift, S.: Refactoring and its relationship with fan-in and fan-out: An empirical study. In: Proceedings of the 16th European Conference on Software Maintenance and Reengineering, CSMR 2012, pp. 63–72 (2012)
22. Java Qualitas Corpus, http://qualitascorpus.com/
23. Tempero, E., Anslow, C., Dietrich, J., Han, T., Li, J., Lumpe, M., Melton, H., Noble, J.: Qualitas corpus: A curated collection of java code for empirical studies. In: 2010 Asia Pacific Software Engineering Conference (APSEC 2010), pp. 336–345 (December 2010)

Social Contracts, Simple Rules and Self-organization: A Perspective on Agile Development

Ken Power

Cisco Systems
Galway
Ireland
ken.power@gmail.com

Abstract. Teams and organizations are complex adaptive systems. Self-organization in complex adaptive systems evolves through a set of Simple Rules. Self-organization is a core tenet of agile teams. Self-organization does not mean everyone gets to do whatever they want to do. Team members create contracts with each other. These contracts create boundaries, or containers, within which self-organization can occur. Teams also create contracts with other teams, the wider organization and other stakeholders. The contracts are both implicit and explicit. Social contracts in complex adaptive systems are more effective if they are based on Simple Rules. Social Contract Theory acts as a lens through which we can better understand these social contracts in agile teams. This paper represents ongoing research that examines the role of Simple Rules and Social Contract Theory in fostering self-organization in agile development teams. The paper discusses four examples of social contracts in agile teams: definition of done, definition of ready, working agreements, and retrospectives.

Keywords: definition of done, definition of ready, simple rules, social contract theory, justice, social contracts, working agreements, agile, complexity, complex adaptive system, human systems dynamics.

1 Introduction

Social contract theory has its roots in part in the work of 18th century political philosopher Jean-Jacque Rousseau [1], and more recently in the work of moral and political philosopher John Rawls, and his Theory of Justice [2]. Rawls' primary focus is the subject of justice in what he calls social organizations, and specifically *"the way in which the major social institutions distribute fundamental rights and duties and determine the division of advantages from social cooperation"*. In other words, people in a social system have rights and benefits that are determined by the system. *"The basic structure is the primary subject of justice because its effects are so profound and present from the start."* [2]. The philosopher and physician John Locke uses the social contract to defend and protect particular values, and to institute an accountable system of authority [3]. This paper discusses how these ideas apply to agile teams and organizations.

G. Cantone and M. Marchesi (Eds.): XP 2014, LNBIP 179, pp. 277–284, 2014.

"*Social contract arguments typically posit that individuals have consented, either explicitly or tacitly, to surrender some of their freedoms and submit to the authority of the ruler or magistrate (or to the decision of a majority), in exchange for protection of their remaining rights*" [4]. This definition is worth analyzing in the context of self-organizing human systems in general, and agile software development teams in particular. In the context of agile development teams:

- The individuals are the team members. They are also employees of the organization.
- The "majority" is the team as a whole. There may also be a wider team, or "team of teams", such as a program where many teams deliver a large product or system.
- The ruler or magistrate is equivalent to the managers of the organization the individuals and teams work for. There is an explicit contract of employment that carries certain explicit and implicit obligations.

The first interpretation relates to "the decision of the majority". A team, in order to be successful, needs to agree how they are going to work together. These agreements set expectations. Although individuals will have their own working style preferences, there is a balance between accommodating individual preferences and doing what is good for the group as a whole. In lean terms, this is an application of systems thinking. So, a team will ideally have a facilitated discussion to agree their social contracts. It is best if these social contracts are created by the people who are most affected by them. There are other types of contracts, such as rules for driving on motorways or taxation laws that are created by a few people and imposed through rule of law. There are similar laws or contracts in the workplace, where people are subject to employment law. The type of contract we are talking about with social contracts is where the people governed by the contracts create, or at least have significant input, into creating the contracts. In a "*well-ordered social structure*", whether a society, team or organization, each citizen of the social structure honors the social contract because it is in their own self-interest, as long as enough of the other citizens of the social structure also honor the contract [5].

Some writers in the agile community have mentioned social contracts. Israel Gat, for example, wrote two Blogs about the advantages of creating social contracts between teams and management, particularly at the start of an agile transition and in the face of difficult situations such as impending layoffs [6, 7]. Alan Atlas writes how social contracts form the basis for interaction between people, and defines a social contract as "*Working Agreement between non-peers. In an Agile context, social contracts are written between a team and its management, or a team and its encompassing organization*" [8]. This paper takes a broader perspective, viewing working agreements as an example of social contract, as described further in section 3.3 below. Jurgen Appelo cites Israel Gat's Blog, and also mentions Social Contract Theory, writing that the ideas translate well to organizations [9]. However, these blog posts do not reference social contract theory, and none of these writers cite the social contract theory literature or the work of Rawls. The research represented by this paper expands on these perspectives to encompass social contract theory, and also to frame social contracts in the context of the Simple Rules that govern emergent behavior and self-organization in teams and organizations. This is the topic of the next section.

2   Teams and Organizations as Complex Adaptive Systems

Dooley notes that *"the prevailing paradigm of a given era's management theories has historically mimicked the prevailing paradigm of that era's scientific theories"* [10]. The complexity sciences have emerged as one of the prevailing paradigms for modern management thinking in general [11, 12], and agile management in particular [13]. Stacey has shown that *"all organisations are complex adaptive systems in which groups and individuals are the agents"* [14], and self-organization is widely acknowledged as a key property of successful agile teams [15]. Agile methods address this directly with Scrum, for example, defined as *"a framework within which people can address complex adaptive problems while productively and creatively delivering products of the highest possible value"* [16]. The creators of the Agile Manifesto recognized this too, with the manifesto stating, *"The best architectures, requirements, and designs emerge from self-organizing teams."*

Human Systems Dynamics (HSD) provides a model for understanding self-organization in human systems. HSD defines a CAS as a *"collection of individual agents who have the freedom to act in unpredictable ways, and whose actions are interconnected such that they produce system-wide patterns"* [17, 18]. Fig. 1 illustrates how system-wide patterns emerge as the agents in the system interact. Fig. 1 is a modified version of the picture used in HSD to represent emergent patterns in complex human systems.

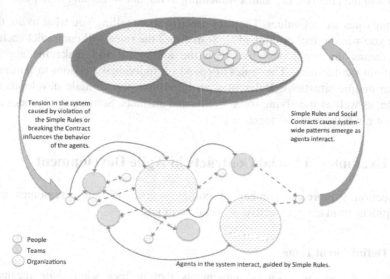

Fig. 1. Agents in a human system interact, guided by Simple Rules, to form patterns

HSD uses three core elements to describe systems: containers, differences and exchanges (CDE). Containers are boundaries within which self-organization of human systems occurs. This is accomplished through focusing and constraining the interactions among the agents in the system. Examples include teams and organizations. Differences establish the potential for change in a human system, creating the possibility for the system to self-organize to a new state. Exchanges, also known as Transforming Exchanges, are interactions between the agents (people, teams, etc.) in a Container, and are *a necessary condition for self-organizing processes to occur*" [19]. Making changes in a system is referred to as making an intervention. For example, a Container intervention might alter the structure or membership of a team, or change the social contract. Improving the communication between the agile team and management is an example of an Exchange intervention.

2.1   Simple Rules

In CAS terms, Simple Rules support coherent actions among the agents in a system. "*If everyone follows the same short list of Simple Rules, then the group behaves in a coherent way as a whole*" [17]. Here are the HSD rules for creating Simple Rules [17]:

- Include no more than 5 rules (plus or minus 2).
- Begin the rule with a verb.
- Work for everyone and every place in the system.
- Need at least one rule for each of the conditions of self-organization, i.e., a Container rule, a Difference rule and an Exchange rule.
- Stated in the positive, i.e., states something to do, not something to not do.

Simple rules are not values. They are specific about telling you what to *do*; they do not tell you what to feel or think [17]. Sometimes the rules will contradict each other, which means the group will live with the ambiguity and make the appropriate tradeoffs in the moment. The "rules" depend on individual freedom to interpret and apply in unique situations. Rules play an important part in agile development. For example, as well as specifying roles, events and artifacts, Scrum also includes a set of rules that binds these things together [16].

3   Examples of Social Contracts in Agile Development

This section explores a number of common artifacts and ceremonies in agile development from the perspective of social contracts.

3.1   Definition of Done

Definition of done is a set of agreements that defines what *done* means for a potentially shippable product increment of a product. Everyone on the team, including Scrum Masters and Product Owners, must have a common understanding of what done means [16]. The line items of the *definition of done* are Simple Rules. *Definition of done* creates a contract between the development team, the product owner and the rest of the organization. The terms of that contract are effectively that the team is committing to satisfying each item in the definition before declaring a user story to be done. When a user story is declared done, and accepted by the product owner, it becomes part of a potentially shippable product. The team commits to getting the user story done by following the Simple Rules, and hence fulfilling their part of the contract. The organization commits to supporting the team and not coercing them into taking shortcuts. The product owner commits to providing feedback, answering questions, and generally being available to support the team in getting to done. The Scrum Master makes sure that everyone is upholding their part of the social contract, and when necessary, reminds people about the Simple Rules. The Scrum Master is effectively the guardian of the Simple Rules and the social contract.

3.2   Definition of Ready

Definition of Ready is a set of Simple Rules adopted by an agile team to help them remember all the things they need to do before a development team starts work on a backlog item [20]. Where the development team is responsible for meeting definition of done, product owners (or equivalent) are responsible for making sure work items meet definition of ready. This creates a similar but different social contract to that created by *definition of done*. This time, the emphasis is on the product owner to meet the terms of the contract, and the team agrees to support them [21].

3.3   Working Agreements

Working agreements are common in healthy agile teams, and the agreements team members make with each other about how they will work together are part of creating the team's culture [15]. There are explicit agreements, e.g., be on time for the daily scrum meeting, don't break the build, no meetings on Fridays. There are also implicit agreements, e.g., be mindful about inviting people to meetings, send meeting invites to named people rather than group aliases. Mike Cohn also describes the different agreements a co-located team and a distributed team might make.

All of these agreements are examples of Simple Rules that create social contracts that in turn influence the behavior of the people in the team. With reference to Fig. 1, as the people (agents) in the system interact based on these Simple Rules, patterns emerge. One such pattern might be that a developer is consistently late for the daily standup. This will cause a tension in the system that in turn will influence the behavior of the actors, or team members. What happens next will depend on the team. They might remind each other of their working agreements (Simple Rules), or the Scrum Master might remind them, and point out that one of the rules is being violated. They have a choice to make around whether the rules are still serving them. If so, the tardy developer might choose to respect the social contract formed by the Simple Rules and start showing up on time. This resulting behavior will cause a new pattern to emerge in the system.

3.4   Retrospectives

Retrospectives are a teams' opportunity to inspect and adapt; to reflect on how they are working and make necessary changes to their system. Teams usually hold retrospectives at the end of each Sprint, and a bigger one at the end of each release.

3.4.1 Retrospective Prime Directive

Retrospectives are intended to drive change. However, a human system cannot evolve if the people are filled with anxiety. As Olsen and Eoyang note, *"leaders and change agents have a role in creating a safe space, at least safe enough for system agents to take risks associated with movement and change"* [22]. Norm Kerth created the retrospective "Prime Directive", which he defined as follows: *"Regardless of what we discover, we must understand and truly believe that everyone did the best job he or she could, given what was known at the time, his or her skills and abilities, the resources available, and the situation at hand."* [23]. The goal of this social contract is to develop safety and trust among the retrospective participants so they can have an open and honest discussion without fear of recrimination. If this contract is broken, and the prime directive violated, the retrospective will fail to meet its goals.

3.4.2 Retrospective Second Directive

Dale Emery coined the Retrospective Second Directive to make explicit the central element of responsibility in the team: *"We accept the responsibility to change at least one of the conditions that made our best less than we now want it to be."* [24]. This creates a social contract in the team to accept the responsibility to make changes in their system.

3.4.3 Ground Rules and Working Agreements

Jean Tabaka writes that Ground Rules *"should be the team's declaration of its self-governance"* [25]. The ground rules belong to the team, not the meeting facilitator, and are *"the boundaries a team believes can help it stay focused on their goal"*. The Ground Rules are an example of Simple Rules that create a social contract between the meeting participants, so that they can work together to meet their goals. Ground Rules are similar to what Diana Larsen and Esther Derby refer to as Working Agreements for retrospectives. Larsen and Derby also emphasize that working agreements belong to the team, not to the retrospective facilitator [26]. In alignment with the guidelines for creating Simple Rules, retrospective working agreements should number no more than five. While it is not possible to predict every situation that will occur, *"most groups can address the majority of situations with five working agreements"* [26].

4   Conclusions

This paper described the connection between Social Contract Theory and agile teams, viewing agile teams as complex adaptive systems. The field of Human Systems Dynamics provides a suitable lens through which to view teams and organizations as complex adaptive social systems, and defines necessary conditions for self-organization using Containers, Differences and Exchanges. The social contracts in agile teams and organizations are based on the Simple Rules that govern emergence and self-organization.

Simple Rules support coherent behaviors in a system. Definition of done, definition of ready, and working agreements are all examples of social contracts, created using Simple Rules, in agile teams and organizations. In addition, there are examples of social contracts to be found in retrospectives, including the prime directive, second directive and ground rules. These Simple Rules and Social Contracts support emergent behaviors and self-organization.

Teams own their own Simple Rules. As teams adapt their Simple Rules, new patterns are formed in the system. These patterns are governed by the social contracts created by the Simple Rules. Violating the Simple Rules creates a tension in the system that can be resolved by the team enforcing the rules or altering the rules (an Exchange intervention), or by the team membership changing (a Container intervention).

Social Contracts exist within agile teams, between agile teams, between agile teams and management, and within management teams.

Further research on this topic will continue to explore social contracts and Simple Rules in human systems, with a particular focus on agile teams and organizations.

References

1. Qvortrup, M.: The political philosophy of Jean-Jacques Rousseau: The impossibilty of reason. Manchester University Press, Manchester (2003)
2. Rawls, J.: A Theory of Justice. Harvard University Press, Cambridge (1971)
3. Jos, P.H.: Social Contract Theory: Implications for Professional Ethics. The American Review of Public Administration 36, 139–155 (2006)
4. Wikipedia, http://en.wikipedia.org/wiki/Social_contract
5. Binmore, K.G.: Game Theory and the Social Contract, Vol 2: Just Playing, vol. 2. The MIT Press, Cambridge (1998)
6. Gat, I.: A Social Contract for Agile, http://theagileexecutive.com/2009/02/03/a-social-contract-for-agile/
7. Gat, I.: Addition to the Social Contract, http://theagileexecutive.com/2009/04/11/addition-to-the-social-contract/
8. Atlas, A.: Teach Your Boss to be Agile with a Social Contract, http://theagileexecutive.com/2009/11/05/teach-your-boss-to-be-agile-with-a-social-contract-guest-post-by-alan-atlas/
9. Appelo, J.: Management 3.0: Leading Agile Developers, Developing Agile Leaders. Addison-Wesley, Upper Saddle River (2011)
10. Dooley, K.J.: A Complex Adaptive Systems Model of Organization Change. Nonlinear Dynamics, Psychology and Life Sciences 1, 69–97 (1997)
11. Snowden, D.J., Boone, M.E.: A Leader's Framework for Decision Making. Harvard Business Review (2007)
12. Vasconcelos, F.C., Ramirez, R.: Complexity in business environments. Journal of Business Research 64, 236–241 (2011)
13. Appelo, J.: Management 3.0: leading Agile developers, developing Agile leaders. Addison-Wesley, Upper Saddle River (2011)
14. Stacey, R.: Emerging Strategies for a Chaotic Environment. Long Range Planning 29, 182–189 (1996)

15. Cohn, M.: Succeeding with Agile: Software Development Using Scrum. Addison-Wesley, Upper Saddle River (2010)
16. Sutherland, J., Schwaber, K.: The Scrum Guide. The Definitive Guide to Scrum: The Rules of the Game. Scrum.org (2013)
17. Eoyang, G.H.: Human Systems Dynamics Professional Certification Training Manual. HSD Institute, Cohort 32 - Roffey Park, UK (2013)
18. Eoyang, G.H., Holladay, R.J.: Adaptive Action: Leveraging Uncertainty in Your Organization. Stanford University Press, Stanford (2013)
19. Eoyang, G.H.: Conditions for Self-Organizing in Human Systems. Doctor of Philosophy. The Union Institute and University (2001)
20. Rubin, K.S.: Essential Scrum: a practical guide to the most popular Agile process. Addison-Wesley, (Pearson Education [distributor]) London, Boston (2012)
21. Power, K.: Definition of Ready: An Experience Report from Teams at Cisco. In: Cantone, G., Marchesi, M. (eds.) XP 2014. LNBIP, vol. 179, pp. 312–319. Springer, Heidelberg (2014)
22. Olson, E.E., Eoyang, G.H.: Facilitating Organization Change: Lessons from Complexity Science. Jossey-Bass/Pfeiffer, A Wiley Company, San Francisco (2001)
23. Kerth, N.: Project retrospectives: a handbook for team reviews. Dorset House Publishing, New York (2001)
24. Emery, D.: The Second Directive, http://cwd.dhemery.com/2003/06/the_second_directive/
25. Tabaka, J.: Collaboration Explained: Facilitation Skills for Software Project Leaders. Addison-Wesley Professional, Upper Saddle River (2006)
26. Derby, E., Larsen, D.: Agile Retrospectives: Making Good Teams Great. The Pragmatic Programmers, Raleigh (2006)

Realizing Agile Software Enterprise Transformations by Team Performance Development

Petri Kettunen

University of Helsinki
Department of Computer Science
P.O. Box 68, FI-00014 University of Helsinki, Finland
petri.kettunen@cs.helsinki.fi

Abstract. Many software-intensive new product development (NPD) based enterprises pursuit nowadays agile transformations in order to sustain and improve their performance and competitiveness. Agile software development teams are by definition striving for high performance. However, in larger organizations there can be a wide diversity of such teams. It is not so straightforward to determine high performance for the teams, but by understanding the overall performance aims of the enterprise, such diverse teams bring competitive advantages to software development organizations. Continuing our prior works, this paper addresses those issues by proposing a performance analysis approach for agile software organizations. The overall goal is to provide means to distinguish different high-performing agile software teams, and consequently practical measures to establish and sustain performance in different organizational transformations. The example cases demonstrate how it is able to align and integrate team performance targets and overall aims of industrial software organizations under agile transformations.

Keywords: agile software enterprise, organization design, team performance management, transformation competencies, capability development.

1   Introduction

Teams and teamwork are central to agile software development. Moreover, not just having teams but consciously concentrating on their performance is what brings the agility benefits. Furthermore, since agile enterprises are by definition proficient at change, it is necessary to understand the impacts of organizational changes to team performance in order to avoid unintended negative effects. The ultimate aim of agile software enterprise transformations is to achieve such ideal performance state of the organization.

High-performing teamwork has been investigated in many fields over the years. In particular, the success factors of new product development (NPD) teams are in general relatively well known. However, the specific concerns and intrinsic properties of modern agile software development teams are essentially less understood in particular in larger scales. In all, it is not clearly understood, what high performance

G. Cantone and M. Marchesi (Eds.): XP 2014, LNBIP 179, pp. 285–293, 2014.
© Springer International Publishing Switzerland 2014

means for agile software development enterprises in total, and how exactly such effects and outcomes are achievable in transformational ways. Such fundamental comprehension would greatly help to justify and execute agile transformations, and leverage diverse teams to scale up at enterprise levels.

This paper approaches those issues by proposing a holistic performance analysis approach for team-based agile software enterprises. The purpose is twofold:

1. Software development organizations can gauge their diverse teams with it for organizational transformations.
2. Software teams themselves may utilize it for their own performance management to support the attainment of the desired transformation state.

The rest of this paper is organized as follows. The next Section 2 reviews software team performance measures in general and agile software enterprise development traits. Section 3 presents the performance-based transformation analysis approach, followed by certain industrial case examples in Section 4. Finally, Section 5 discusses the proposition with implications and concluding pointers to further work in Section 6.

2   Software Team Performance and Agile Enterprises

Industrial-strength software product development is almost always done in teams, even in globally virtual set-ups. Furthermore, software teams do not exist in isolation in particular in larger product development enterprises. Moreover, in large-scale organizations there are typically not just single teams but a network of interdependent teams, passing even external company boundaries. In general, it is not reasonable to attempt to define (high) performance of software teams without taking into account the context. In all, the domain of the software (products) sets the main performance criteria. There may considerable differences in different industries and competitive environments (e.g., automotive embedded software vs. mobile games). Nevertheless, it is possible to find many generally applicable ways and measures to device and guide agile software teams towards high performance for the enterprises.

All in all, high performance of agile software enterprises and development teams is apprehended in multidisciplinary ways spanning many areas of modern business competence and R&D management, in particular: software engineering management and leadership, knowledge-intensive NPD teamwork, and high-technology business strategy and organizational development.

This paper focuses on software engineering (management) discipline. However, it is fundamental to understand the connections to those related fields for instance with respect to knowledge workers in general.

In practice there are usually many ways to affect the (high) performance with agile software teams. In general, there is no one universal measure of software team performance. To begin with, software teams can be seen as general work teams and their performance accordingly [1].

Typically software team performance is associated with productivity [2]. However, software development teams have usually multiple enterprise stakeholders – including the team members themselves – and consequently multiple different dimensions of performance [3]. Agile software teams excel in their value creation not only for the customers, but also for their organizations and for the team itself [4]. Conversely, while waste lowers performance it is relative to the defined value.

Moreover, the measurement scales (high vs. low performance) vary for instance in different product development domains. Multivariate measures are thus usually more applicable. Consequently, different teams may have different performance targets even within same larger organizations.

Prior literature has described many such possible software team performance measures. Typical performance measures used in software-intensive organizations are like the following ones: stakeholder-rated performance (e.g., product quality, contribution to the firm performance), meeting user needs and company demands, and process performance (development schedule, budget).

Although it is difficult to define general-purpose performance metrics for specific software teams, the measurement systems can be developed based on existing general-purpose frameworks to begin with. In particular, the ISO/IEC 15939 standard provides such a platform [5]. It is imperative to know, who judges the success and when [6].

There is no universal recipe for creating and improving high-performing software teams. However, such means can stem from the processes, tools, organization, and most importantly the people in the team. Typical performance factors presented in the extant literature are as follows: extensive sharing of financial and performance information throughout the organization (with trust, open-book management) [7], organizational constructs to facilitate longer-term process development and improvement [8], clear mission, appropriate software life-cycle models [9], and empowering leadership [10].

Notably many negative factors (weaknesses and impediments) can be inverted to positive ones (strengths). Furthermore, those positive influences require typically certain supporting organizational enablers on the one hand, and removing possible hindrances and impediments on the other hand. Larger organizations should also be able to take a competitive advantage of its diverse software teams and their unique strengths.

Finally, advancing from the software team level up to the enterprise level, organizational development may comprise large-scale transformations. In general, such enterprise transformations are radical changes in what business the organization conducts and how it operates in total. The drivers for such transformations stem from the need to respond to radical changes in the competitive environment, strategic repositioning of the company, and the pressures for cost reductions and performance improvements [11]. Conceptually, they can be defined as value deficiencies [12].

There are certain general-purpose enterprise transformation models published. For instance Rouse defines such a transformation framework with the dimensions of scope (ranging from the entire enterprise to work activities), ends, and means [12].

In case of software organizations, so-called agile transformations usually mean adoption of agile software development methods and possibly also some more general principles of the Agile Manifesto defined way of working. However, there are no comprehensive models for realizing systematic transformations of large-scale agile software enterprises [13], [14]. The purpose of this work is to address that integration gap.

3   Framework for Team-Based Transformations

The approach proposed here integrates and further develops our prior works as outlined in Table 1. The key idea here is that once the overall performance goals are determined for the desired future state of the enterprise transformation (1), the software team performance management can be oriented accordingly (2). There are then typically different needs and opportunities for diverse agile software teams in the enterprise (3).

Table 1. Framework foundations

BASE	Groundwork	Key Elements
1	Enterprise-level performance goals determination [15]	• systematizing the strategic needs • means / enablers to fulfill them
2	Software team performance aiming [16]	• determining software team performance portfolio in the overall product development constellation
3	Team performance self-monitoring and improvement [17]	• gauging software teams with respect to their desired performance

Following that line of thinking in Fig. 1, agile teams and their performance can be seen in a multidimensional space.

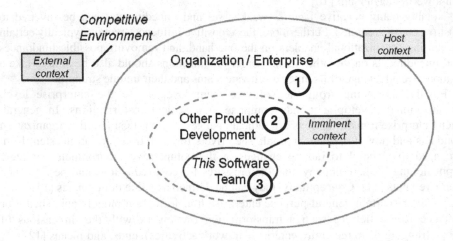

Fig. 1. Software development team contextual dimensioning[1]

Based on the prior works reviewed in Sect. 2 coupled with our groundwork presented in Table 1, Table 2 charts such a conceptual dimensioning grid to address

---

[1] The points 1-3 refer to Table 1.

the objectives set in Sect. 1. It compiles a three-dimensional space for agile software team transformational performance excellence.

Table 2. Team-based transformation management grid

DIM	Scope (Fig. 1) Emphasis	(Agile) Transformation Traits	Measures INSTRUMENTS (c.f., Table 1)
1	Company	• needs and goal attainment strategies	• ratings of (business) drivers and (agility) goals
	Goals		• *Agility Profiler* [15]
2	R&D / Software Development	• team diversity port- folio coordination and	• team performance positioning (key capabilities)
	Means	alignment	• *Orientation Frame* [16]
3	Teams	• team performance	• performance profile gauges
	Enablers	(self-)management	• *Capability Analyzer, Monitor* [17]

The suggested way of realizing the frame (Table 2 dimensions 1-3, respectively) is:

1. Determine the strategic needs and goals for the (next) future desired state.
2. Discern the different software teams of the organization according to their main orientation and purposes for achieving the future state (in particular with respect to business excellence, operational excellence and growth objectives).
3. Set and guide the individual team performance targets accordingly.

Notably in larger enterprises with multiple teams, there are typically many interdependencies. Such relations may affect the performance of individual software teams both positively or negatively. For instance, if one team may have to wait for high-quality, novel software assets (e.g., components) from an apparently slower platform development team. It follows that not all teams need to improve in the same respects (dimension 2) simultaneously. Agile software organizations realize that their teams work in co-operation as a system, which should be optimized as a whole rather than suboptimally as separate teams. Overall, the enterprise can also increase its business agility by leveraging the diversity of its teams in the portfolio configuration.

In general, transformations are continuous processes since the drivers of the transformations for modern software organizations tend to be in constant flux. The three different dimensions in Table 2 can furthermore be viewed from an enterprise system development perspective as follows:

- Industrial software development organizations have business goals to achieve.
- Their operational capabilities provide means to satisfy them.
- Agile software development organizations develop and improve continuously their team capabilities, competence, and assets (including people) for sustainable future excellence.

Specific performance measures on each dimension and also linkage relations between them can be defined with such approaches as advanced Balanced Scorecards

(BSC), Baldrige and EFQM Excellence Models [18]. Considering the dimension 2 in Table 2, typical performance measures for the operational excellence are in terms of outputs, while the business excellence should be managed with respect to outcomes and business impacts. The growth calls for more holistic measures – in particular on intellectual capital (IC) [19]. In all, it follows that the measurement timescales are key considerations in each dimension for interpreting the performance.

4   Case Examples

We have been working on agile/lean transformations for several large software development enterprises. Although the framework presented here was not available when those transformations were conducted, we can revisit them retrospectively as partially validating examples.

Table 3 demonstrates how their identified transformation goals and strategies can be conceived with the dimensioning frame presented in Table 2.

Table 3. Industrial agile enterprise transformation goal mappings

COMPANY	Objectives	Dimension (Table 2)		
		1	2	3 (Teams)
A	Increase customer satisfaction	×		
	Better response to changes		×	
	Release promptness			×
	Short, visible feedback cycle			×
	Lean organizational model		×	
	Agile/Lean Adoption		×	
B	Continuous learning		×	
	Continuous improvement		×	
	Flexible frequent releases	×		
	Continuous velocity improvement		×	
	Better quality			×
	Frequent code commits			×
C	Increased customer satisfaction	×		
	Faster service delivery		×	
	Less efforts in service development			×

Table 3 illustrates how various informally identified transformation objectives can be distinguished and leveled systematically. The next step would be to link the rows and then to discern potentially missing ones following the three-step procedure outlined in Sect. 3 to get a comprehensive set of team performance targets (dimension 3) supporting the strategic goals (dimension 1).

Often such linkages are not apparent. For instance the strategic business goal (dimension 1) of increasing customer satisfaction (A and C) may be linked to multiple items of the dimensions 2 and 3.This suggests the usefulness of our framing approach. The linkages can further be developed with such methods as GQM$^+$Strategies [20].

Notably the case company transformations have been by and large successful with respect to most of their objectives in Table 3. However, because of the retrospective, theory-fitting approach done here, it is not possible tell conclusively how the outcomes could have improved and the particular team performances impacts, if the framework proposed here had been available when they proceeded.

Nevertheless, the case companies could now use it for continuing their transformations. One of our key suggested insights based on the information here is thereby that the different objectives in Table 3 can actually be conceived as goals, means, and enablers like outlined in Table 2. The particular software team performances should be guided accordingly.

5   Discussion

The fundamental tenet of this team-based transformation management approach is that each team should be able to position itself in their particular organizational context. Not all teams (in large organizations) have to be equal. It follows that the company should continuously manage the performance portfolio of their teams. The company may then choose to develop their total team capabilities for the desired transformation state. Moreover, the company may also direct the transformation strategies based on their current software team assets.

In more general, the teams of the enterprise can be seen as dynamic resources. That kind of reconfigurability is one of the key premises of agile enterprises [21]. Our approach supports that by providing systematic ways of managing the performance portfolio of the teams.

Notably, since our approach is based on teams, we are also dealing with people factors. This brings up organizational culture issues. Different configurations in the transformation frame (Table 2) may require different organizational values and operation principles. However, group culture is the underlying premise of the whole.

Our framing approach can be related to the transformation framework proposed by Rouse [12]. However, while they emphasize work process changes (redesign) being the core for transformations, we put teams to the epicenter. In contrast, our key proposition here is that since software work processes are actually performed by teams (and their individuals), the transformations are ultimately realized by addressing them.

In sum, the conceptual transformation analysis frame constructed here is holistic but necessarily coarse-grained. The intention is certainly not to suggest particular transformation recipes for all organizations since transformational software team performance is relative and organization-specific. However, the key idea is to guide the moves in organizations to see their team performance in their overall enterprise constellation from different perspectives and time horizons.

6   Conclusion

Most agile software development organizations are nowadays team-based. It follows that such enterprises can be improved and even transformed by orienting the teams and gauging their performance accordingly towards the desired states.

In this paper, we have proposed a team-based transformation analysis framework for supporting such aims. It facilitates rationalizing the current team performance goals and consequently (re)positioning and aligning the diverse teams of the organization to achieve the desired transformation states. This makes it possible to realize software enterprise transformations based on their existing and future teams. The industrial case examples presented here illustrate how such team-based transformational development can be conceived in practice.

Acknowledgements. This work was supported by TEKES as part of the Cloud Software Program of DIGILE (Finnish Strategic Centre for Science, Technology and Innovation in the field of ICT and digital business).

References

1. Hackman, J.R.: Leading Teams: Setting the Stage for Great Performances. Harvard Business School Press, Boston (2002)
2. Petersen, K.: Measuring and predicting software productivity: A systematic map and review. Information and Software Technology 53, 317–343 (2011)
3. Chenhall, R.H., Langfield-Smith, K.: Multiple Perspectives of Performance Measures. European Management Journal 25(4), 266–282 (2007)
4. Patanakul, P., Shenhar, A.: Exploring the Concept of Value Creation in Program Planning and Systems Engineering Processes. Systems Engineering 13(4), 340–352 (2009)
5. Staron, M., Meding, W., Karlsson, G.: Developing measurement systems: an industrial case study. J. Softw. Maint. Evol.: Res. Pract. 23, 89–107 (2010)
6. Agresti, W.W.: Lightweight Software Metrics: The P10 Framework. IT Pro., pp. 12–16 (September-October 2006)
7. Pfeffer, J.: Seven Practices of Successful Organizations. California Management Review 40(2), 96–124 (1998)
8. Glazer, H.: Love and Marriage: CMMI and Agile Need Each Other. CrossTalk 23(1), 29–34 (2010)
9. Allen, M.: From Substandard to Successful Software. CrossTalk 22(4), 29–32 (2009)
10. Faraj, S., Sambamurthy, V.: Leadership of Information Systems Development Projects. IEEE Trans. Engineering Management 53(2), 238–249 (2006)
11. Purchase, V., Parry, G., Valerdi, R., Nightingale, D., Mills, J.: Enterprise Transformations: Why Are We Interested, What Is It, What Are the Challenges? Journal of Enterprise Transformation 1, 14–33 (2011)
12. Rouse, W.B.: A theory of enterprise transformation. Systems Engineering 8(4), 279–295 (2005)
13. Kettunen, P.: Agile Software Development in Large-Scale New Product Development Organization: Team-Level Perspective. Dissertation, Helsinki University of Technology, Finland (2009)

14. Laanti, M.: Agile Methods in Large-Scale Software Development Organizations – Applicability and Model for Adoption. Dissertation, University of Oulu, Finland (2012)
15. Kettunen, P.: Systematizing Software-Development Agility: Toward an Enterprise Capability Improvement Framework. Journal of Enterprise Transformation 2(2), 81–104 (2012)
16. Kettunen, P.: Orienting High Software Team Performance: Dimensions for Aligned Excellence. In: Heidrich, J., Oivo, M., Jedlitschka, A., Baldassarre, M.T. (eds.) PROFES 2013. LNCS, vol. 7983, pp. 347–350. Springer, Heidelberg (2013)
17. Kettunen, P.: Directing High-Performing Software Teams: Proposal of a Capability-Based Assessment Instrument Approach. In: Winkler, D., Biffl, S., Bergsmann, J. (eds.) SWQD 2014. LNBIP, vol. 166, pp. 229–243. Springer, Heidelberg (2014)
18. Malz, A.C., Shenhar, A.J., Reilly, R.R.: Beyond the Balanced Scorecard: Refining the Search for Organizational Success Measures. Long Range Planning 36, 187–204 (2003)
19. Athey, T.R., Orth, M.S.: Emerging Competency Methods for the Future. Human Resource Management 38(3), 215–226 (1999)
20. Basili, V.R., Lindvall, M., Regardie, M., Seaman, C., Heidrich, J., Münch, J., Rombach, D., Trendowicz, A.: Linking Software Development and Business Strategy through Measurement. IEEE Computer 43(4), 57–65 (2010)
21. Goldman, S.L., Nagel, R.N., Preiss, K.: Agile competitors and virtual organizations: strategies for enriching the customer. Van Nostrand Reinhold, New York (1995)

A Test-Driven Approach for Model-Based Development of Powertrain Functions

Henrik Peters[1], Christoph Knieke[1], Oliver Brox[2], Stefanie Jauns-Seyfried[2], Michael Krämer[2], and Andreas Schulze[2]

[1] Clausthal University of Technology, Department of Informatics, Julius-Albert-Str. 4, 38678 Clausthal-Zellerfeld, Germany
henrik.peters,christoph.knieke@tu-clausthal.de
[2] Volkswagen AG, Post box 15000, 38436 Wolfsburg, Germany
{oliver.brox,stefanie.jauns-seyfried, michael.kraemer1,andreas.schulze}@volkswagen.de

Abstract. Vehicle functions for engine control units are modeled using a set of software units, so-called modules, specifying the discrete and continuous behavior of the corresponding function. As required by ISO 26262, each module needs to be tested separately. Established techniques for model-based testing necessitate a requirements specification from which a test model can be derived. In practice, requirements are specified by natural language and on the level of whole vehicle functions instead of modules so that test models on module level can not be derived directly. Therefore, we propose a systematic model-based, test-driven approach to design a specification on the level of modules, which is directly testable. We demonstrate our approach on a Selective Catalytic Reduction system, a real world case study from automotive software engineering.

Keywords: model-based testing, test-driven development, automotive software engineering, embedded systems.

1 Introduction

There is a new trend in the automotive industry towards model-based development. Software components are modeled with ASCET, MATLAB/Simulink, Statemate or similar tools. Quality assurance is an important aspect in software development for embedded systems. The ISO 26262 standard ("Road vehicles – Functional safety") [5] makes special demands on software development for all safety-critical automotive systems. Besides model-based development, model-based testing (MBT) is increasingly becoming an integral part of the development process.

Part 6 ("Product development: software level") of the ISO 26262 standard requires every software unit to be tested separately. In order to apply an MBT approach at module level, a sufficient, detailed specification is required. However,

G. Cantone and M. Marchesi (Eds.): XP 2014, LNBIP 179, pp. 294–301, 2014.

requirements are often documented only at the function level. In addition, the requirements documentation is usually performed exclusively in natural language and therefore complicates the construction of a test model. Thus, the systematic validation at module level is insufficient or accompanied by high efforts.

The testers' and the developers' roles in the development process need to be filled by the same person, because the specification is not fine grained enough. The actually required independent construction of a test model for testing against a specification is therefore not given. This leads to the risk of missing the same corner cases during software development as during testing. From the very static software development process in model-based development follows the every day life fact that all test activities are carried out after the actual development is finished. Especially if there are just small changes in the software, there is a danger that testing is completely omitted.

Integrating ideas of test-driven development (TDD) can help to tackle these problems. The previously missing specification at module level is generated throughout requirements engineering accompanying the concept phase and especially the development phase of every module. In this way, a testable specification is generated in the form of a test model. Although the test model is still not constructed by an independent tester role (in TDD, no independent developer and tester roles exist), "routine-blindness" is reduced by anticipating test activities.

This paper is organized as follows: First, we give an overview on related work and introduce a real-world example from automotive software engineering at Volkswagen AG which serves as running example throughout this paper. Next, some fundamentals concerning model-based testing, the tool Time Partition Testing (TPT), and test-driven development are given. Section 3 introduces our test-driven approach for model-based development. The results of a case study are discussed in Section 4. Section 5 concludes.

1.1 Related Work

There are many model-based testing approaches, but only a few are specialized in testing the continuous behavior of closed-loop control systems.

An approach for functional black-box tests based on test models is developed in [10]. A signal-feature-oriented paradigm is generated enabling abstract descriptions of signals and their properties. The introduced test framework is realized in the MATLAB/Simulink environment.

In [6] a model-based testing approach for embedded automotive software is proposed. A method and a tool called MTest is introduced. MTest provides graphical notations for the development of test scenarios. Also MTest is a part of AutomationDesk and therefore works mainly with MATLAB/Simulink.

The requirements for a test technology for discrete signals and continuous flows are discussed in [8]. The requirements are compared with the only standardized test specification and implementation language TTCN-3 and TTCN-3 is extended to Continuous TTCN-3. Additionally, [8] presents concepts for specifying continuous and hybrid test behavior.

Agile software development in automotive embedded systems is introduced in [4]. This paper focuses on specialties of mass-produced systems where product development as a whole is motivated by a plan-driven process. However, this approach is tailored to infotainment systems whereas we focus on continuous control systems.

For the integration of test-driven development in a model-based process, other model-based test approaches can be used. However, our focus lies on TPT, because it suits particularly well due to the ability to describe continuous behavior.

1.2   Running Example

The reduction of pollutant emissions is an important challenge in the automotive domain. An exhaust after-treatment system is the Selective Catalytic Reduction (SCR). SCR is a means of reducing nitrogen oxides (NO_x) contained in the exhaust emissions.

Nitrogen oxides are converted into diatomic nitrogen (N_2) and water (H_2O). For that purpose, a reducing agent is pumped through a heatable feed line to the reducing agent injection valve. The reducing agent is carried in a separate tank. In addition, the reducing agent injection valve is controlled by the ECU and injects the reducing agent dosed into the exhaust tracts.

The SCR system consists of different sensors and actuators. The sensors include certain pressure and temperature sensors, and there are actuators like pumps, heatings and valves.

We use SCR as a running example in this paper and demonstrate our approach by an SCR case study. SCR is a typical medium-sized powertrain electronic function and shares several characteristics with other automotive systems: The SCR function contains continuous control, interaction with actuators, and sensors, user interaction (via displayboard), interaction with further subsystems, and includes state-based behavior.

2   Fundamentals

2.1   Model-Based Testing

MBT can be divided into four main categories [9]:

1. Generation of test cases from an environment model
2. Generation of test cases with oracles from a behavioral model
3. Generation of test input data from a domain model
4. Generation of test scripts from abstract tests

Model-based testing approaches often focus on the second category, mainly due to the ability to assess the executed test cases directly. All other approaches cannot evaluate the test results without extra effort.

Fig. 1 shows how we apply MBT. Since we use the tool Time Partition Testing, we are confronted with the third category. TPT extends the idea of domain modeling, using *testlets*, to the opportunity of assessing test results automatically, using *assesslets*.

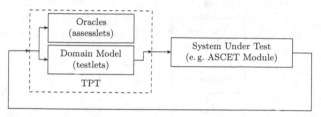

Fig. 1. MBT in the context of software development for powertrain electronics

2.2 Time Partition Testing

Continuous behavior and its testing are having some specialties [2]. TPT is both a new testing methodology for testing continuous behavior of embedded systems in the automotive domain and a tool for supporting that methodology. TPT supports the activities modeling, execution, evaluation, and documentation of tests [7].

The platform-independent construction of test models is performed using a graphical, state-based notation. Entire sequences of test scenarios are decomposed to phases with states and transition conditions. To execute test cases automatically formal definitions are assigned to each element. All test cases of a scenario are derived from a single state machine using the classification tree method by combining the variation points.

The execution of test cases is platform-dependent by means of a test engine. To run the same test cases in a model-in-the-loop (MiL), a software-in-the-loop (SiL) or a hardware-in-the-loop (HiL) test, an abstract intermediate code is used. During execution all signals involved are recorded.

To evaluate the recorded signals properties have to be specified that must be met. The definition of a test oracle is difficult if the recorded signals are complex and often it is impossible to define the systems' behavior based only on the outputs. Therefore, the recorded signals are abstracted in order to extract information and to allow general statements. For example, TPT enables the simple evaluation of threshold crossing or the simple comparison with reference signals. Any assessment can be valid globally or temporarily.

Finally TPT allows a platform-independent documentation of the testing activities in various formats, e.g. HyperText Markup Language (HTML) or Portable Document Format (PDF).

2.3 Test-Driven Development

The idea of TDD is to write a test case first for any new code that is written. The approach is based on a development cycle [1] that is represented in Fig. 2 [3].

As an advantage of this approach the newly generated source code is pre-specified. In addition, a high coverage is achieved on the basis of unit tests.

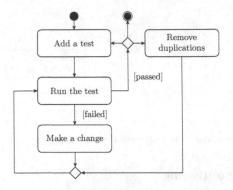

Fig. 2. Test-driven development cycle

3 Test-Driven Approach

To start with our approach, some preparatory work is needed. The aim of the development is to implement a complete function of the engine control unit (ECU). However, currently our approach is limited on the development of a single module. Therefore, the function to be developed has to be decomposed into components, which are further divided into modules. For the decomposition of the function, an established procedure is used in the development process. During the first and the second decomposition, the respective interfaces have to be specified (between components and modules respectively). The result is a complete module architecture in which each module can be designed.

We have adapted the TDD cycle for model-based development, as well as enhanced it for MBT. Fig. 3 shows the extended TDD cycle.

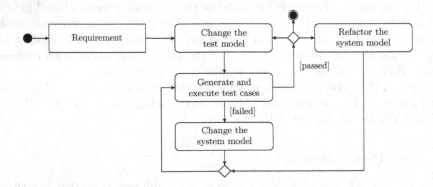

Fig. 3. Extended TDD cycle for model-based development

Each cycle starts with a requirement, which has to be implemented. Instead of writing a test directly, the test model is extended – based on criteria which are described in more detail later. In this step, the necessary assesslets for specifying and checking the requirement and the necessary testlets to produce the desired input data for the system under test (SUT) are modeled. In the following the test cases are derived. TPT allows a manual selection of test cases and enables an automatic generation based on the classification tree method. The following steps are closely related to the original TDD approach (see Section 2.3), except that we refer to models instead of code.

TDD focuses on unit tests to check the implementation. Since we use TDD to design a testable specification, we are focusing on acceptance tests. To ensure a high coverage of the generated code, we use coverage metrics like decision coverage for measuring the test quality.

Requirements are formulated with the aid of assesslets in TPT so that they can be viewed directly as a testable specification. Therefore, some properties have to be met. At module level the specification describes a required behavior. In order to observe behavior, signals are required, so that we define two rules:

1. We demand at least one requirement per signal.
2. We demand at least one signal per requirement.

It should be pointed out that the behavior of the respective signal may depend on other signals, characteristic values, curves, maps or system constants, which has to be considered.

In addition to these optional dependencies, a requirement has a unique name and via the documentation capabilities of TPT it is possible to add further descriptions (e.g., natural language comments, behavior or context diagrams, etc.). Furthermore, the conventional rules for requirements engineering apply (atomicity, consistency, etc.).

Each requirement must be covered by an acceptance test. According to the TDD cycle a new requirement may only be implemented if the corresponding acceptance test fails. This implies that defects which are not detected by a test have to be reproduced by a test before the adaptation of the system model is done [3]. Although acceptance tests are usually a kind of black-box testing, these rules also apply to local signals of the respective module. That means that the specification includes not only interface-related behavior. The test aspects of our approach can be classified as a modification of grey-box testing.

4 Case Study

The software of SCR is divided into different components, e.g., the heater, the pump, and the coordinator. The components itself are divided into modules. The pump component, for instance, consists among other things of a module for the pressure build-up after start, the controller, and the post-drive. We demonstrate the approach exemplarily on an excerpt of the module for the pressure build-up after start.

The interface of the module consists of an input, which provides the pressure in the reducing agent line. Outputs are the required mass flow and the required duty cycle needed for the pressure build-up. The starting point is an unspecified module except for the interface definition. Therefore, we begin to specify the behavior of the mass flow signal. The behavioral specification of the signal consists of four assesslets, where the first one specifies the valid range of the signal. The other three assesslets specify the behavior of the signal. During the specification of the output it turns out that the modules' behavior is dependent on an internal state of the module. Therefore, a new, local signal for the specification of this state is introduced. Further outputs are specified step-wise in the same manner.

In parallel with the behavioral specification using assesslets the domain model is extended by means of testlets. Fig. 4 shows the decomposition of the modules' test scenario into phases. Moreover, Fig. 4 demonstrates the selection of specific variation points and therefore represents a concrete test case. Each testlet within the test case is responsible for the generation of temporarily valid input data.

All test cases are generated using the classification tree method of TPT. The execution takes place within a MiL test in ASCET.

In addition to the formal specification of the assesslets a natural language description is added, which is used for the test documentation and which can also be used for the modules' documentation.

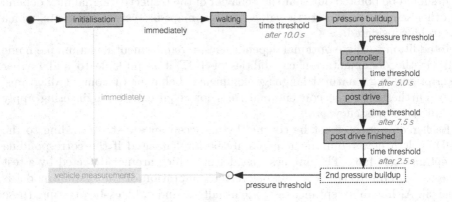

Fig. 4. The modules' domain model with selected variation points

Results. Several modules within the SCR functionality have been successfully developed. The test quality was evaluated by means of decision coverage. 109 of 111 branches were irrelevant[1] or were covered. A coverage of 98 percent was achieved without regarding the control flow, i. e. the programs' structure.

5   Conclusion

Applying a test-driven approach to model-based development has turned out to cope with the missing requirements specification on module level. The systematic

---

[1] Some branches only were generated for the simulation code.

anticipation of testing activities successfully allows the construction of a testable specification while preventing the neglection of tests. In addition, misinterpretations of the requirements are already reduced at module level. Furthermore, the domain models provide valuable information for the further integration of modules, e.g., for implementation in fixed-point arithmetic.

For the refactoring steps tool support is recommended [1]. As refactoring is not supported by ASCET, however, refactoring had to be done manually for the SCR function. During the following developments the effort of refactorings has to be measured in order to decide on additional tool support.

Due to still missing vehicle measurements, the quality of the functionality is difficult to evaluate. In the future, rapid prototyping experiments should assess this quality after MiL tests.

In addition to further developments of the approach the existing limitation on modules will be extended initially to components and then to functions.

References

1. Beck, K.: Test Driven Development. By Example. Addison-Wesley Longman (2002)
2. Bringmann, E.: Testing the Continuous Behavior of Embedded Systems. In: Proceedings of the 4th Workshop on System Testing and Validation (2007)
3. Dohmke, T.: Test-Driven Development of Embedded Control Systems: Application in an Automotive Collision Prevention System. PhD thesis, Department of Mechanical Engineering, Faculty of Engineering, University of Glasgow (2008)
4. Eklund, U., Bosch, J.: Applying Agile Development in Mass-Produced Embedded Systems. In: Wohlin, C. (ed.) XP 2012. LNBIP, vol. 111, pp. 31–46. Springer, Heidelberg (2012)
5. International Organization for Standardization. ISO/DIS 26262: Road vehicles – functional safety (2009)
6. Lamberg, K., Beine, M., Eschmann, M., Otterbach, R., Conrad, M., Fey, I.: Model-based Testing of Embedded Automotive Software Using Mtest. In: SAE World Congress 2004, Detroit, US (2004)
7. Lehmann, E.: Time Partition Testing – Systematischer Test des kontinuierlichen Verhaltens von eingebetteten Systemen. PhD thesis, Fakultät IV – Elektrotechnik und Informatik, TU Berlin (2004)
8. Schieferdecker, I., Bringmann, E., Großmann, J.: Continuous TTCN-3: Testing of Embedded Control Systems. In: Proceedings of the 2006 International Workshop on Software Engineering for Automotive Systems, SEAS 2006, pp. 29–36. ACM, New York (2006)
9. Utting, M., Legeard, B.: Practical Model-Based Testing – A Tools Approach. Morgan Kaufmann (2007)
10. Zander-Nowicka, J.: Model-based Testing of Real-Time Embedded Systems in the Automotive Domain. PhD thesis, Fakultät IV – Elektrotechnik und Informatik, TU Berlin (2009)

Archinotes: A Global Agile Architecture Design Approach

Juan Urrego, Rafael Muñoz, Mauricio Mercado, and Darío Correal

Systems and Computer
Engineering Department
Universidad de los Andes
Cra 1E No 19A-40, Bogotá, Colombia
{js.urrego110,r.munoz92,md.mercado49,dcorreal}@uniandes.edu.co

Abstract. Currently, many software developing organizations have adopted work methodologies around Global Software Development (GSD) in which the members of a geographically sparse team can coordinate their activities through collaboration tools. Nevertheless, these tools are focused primarily on the construction process rather than on the concrete design. It is usual that this kind of organizations have teams where its members are located in different cities or even countries. Due to this, architects must forcefully adjust their calendars to schedule face-to-face or virtual meetings where they can define the architecture together. This paper's objective is to propose a tool that supports Global Agile Architecture Design (GAAD) approaches where architects can coordinate, communicate and control a software architecture design process while being geographically apart. To validate our proposal, we used the Universidad de los Andes' Software Architecture and Design course, were the students had to design a software architecture based on a concrete case study and an enterprise software development project to support an electoral process in a public Colombian university. The tool that supported the GAAD process was Archinotes, a platform that allows the design and documentation of software architectures in a collaborative manner.

Keywords: Global software development, Software architecture, Agile Architecture.

1 Introduction

Conway's law states that the structure of a software mirrors the structure of the organization that designed it [1]. For that reason, a lack of communication and cohesion in an organization produces software with the same characteristics. Therefore, engaging in projects that involve distributed teams, such as those applying Global Software Development (GSD) approaches, can be too risky and produce software without adequate integration between its components, if it is not addressed properly. Conway [2] states that large distances imply problems

G. Cantone and M. Marchesi (Eds.): XP 2014, LNBIP 179, pp. 302–311, 2014.

regarding first contact between distributed members, effective communication, lack of trust, and issue resolution.

Currently, many software development organizations have adopted work methodologies around GSD seeking for the members of geographically sparse teams to coordinate their activities through collaboration tools. According to [3], a lot of enterprises offshore their software development, and this trend becomes stronger each day. Nevertheless, this approach and the tools used in the GSD process, are focused primarily on the product development process rather than on the architecture of the system.

During software architecture design processes (SADP), many architects are involved (i.e data architect, security architect, infrastructure architect, etc.) and their activities and designs must be coherent and coordinated between them. Moreover, most of the time these architects are located in different cities or countries, thus they are forced to adjust their calendars to schedule face-to-face or virtual meetings where they can define the architecture. The previous scenario gets even more complex if the architecture team works in a traditional big-design up-front approach to produce the complete architecture of the system, which demands months of work from distributed people working on architectural models. Furthermore, during the development phase, it is difficult to maintain the architecture updated and to understand the rationale behind architectural decisions.

We use the Global Agile Architecture Design (GAAD) term to describe geographically distributed architecture teams involved in the process of designing software architectures following agile principles. In GAAD, architecture teams avoid following a big-design up-front model by working in short sprints and producing minimal architectural models to support the user histories selected for each sprint. This paper presents Archinotes, a tool to support Global Agile Architecture Design (GAAD) approaches where different architects can coordinate, communicate and control an agile SADP while being geographically apart. This document reports our experience using Archinotes in an educational and industry contexts and the results and conclusions obtained so far.

The rest of this paper is structured as follows: Section 2 provides a general description of the functionalities of Archinotes. Section 3 explains how Archinotes supports distributed teams following an agile approach. Section 4 reports our experience after using Archinotes in an educational and enterprise scenarios. Finally, Section 5 presents the related work and Section 6 states conclusions and future work.

2   Archinotes Overview

Archinotes is a platform to help geographically distributed architects build software architectures collaboratively using mobile devices and following an agile approach. Archinotes' main goal is to facilitate the software architecture design and documentation process for distributed agile software development methodologies.

2.1 Archinotes Architecture

Archinotes has 3 main components: (1) a mobile application for the architects, (2) a storage system, and (3) the main processing server; as presented in Figure 1. The storage system and the main processing server store all of the platforms project data and user information. The architects mobile application allows the definition and prioritization of the quality requirements, stakeholders, user story backlog, business drivers and architectural viewpoints.

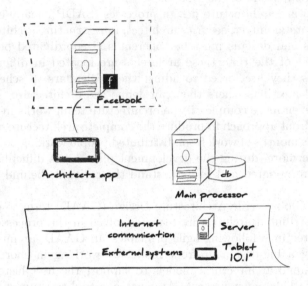

Fig. 1. Architecture of the system

2.2 Archinotes Main Features

Taking into account the information display models defined in [4], we designed Archinotes to avoid using conventional graphical representations of information (tables, list, etc). To accomplish this, Archinotes main menu presents all available options by dividing them in two parts: the documentation that must be defined before the construction of a software architecture, and the architectural viewpoints (Figure 2).

According to this approach, a distributed architecture team can perform the following actions:

1. **Stakeholder identification and prioritization:** During a SADP, the identification and prioritization of stakeholders is one of the most important tasks. Archinotes merges the stakeholder theory of [5,6,7] resulting in a set of predefined stakeholders and a new stakeholder prioritization method called Stakeholder Atomic Model (SAM).

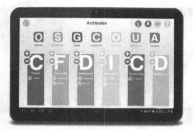

Fig. 2. Archinotes main menu

2. **Business goals definition:** In every software architecture project is very important to identify and document the main concerns and business goals of the organization and project. In Archinotes, we decided to use some similar metrics of the Business Motivation Model (BMM) [8] to document and identify the main business goals and drivers of the project.

3. **Definition of constraints:** Every engineering project has different constraints that we must document. In the case of Archinotes, as [5] recommends, there are two kinds of constraints: (1) business constraints, which are all the restrictions of the project itself; and (2) technological constraints, which are software, hardware and development restrictions.

4. **User stories:** Using this module, the user can create a complete Product Backlog using Epics, Features and User Stories. Each component will be also associated with a concrete sprint, so the architecture owner (or scrum master) can coordinate and document the design and development process of the project.

5. **Quality requirements:** Archinotes users can define and create quality scenarios based in predefined quality attributes or design their own. In this stage, the user will be able to define the utility tree together with quality attributes and quality scenarios.

6. **Modeler:** Archinotes gives the possibility to design and coordinate architecture teams in real-time, despite geographical and temporal differences, through architectural daily meetings. During a meeting, the users can see their partners' movements and add, edit or remove any architectural element or relationship, at the same time that they track the architectural decisions through the creation of annotations (Figure 4a). Archinotes allows to track all the changes of the architecture by saving model changes during a daily meeting, so the user can return to previous versions of the model as base of newer versions (Figure 5b).

7. **SAD print:** Finally, after the SADP has finished, the user can automatically generate a PDF version of the Software Architecture Document (SAD) that presents a typical SAD template using the images and information provided in previous modules.

(a) New quality scenario   (b) New quality scenario

Fig. 3. Archinotes Modeler

3   Archinotes: A Supporting Tool for GAAD

As we previously stated, we introduce the GAAD term to describe the software architecture design process applied by a distributed team. This process' main characteristic is the adoption of shorts periods of work (sprints) to incrementally design and model the system's architecture. In this section we explain how Archinotes supports distributed teams and how agile principles are used in our tool.

3.1   Distributed Teams Support

Archinotes supports collaborative work of distributed teams engaged in the design of software architectures in two different ways. Firstly, Archinotes provides a collaboration mechanism to design architecture models in a synchronous way. Distributed teams can participate remotely in synchronous working sessions to create architectural views and architectural models. Figure 4a presents the model editor provided by Archinotes to define collaborative modeling sessions.

Secondly, Archinotes supports asynchronous collaboration sessions by means of text, audio and video annotations attached to architectural models in an architectural view to store the rationale behind architectural decisions, which can be revised by members of the team working at different time zones. Figure 4b presents an example of an annotation associated to a component in a functional architectural view.

3.2   Agile Architecture Design Support

Archinotes incorporates some of the agile principles followed by agile development groups. For starters, Archinotes supports the definition of different architecture team roles, one of them being the Architecture Owner (AO) [9]. This role is in charge of leading the daily architecture review sessions, which are limited in time by Archinotes (usually 10 minutes) to focus the team on the critical points to be designed each day. Figure 5a presents an example of an invitation to an architectural review meeting scheduled by the Architecture Owner.

(a) Context model   (b) Architectural annotations

Fig. 4. Archinotes Modeler

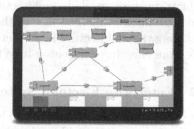

(a) Daily architectural review   (b) Model timeline

Fig. 5. Agile Architectures

4 Lessons Learned

We used Archinotes in two different scenarios: an educational context and a real-life project. In this section we report the two experiences using Archinotes and highlight the results and difficulties learned so far.

4.1 Educational Scenario

At Universidad de Los Andes, the Systems and Computer Engineering Department offers a Software Architecture course in its bachelor's degree since 2004. This course seeks to sharpen quality-requirement identification skills, as well as tactics and strategies relevant to the design of mid-sized information systems [10]. During the semester, students validate their architectures through the development of experiments in four different sprints. For each experiment, the students must develop a software that addresses a specific set of quality attributes. These students usually have different schedules between them (they might not all take the same classes), and may not always be attentive to the projects progress. For that reason, we introduced them to Archinotes so they could design a software architecture in a distributed manner.

After using Archinotes during one semester, we developed an informal survey to understand the perception of the students and how they qualify their experience with the tool and register improvement aspects to take into account.

Additionally, we compared the results obtained using Archinotes with the results obtained in previous semesters.

Among the main conclusions we found that the students valued the idea of avoiding synchronous, face-to-face meetings to work in the project. However, they stated that they felt insecure of taking critical decisions on the architecture while working alone. They stated that it is necessary to have face-to-face meetings to solve critical problems. The use of the tool for non critical decision and the fact that the client used was a mobile device were highly valued for the students.

Additionally, the agile approach proposed by the tool was not performed by the students as expected. In the first place, they argued that the main difficulty to have synchronous daily architecture review meetings was the impossibility to find a common available space in their agendas. On the other hand, the idea of designing the architecture in an incremental basis, avoiding big-design up-front, was more effective, comparing it to the results obtained in previous semesters.

4.2   Enterprise Electoral System

We wanted to analyze how agile architecture iterations changed according to the development sprints and how Archinotes benefits de architecture design process. In most public colombian universities, the selection of administrative roles such as principal, faculty deans, and others, are done via internal elections, where the teaching and administrative staff, as well as the students, select the succeeding administrative roles of the university. For that reason, the university decided to hire a software company to develop an electoral system, while preserving the physical vote, to enhance the electoral process. The problem encountered was that the university and the development team are located at the north-west coast of Colombia, while the software architects are located at the center of the country. To reduce travel costs and time, the company decided to use Archinotes to have daily meetings and design the architecture in a remote, asynchronous, real-time fashion.

To reduce geographical distances, Archinotes was used during the design and development process of the electoral system. In this case, the software company decided to use Discipline Agile Delivery (DAD) as working framework and support all the architecture and business documentation using Archinotes. Part of the communication was supported via Archinotes and the rest using Google Hangout. The idea was that they had two Software Architects, which design and control de software architecture and development process remotely, in the main head quarters in the capital and the development team of 3 junior developers and a team leader in the north-west.

During the project, the architects designed a preliminary architecture using Archinotes, including stakeholders and quality requirements identification. This design was made co-located in a face-to-face meeting and the only participants were the architects. Based on the architecture and stakeholder concerns, the architects and the team leader, who is in a different city, defined the product backlog through Archinotes. In this stage, a first sprint was released and the developers began work. Every day, the architects and developers had coordination meetings through Google Hangout, where the members described their work done. Sometimes, during this coordination meetings, the developers and/or architects would identify errors in the architecture. When this occurred, the architects decided to make an architectural daily review using Archinotes. In this meting, the members of the team were involved, but architects were the only ones with permissions to change the models. Nevertheless, the developers were able to create annotations on the model, which would later be revised by the architects to track all the questions, doubts and architectural decisions.

After 6 sprints of two weeks each, the development and architecture design of the system were finished. During this process, the developers and architects used Archinotes to support all the business and quality definitions, as well as the software architecture. Our idea was to collect the project information and analyze how the architecture changed through the development process, and how that affected the team performance. During the project, we observed that at the beginning of the development, the architecture changed frequently and developers created a big amount of clarification annotations. This means that the team did not have the best performance when the architecture was not clear or incomplete. Figure 6 shows how the amount of annotations impacted the development team performance. When the development team has doubts the performance is low, but when the architecture was complete an clear, the development process improves. In some cases the amount of annotations implied a redefinition of user stories.

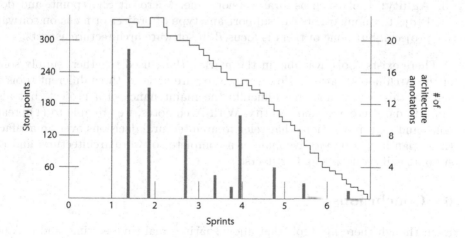

Fig. 6. Development process vs. architecture annotations

4.3 Limitations

Archinotes has been used so far in two different projects. We need more information and data to present statistically significant results. The conclusions presented here have been gathered during the last six months of work and it's not enough to provide decisive conclusions.

5 Related Work

In this paper we proposed a tool called Archinotes that seeks to unify three core concepts: geographic distribution, software architecture design and agility. We researched different approaches and noticed that none of them is able to satisfy the three core concepts. Next, we present the tools that try to solve each core concept.

1. **Geographic distribution:** There are many tools that support geographically distributed teams such as Skype, Google Hangout, and WebEx, among others. However, none of them help us design a software architecture or monitor the state of a project. These tools help us communicate via text, audio, and video in real-time.
2. **Software architecture design (SA):** There are many tools that helpe SADPs such as Enterprise Architect, Microsoft Visio, and Papyrus, among others; but none provide real-time functionalities. Other design tools such as Cacoo, GenMyModel and Gliffy, provide real-time features and global change tracking but bring only the basic models (mostly UML) without a concrete work or framework context.
3. **Agility:** Tools such as Jira, Version One, Microsoft Sharepoint, and dot-Project, among others can support any type of project or focus on software projects, but none of them is focused in software architecture aspects.

There exists tools available in the market that, used together, supply some of the Archinotes features. However, we require at least three different tools to achieve this, which not only difficults the maintenance of a project, but also impacts data integrity and security. With Archinotes, we are able to (1) create voice and text annotations that refer to architectural decisions over an artifact; (2) design in a collaborative manner a complete software architecture; and (3) support agile concepts and artifacts.

6 Conclusions

Even though there are tools that allow sharing, real-time editing, and collaborating, Archinotes makes it easy for architects and development teams to work in a distributed manner. Additionally, its granularity allows better revisions and work tracking.

One major result of Archinotes is that users were more inclined to have daily meetings to review the overall architecture of the project, meaning that

Archinotes helps users that are not familiar to agile methodologies. Software architecture is in fact needed all around the world, but the offer is focused where the demand is low, so architects must travel long distances to be able to work with teams of developers. Bringing a distributed tool like Archinotes allows software architects and developers to work together without the hassle of traveling.

Another point worth mentioning is that users were satisfied with the use of mobile devices to interact with Archinotes, However, most of them asked for a desktop version of the tool stating that this version is better in terms of usability. Given that, we are planning to include a desktop version in the next major release of Archinotes.

References

1. Herbsleb, J.D., Grinter, R.E.: Architectures, coordination, and distance: Conway's law and beyond. IEEE Softw. 16(5), 63–70 (1999)
2. Conway, M.E.: How do committees invent. Datamation 14(4), 28–31 (1968)
3. Aspray, W.: Globalization and Offshoring of Software: A Report of the ACM Job Migration Task Force; the Executive Summary, Findings, and Overview of a Comprehensive ACM Report on the Offshoring of Software Worldwide. ACM (2006)
4. Yau, N.: Visualize This: The FlowingData Guide to Design, Visualization, and Statistics. Wiley (2011)
5. Rozanski, N., Woods, E.: Software Systems Architecture: Working with Stakeholders Using Viewpoints and Perspectives. Pearson Education (2011)
6. Post, J., Preston, L., Sauter-Sachs, S.: Redefining the Corporation: Stakeholder Management and Organizational Wealth. Stanford Business Books (2002)
7. Bourne, L.: Stakeholder Relationship Management: A Maturity Model for Organisational Implementation. Ashgate Publishing, Limited (2012)
8. Group, B.R.: The business motivation model - business governance in a volatile world, release 1.2. Technical report, Business Rules Group (2005)
9. Lines, M., Ambler, S.: Disciplined Agile Delivery: A Practitioner's Guide to Agile Software Delivery in the Enterprise. IBM Press (2012)
10. Urrego, J., Correal, D.: Archinotes: A tool for assisting software architecture courses. In: 2013 IEEE 26th Conference on Software Engineering Education and Training (CSEE T), pp. 80–88 (2013)

Definition of Ready: An Experience Report from Teams at Cisco

Ken Power

Cisco Systems
Galway
Ireland
ken.power@gmail.com

Abstract. Definition of Ready is a set of simple rules adopted by an agile team to help them remember all the things they need to do before a development team starts work on a backlog item. Not having a *definition of ready* can seriously impede the flow of work through your system. This paper describes where definition of ready fits in a team's process, and how it can be used as a synchronization point for teams and product owners. This paper presents an example of definition of ready used by agile teams in Cisco. These teams have developed three levels of ready that apply for user stories, sprints and releases. The paper describes how definition of ready provides a focus for backlog grooming, and some consequences of not meeting definition of ready. The paper finishes with perspectives from different roles in the organization and how they are affected by definition of ready.

Keywords: definition of ready, definition of done, simple rules, product ownership, waste, flow, impediment to flow.

1 Introduction

This paper describes the concept of *definition of ready*, and shows how it is used in agile teams. The paper uses a case study to describe the experiences of teams at Cisco with adopting definition of ready. The experiences include situations where definition of ready was not adopted.

1.1 What Is Definition of Ready?

Definition of ready is a set of agreements that define what *ready* means for a backlog item. *Ready* in this context means the backlog item is sufficiently prepared that a team can start to work on it [1]. The development team is responsible for meeting *definition of done*; product owners (or equivalent) are responsible for making sure work items meet *definition of ready*. Conceptually, the definition of ready is a checklist of the types of work that the product owner is expected to successfully complete before the work item can declare the work item is ready to be pulled in by the team. Being

G. Cantone and M. Marchesi (Eds.): XP 2014, LNBIP 179, pp. 312–319, 2014.

"ready" does not mean the user story or feature must be 100% defined; it needs to be "ready enough" so that the team is confident they can successfully deliver the user story, or that everyone has a common understanding of the risks.

Kenny Rubin provides an example definition of done [2]:

- Business value is clearly articulated.
- Details are sufficiently understood by the development team so it can make an informed decision as to whether it can complete the PBI (Product Backlog Item).
- Dependencies are identified and no external dependencies would block the PBI from being completed.
- Team is staffed appropriately to complete the PBI.
- The PBI is estimated and small enough to comfortably be completed in one sprint.
- Acceptance criteria are clear and testable.
- Performance criteria, if any, are defined and testable.
- Scrum team understands how to demonstrate the PBI at the sprint review.

Roman Pilcher mentions the idea of capturing "operational qualities" of a story as constraint cards and attaching them to the story as part of getting the story ready [3].

1.2   Goals of Definition of Ready

Definition of Done and *Definition of Ready* act as social contracts in agile teams. Together, they provide a boundary that stabilizes the team's working environment, prevents waste (time, delays, churn, working on the wrong things), remove impediments, and avoids the accumulation of technical debt and quality debt. The diagram in Fig. 1 shows how work passes through Sprint boundaries as it flows through the system. *Definition of ready* acts as a check before work is allowed to enter the Sprint. *Definition of done* acts as a check before work is allowed to leave the Sprint. There is a saying we use from the agile community: *"Let nothing into a Sprint that is not Ready; let nothing out of a Sprint that is not Done"*. Following these simple rules avoids many frustrations and challenges (see section 2.3 below).

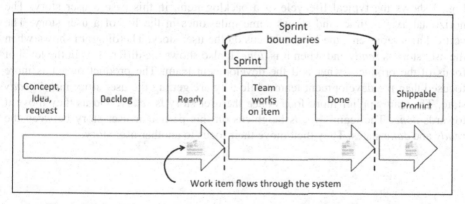

Fig. 1. Work passes through Sprint boundaries as it flows through the system

1.3   Teams Using Kanban or Flow-Based Methods

Teams using Kanban or flow-based methods have a "Ready" queue in their workflow, as shown in Fig. 2. The "ready" queue is the place from which teams pull work. Product owners add work to the ready queue as the work items meet definition of ready. Many teams use a Work In Progress (or WIP) limit on the ready queue to prevent it from getting too full, and to recognize there is no point overfilling the ready queue if the team cannot pull work through. The explicit WIP limit avoids an impediment to the flow of work.

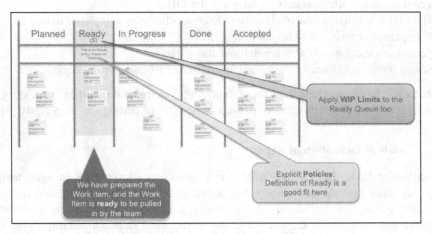

Fig. 2. Kanban board with a "ready" queue

Kanban teams also use explicit entry and exit policies for their workflow states. Definition of ready serves as an explicit entry policy for the ready state.

1.4   The Lifecycle of Backlog Items

Fig. 3 shows the typical lifecycle of a backlog item, in this case a user story. The horizontal axis is time, and shows some milestones in the life of a user story. The vertical axis represents the level of focus on the user story. The diagram shows when the user story is *ready* and when it is *done*. It also shows the differences in the level of focus of the product owner and the development team. The product owner is more focused than the development team while they are getting the user story into a *ready* state. The team applies more focus once the user story is *ready*, and as they move it towards *done*. The team's focus heightens on this particular user story between the *ready* and *done* states. They then move their focus to another user story.

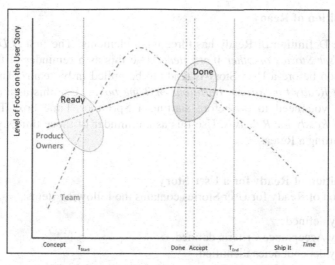

Fig. 3. Levels of focus on a user story over time

1.5   Cadence and Synchronization Points

The product owner and development team work at different cadences. They focus on different things at different times. Time-boxed iterations (or Sprints) are one way to synchronize their different areas of focus. Having a *definition of ready* that serves as a set of mutual agreements between Product Owner and the rest of the team brings a focus to upcoming Sprint synchronization points.

2   Case Study: Definition of Ready in Cisco

This section presents a complete example of definition of ready from a business unit of over 400 people in Cisco. The teams are largely based in the US, Europe and China. When teams in the business unit start using definition of ready in 2008, each team would develop its own version. There were some teams that chose not to use definition of ready. The teams that did not employ Definition of Ready at all faced many consequences, some of which are mention in section 2.3. The teams are responsible for the development of a portfolio of products and components with many interdependencies across the teams. Because of these interdependencies, and because of the challenges and impediments to flow the organization was seeing, they decided to employ a common baseline definition of ready that applies to all teams.

Definition of Ready applies no matter what process the team is using. Teams have a discussion about Definition of Ready, making sure they understand each point, and the responsibilities this creates for their team. This discussion generally takes place at the start of a new release, or when a new team is formed.

2.1   Definition of Ready

The baseline Definition of Ready has three main elements. The first is *Definition of Ready for User Stories or other Work Items*. Use this as a reminder of those things you need to do before a User Story is ready to be pulled in by teams. The second is *Definition of Ready for Sprints, Iterations or Time boxes*. Use this as a reminder of those things you need to do before starting a Sprint or Time box. The third is *Definition of Ready for Releases*. Use this as a reminder of those things you need to do before starting a Release.

2.1.1   Definition of Ready for a User Story
The Definition of Ready for User Stories contains the following items:

- User Story defined
- User Story Acceptance Criteria defined
- User Story dependencies identified
- User Story sized by Delivery Team
- User Experience artifacts are Done, and reviewed by the Team
- Architecture criteria (performance, security, etc.) identified, where appropriate
- Person who will accept the User Story is identified
- Team has reviewed the User Story
- Team knows what it will mean to demo the User Story

2.1.2   Definition of Ready for a Sprint, Iteration or Time box
The Definition of Ready for a Sprint, Iteration or Time box contains the following items:

- All User Stories meet Definition of Ready
- The team has made a forecast of what they think they can deliver
- The Sprint/Iteration/Time box goals are defined, understood and agreed
- The Sprint/Iteration/Time box Backlog is prioritized
- The Sprint/Iteration/Time box Backlog contains all defects, User Stories and other work that the team is committing to, with no hidden work
- All team members have noted their capacity for the Iteration
- Capacity is filled to no more than 70% so there is some room to adapt
- The backlog contains Continuous Improvement items

2.1.3   Definition of Ready for a Release
Definition of Ready for Releases' contains the following items:

- The Release has been categorized as 'Fixed Scope' or 'Fixed Date' but not both
- The Release Backlog is prepared
- Work is sized
- Work is prioritized
- Market Value is understood and communicated
- The Release Themes are identified

- The MVO (Minimal Viable Offer) is identified
- The MVO is not the full target release content, i.e., allow scope for negotiation
- Release Planning has taken place, and the team has been involved
- Team and Product Owners agree the Release Plan is a realistic forecast
- Customers are engaged and prepared to take the output of the release, as well as interim drops of the release
- Risk analysis is under way
- Interim milestone deliveries are identified
- The Release backlog contains Continuous Improvement items
- Quality targets are defined
- The team's capacity is not planned to 100%
- Capacity is planned for multiple different areas
- New feature work, fixing defects, reducing Quality Debt, reducing

  Technical Debt, supporting previous releases, and handling unknown requests
- The right technical infrastructure is in place to support the team
- All known dependencies are aligned
- Architecture changes are understood
- Stakeholders are identified
- Definition of Done is agreed
- Definition of Ready is agreed
- Communication and Coordination model is defined
- Means of tracking progress is understood
- Lessons learned from previous Release Retrospective have been incorporated
- Playtime / Innovation time is included in the Release Plan
- Celebrations are included in the Release Plan

2.2 Keeping the Backlog Ready

Backlog management or backlog grooming is the ongoing process of looking after the product backlog and ensuring it is well maintained and up to date [4]. Product owners will generally prepare backlog items in a grooming session, bringing in the team and other people as needed. Definition of ready provides a focus for backlog grooming sessions. At least once per sprint the team will attend a backlog grooming session to participate in preparing upcoming user stories.

Getting user stories to meet Definition of Ready provides a focus for backlog grooming sessions. Before the team will pull a user story into the current sprint, the story must meet *definition of ready*. Backlog grooming needs to be continuous. The closer the team is to implementing a user story, the higher their confidence should be that they understand it, and can size it appropriately. The farther away in time they are from implementing the user story, the lower the certainty we have in our estimates and understanding. This is one reason why it is important to do continuous, rolling planning. As more work is done to prepare the user stories and get them *ready*, the teams confidence in their ability to deliver the stories increases. Part of the reason for this is that working together to get a set of user stories *ready* facilitates shared learning and collaboration.

2.3   Consequences of Not Being Ready

Jeff Sutherland highlights some of the consequences of not being ready [5]. These include estimating and forecasting problems, wasted time and energy, frustration, working on the wrong things, and forced rework. The teams in this case study have experienced all of these consequences. There were cases where teams would see user stories for the first time at the Sprint planning meeting, where user stories were little more than one-line phrase.   The biggest gains seen through employing Definition of Ready is reduction in churn, reduced delays and overall smoother flow of work.

2.4   Different Perspectives on Definition of Ready

This section presents perspectives on definition of ready from people playing different roles in the organization.

Developer: *"If a work item meets Definition of Ready then I have more confidence that Product Owners know what they want, and we'll spend less time churning. It helps get everyone aligned, so we're all focused on the feature I am developing."*

Tester / QA: *"I know that the test scenarios and deployment scenarios have been considered. Performance, interoperability and security criteria are known, and there will be fewer surprises."*

Product Manager or Product Owner: *"It requires me to put sufficient thought into the features I am asking for. One-liners are not enough."*

Engineering Manager: *"I want my teams to work in a productive environment, where we can deliver at a sustainable predictable pace. I don't want my teams churning trying to figure out what it is we are meant to be delivering. Definition of Ready helps me and my teams be more effective."*

Program Manager: *"If I get a clear picture on which backlog items are 'Ready' then I can extrapolate data from that. I can see, for example, if we are likely to meet a delivery date or incremental milestone based on the state of the backlog. I can help the team forecast potential problems and pitfalls that will hold them back."*

Director: *"I want to understand my organization's capacity to deliver. I want my organization to be effective. For Portfolio-level items, I want to know when we are done with the Portfolio-level analysis and work is ready for our teams to consume. I need to be able to create reliable roadmaps that I can use to converse with customers and other stakeholders. Knowing we're really 'Ready' to begin a feature or initiative helps me keep those roadmaps up-to-date."*

Scrum Master: *"I want to help my Product Owners in meeting Definition of Ready any way I can. I can do this in many ways, including helping with Backlog grooming, user story splitting, etc. I want to help my team by not having them waste time on work items that are not really 'Ready'. When the going gets tough, and its tempting to take short cuts, I'll remind everyone of that we agreed to use Definition of Ready. I'll help tailor our Definition of Ready, and look for improvements."*

User Experience Designer: *"For many work items, they are not Ready until my work is Done. There's a natural dependency. I have a responsibility to help the user story* *get to 'Ready' so our teams can start work. Sometimes, maybe due to capacity issues, we will decide together that the team will start before I am Ready. In those cases, we should all understand and accept the situation."*

Architect: *"Sometimes I work on Portfolio or Cross-BU level initiatives that eventually end up as features or other work on the backlogs of one or more teams. Part of my responsibility is contributing to the work items being 'Ready' for teams to pull in."*

Technical Writer: *"Seeing a set of stories that are* ready *allows me to start writing about the features, and work with the team to understand what it will do, before its done. This lets me work more in parallel with the team, rather than lagging behind."*

3   Conclusions

Neglecting Definition of Ready creates waste and impediments to flow in teams and organizations. The larger the teams and organization, and the larger the products they are creating, the more there is potential for harmful waste. Use *Definition of Ready* to bring a focus to Backlog Grooming meetings and Look-Ahead planning activities. Product Owners can use it as a guide when preparing user stories for upcoming Sprints. Teams can use it as a checklist to make sure that they have an increased chance of success in delivering the completed user story, and that there is enough thought gone into the user story before they start to deliver it.

Get your team together to agree a definition of ready. The simple rules form a type of social contract in the team. It is important there is consensus to meeting definition of ready. Understand what it means to be 'ready' to start a user story, a sprint and a release. Look to your retrospectives to see what problems might be addressed by having a definition of ready. Evolve your definition of ready as you learn more about what works for you and your teams.

References

1. Power, K.: Definition of Ready,
   http://systemagility.com/2011/05/17/definition-of-ready/
2. Rubin, K.S.: Essential Scrum: A practical guide to the most popular Agile process. Addison-Wesley, Pearson Education [distributor] London, Boston (2012)
3. Pilcher, R.: The Definition of Ready, http://www.romanpichler.com/blog/product-backlog/the-definition-of-ready/
4. Cohn, M.: Succeeding with Agile: Software Development Using Scrum. Addison-Wesley, Upper Saddle River (2010)
5. Sutherland, J.: The Dangers of Not Being Done, Or Ready for that Matter, http://scrum.jeffsutherland.com/2012/02/on-march-9-jeff-will-be-giving-webinar.html

Specification by Example with GUI Tests - How Could That Work?

Emily Bache[1] and Geoffrey Bache[2]

[1] Bache Consulting, Göteborg, Sweden
[2] Jeppesen Systems, Göteborg, Sweden
emily@bacheconsulting.com, geoff.bache@jeppesen.com

Abstract. Specification by Example is a collaborative method for developing software. It involves a workshop where people representing various roles and viewpoints discuss what is to be built, and come up with concrete example scenarios. These scenarios later form the basis for automated (functional) acceptance tests, and are sometimes called "Living Documentation", as they are written in a Domain Specific Language and can be read by non-programmers. GUI testing has traditionally used a record-replay paradigm that requires the user interface exists before the tests can be created, and hence have been considered incompatible with a Specification by Example approach. In this experience report we will discuss how we have overcome this apparent contradiction at Jeppesen, and relate an experience using the tool TextTest for GUI testing of Jeppesen's next-generation Crew Management System.

Keywords: Specification by Example, GUI testing, ATDD, Capture-Replay Testing.

1 Experiences Testing CMS at Jeppesen

Jeppesen has several successful products for crew planning and optimization, which are in use at many airlines around the world. Some of the development teams in Göteborg are working on a next-generation Crew Management System, (CMS), where Geoff is a test automation specialist. Emily has worked as an external consultant at Jeppesen, creating automated test cases and coaching testers and developers.

CMS, is a rich-client application, with a large and complex GUI, comprising tens of screens, several novel GUI widgets for presenting crew schedules, and over 150 000 hours of development. Development is currently proceeding using an agile approach including Specification By Example, and Geoff has invented a testing tool, TextTest, which is being used. In this paper we'll describe the approach and benefits.

G. Cantone and M. Marchesi (Eds.): XP 2014, LNBIP 179, pp. 320–326, 2014.

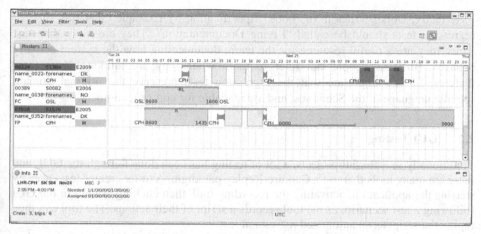

Fig. 1. Screenshot of the CMS user interface

2 Background to the Approach

2.1 Specification by Example

Specification by Example is a collaborative method for developing software, that should help you to build the right software. Gojko Adzic has written several books [1], about this method. He describes in some detail how you can hold specification workshops where you collaboratively come up with example scenarios to help you build the right thing.

In any agile method, the requirements process is a little different than with a traditional, (waterfall), method. In agile, you can think of a "requirement" as having three parts - the User Story, the Conversation, and the Example Scenarios.

The User Story is just a sentence or two written on an index card or similar. This represents a small piece of functionality the user wants to be built. The index card is actually just a promise of a Conversation.

The Conversation is the next part of the requirement. You get together several people representing different perspectives, and discuss what is to be built. Usually this includes at least three people representing different roles - the programmer who'll be writing the code, the tester who'll test it, and the business analyst or product owner who understands what the user is trying to achieve. Usually one of the concrete outcomes of the Conversation is a list of Scenarios.

The Scenarios are example cases illustrating the feature and how it's going to be used. The idea is the programmer will be able to translate these examples directly into test cases to use in a Test-Driven Development process as they build the code. The Tester will be able to use them as a basis for further, exploratory testing, once the feature is built. The Scenarios document for the business people how the feature is supposed to work in practice. Some or all of the scenarios will be automated as regression tests and continue to be run regularly as development of new features continues.

Actually, Gojko writes in his book "Specification by Example" that this suite of regression tests should be called "Living Documentation". They are more than test cases, they are a useful resource for the team, documenting how the system actually behaves. Business people can refer to them when they are thinking about new features. So it's important that the regression tests preserve the original domain specific language of the Scenarios, and are readable for non-programmers.

2.2   GUI Testing

Traditionally in waterfall projects, a lot of testing has been done through the GUI, and there are many tools that use a Capture-Replay paradigm. A tester creates test cases by starting the application, activating the recording tool, then clicking around in the GUI following a test scenario, as the tool records a script of their actions. The tool can then replay the script as an automated regression test.

Creating these kinds of tests is often left until near the end of the project, since they require the GUI to be usable before the test can be recorded. This means the tests are usually only used for critiquing the product, (finding defects), and give little support to the team. As Janet Gregory and Lisa Crispin point out [2], in an agile project, supporting the development team is an important role for automated tests. This mean that the tests should be designed before the code they test.

Another problem with capture-replay tests like this is that the maintenance costs are often prohibitive. The scripts that the tool creates are generally written in a programming language, and are often fairly impossible to read or refactor. They are tighly coupled to the exact widgets that the user clicked on, and break as soon as anything in the GUI changes. The GUI is usually one of the most volatile parts of the application, and particularly in an agile project where functionality is continually being updated, widgets get moved, workflows get changed, and all test scripts that are tightly coupled to them will need to be re-recorded.

One solution people have come up with is a pattern called "Page Objects". For example this is the recommended way to work with Selenium WebDriver, [3]. The idea is you create an intermediate layer of code between the UI and your test cases. It's basically a layer of indirection to keep your test cases isolated from the volatility of the GUI. What you end up with is test cases that read like a high-level domain language description of what the user is doing, and Page Objects that abstract away all the details of how they interact with widgets in the GUI.

Emily has done this on a previous project, and found it works pretty well, the maintenance costs are managable. You still have to create and maintain this abstraction layer of Page Objects, but now your test scripts are decoupled from the details of the GUI. When a widget is moved or a workflow changed, you have only to update a few Page Objects, not every single test script that uses that widget. With a tool like Selenium, you design and code your Page Objects by hand, and once you've got some, your recording tool becomes much less useful. It won't let you record test scripts that use your Page Objects to access your GUI. You find that test creation takes longer than with a pure capture-replay approach, but on the other hand, the test maintenance becomes managable.

2.3   Tools for Specification by Example

Many people are doing Specification by Example using tools like Cucumber and Fitnesse. These tools are set up to let you specify tests in a domain specific language that is readable for non-programmers. In Cucumber, you have "feature" files which contain the Feature descriptions and Scenarios from the "User Story" and "Conversation" parts of your requirement.

As the programmer develops the feature, they will turn this file into an executable test, by adding little pieces of code called "step definitions". By the time the feature is finished, the "feature" file is executable as a regression test.

Fitnesse works in a similar way, but this time the User Story and Scenarios are written into a special wiki and formatted as tables. As the programmer builds the code, they implement "fixture" code for each kind of table, connecting them to the system under test.

So in both these tools you have a layer of indirection between the test case and the system under test. Just like with Page Objects, there is a fair amount of time spent writing and maintaining this layer.

When it comes to systems with a GUI, often the advice is to avoid testing via the GUI. If you're using Cucumber or Fitnesse and the test is written in a domain language, there's actually no need to use the same interface as the user, you can create an API under the GUI that the tests use to access the business logic directly. This can make your tests much more reliable and quick to execute.

In Jeppesen's CMS, going under the GUI seems like a poor option. There is a lot of functionality and visual information there that absolutely needs to be tested.

3   TextTest

This is a tool that Geoff has created and is being used for testing CMS at Jeppesen. It has both a Capture-Replay tool for GUI testing, and is suitable for use with Specification by Example. It's open source and freely available to download - see http://texttest.org [4]. Let's look at how it works.

3.1   Record Tests in a Domain Specific Language

In Specification by Example, you need a way to take the Scenarios you come up with before coding starts, and as coding progresses, make them executable as regression tests. Usually this is the job of the programmer. As they develop the User Interface, they follow a Scenario, and record steps in a test case. This involves clicking in the GUI just like a real user would. Underneath, TextText is recording a script of actions, but not in a programming language. TextTest uses a library of named domain actions, that match the terms being used in the Scenario. As you're recording, if you use a new feature or widget that has no associated domain language action, TextTest prompts you to create and name new ones.

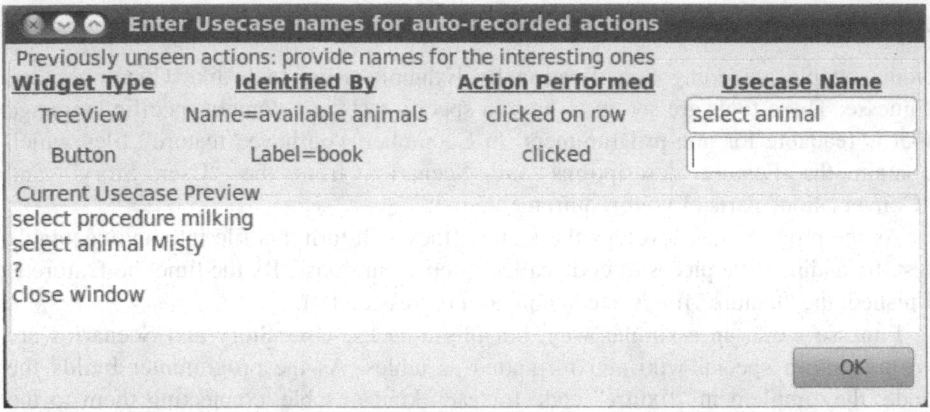

Fig. 2. Screenshot of TextTest prompting you to create domain language

So now you can record test cases in your domain language. The "fixture code" - that intermediate layer also known as Page Objects, Step Definitions, glue code - that is all created for you by TextTest, in the form of configuration files. When you record your test cases, you focus on creating the domain language, making test cases expressive and readable.

```
open default plan and show rosters
change service type of activity JPO 503 for
Alpickney to K
change service type of activity JPO 2537 for
Brogan to M
undo
wait for completion of undo
close and discard changes
```

Fig. 3. Sample "use case" from a test case for CMS

Each of the steps in the example above is actually composed from a number of lower-level interactions with particular widgets. TextTest lets you group and name a sequence of domain language actions into a higher level domain term, so you can easily raise the abstraction level of your test cases. The information connecting the lower-level domain terms to actual widgets is achieved with a simple configuration file.

This works because there's a lot going on under the covers - TextTest hooks into the GUI library to discover widget names and what data they are presenting. It does a lot of work helping you to link up your user domain actions with runtime code objects. That's why TextTest at present only supports a few GUI libraries - notably Eclipse Rich Client Platform.

3.2   The GUI Log

The domain language part of the test is only half the story though. TextTest also handles assertions rather differently than other tools, as you'll notice by reading the "use case" above - there are no "assert" or "check" statements in it. Most Capture-Replay tools have you pause occasionally while recording a test case, and indicate you want to check a particular widget or text is shown on the screen. TextTest doesn't do that. You just concentrate on recording what the user does.

All the while you're recording a scenario, TextTest is generating a plain text log of how the user interface looks, and what is changing. Conceptually, it's as if it takes a screenshot any time anything significant happens. The test case then comprises two parts - the recorded actions, and the recorded GUI log. When you execute the test case, TextTest replays the actions, and does a diff of the resulting GUI log against the recording. Any diff will cause the test to fail, and report which part of the GUI has changed.

```
...
Updated Gantt Chart :

                                                Tue 24
                                                00 01 02 03 04 05 06 07 08 09 10        11    12 13 14        15 16 17      18
00224(red*) E1384(red*)              E2009                                    -(blue)-----[--------]--[--------]--[--------]--
name_00224  forenames_00224          DK                                      -(green+)----[ green- ] [ green-     ] [ green- ]
FP          CPH                      M(blue-)                 CPH                        [     ][     ]     [     ][     ]

00389       K0082                    E2006                    [-(blue)----RL--------------------------------]
name_00389  forenames_00389(green-)  NO                       [       brown-                                ]
FC          OSL                      M(blue-)      OSL [ 0600                                     1600     ] OSL

03528(red*) S1576(red*)              E2005                    [-(blue)----R------------------]--------------[--------------]-[
name_03528  forenames_03528          DK                       [       brown-                  ]  -(green+)----[ green-    ] [
FP          CPH                      M(blue-)      CPH [ 0600                          1435    ] CPH            [          ] [

Row count label '3'

Updated Text Field
========== Browser ==========
LHR-CPH     SK 504   Nov24  MBC  J
2:05 PM  -  4:00 PM  Needed      1/1/0/0//0/0/1/3/0//0/0
            -        Assigned    0/1/0/0//0/0/0/0/0//0/0
==================================

New widgets have appeared: describing common parent :

'Crew: 3, trips: 6' | 'UTC'
...
```

Fig. 4. Excerpt from a GUI log of a test case for CMS

If you look at the GUI log excerpt above (figure 4), and compare it with the screenshot shown in figure 1, I hope you'll see the correspondence between the two.

For Jeppesen's CMS, this means the test cases give us a very high assurance that the GUI looks the way it's supposed to. For this application, it's crucial that all these little green lines and boxes and pink blobs are all in exactly the right positions, and are updated correctly when the user edits the Plan. Instead of each test case having to pick out a few small things to check, by default each test case checks everything on the screen.

Of course in practice it is useful to filter the GUI log, so most test cases ignore common screens, and only actually check for screens that are important or different in their particular scenario. We do find though that the default setting of checking everything does mean we find subtle differences and bugs the test designer wasn't intending to find.

Because we're using an ASCII representation of the screen, not a screenshot, it makes it much easier to handle the test cases - they're just plain text. You can store, version control, update, diff and bulk-update these files with commonly available tools. It also makes it straightforward to test your application using a virtual display, and the tests execute very quickly and efficiently on a large compute cluster.

4   Conclusions

At Jeppesen we are developing a tool, TextTest, which can be used for GUI testing of a rich-client applications. It lets you translate the kind of Scenarios you come up with in Specification by Example into executable test cases, written in a Domain Specific Language. These test cases are created using a Capture-Replay approach.

TextTest is suited to GUI-intensive applications where it really matters what is shown on the screen, since it will record and assert against a textual representation of the whole user interface. Creating ASCII-art "screenshots" makes the tests easier to maintain compared with approaches that use an actual pictorial screenshot.

At present this approach and tool are being successfully used at Jeppesen to test their next generation Crew Management System. We have an extensive suite of end-to-end full system automated tests that are written in a Domain Specific Language that is readable by non-programmers and business people. The full suite runs in parallel on a linux cluster in under 15 minutes, as part of a Continuous Integration setup. It often detects important regression errors just minutes after insertion.

References

1. Adzic, G.: Specification by Example, Bridging the Communcation Gap
2. Crispin, L., Gregory, J.: Agile Testing
3. Fowler, M.: Fowler's bliki,
   http://martinfowler.com/bliki/PageObject.html
4. http://texttest.org

Towards Agile and Beyond: An Empirical Account on the Challenges Involved When Advancing Software Development Practices

Helena Holmström Olsson[1] and Jan Bosch[2]

[1] Department of Computer Science, Malmö University, Malmö, Sweden
`helena.holmstrom.olsson@mah.se`
[2] Department of Computer Science and Engineering, Chalmers University of Technology,
Gothenburg, Sweden
`jan.bosch@chalmers.se`

Abstract. During the last decade, the vast majority of software companies have adopted agile development practices. Now companies are looking to move beyond agile and further advance their practices. In this paper, we report on the experiences of a company in the embedded systems domain that is adopting agile practices with the intention to move beyond agile and towards continuous deployment of software. Based on case study research involving group interviews and a web-based survey, we identify challenges in relation to (1) the adoption of agile practices, (2) testing practices, (3) continuous deployment, and (4) customer validation.

Keywords: Agile practices, beyond agile, continuous deployment, challenges.

1 Introduction

During the last decade, the vast majority of software development companies have adopted agile development practices. With characteristics emphasizing the use of short iterations and the development of small features, agile practices have increased the ability for software development companies to better accommodate changing customer requirements and fast changing market needs [1]. While there are a number of studies focusing on different agile methods and techniques, and best practices in relation to the adoption of these [2, 3, 4, 5], research focusing on the way in which the adoption of agile practices is a means for achieving something else, i.e. how to move beyond agile practices, is scarce.

In this paper, we share the experiences of a company in the embedded systems domain that is in the process of adopting agile practices with the intention to move towards continuous deployment of software. Our study provides an empirical account of the company's experiences so far, and it identifies challenges related to four areas, i.e. the adoption of agile practices, testing practices, continuous deployment and customer validation. Although this study is based on a single case, we have significant experience from other similar companies that we use as a background and as part of

G. Cantone and M. Marchesi (Eds.): XP 2014, LNBIP 179, pp. 327–335, 2014.

the theoretical framework underlying this research [6, 7, 8]. The contribution of this paper is two-fold. First, we share the experiences of a large-scale software development company in the process of adopting agile practices. Second, our study outlines challenges that typically face companies adopting agile practices with the intention to move towards continuous deployment of software.

The paper is organized as follows. In section 2, we outline the typical evolution path for software development companies moving towards agile practices and beyond. In section 3, we describe our research site and method. Section 4 presents the findings, and in section 5 we discuss these findings. Finally, in section 6 we present the conclusions.

2   Background

Based on our earlier work [6], we developed a model that most companies follow when advancing their software development practices. We refer to this as the "Stairway To Heaven" (see Figure 1).

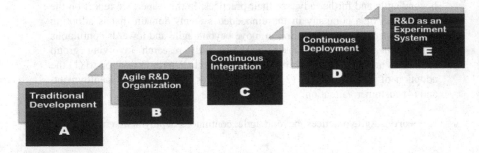

Fig. 1. The 'Stairway to Heaven', i.e. the typical evolution path for software development companies when moving towards agile practices and beyond

Our model depicts the transition from traditional development to agile practices and beyond. We use this model as a background for understanding the challenges associated with moving beyond agile practices and towards continuous deployment of software.

2.1   Climbing the 'Stairway to Heaven'

Traditional development is characterized by long development cycles and slow customer feedback loops [9]. A company interested in moving towards agile practices needs to re-organize large project groups into smaller cross-functional teams focusing on features rather than components [6]. An agile development organization is characterized by small cross-functional teams working in short development cycles [2]. To move to continuous integration, companies need to develop automated tests and code needs to be frequently checked in [6]. Continuous integration implies practices that allow for frequent integration of work [10, 11]. To move towards continuous deployment, companies need to involve product management and release in the short feedback cycles. Continuous deployment is where software functionality is deployed continuously to customers [10]. At this point, product management and customers are involved in short feedback cycles. The final step is where deployment of software is seen as a starting point for development rather than delivery of the final product. Recently, the concept of 'experiment systems' was defined as an experiment-centric approach with the purpose of accelerating innovation through systematic and continuous collection of user feedback [12, 13]. As a result, requirements evolve in real-time based on data collected from customer use instead of being frozen early as part of requirements prioritization [12].

3   Research Site and Method

This paper presents a case study conducted at the world leading company in network video. The company offers products such as network cameras, video encoders, video management software and camera applications for video surveillance. Currently, the company is adopting agile development practices with the intention to advance towards continuous deployment of software. From releasing products every 18 months, the company releases software at least twice a year using agile practices such as sprints and daily stand-up meetings. When initiating this study, we met with a management group including top-level managers, two team leaders, a test manager and two software architects. During this meeting, the company representatives expressed an interest in conducting an assessment of their adoption of agile practices. They were interested in learning about peoples' experiences so far, and what challenges they face in moving further. As a result of the meeting, there was an agreement to focus our study on four areas, i.e. (1) adoption of agile practices, (2) testing practices, (3) continuous deployment, and (4) customer validation. These four areas correspond to the second to fifth step in the 'Stairway to Heaven' model [6]. In relation to area (1) we investigate to which extent the development organization has adopted agile practices. In area (2) we investigate the testing practices and to what extent these are being automated to allow for continuous integration. In area (3) we investigate the frequency of software delivery, and in area (4) we investigate the feedback loop to customers and to what extent customers validate software functionality.

Our paper reports on a case study [14, 15] conducted between April – October 2013. The data collection methods used were semi-structured group interviews with open-ended questions [15] and a web-based survey using a 7-point Likert scale [16]. For the group interviews, we met with a total of 44 people including developers, testers, system architects, product owners, project managers and product specialists. All group interviews were conducted in English and lasted for two hours. In total, we have 10 hours of recordings and 40 pages of summarizing notes. Also, we conducted a web-based survey. The survey was designed using a 7-point Likert scale where '1' is 'strongly disagree' and '7' is 'strongly agree'. In total, the survey was distributed to 300 employees and after having had it accessible from late May to early September 2013 we got 115 responses.

4   Findings

In this section, we present the interview and survey findings. Our findings are related to the four focus areas, i.e. (1) adoption of agile practices, (2) testing practices, (3) continuous deployment, and (4) customer validation. These areas correspond to the 'Stairway to Heaven' model, which we use as a framework to assess the challenges the company faces when moving further.

Adoption of agile practices: All groups within the company are experienced in working agile. Especially, Scrum practices are widely adopted. The most common practice is to organize work in sprints, and as can be seen in Figure 2, a majority of the survey respondents agree when asking if they organize their work in sprints.

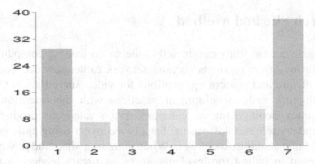

Fig. 2. "We organize our work in sprints" (1= strongly disagree and 7= strongly agree)

A common challenge is to have resources available within each agile team. Most of the interviewees experience a situation in which they have to share important resources, such as configuration, test and administration, with other teams. Another challenge is to find a balance between expertise and general knowledge. As experienced in some teams, expertise can be lost when trying to broaden knowledge within a cross-functional team. At the same time, many people find the agile practices helpful in that they encourage people to take on new tasks.

Testing practices: The inclusion of test activities in the sprints is a challenge. In some of the teams, continuous integration practices are established and there is always a shippable piece of functionality. On a team level, automated tests are common and this is reflected in the survey (see Figure 3).

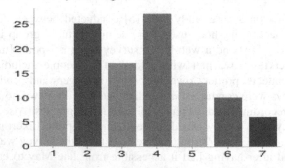

Fig. 3. "Verification and validation of code is fully automated on a team level" (1= strongly disagree and 7= strongly agree)

However, while automated tests are common in parts of the organization and while some teams have full coverage, other parts of the organization find automated tests difficult to apply. Also, analysis of tests is difficult and the interviewees wish for better tools for this.

Continuous deployment: In the company, the ambition is to increase the frequency of delivery. Currently, new functionality is released once or twice a year and the company has already succeeded in shortening the release cycles that used to be close to 18 months. The motivation for more frequent releases is the demand from customers. According to the interviewees many customers ask for functionality once per month and that is a frequency in which the company needs to be able to release. When discussing rollback mechanisms, the only solution the company uses is to degrade to a previous version. Currently, there are no other efficient mechanisms if new functionality causes problems (Figure 4):

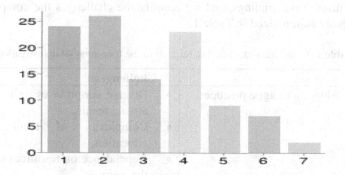

Fig. 4. We have effective mechanisms to rollback deployment of new functionality that causes problems" (1= strongly disagree and 7= strongly agree

Customer validation: Our study reveals that customer feedback is scarce. The main input from customers is service and trouble reports that indicate an error in the system. Most respondents feel distant from the customers and when asking whether they know what features of the system that customers use, the answer is that the majority does not (Figure 5). As a result of this, the company only gets feedback when something doesn't work, and this is not necessarily an indication of what features that are used the most. Furthermore, data collected from the products is only used to help troubleshooting and support activities but not for informing the development organization about how individual features are used.

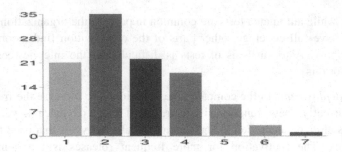

Fig. 5. "We know what features of our products that our customers use" (1= strongly disagree and 7= strongly agree)

5   Discussion

Below, we discuss our findings, and we identify the challenges the company faces. Our findings are summarized in Table 1.

Table 1. Challenges identified in relation to the four areas of investigation

Area:	Challenges:
Scaling adoption of agile practices	• Diverse adoption of agile practices among teams. • Complexity of team resource allocation. • Dependence on resources outside of the team.
Automated testing of functionality	• Difficulties in analyzing and maintaining automated tests. • Difficulty in removing or reducing old tests.
Continuous deployment	• Difficulties in establishing efficient rollback mechanisms.
Data collection and use	• No effective mechanisms for analysis of customer data. • Lack of understanding about feature use. • No pro-active use of customer data.

5.1   Scaling Adoption of Agile Practices

Our respondents experience a diverse adoption of agile practices, and a situation where different products have different processes. One reason for this is the characteristics of the products. The products are embedded systems that include hardware as well as software, meaning that the lengths of development cycles are different for different parts of the system. As recognized by Bosch and Eklund [13], many companies developing mass-produced embedded systems view software as a necessity rather than as a strategic opportunity. While development of hardware is part of well-established traditions, software introduces both opportunities and challenges that have not been encountered before. Also, most companies in the embedded systems domain have extensive supplier and subcontractor relationships and the cost, effort and unpredictability of the deliverables from these external partners are experienced as a true challenge for adoption of agile practices [13]. In our case company, a majority of the teams experience a situation in which they are dependent on resources outside of the team. This brings with it a number of challenges. First, the efficiency of the organization is hampered [6, 17]. Furthermore, the dependency on external resources makes team empowerment more difficult [2, 4].

5.2   Automated Testing of Functionality

Currently, the company experiences great variety in the adoption of automated tests. While groups working with software-intensive parts for which they own the entire development cycle have automated tests with full coverage, other groups operate in an environment where manual testing is still the dominant practice. As reported in literature, continuous integration is expected to improve release frequency and predictability and increase developer productivity [18]. In the transition towards automated testing practices, our study identifies two major challenges. First, one difficulty is the analysis and maintenance of automated tests [11, 19]. Second, our study reveals a situation in which it is easy to increase the number of tests, but very difficult to remove or reduce the number of old tests. While the concept of continuous integration is complex [11], our study shows that adopting these practices is a step necessary in order to advance the adoption of agile practices.

5.3   Frequent Delivery of Software

The goal for our case company is to advance towards more frequent delivery of software. In continuous deployment you automatically deploy code changes into the software production line [10]. Based on our findings, we see a situation in which customers to a greater extent ask for new functionality, and the overall experience is that customers ask for new functionality as soon as they know they can get it. The challenge is to have efficient rollback mechanisms to manage potential problems with the deployment of new software. Our respondents report on a situation in which the only way to rollback is to de-grade to the previous system version. While this is common practice it is not considered a sufficient mechanism when moving to more frequent deployment of software.

5.4   Data Collection and Use

With connected systems the opportunity to collect post-deployment data from customers has significantly increased [8, 12, 20], and the cost of collecting data from the customer is low [12]. Our study reveals that a huge amount of data is collected after deployment at customer site. However, the use of this data is limited and it is not used as input for the development organization. As a result, there is no general understanding for what features that are actually used by customers [8]. Another problem is that the feedback loop is slow and product management does not view customer data as a mechanism for continuous customer validation of software functionality.

6   Conclusions

In this paper, we share the experiences of a company in the embedded systems domain that is adopting agile practices with the intention to move beyond agile and towards continuous deployment of software. We identify the challenges they face in relation to (1) the adoption of agile practices, (2) testing practices, (3) continuous deployment, and (4) customer validation. Although our study is based on a single case company, we believe that our findings are relevant for other companies with an interest in adopting and advancing agile practices. Our results serve as input to companies when assessing the maturity of their processes, and as input when planning what actions need to be taken when transitioning towards agile and beyond.

References

1. Fogelström, N.D., Gorschek, T., Svahnberg, M., Olsson, P.: The Impact of Agile Principles on Market-Driven Software Product Development. Journal of Software Maintenance and Evolution: Research and Practice 22, 53–80 (2010)
2. Highsmith, J., Cockburn, A.: Agile Software Development: The business of innovation. In: Software Management, pp. 120–122 (September 2001)
3. Beck, K.: Embracing Change with Extreme Programming. Computer 32(10), 70–77 (1999)
4. Larman, C.: Agile and Iterative Development: A Manager's Guide. Addison-Wesley (2004)
5. Abrahamsson, P., Warsta, J., Siponen, M., Ronkainen, J.: New Directions on Agile Methods: a comparative analysis. In: Proceedings of the 25th International Conference on Software Engineering, Portland, Oregon, pp. 244–254 (2003)
6. Olsson, H.H., Alahyari, H., Bosch, J.: Climbing the Stairway to Heaven. In: Proceedings of the 38th Euromicro Software Engineering Advanced Applications (SEAA) Conference, Cesme, Turkey, September 5-7 (2012)
7. Olsson H.H., Bosch, J.: Towards, R.&D. as Innovation Experiment Systems: A Framework for Moving Beyond Agile Software Development. In: Proceedings of the IASTED International Conference on Software Engineering (SE 2013), Innsbruck, Austria, February 11-13 (2013)
8. Olsson, H.H., Bosch, J.: Post-deployment Data Collection in Software-Intensive Embedded Products. In: Herzwurm, G., Margaria, T. (eds.) ICSOB 2013. LNBIP, vol. 150, pp. 79–89. Springer, Heidelberg (2013)
9. Sommerville, I.: Software Engineering, 6th edn. Pearson Education, Essex (2001)
10. Humble, J., Farley, D.: Continuous Delivery: Reliable Software Releases through Build, Test and Deplyment Automation. Addison-Wesley, Boston (2011)

11. Ståhl, D., Bosch, J.: Modeling continuous integration practice differences in industry software development. Journal of Systems and Software, 48–59 (2014)
12. Bosch, J.: Building Products as Innovation Experiment Systems. In: Cusumano, M.A., Iyer, B., Venkatraman, N. (eds.) ICSOB 2012. LNBIP, vol. 114, pp. 27–39. Springer, Heidelberg (2012)
13. Bosch, J., Eklund, U.: Eternal embedded software: Towards innovation experiment systems. In: Margaria, T., Steffen, B. (eds.) ISoLA 2012, Part I. LNCS, vol. 7609, pp. 19–31. Springer, Heidelberg (2012)
14. Walsham, G.: Interpretive case studies in IS research: Nature and method. European Journal of Information Systems 4, 74–81 (1995)
15. Runesson, P., Höst, M.: Guidelines for conducting and reporting case study research in software engineering. Empirical Software Engineering 14 (2009)
16. Allen, E., Seaman, C.: Likert Scales and Data Analyses. Quality Progress 2007, 64–65 (2007)
17. Williams, L., Cockburn, A.: Agile Software Development: It's about feedback and change. Computer 36(6), 39–43 (2003)
18. Goodman, D., Elbaz, M.: "It's not the pants, it's the people in the pants" Learnings from The Gap Agile Transformation. In: Agile 2008 Conference, pp. 112–115 (2008)
19. Ablett, R., Sharlin, E., Maurer, F., Denzinger, J., Schock, C.: BuildBot: Robotic Monitoring of Agile Software Development Teams. In: 16th IEEE International Symposium on Robot and Human interactive Communication, pp. 931–936 (2007)
20. Kohavi, R., Longbotham, R., Sommerfield, D., Henne, R.M.: Controlled experiments on the web: survey and practice guide. Data Mining and Knowledge Discovery 18(1), 140–181 (2009)

Author Index